Latina/o Communication Studies Today

PETER LANG
New York • Washington, D.C./Baltimore • Bern
Frankfurt am Main • Berlin • Brussels • Vienna • Oxford

Latina/o Communication Studies Today

Angharad N. Valdivia, Editor

PETER LANG
New York • Washington, D.C./Baltimore • Bern
Frankfurt am Main • Berlin • Brussels • Vienna • Oxford

Library of Congress Cataloging-in-Publication Data

Latina/o communication studies today / edited by Angharad N. Valdivia.
p. cm.
Includes bibliographical references and index.
1. Hispanic American mass media. 2. Hispanic Americans and mass media.
I. Valdivia, Angharad N.
P94.5.H58L36   302.23089'68—dc22   2007044391
ISBN 978-0-8204-8632-1 (hardcover)
ISBN 978-0-8204-8628-4 (paperback)

Bibliographic information published by **Die Deutsche Bibliothek**.
Die Deutsche Bibliothek lists this publication in the "Deutsche Nationalbibliografie"; detailed bibliographic data is available on the Internet at http://dnb.ddb.de/.

Cover design by Clear Point Designs

© 2008 Peter Lang Publishing, Inc., New York
29 Broadway, 18th floor, New York, NY 10006
www.peterlang.com

All rights reserved.
Reprint or reproduction, even partially, in all forms such as microfilm, xerography, microfiche, microcard, and offset strictly prohibited.

To *Ailín del Carmen Valdivia McCarthy,*
the coolest and hippest Latina girl in the universe.

Table of Contents

Acknowledgments ix

Part I. The Production of Latinidad

Chapter 1. Is My Butt Your Island? The Myth of Discovery
and Contemporary Latina/o Communication Studies 3
Angharad N. Valdivia

Chapter 2. When Dolores Del Rio Became Latina: Latina/o Stardom
in Hollywood's Transition to Sound 27
Mary Beltrán

Chapter 3. The Importance of Spanish-Language and Latino Media 51
Mari Castañeda

Part II. Performance and the Self

Chapter 4. Performing the Responsible Sponsor: Everything You
Never Wanted to Know About Immigration Post-9/11. 69
Bernadette Marie Calafell

Chapter 5. Hybrid Performativity, South and North of the Border:
Entre la teoría y la materialidad de hibridación. 91
Shane T. Moreman

Part III. Contextually Representing the Heterogeneity

Chapter 6. Policing the Latina/o Other: Latinidad in Prime-Time
News Coverage of the Elián González Story 115
Isabel Molina Guzmán

Chapter 7. Real Women and Their Curves: Letters to the Editor
and a Magazine's celebration of the "Latina Body" 137
Katynka Z. Martínez

Chapter 8. A Morning Dose of Latino Masculinity:
U.S. Spanish-language Radio and the Politics of Gender 161
Dolores Inés Casillas

Part IV. Latina Women as Cultural Readers

Chapter 9. Media Practices and Gendered Identity
among Transnational Latina Teens 187
Lucila Vargas

Chapter 10. Watching Over the Border: A Case Study
of the Mexico-U.S. Television and Youth Audience 219
David González Hernández

Chapter 11. Survival Aesthetics: U.S. Latinas and the Negotiation
of Popular Media 237
María Elena Cepeda

Chapter 12. Mexican (American) Women Talk Back:
Audience Responses to Latinidad in U.S. Advertising 257
Jillian M. Báez

About the Authors 283

Index 287

Acknowledgments

This book is part of a community and social movement. Intellectual property, that misnomer of capitalism, belongs to a people and culture, not an individual. This book, or my work, would not be possible without those scholars who wrote before me. I want to single out Jacqueline Bobo for she opened up a space for women of color to write in the fields of cinema and media studies. Without the "*Color Purple*" essay and the extensive work that she has continued to publish, I doubt many of us would be taken seriously as we continue to purse research on women of color as cultural beings. I want to thank the wonderful contributors to this volume. Their great work inspires me. Closer to home, my outstanding colleagues at the Institute of Communications Research at the University of Illinois continue to provide the fertile ground on which many of us can work and carve out a little piece of research. The support of John Nerone, Clifford Christians, Norman Denzin, and Paula Treichler is, to quote the Master Card commercials, priceless! In terms of the intersection between communications and ethnicity I am such a fortunate soul to be able to discuss matters with and learn from Kent Ono. And then when you add gender and transnationality to the mix, I count my lucky stars to have Isabel Molina Guzmán as my colleague, friend, and incredibly insightful partner in crime in the area of Latina Media Studies. The work of fabulous doctoral students such as Jillian Báez and Diem-my Bui nourishes and energizes my own. Most thankful I am to my colleague and partner Cameron McCarthy for his patient conversations, theoretical guidance (what was that thing about Kant again?) and overall support. I have had incredible students work to help me carry out this project. Kortney Ziegler and Shivali Tukdeo provided the essential assistance without which this manuscript would have never been finished. Cindy San Miguel helped in the final push. Both Greg Zike and James Salvo provided technical assistance. My thanks go to all who helped, and I take any shortcomings of this volume to be my own.

Part I. The Production of Latinidad

CHAPTER ONE

Is My Butt Your Island? The Myth OF Discovery AND Contemporary Latina/o Communication Studies

ANGHARAD N. VALDIVIA

The making of an academic field seldom is secured without struggle. Arising out of extensions, revisions, and challenges to previous paradigms a new field must make way for itself (Kuhn, 1996). This is even more so the case in a time of war when any public expenditures must suffer in relation to defense spending, and when within public education the humanities and social sciences are under fire (Bérubé & Nelson, 1995). If we are to follow a communication ritual approach such as that outlined by James Carey (1992) we must bring up a seat to the table—the place where the conversation is taking place. However, to do so we must find a seat, and we must make a space, for the table participants may not be so willing to welcome newcomers (Valdivia, 2007b). Such is the situation for Latina/o Communication Studies today. So many articles, essays, chapters, and books have been written predating and postdating the 2003 U.S. Census announcement that as of 2000, the date of the last national census, Latina/os had become the most numerous minority in the country. Mobility has resulted in increased forced and voluntary migration of Latin American populations up and out of their countries of origin, both recently and historically. Just as the Latina/o population is numerous and here to stay—indeed, as Latina/o Studies scholars note, it precedes the Anglo population in this part of the American continent—so are scholars of Latina/o Studies in our field rewriting the study of communication and ethnicity. However, this is not easy, nor does it go unchallenged. To bring up a chair to the table unsettles previous arrangements. To accept newcomers, take them seriously, acknowledge that the new seat at the table brings new insights *and* enriches previously existing paradigms all indicate acceptance of an academic intervention, an intellectual form of social change.

The time is ripe for a volume on *Latina/o Communication Studies Today*. This volume speaks to a number of constituencies. First, it provides an invaluable resource to those already conducting research and teaching in Latina/o Communication Studies. The chapters in this volume will prove immensely informative to scholars in the field. Second, this volume speaks to those within the communications interdiscipline who may not be familiar with this large area of scholarship. Too often when communication scholars think about or approach issues of race and ethnicity, they still think in binary terms of black and white. Latina/os fall out of the picture. Third, this volume speaks to Latina/o Studies scholars, urging them to take Communication and Media Studies seriously. Within Latina/o Studies, many scholars take Communication and Media Studies rather lightly, as if watching television and movies qualifies any historian, anthropologist, or psychologist to talk as if media and communication were transparent and not sophisticated fields with theories, methodologies, and findings. Fourth, all chapters in this volume are written in a clear and accessible manner for a general audience of informed readers.

As a way to illustrate some of the issues facing Latina/o Communication scholars I begin with three vignettes that shed light on some of the lived experiences of those who embody this intellectual formation. The following speak to resistance of the practice of social change and the rise of Latina/o Communication/Media Studies in the academy.

VIGNETTE #1: PAULO FREIRE VISITS THE UNIVERSITY OF ILLINOIS

In December 1987 the renowned education scholar Paulo Freire, author of the canonical *Pedagogy of the Oppressed* (1993), visited the University of Illinois. His lectures had overflowing audiences. In the midst of the most highly attended, "A Conversation with Paulo Freire ... A Teacher with Profound Insights into the Learning Process and a Passion for Social Justice" on December 10, a graduate student challenged him about his implicit support of violence in the name of social change. Freire replied that he did not know of one instance when the ruling class had willingly given up its privilege. The student followed up this line of questioning later on that night at dinner. Paulo this time asked whether she knew about snow. It was, after all, a rather snowy winter in Champaign. She was a bit puzzled but replied, "Yes." At which point Paulo said, "Then let's talk about snow since we can both agree it is white." This prompted the student to walk out.

Freire articulated a missing element from the Carey vision—namely, bringing that chair to the table is not done without stress, challenge, and/or resistance. The graduate student's initial verbal challenge, followed by a physical and symbolic walkout, attests to the fact that while theories of social change may be palatable, the methods and struggles that these might entail are not. While this particular graduate student and Freire were talking about social and political revolutions, in this book we are talking about an intellectual revolution—one that unsettles previous areas of studies and promises to create new ones. Adding an area of study to a field, such as the interdiscipline of communication, is a form of social change. In theory many of us might be amenable to such a move. Yet those of us engaged in this enterprise encounter stress, challenge, and resistance. How many of us have been met by a lukewarm reception or, worse, outright rejection when trying to revise the curriculum or suggest a new faculty line for Latina/o Studies in our field? In an ideal world the table would expand—an unlimited growth model. But in the present condition of shrinking budgets and embattled social sciences and humanities, new areas of research usually butt up against older traditions whose practitioners do not care to share a pool of scarce resources and who may additionally be ideologically resistant to expanding the ethnic register. Seldom do we hear the latter, as the former becomes the most immediate rationale for vetoing change. Theoretically, race and ethnicity are important to pursue. Practically, where do we come up with the funding? I have actually been asked by a white colleague, "We study blacks and now you propose Latina/os. When will this end?" Going back to Freire, we can all agree that diversity is important, yet privilege is not relinquished or shared without struggle.

VIGNETTE #2: SEARCHING FOR A LATINA/O HISTORIAN

Last year I co-chaired a search committee for a junior Latina/o historian. The application pool had great, indeed mind-blowing, depth and breadth. It was a very rewarding experience given that I remembered a similar search more than ten years ago when there were very few applicants and fewer yet with the credentials to survive in a Research One setting. Five senior historians accounted for the mentoring and reference letters of nearly all of the top ten applicants. We preinterviewed ten fantastic junior scholars at a major convention before selecting the four who would be extended campus invitations. To one of our preset questions—"What is the connection between Latina/o Studies and History?"—one after another brilliant junior scholar asserted that "Latina/o history is American history." To connect this vignette to the previous one, we had a situation where the newcomers to the table asserted not only their right to belong but also the fact that they were not merely another voice but the connecting thread to the entire intellectual formation of "American" history. Their confidence and the quality of their research were unassailable. It literally gave me goose bumps to hear this and I am reminded of it by the contributors to this volume as they confidently assert that Latina/o Communication and Media Studies are equally central to our discipline. Another thing nearly all of the history applicants did was move into the study of media and/or popular culture. Yet their engagement with the literature of Communication and Media Studies was minimal. It was as if they did not feel a need to take this scholarship seriously. Certainly when media historians write, they take history as seriously as possible. But the reverse was not happening. This volume is an intervention into the twin processes observed in that search. First, Latina/o Communication Studies is communication studies. It is not something that can be reduced to representational analysis, cultural studies, qualitative studies, or first-person testimony—all four usual dumping grounds, from a positivist mainstream perspective, of marginal pursuits in the field. The brilliant work of all these contributors attests to this. Second, Latina/o Studies scholars need to seriously engage with Latina/o Communications scholarship if they choose to pursue issues of media and popular culture. This is a complex field that provides insight into what is usually treated as simplistic and transparent media processes.

VIGNETTE #3: WHAT DOES IT TAKE TO DO ETHNIC STUDIES?

I was recently in a situation where I was asked, "What does it take to conduct ethnicity and diversity research in communication?" My answer was, to do the leg work, to read the literature as it now exists, including its methodological and theoretical diversity, and to follow a research path that is informed by this research and formulate innovative and creative questions that also intersect with issues of social justice in a transnational world that is most often, but not always, lived in a local situation (or situations). I was pretty proud of that answer [in fact, I thought, Note to self—write that out and add it to whatever paper I am working on]. However, my questioner was not satisfied. "What else," he continued, "does it take to do research on diversity and communication—are you missing something?" I thought to myself, well I must be, and rephrased my answer something to the effect of "The approach must be as dedicated as possible—since it is likely to be an interdisciplinary and multi-methodological pursuit, one has to come to terms with incompleteness—but like all other research in the academy it must build on and extend previous work—even if that takes the form of rejection." I was hoping my inquisition was over, but it was not—"But is there anything else you are missing?" he continued. At this point I was a little skeptical of where this was going—maybe I also had lost my patience—and said, "If you are steering me in the direction of some essentialist answer to the effect that it takes a person of color to conduct research on diversity, I just won't and can't go in that essentialist direction. Is that where you are going?" At that point he, of course, said "no" as "essentialist" is kind of a naughty word that no scholar, at least in public, wants to agree to—but he did not continue his pursuit. This happened in 2007 in a major university in the field of communication.

The three vignettes illustrate issues that comprise part of our lived experience and continue to challenge us. In "us" I include at least two groups of scholars with a fairly wide swath of intersection. The first group is composed of those who conduct research on issues of ethnicity and race. The second group is composed of scholars who are racialized or ethnicized in the contemporary Western academy. While there is an overlap between these two groups, it does not naturally or essentially follow that Ethnic and Race Studies has to be conducted by racialized or ethnic people (the direction I think my questioner in vignette #3 was heading). Similarly, it does not naturally or essentially follow that ethnic and/or racialized people will conduct research only on race and ethnicity.

So what does it take to conduct our research? Tremendous dedication. We are not asking simple questions. To conduct this type of research one has to engage in interdisciplinary questions and multiple methodologies and bring together literatures that may use different languages [a tip—some use "race" instead of " ethnicity"; some think race and ethnicity are the same thing; others are post-race]. But the questions that we are asking must be asked—beginning with what are ethnicity and race in communications? How are ethnicity and race constructed through communications? How do these intersect issues of nationality, gender, and sexuality? Together the three vignettes speak to resistances, erasures, assumptions, and narratives that tend to structure the development of the interdisciplinary pursuit of Latina/o Communication Studies. As with all people and organizations, scholars and scholarships exist through the tension between agency and structure. Scholars must answer to their disciplines. Departments must answer to their deans. Deans must answer to their chancellors. Chancellors must answer to their boards of trustees and legislatures. Along that hierarchy all are more or less constrained by financial resources, yet many envision an expanding scholarship that leads to greater social justice. The changes will not be made easily, but interventions, such as this book, will contribute to change in scholarship, the academy, and social understanding, for Latina/o Communication Studies speaks to historically grounded yet contemporary issues that affect the knowledge and experience of everyone.

NAMING OURSELVES WITHIN THE ACADEMIC TERRITORY

Latina/o Studies challenges previous categories of race and ethnicity. Although the U.S. Census continues to struggle with racial and ethnic categories, until recently the U.S. national imaginary rested on a binary conception of self: black and white. This, of course, does not imply equality or parity, but it does document that there was an acknowledgment of a presence and history of blackness in relation to mainstream whiteness. As a discursive formation, Latina/o Studies names and authorizes a field of study about a population that was here long before the naming of the field. It is important to remember that just because the Census announced in 2003 that Latina/os were the most numerous U.S. minority does not mean that Latina/o arrival and participation in the United States started anywhere near that date. Nonetheless the Census documents increased migration through Mexico, though certainly not only from Mexico, for mostly economic reasons that can be elsewhere explained by the combination of global neoliberal policies of transnational capital in concert with relevant nation-states (Mexico, Canada, and the United States) that at the local level translated into the North American Free Trade Agreement (NAFTA) in 1994. The symbiotic relationship between demographic change and political economy generated the latest Latina/o boom as exemplified primarily by popular culture figures such as Selena, Ricky Martin, and Jennifer Lopez (Beltrán, 2009, 2002; Calafell & Delgado, 2004; Cepeda, forthcoming [a], 2003a, 2000; Paredez, 2002; Vargas, 2002). The hotness of hip Latina/os can be contrasted with the cool reception to new and long-standing immigrants that continues to be a crucial component of contemporary U.S. politics. This is the context that undergirds the study of Latina/os in the academy as well as the inclusion of Latina/o Studies scholars. While spurious talk about the ivory tower is still widely circulated, those of us inside it can attest to the fact that larger social and global issues influence the operation of university life in ways that are enabling and restricting. In 2004 I wrote the following:

> As a result of the twin forces of institutional and marketing needs to construct, survey, and sell to an identifiable ethnic group as well as internal Latina/o community strategies to forge a pan-national, pan-ethnic political and cultural group from which to make demands on the state and other social institutions, we now have the category Latina/os, the cultural identity of *Latinidad*, the state of being or performing a Latina/o identity, and the formation of Latina/o Studies within the academy. (Valdivia, 2004a, p. 108)

This complex set of influences and tensions has to be acknowledged to understand the location and development of Latina/o Studies in general and Latina/o Communication Studies in particular (Del Río, 2007; Molina Guzmán, 2007a).

The naming of "Latina/o Studies" as well as the impetus comes both from above and from below (or from within and without). Heterogeneity within this category is something that is acknowledged, yet both internal and external forces find reasons to subsume it and gloss over it. While it has been common to define Latina/os as the U.S. population of Latin American origin, recent or past, I am becoming more and more convinced that this nationalist definition does not serve us well. Transnational approaches within Latina/o Studies are common (see, e.g., the extensive work of Báez, Casillas, Cepeda, González, Molina Guzmán, and Valdivia both in this volume and elsewhere), yet we have continued to reduce the possibility of Latinidad to the United States. The fact is that in the contemporary and historical global mobility situation Latina/os have migrated not only through Mexico into the United States but also into Canada and over the Atlantic to Europe, the Pacific to Australia, with pockets in Asia and, less often, in Africa. We must begin to talk of Latina/os as a diaspora. Otherwise, how to make sense of such lovely work as Patria Roman Velazquez's *The Making of Latin London: Salsa Music, Place and Identity* (1999)? Latina/o Studies is a global pursuit, as all serious academic enterprises are.

Careless commentators can speak to the erasure or flattening of difference, yet as the contributors to this volume highlight, this is not something that can be blamed on our research. Collapsing the difference between Latina/os, Latinidad, and Latina/o Studies further contributes to unsophisticated approaches.[1] If we can understand Latinidad to mean the set of practices and subjectivities that cohere, albeit dynamically and temporarily, in relation to a range of Latina/o peoples and their histories and experiences, then, once more, we are right back at the point where we must consider historical and regional specificity. Expanding the geographic reach of the Latina/o diaspora serves to strengthen the field and make more connections to overlapping areas of study. The global perspective supports a focus on hybridity, for we have to take diaspora not as a drop of oil in a pool of water but rather as a fluid, dynamic, and permeable concept. Hybridity as a concept forces us to consider mixed race and the overlaps between Latina/os and all other ethnic categories. Latina/o Studies scholars build on this edifice of intersectional subjectivity. For instance, extending Aparicio (2003), Báez (2007b, p. 124) urges us to study the "multiple and intersecting identity politics" generated by the hybridity within Latinidad. Shugart (2007) cautions us not to get too carried away with hybridity as it serves to reinforce the privilege of whiteness, especially by displacing Mexicanidad and blackness (Calafell, 2006; Valdivia, 2005a). The latter warning must be heeded lest we lapse into some relativist celebration of the hybrid without attention to issues and histories of unequal power.

Latina/o Studies scholars must and do focus on specificity and interrelationality both within and without Latinidad. After all this ethnic category challenges the previous binary *not just* because it falls in between black and white—that would be so simple. Latina/os as a category challenges previous formations of ethnicity because it bleeds into all other categories—belying the effort to treat ethnicity as discrete groups of people. To wit, Latina/os are white, black, Native, Asian, Middle Eastern, and so on. Latina/os are a hybrid lot whose existence and experience cover the gamut of ethnicity. Thus theorizing the panethnicity of Latinidad forces us all to face the impurity of populations and cultures and the inability to keep the boundaries clean and static. Whereas Gitlin (1995) finds fault with "identity politics" for its tendencies to particularize and fragment the Left's universalist political program (faculty fighting over the English department while the Right took over the White House), McCarthy (1995) responds that identity politics are discussed as if they benefit only people of color while they, in fact, stand to benefit everyone. At that time, in popular film he found that identity politics were being used to reify white privilege. Since Latina/o Studies is really about the global condition, then maybe Gitlin's worries about the lack of universality can be now assuaged. We are actually talking about issues that concern us all. Still the task of scholars is to understand and explore how and when these boundaries hold and give meaning to people in terms of subjectivity and open up spaces for interventions into discourse, public policy, and life.

While Latina/o Studies scholars do not necessarily read Communication and Media Studies when pursuing research on such topics, in Communication Studies, the reception of Latina/o Studies has been uneven and slow, although Latina/o Studies informs all areas of communications. There are several reasons for this, both practical and ideological. To construct a research project, scholars inevitably encounter interdisciplinary contributing streams. That is, seldom can Latina/o Communication scholars read only within communications. They must read in Latina/o Studies, American Studies, Ethnic Studies, and, depending on the paradigm, in cognate disciplines such as history, psychology, literature, anthropology, and sociology, to name a few. This does not just apply to Latina/o Studies scholars. One of the things that make the field of communications so compelling is its holistic and integrally interdisciplinary approach to research (Valdivia, 2003a). Communications scholarship is itself interdisciplinary; Latina/o Communication Studies is doubly so. The additional labor of Latina/o Studies lies in the complex, heterogeneous, and inescapably hybrid composition of this category that often leads scholars to read and conduct research in African American, diaspora, Asian American, Native American, transnational, and other areas of study. Truth be told, this is quite a handful, and, given that we are just beginning to see a generation of scholars trained in this interdisciplinarity, it is not surprising that our scholarship has had a slow and difficult road to travel. Contributors to this volume demonstrate the possibilities of this task and provide models for research for all of us.

Writing from a Latina/o Media Studies perspective, del Río (2006) asserts, "Latina/o Media Studies offer an important opportunity to interrogate the construction of broad cultural categories in mainstream media representations and to examine how subaltern or vernacular texts contest, negotiate, or integrate dominant meanings" (p. 391). Latina/o Communication Studies belongs in any of the areas of communication research such as interpersonal, organizational, intercultural, international, political, health, cultural, and so on. The methodology can be quantitative, qualitative, or combined. The approach can be historical or contemporary. The theoretical bent can be Gramscian, Foucaultian, Mertonian, Deleuzian, or from any other tradition. Ideally the theoretical approach would include a broader register than the European theorists, but more on that in the next section. As Latina/o Studies scholars document, there have been Latina/o booms before this latest one (see, e.g., Beltrán, this volume and 2005a and b). This latest boom coincides with a field that continues to secure its foothold in academia. My concern here is not so much with the entire academy as within communications. I believe the chapters that we have in this book go a long way toward claiming that centrality that del Rio alludes to in the above quotation, built on an accumulating field of knowledge written by the same scholars and highlighted in this volume.

This is not the place to outline all of the many vectors of contemporary research in this burgeoning field—that deserves entire books (Valdivia, forthcoming a and b)—but some of the main ones already conducted by contributors to this volume are as follows: latinization (Báez, forthcoming); examining the Latino South (Calafell, 2004); Latina/os and hybridity (Valdivia, 2003b, 2004b, 2005a); Spanish-language radio (Casillas, forthcoming; Castañeda Paredes, 2001, 2003); transnational approaches to popular music (Cepeda, 2008, forthcoming a); salsa as latina/o formation (Valdivia, 2003b and c); border television (González, 2006); media industries (Beltrán, Park, Puente, Ross, & Downing, 2005: Molina Guzmán, 2007a); performance of Latina/o subjectivities and history (Calafell, 2005; Holling & Calafell, 2007; Moreman, 1999); Latina/os in media and popular culture in relation to mixed race (Beltrán, 2005c; Beltrán & Fojas, 2008; Valdivia, 2008); popular music in general (Casillas, 2005a; Cepeda 2005a, 2005b; Martínez, 2006); Latina girls and popular music (Valdivia & Bettivia, 1999b); reggaetón in particular (Báez, 2006; Cepeda, forthcoming); magazines and coffee table books (Calafell, 2001; Calafell & Delgado, 2004; Martínez, 2004), the press in general (Molina Guzmán, 2006a; Subervi-Velez, Báez, & Saenz, 2005; Vargas, 2000) and the Elián spectacle in particular (Molina Guzmán, 2005, 2007b); Latina/o youth in general (González, 2007a and 2007b; Valdivia, 2007c; Valdivia & Bettivia, 1999a) and Dora the Explorer in particular (Harewood and Valdivia, 2005); Latina feminist approaches in Media Studies (Báez, 2007b;

Beltrán, 2004), the Latina body in general (Báez, 2007b; Beltrán, 2002), Rosie Perez (Valdivia, 1996, 1998), Penélope Cruz (Valdivia 2005a, 2007b), and Salma Hayek (Molina Guzmán, 2006b, 2007c); and mentoring and classroom issues in the field (Calafell, 2008). This should give the reader some sense of the prolific work being conducted by these scholars.

TOKENS, STATIC FOSSILS, AND THE MYTH OF DISCOVERY; OR, JENNIFER, THY BUTT IS MY ISLAND

Scholars such as Shohat and Stam (1994) carefully and brilliantly expose how the myth of discovery is deployed through Hollywood film on the South American, African, and Asian continents as if the land and peoples were there for the taking. "Natives" are represented as static fossils, waiting for the Euro discoverer to deliver them from their situation. This myth of discovery continues to be played out in myriad ways. For example, Katerí Hernandez (2002) finds that both Ry Cooter's "discovery" of the Buena Vista Social Club (BVSC) and the accompanying press discussion of that musical formation are present-day examples of the myth. BVSC and Cuba were waiting to be "discovered," and their global circulation was discussed in a context of political and historical amnesia regarding the Cuban-U.S. political situation. We also can still see this myth being carried out by academics when they pursue research on "natives."

While one of the reasons for this volume is the overwhelming amount of reading that one needs to do to keep up with this burgeoning field—a primer function—another is to highlight the fact that this research is already being produced—as a function of asserting presence and existence. We can see a generational process in the production of knowledge by Latina/o Communication scholars. The first generation extends back for decades and stands out in terms of its foundational work and continued relevance. Self-taught, indeed building the framework of Latina/o Studies, in this group I include Federico Subervi-Velez, Félix Gutiérrez, and Rosa Linda Fregoso. The second generation, the one I belong to, had access to disciplines such as history and literature, the location or origin of much of the work about film, popular culture, and cinema studies, and extrapolated into media and communication studies (e.g., Aparicio and Chávez-Silverman, 1997; Jáquez & Aparicio with Cepeda, 2003; Valdivia, 1995, 2000).[2] We put together stuff from a range of disciplines, often without any mentoring or assistance as our very capable faculty and mentors were not schooled in or familiar with ethnic or Latina/o Studies. Quite often there was a bit of reinventing the wheel as less than interdisciplinary arrangements did not facilitate the reading in other fields that might have informed the work within our intellectual home spaces. In fact, unyielding disciplinarity outright prevented many of us from crossing disciplinary borders as that could translate into career suicide, especially before tenure. Despite declarations to the contrary, most U.S. universities talk a big talk about interdisciplinarity but that is the last thing they want. Contemporarily we are beginning to see third-generation scholars trained in Latina/o Communication Studies. All of the contributors to this volume straddle the second and third or firmly exist within the third generation. The third generation has the full benefit of a large body of interdisciplinary work as well as communication scholarship from which to draw and the burden of carrying the field to a next stage against the backdrop of a rather lively, if not outright divisive, set of constituencies within Latinidad and Latina/o Studies. Yet when I look at reference texts, review articles for journals, or syllabi on the Internet (both for Communication and for Latina/o Studies), the brilliant work of these contributors seldom if ever shows up.

In sum, few who write about and teach Latina/o Communication Studies read the work of the first-, second-, or third-generation scholars mentioned above. Rather like planting a flag on an island and claiming it as their own, many a mainstream scholar uses Jennifer's butt as the metaphorical island to lay their claim on new knowledge. I have reviewed many essays for journals where the authors have not done the basic task of scholarship: a literature review. This is another version of the myth of discovery. Looking up keywords such as "Latina/o Studies" and "Jennifer Lopez" would generate a range of articles and books in Google™ Scholar. However, what often happens, especially in the stuff submitted by the fellowship of the British,[3] is that the analysis of Latina/os, Latinidad, and communication is conducted without any reference to the scholarship of Latina/o Studies. I have a reference sheet prepared for such occasions. I have reviewed the "I Just Discovered the Jennifer Lopez Phenomenon" paper at least seven times. Negrón-Muntaner published her now famous "Jennifer's Butt" in 1997; Barrera her equally compelling "Hottentot 2000: Jennifer Lopez and Her Butt" in 2000; Aparicio her trenchant analysis of Jennifer in relation to Selena and the construction of Latinidad in 2003. I and Molina Guzmán (2004) have elaborated on the politics and economics of the booty; I have also explored her in relation to Penélope Cruz (2007a); and Durham and Báez (2007) have brought the analysis full circle back to Hottentot by conducting a relational analysis between Lopez and Beyoncé. And these are only some of the articles about Jennifer Lopez (e.g., Báez, 2007a; Beltrán, 2002; Fiol-Matta, 1999/2002). I have encountered a similar situation, though less often, with scholars submitting "just discovered" articles about the Ciudad Juarez femicide when Latina/o Studies scholars such as Alejandro Lugo and Rosa Linda Fregoso, among others, and Latina filmmaker Lourdes Portillo have been writing and producing videos (e.g., *Señorita Extraviada*) about this crisis for years. Yet scholars continue to submit essays to major communication journals without doing what we teach our students, at the undergraduate level, is the most basic step in research, *a thorough literature review*. However, we cannot be surprised at this tactic for it is part of a cultural regime where peoples of color are assumed not to produce our own knowledge, not to have complexity. Our reality has traditionally been written by those without—who assume themselves to be the privileged purveyors of knowledge production. So it is no surprise that one after another mainstream scholar decides to write about Latina/os without doing the literature review in Latina/o Studies. This book challenges scholars to take our work seriously—to read this before you submit another article on Jennifer's butt, Dora the Explorer, Ciudad Juarez, border/immigration coverage, or any latest Latina/o media thing.

Another component of the myth of discovery strategy is that our scholarship has to be written in reference to mainstream approaches, a practice that privileges whiteness and mostly white scholars. Some of the essays I spoke about above drew their entire analytical force from, for instance, Judith Butler and/or Michel Foucault. Yet they did not draw on Jacqueline Bobo, Gloria Anzaldúa, Nestor García Canclini, Jesus Martín Barbero, George Lipsitz, or any of the people who have contributed to this volume. A similar deployment of this tactic is the policing of minority scholarships by demanding connection to mainstream literature. It is fine to write about Latina/o Studies and reference that scholarship, but you must connect it to whiteness. Moreover, most mainstream research need not connect to issues of race and ethnicity. In this way whiteness remains the privileged space of knowledge against or in relation to which all must write.

Another version of whiteness privileging is what I call *static token fossil practice*. In reference to Latina/o Studies, it most often takes the form of: "I referenced Gloria Anzaldúa therefore I have fulfilled my Latina/o Studies, gender, diversity debt." What this means is that *This Bridge Called My Back* (1983) literally serves as the static token fossil representative of issues of difference. Never mind that Anzaldúa herself wrote so many more things after that. Never mind that the book was coedited by Cherríe Moraga, who also has continued to write. Never mind that there have been scores of other scholars writing about issues of gender, class, transnationality, sexuality, and Latina/o Studies. Never mind that many in Communications have written about these issues. None of this matters, as the Anzaldúa reference serves as the static token fossil to fulfill any engaged approach with these issues.

While Anzaldúa serves as the general Latina reference, Bobo (1988) provides a similar service as the resource for women of color in Communications. At the 2007 International Communication Association (ICA) convention, the Ethnicity and Race in Communication (ERIC) interest group hosted a mentoring panel that included Jacqueline Bobo. Attendance was high, as it should have been, and scholar after Communications scholar came up to her after the panel and remarked, "Of course I read your *'Color Purple'* piece." Granted that piece is canonical, but Bobo has had a prolific and distinguished trajectory of research and publications on issues of black women as cultural readers, producers, and creators (e.g., 1995, 2001, 2004; Bobo, Hudley, and Michel, 2004). *The Color Purple* piece (1988), while undeniably groundbreaking and canonical, was just the beginning!

Syllabi on the Internet is another location for seeing this form of tokenizing and fossilizing. While other areas such as Girl Studies [read—mostly white Girl Studies] are fervently updated, many syllabi still use a chapter from Félix Gutiérrez's *Minorities and the Media: Diversity and the End of Mass Communication* (1985) for their "Hispanics in Communications" lecture, though to be fair some use his updated *Racism, Sexism, and the Media: The Rise of Class Communication in Multicultural America* (2003). While we all draw on our esteemed colleague's groundbreaking work, we urge you to consider that other research on Latina/os and the media has been conducted since 1985—but if you are very fond of this canonical text, we all build on its solid groundwork. Come to think of it, maybe it is a fixation with the 1980s that drives contemporary academia. Seriously though, as scholars we need to take our blinders off. Might we consider what our colleagues with expertise in a certain area of our field are doing before writing in that area? Certainly! Then please read the work of our colleagues who conduct serious work in Latina/o Communication Studies.

The discussion about the myth of discovery, like all discussions about culture and power, has real-life implications. Most of the third-generation scholars in Latina/o Communication Studies are junior scholars. Not only is it important for all of us to read their engaging and important work, but also they need you to do it for their continued membership in our field. The pragmatics of the situation are that reference indexes in some cases can make or break a hiring or a promotion decision. Furthermore, as members of a democratic and engaged scholarly community, all of us need to stay abreast of the ongoing intellectual production in ours and relevant fields. The practices of fossilizing and tokenizing mentioned in the previous section actually subvert such engagement. Reading the work of the scholars entering into the field serves to invigorate us individually and collectively. Undergraduate and graduate students need to learn about the changing demographic composition of our country. From a Communications perspective, how can we train new journalists, for example, if they know little or nothing about the most numerous minority? From a Latina/o Studies perspective, how can we train our students if they do not understand basic issues about media and popular culture from a theoretically and methodologically rigorous approach?

ORGANIZATION OF THE BOOK

This book is divided into four parts. At the outset I want to acknowledge that it focuses primarily on qualitative approaches to the study of communication and Latina/os. This is not meant to imply that quantitative methodologies are not relevant or important. Rather, the contributors to this volume concentrated on qualitative approaches. Given that within Communication Studies in the U.S. the dominant paradigm remains quantitative, it would certainly be a welcome contribution to have another book highlighting that area of expertise for we all need to be in conversation with one another, and Latina/o Communication Studies is certainly not exhausted with this one book. Personally I definitely could use much more statistically rigorous data about media use, participation in production, and so on in relation to Latina/os and the media to give more force to some of the findings at the cultural level of analysis. Within the qualitative approaches that this book represents, four general areas are highlighted in this volume.

The first part, "The Production of Latinidad," explores the formation of the field as well as the production of the category "Latina/o" both historically and across languages within communication. After this first chapter, Mary Beltrán's chapter, "When Dolores del Rio Became Latina: Latina/o Stardom in Hollywood's Transition to Sound," documents that early and largely forgotten Latina/o boom in the mid- to late 1920s when Latina/o actors were prominent in the film industry prior to the introduction of sound technology. This technological advance facilitated, and indeed initiated, the coding of Latina/os as others while simultaneously marginalizing major stars such as Dolores del Rio who could only be portrayed as a stereotype. Accent or no accent, Latina/os became dark ladies and Latin lovers. It is not so much that these stereotypes did not exist prior to sound, but that the status of star was removed and precluded from these roles after sound. The popular culture representation of Latina/os as eternal outsiders, through language practices, can be traced back to the transition to sound in Hollywood film. Dolores del Rio's personal career in Hollywood dwindled, prompting a return to Mexico for continued stardom. Her attempts to crossover later on were not as successful as her original forays in the 1920s. Thus Beltrán through careful historical research demonstrates that the coding of Latina/os was rooted in a particular historical and technological situation. In fact, her essay reads like a reverse script for *Singing in the Rain* (1952). Mari Castañeda explores the convergence of media around the difference of language. Deploying political economic methodology, Castañeda links the rise of Spanish-language media to contemporary transnational issues of audiences and profit maximization. The convergence in ownership of both Spanish- and English-language newspapers and radio stations makes total sense in an era in which demographic growth of the Latina/o diaspora is undeniable and ultimately, as many including Dávila (2001) have amply documented, highly profitable and therefore desirable from the perspective of transnational capital. Castañeda is one of two authors in this book (the other is Casillas) who touch on issues of radio (see also Casillas, 2005b; Castañeda Paredes, 2003; Gutiérrez and Schement, 1979), an understudied medium that remains prominent across the world and nationally. Together these three chapters illustrate how approaches from a variety of perspectives within communications—history, political economy, and structuring myths and narratives—flesh out the construction of a body of research that takes Latina/o Studies issues centrally and seriously.

The second set of chapters, "Performance and the Self," draws on auto-ethnography and performance studies within communications. In "Performing the Responsible Sponsor: Everything You Never Wanted to Know about Immigration Post-9/11," Bernadette M. Calafell connects Latina/o identity to Middle Eastern subjectivity in this post-9/11 world where all are assumed to be traitors until proven patriots. In accompanying her partner to get immigration papers, Calafell experiences firsthand the inspections border crossers face as they navigate the bureaucracy.[4] The combination of Chicana—read suspect—yet light skinned professor—read acceptable—favor Calafell's subjectivity versus her partner's Egyptian country of origin plus his name, Mohamed. All of these vectors of difference add up to a complex set of belongings and outsider status for Calafell and her partner as well as for successive agents they have to meet, who include dominant culture ones as well as an African American woman. This is no simple process of black and white, but an intricate matrix of hybrid experiences and histories that are all the more intense once Calafell travels to Mexico, where she is told her name is Arab, thus making the transnational connection between the couple come full circle! Shane Moreman's "Hybrid Performativity, North and South of the Border: *Entre la teoría y la materialidad de la hibridación*" follows Paulina Rubio's trajectory as a transnational star attempting that important crossover into U.S. markets and maps it over Shane's own personal trajectory as a gay Latina/o scholar as he crosses over into Mexico and into academia. Taking hybridity as a central concept and infusing it with the lived experience of struggle and contestation of hybrid bodies, Moreman reminds us that border crossing is easier for some than others (Cepeda, 2001, 2000). Even so, Paulina Rubio, despite possessing assets that usually count for the mainstream crossover such as gender, beauty, and whiteness, is finding it difficult to gain a foothold of the type that Shakira has achieved (Cepeda, 2003b). Similarly, Moreman's body gets checked at both sides of the border in spaces ranging from clubs to academia. In both of these chapters it is explained how global policies are lived locally by particular bodies. The knowledge derived from such deeply courageous and personal accounts highlights the necessity for a broad range of methodologies in our field. The chapters in this section of the book complement those in the three other sections, reminding us of the importance of diversity in qualitative approaches.

The third section of the book, "Contextually Representing the Heterogeneity," contains three excellent examples of representational analysis of contemporary Latina/os in the media and Latina/o media. These are two different categories: the first refers to Latina/o representation in mainstream media and the second to Latina/o representation in media produced for, and less often by, Latina/os. While it has become nearly commonplace for communication scholars to deride representational analysis as easy or lazy,[5] these three chapters should dispel those two derogatory adjectives. Quality representational analysis is deceptively simple, but any scholar who has tried it can attest to its complexity. To begin with, it has to be conducted in relation to context, and that is a difficult yet integral component of the process. Thus it remains an important part of our field precisely because of the rich knowledge that it yields. Focusing on primetime television news and the process of "symbolic colonization," Isabel Molina Guzmán's research ("Policing the Latina/o Other: Latinidad in Primetime News Coverage of the Elián González Story") finds that the Elián González spectacle serves to gender, racialize, and infantilize the Cuban American community that had until then, 1999–2000, filled the position of "exceptional minority" within the U.S. Latina/o population and national imaginary. This move restored binary categories so useful to mainstream news that once again privilege values and norms of whiteness. Symbolically dislodged from their privileged position, Cuban Americans can now be subject to the type of coverage that other Latina/os routinely receive. Katynka Z. Martínez's "Real Women and Their Curves: Letters to the Editor and *Latina* Magazine's Celebration of the 'Latina Body'" analyzes the pages of *Latina* magazine. Having recently celebrated its tenth anniversary, *Latina* has a traceable history of approaches to identity and nationality. Martínez focuses on the letters to the editors and thus this chapter straddles the media studies categories of representation and audience. Nonetheless the chapter demonstrates that *Latina* has sought to represent Latinas in their heterogeneity, both national and corporeal, within the limits of a national circulation, advertiser-supported mainstream magazine. In sum, both Latinas and the magazine must walk the tightrope between agency and structure as well as a tension between a sociopolitical and cultural-political activism in order to resolve commodity discourses, transnational alliances, and normative versions of the female body. This chapter charts the evolving approaches that *Latina* takes from pan-nationality to hybrid ethnicity. To round out this section Dolores Inés Casillas in "A Morning Dose of Latino Masculinity: U.S. Spanish-Language Radio and the Politics of Gender" examines masculinity in talk show radio. After the April 2007 Don Imus incident[6] nearly all of us are much more familiar with shock jock radio, but Casillas shines light (to those who may not know about it, it is quite a popular form of media) on the existence of Latina/o morning radio. Bringing to bear issues of global labor circulation, masculinity, Latina/o male emasculation as they enter underpaid labor in the United States, and the articulation of a voice through commercial radio that thrives on gendered and sexist discourse, Casillas reminds us that radio's day is not yet over. In fact in terms of audience and profits, radio remains at the center of media importance. For Latina/o Communication Studies the study of radio and masculinity illuminates gender relations within Latinidad as a result of global issues of the circulation of labor power. Much like Moreman, Casillas relates the global to the local in an innovative yet absolutely essential way if we are to begin to understand the endurance and perhaps resurgence of patriarchal practices in the new Latina/o America and the fact that shock jock radio is not just a white boy business.

The fourth section, "Latina Women and Youth as Cultural Readers," contributes to a growing area of studies charted out by Rojas (2004) and Mayer (2003) within Latina/o media studies and much earlier, of course, by the foundational work of Bobo (1988). In "Media Practices and Gendered Identity among Transnational Latina Teens," Lucila Vargas engages girls/young women in the production of collages to speak to their own identity as gendered subjects. The richness of these collages speaks to their understanding of the complex intersectionality they face as well as to youth's facility with visual approaches to understanding experience[7] and their deep engagement with popular culture in very sophisticated ways. David Hernández González talks to youth at the Tijuana, Mexico-San Diego, California, border about their media use. In "Watching over the Border: A Case Study of the Mexico-United States Television and Youth Audience" he finds that middle-class Tijuanense youth see themselves as cosmopolitan and modern, especially in relation to internal immigrants to the border city, whom they interpret as traditional and backward. In turn they interpret U.S. programming as more fun and desirable, relating more to their lives than what is produced in Mexico. In "Survival Aesthetics: U.S. Latinas and the Negotiation of Popular Media," María Elena Cepeda pursues the comparative analysis of two Latina communities, one in Minnesota and the other in Massachusetts, through a combination of focus group methodology and analytical literature of media and fandom. She finds that Latinas, as active readers and interpreters of popular culture, develop a "form of (un)conscious 'survival aesthetics'" to make sense of their own position and of popular culture. Still some of them while recognizing the hegemonic sexualizing tendencies of the mainstream, underestimate their oppositional potential. Last, but certainly not least, Jillian Báez also uses focus groups to generate Mexican American women's relation to popular culture. One of the components of the Cepeda project is that in both university settings that she studied, Caribbean Latinas were overrepresented within the focus groups. Báez actively seeks the Mexican American component of the female audience as Mexican Americans still make up the majority of the U.S. Latina/o population yet continue to be underrepresented in media and popular culture (Valdivia, 2004b, 2005a; Zimmerman, 2003). In "Mexican American Women Talk Back: Audience Responses to Representations of Latinidad in U.S. Advertising," Báez finds that the "the women's engagement with the ads functions as awareness of and resistance to a colonial legacy of the commodification of racialized sexuality and contemporary expectations of sexualized performances." For these women the hybridity of femininity and sexuality had to be balanced against hegemonic discourses of authenticity. As overall themes, class and nation functioned prominently in these women's interpretations of Latina/os in popular culture. Their special engagement with Salma Hayek spoke of issues of perceived and desired class mobility as well as connection to one of the few Mexican Americans composing this latest Latin boom.

Together these chapters should give any Communication and/or Latina/o Studies scholar plenty of resources, not to mention excellent case studies, to be able to incorporate the work of Latina/o Communication Studies into their research and curriculum. For Latina/o Studies scholars, these chapters provide the best research that is coming out from the field of Communication and Media Studies. For Communications scholars these chapters introduce you to the interrelational work being conducted by Latina/o scholars. All of these chapters are sophisticated interventions integrally and thoroughly combining Latina/o and Communication Studies. While foundational scholarship should never be ignored, these are third-generation scholars of a field that has a history, a broad range of methodologies and accumulating set of findings, and a still wide-open set of questions begging to be pursued. We certainly need more research, more scholars. Acceptance of the newcomers entails meaningful engagement. The table at which we carry on our conversation will have to include more seats. Latina/o Communication scholars will take some of those seats and bring their work to the table, their ideas to the discussion. They/we encourage you to read the work—it is the only way to become familiar with it. Once you do that you will realize that we are here, and if you are one of those discoverers, please get you flag off our butts!

NOTES

1. Not all Latina/os do Latina/o Studies; not all of Latina/o Studies is conducted by Latina/os; Latinidad is complex, tension-full, and unstable.
2. At this point I will not delve into the differences between Communication and Media Studies and Film and Cinema Studies. Quite often to the outsider they are the same, much as to the outsider

all Latina/os are alike. However, the theories, methods, questions, and levels of analysis are quite different.
3. I say this because quite often the articles, which are of course submitted for blind review, use British spelling, which suggests to me they are not written by U.S. scholars.
4. I use the word "bureaucracy" because they keep changing the name of what used to be called the INS (Immigration and Naturalization Services).
5. I was astounded when a panelist sitting next to me in the 2007 ICA (International Communication Association) conference said rather flippantly that representational analysis is really a lazy way of doing research. This was said in reference to "girls' studies," despite the wonderful work done in this area by scores of scholars, including Sarah Projansky and Sharon Mazzarella, and others.
6. In April 2007 Don Imus called a women's NCAA basketball team "nappy-headed hos," prompting his firing by CBS radio and a national debate about ethics, race, and gender.
7. I used this chapter as the background for an assignment of a "digital collage of self and subjectivity" on the first day of class of my "Latinas in Popular Culture" course, and the results were outstanding! Students put together fabulous collages and then proceeded to write long narratives about the collages. I thoroughly recommend this exercise.

REFERENCES

Aparicio, F. R. (2003). Jennifer as Selena: Rethinking Latinidad in media and popular culture. *Latino Studies, 1*, 90–105.

Aparicio, F. R. & S. Chávez-Silverman (Eds.). (1997). *Tropicalizations: Transcultural representations of Latinidad.* Hanover, NH: University Press of New England.

Báez, J. M. (2006). "En mi imperio": Competing discourses of identity in Ivy Queen's reggaetón. *CENTRO: Journal of the Center for Puerto Rican Studies, 18*(2): 62–81.

Báez, J. M. (2007a). Speaking of Jennifer Lopez: Discourses of iconicity and identity formation among Latina audiences. *Media Report to Women, 35*(1), 5–13.

Báez, J. M. (2007b). Towards a *Latinidad feminista*: The multiplicities of Latinidad and feminism in contemporary cinema. *Journal of Popular Communication, 5*(2), 109–128.

Báez, J. M. (2007c). (Re)membering the Latina body: A discourse ethnography of gender, Latinidad, and consumer culture. In C. McCarthy, A. S. Durham, L. C. Engel, A. A. Filmer, M. D. Giardina, & M. A. Malagreca (Eds.), *Globalizing cultural studies: Ethnographic interventions in theory, method and policy* (pp. 189–203). New York: Peter Lang.

Báez, J. M. (forthcoming). Latinization. In C. Lugo-Lugo & D. Leonard (Eds.), *Latinos and Latinas in U.S. history and culture: An encyclopedia.* Armonk, NY: M. E. Sharpe.

Barrera, M. (2000). Hottentot 2000: Jennifer Lopez and her butt. In K. Phillips & B. Reay (Eds.), *Sexualities in history: A reader* (pp. 110–133). New York: Routledge

Beltrán, M. (2002). The Hollywood Latina body as site of social struggle: Media constructions of stardom and Jennifer Lopez's "cross-over butt." *Quarterly Review of Film and Video, 19*(1), 71–86.

Beltrán, M. (2004). *Más Macha*: The new Latina action hero. In Y. Tasker (Ed.), *Action and adventure cinema* (pp. 186–200). London: Routledge.

Beltrán, M. (2005a). Commemoration as crossover: "Remembering" Selena. In S. Jones & J. Jensen (Eds.), *Afterlife as afterimage: Understanding posthumous fame* (pp. 81–96). New York: Peter Lang.

Beltrán, M. (2005b). Dolores del Río, the first "Latino invasion," and Hollywood's transition to sound. *Aztlán: The Journal of Chicano Studies, 30*(1), 55–86.

Beltrán, M. (2005c). The new Hollywood racelessness: Only the fast, furious (and multi-racial) will survive. *Cinema Journal, 44*(2), 50–67.
Beltrán, M. (2008). Mixed race in Latinowood: Latino stardom and ethnic ambiguity in the era of *Dark Angels*. In M. Beltrán & C. Fojas (Eds.), *Mixed race Hollywood: Multiraciality in film and media culture*. New York: New York University Press.
Beltrán, M. (2009). *Hollywood Latinidad: Latina/o Stars, Shifting Borders*. Urbana: University of Illinois Press.
Beltrán, M. & C. Fojas. (Eds.). (2008). *Mixed race Hollywood: Multiraciality in film and media culture*. New York: New York University Press.
Beltrán, M., J. C. H. Park, H. Puente, S. Ross, & J. Downing. (2005). Pressurizing the media industry. In J. D. H. Downing & C. Husband (Eds.), *Representing "race": Racisms, ethnicity, and the media* (pp. 160–193). London: Sage.
Bérubé, M. & C. Nelson. (1995). *Higher education under fire: Politics, economics, and the crisis of the humanities*. New York: Routledge.
Bobo, J. (1988). *The color purple*: Black women as cultural readers. In D. Pribram (Ed.), *Female spectators: Looking at film and television* (pp. 90–109). London: Verso.
Bobo, J. (1995). Black women as cultural readers. New York: Columbia University Press.
Bobo, J. (Ed.) (2001). *Black feminist cultural criticism*. Malden, MA: Blackwell.
Bobo, J., C. Hudley, & C. Michel (Eds.). (2004). *Black studies reader*. New York: Routledge.
Calafell, B. M. (2001). In our own image?!: A rhetorical criticism of *Latina* magazine. *Voices: A Journal of Chicana and Latina Studies, 3*(1/2), 12–46.
Calafell, B. M. (2004). Disrupting the dichotomy: "Yo soy Chicana/o?" in the new Latina/o south. *The Communication Review, 7*, 175–204.
Calafell, B. M. (2005). Pro(re-)claiming loss: A performative pilgrimage in search of Malintzin Tenépal. *Text and Performance Quarterly, 25*, 43–56.
Calafell, B. M. (2006). Mocking Mexicans for profit. *Latino Studies, 4*, 162–165.
Calafell, B. M. (2007). "Your education wipes out your ethnicity": A "white woman of color" in the classroom. In. D. Cleveland (Ed.), *When minorities are especially encouraged to apply*. New York: Peter Lang.
Calafell, B. M. (2008). Mentoring and love: An open letter. *Cultural Studies: Critical Methodologies, 8*, 1.
Calafell, B. M. & F. Delgado. (2004). Reading Latina/o Images: Interrogating Americanos. *Critical Studies in Media Communication, 21*, 1–21.
Carey, J. (1992). *Communication as culture: Essays on media and society*. New York: Routledge.
Casillas, D. I. (2005a). Latin Grammys. In S. Oboler & D. Gonzalez (Eds.), *Encyclopedia of Latinas and Latinos in the United States*, Vol. 2 (pp. 477–478). New York: Oxford University Press.
Casillas, D. I. (2005b). Radio, Spanish-language. In S. Oboler & D. Gonzalez (Eds.), *Encyclopedia of Latinas and Latinos in the United States*, Vol. 3 (pp. 548–552). New York: Oxford University Press.
Casillas, D. I. (forthcoming). Broadcasting Trans(Nationalism): An acoustic remapping of U.S. Spanish-language radio. *SYMBOLISM: A Journal of Critical Aesthetics*.
Castañeda Paredes, M. (2001). The Reorganization of Spanish language media marketing in the United States. In V. Mosco & D. Schiller (Eds.), *Continental order? Integrating North America for cybercapitalism*. Lanham, MD: Rowman and Littlefield.
Castañeda Paredes, M. (2003). The transformation of Spanish-language radio in the United States. *Journal of Radio Studies, 10*(1), 5–16.
Cepeda, M. E. (2000). *Mucho loco* for Ricky Martin, or: The politics of chronology, crossover and language within the Latin(o) music "boom." *Popular music and society, 24*(3), 55–71.

Cepeda, M. E. (2001). "Columbus effects": The politics of crossover and chronology within the Latin(o) music "boom." *Discourse, 23*(1), 242–267.

Cepeda, M. E. (2003a). *Mucho loco* for Ricky Martin, or: The politics of chronology, crossover and language within the Latin(o) music "boom." In M. T. Carroll & H. Berger (Eds.), *Global pop, local talk* (pp. 113–129). Jackson: University of Mississippi Press.

Cepeda, M. E. (2003b). Shakira as the idealized, transnational citizen: A case study of *Colombianidad* in transition. *Latino Studies, 1*(2), 210–232.

Cepeda, M. E. (2005a). Marc Anthony. In S. Oboler & D. J. González (Eds.), *The Oxford encyclopedia of Latinos and Latinas in the United States* (pp. 83–85). Oxford: Oxford University Press.

Cepeda, M. E. (2005b). Shakira. In S. Oboler & D. J. González (Eds.), *The Oxford encyclopedia of Latinos and Latinas in the United States* (pp. 120–122). Oxford: Oxford University Press.

Cepeda, M. E. (2008). *Musical imagi/nation: U.S. Colombians and the Latin(o) music "boom."* New York: New York University Press.

Cepeda, M. E. (forthcoming). Whose musical imagi/nation?: Contradictory discourses of belonging in "Nuestro Himno" and "Reggaetón Latino." *Identities: Global studies in culture and power*.

Dávila, A. (2001). *Latinos inc.: The marketing and making of a people*. Berkeley: University of California Press.

Delgado, F. & B. M. Calafell. (2004). From Rico Suave to livin' *La Vida Loca:* A decade of evolution for Latino pop star images. In R. A. Lind (Ed.), *Race/gender/media: Considering diversity across audiences, content, and producers* (pp. 235–242). New York: Longman.

Del Río, E. (2006). The Latina/o problematic: Categories and questions in media communication research. In C. Beck (Ed.), *Communication yearbook 30* (pp. 387–429). Mahwah, NJ: Lawrence Erlbaum Associates.

Durham, A. & J. M. Báez. (2007). A tail of two women: Exploring the contours of difference in popular culture. In S. Springgay & D. Freedman (Eds.), *Curriculum and the cultural body* (pp. 131–145). New York: Peter Lang.

Fiol-Matta, L. (2002). Pop Latinidad: Puerto Ricans in the Latin explosion. *Centro Journal, 14*(1), 27–51.

Freire, P. (1993). *Pedagogy of the oppressed*, 20th anniversary ed. New York: Continuum.

Gitlin, T. (1995). The rise of "identity politics": An examination and a critique. In Bérubé, M. & C. Nelson (Eds.), *Higher education under fire: Politics, economics, and the crisis of the humanities* (pp. 308–318). New York: Routledge.

González, D. (2006). Televisión y frontera: el espacio audiovisual en Tijuana. In M. Ortiz (Ed.), *Los medios de comunicación en Baja California* (pp. 143–156). México: Universidad Autónoma de Baja California/Porrúa, 2006.

González, D. (2007a). Aquí, allá y en todas partes: las audiencias juveniles en la frontera norte. In G. Orozco (Coor.), *Un mundo de visiones. Interacciones de las audiencias en múltiples escenarios mediáticos y virtuales* (pp. 117–131). México, DF: Instituto Latinoamericano de Comunicación y Educación (ILCE).

González, D. (2007b). *El sueño americano en México. Televisión y audiencias juveniles en Tijuana*. Mexicali, Baja California: Universidad Autónoma de Baja California.

Gutiérrez, F. & R. Schement (1979). *Spanish language radio in the Southwestern United States*. Austin: Center for Mexican American Studies, University of Texas.

Harewood, S. J. & A. N. Valdivia (2005). Exploring Dora: Re-embodied Latinidad on the web. In S. R. Mazzarella (Ed.), *Girl wide web: Girls, the internet, and the negotiation of identity* (pp. 85–104). New York: Peter Lang.

Hernandez, T. K. (2002). The Buena Vista social club: The radical politics of nostalgia. In M. Habell-Pallán & M. Romero (Eds.), *Latino/a popular culture* (pp. 61–72). New York: New York University Press.

Holling, M. A. & B. M. Calafell. (2007). Identities on stage and staging identities: Chicano Brujo performances as emancipatory practices. *Text and Performance Quarterly, 27*, 58–83.

Jáquez, C. F. & F. R. Aparicio, with M. E. Cepeda. (2003). *Musical migrations: Transnationalism and cultural hybridity in Latin(o) America*. New York: St. Martin's Press.

Kuhn, T. (1996). *The structure of scientific revolutions*, 3rd ed. Chicago: University of Chicago Press.

Martínez, K. Z. (2004). Latina magazine and the invocation of a panethnic family: Latino identity as it is informed by celebrities and Papis Chulos. *The Communication Review, 7*(2), 155–174.

Martínez, K. Z. (2006) American idols with Caribbean soul: Cubanidad and the Latin Grammys. *Latino Studies, 4*, 381–400.

Mayer, V. (2003). *Producing dreams, consuming youth: Mexican Americans and mass media*. New Brunswick, NJ: Rutgers University Press.

McCarthy, C. (1995). Contradictions of existence: Identity and essentialism. In M. Bérubé & C. Nelson (Eds.), *Higher education under fire: Politics, economics, and the crisis of the humanities* (pp. 326–335). New York: Routledge.

Molina Guzmán, I. (2005). Gendering Latinidad in the Elián news discourse about Cuban women. *Latino Studies, 3*, 179–204.

Molina Guzmán, I. (2006a). Covering ethnic conflicts: Tracing the discourses of race, ethnicity and difference in the local press. *Journalism: Theory, Practice, Criticism, 7*(3), 281–299.

Molina Guzmán, I. (2006b). Mediating Frida: Negotiating discourses of Latina/o authenticity in global media representations of ethnic identity. *Critical Studies in Media Communication, 23*(3), 232–251.

Molina Guzmán, I. (2007a). Mapping the academic terrain of US Latinas/os in the general-market and Latina/o media. In H. Rodriguez, R. Saenz, & C. Menjivar (Eds.), *The Experiences of Latinas/os in the United States* (pp. 199–209). New York: Springer Press.

Molina Guzmán, I. (2007b). Marisleysis: Discourses of disorderly bodies in the Elián story. In Myra Mendible (Ed.), *From bananas to buttocks: The Latina in popular film and culture* (pp. 221–243). University of Texas: Austin.

Molina Guzmán, I. (2007c). Salma's Frida: Latinas as transnational bodies in US popular culture. In Myra Mendible (Ed.), *From bananas to buttocks: The Latina in popular film and culture* (pp. 117–129). University of Texas: Austin.

Molina Guzmán, I. & A. N. Valdivia. (2004). Brain, brow or bootie: Latina iconicity in contemporary popular culture. *Communication Review, 7*(2), 203–219.

Moreman, S. (1999). *Chupa Mi Cacahuate*: The terms of my Latino identity. In N. K. Denzin (Ed.), *Studies in symbolic interaction, a research annual*, Vol. 22. Greenwich, CT: JAI Press.

Negrón-Muntaner, F. (1997). Jennifer's butt. *Aztlán, 22*(2), 182–195.

Paredez, D. (2002). Remembering Selena, re-membering Latinidad. *Theater Journal, 54*(1), 63–84.

Rojas, V. (2004). The gender of Latinidad: Latinas speak out about Hispanic television. *Communication Review, 7*(2), 125–154.

Shohat, E. & R. Stam. (1994). *Unthinking eurocentrism: Multiculturalism and the media*. New York: Routledge.

Shugart, H. A. (2007). Crossing over: Hybridity and hegemony in the popular media. *Communication and Critical/Cultural Studies, 4*(2), 115–141.

Subervi-Vélez, F. (1999). The mass media and Latinos: Policy and research agendas for the next century. *Aztlan, 24*(2), 131–147.

Subervi-Velez, F., J. Báez, & N. Saenz. (2005). News networks. In D. Gonzalez & S. Oboler (Eds.), *The Oxford encyclopedia of Latinos and Latinas in the United States* (pp. 265–266). New York: Oxford University Press.

Valdivia, A. N. (Ed.) (1995). *Feminism, multiculturalism and the media: Global diversities.* Newbury Park: Sage.

Valdivia, A. N. (1996). "Rosie Goes to Hollywood: The Politics of Representation." *Education/Pedagogy/Cultural Studies*, 18: 2, 122–141.

Valdivia, A. N. (1998). Stereotype or transgression? Rosie Perez in Hollywood film. *The Sociological Quarterly*, *39*(3), 393–408.

Valdivia, A. N. (2000). *A Latina in the land of Hollywood and other essays on media culture.* Tucson: University of Arizona Press.

Valdivia, A. N. (2003a). *A companion to media studies.* Malden, Blackwell.

Valdivia, A. N. (2003b). Radical hybridity: Latina/os as the paradigmatic transnational post-subculture. In D. Muggleton & R. Weinzierl (Eds.), *The Post-subcultures reader* (pp. 151–165). London: Berg Publishers.

Valdivia, A. N. (2003c). Salsa as popular culture: Ethnic audiences constructing an identity. In A. Valdivia (Ed.), *Media Studies Companion* (pp. 399–418). Oxford: Blackwell.

Valdivia, A. N. (2004a). Latina/o communication and media studies today. *Communication Review*, 7(2), 107–112.

Valdivia, A. N. (2004b). Latinas as radical hybrid: Transnationally gendered traces in mainstream media. *Global Media Journal*, *2*(4). Retrieved from (http://lass.calumet.purdue.edu/cca/gmj/OldSiteBackup/SubmittedDocuments/archivedpapers/Spring2004/refereed/Valdivia.htm, September 12, 2007.

Valdivia, A. N. (2005a). Geographies of Latinidad: Constructing identity in the face of radical hybridity. In W. Critchlow, G. Dimitriadis, N. Dolby, & C. McCarthy (Eds.), *Race, identity, and representation* (pp. 307–317). New York: Routledge.

Valdivia, A. N (2005b). The Location of the Spanish in Latinidad: Examples from contemporary U.S. popular culture. *Letras Femeninas*, *31*(2), 60–78.

Valdivia, A. N. (2007a). Is Penélope to J-Lo as culture is to nature? Eurocentric approaches to "Latin" beauties. In M. Mendible (Ed.), *Bananas to buttocks: The Latina body in popular culture.* Austin: University of Texas Press.

Valdivia, A. N. (2007b) Long live Jim Carey! *Popular Communication*, 5(1): 13–15.

Valdivia, A. N. (2007c). Popular culture and recognition: Narratives of youth and Latinidad. In N. Dolby & F. Rizvi (Eds.), *Youth moves: Identities in global perspective* (pp. 101–114). New York: Routledge.

Valdivia, A. N. (2008). Mixed race on Disney Channel: From *Johnnie Tsunami* to the *Cheetah Girls.* In M. Beltrán & C. Fojas (Eds.), *Mixed race Hollywood: Multiraciality in film and media culture.* New York: NYU Press.

Valdivia, A. N. (forthcoming a). *Latina/os and the Media.* Cambridge, U.K.: Polity Press.

Valdivia, A. N. (forthcoming b). *Latinas in popular culture: Uses and abuses of hybridity.* Oxford: Blackwell.

Valdivia, A. N. & R. S. Bettivia. (1999a) "A Guided Tour through the World of One Adolescent's Girl Culture." In S. Mazzarella & N. Pecora (Eds.), *Growing Up Girls: Popular Culture in the Creation of Identities* (pp. 159–174). New York: Peter Lang.

Valdivia, A. N. & R. S. Bettivia. (1999b) "Gender, generation, space, and popular music." In C. McCarthy, G. Hudak, S. Miclaucik, & P. Saukko (Eds.), *Sound Identities: Music and the Cultural Politics of Education* (pp. 429–446). New York: Peter Lang.

Vargas, D. R. (2002). Bidi bidi bom bom: Selena and Tejano music in the making of *Tejas*. In M. Habell-Pallán & M. Romero (Eds.), *Latina/o popular culture* (pp. 171–226). New York: New York University Press.

Vargas, L. (2000). Genderizing Latino news: An analysis of a local newspaper's coverage of Latino current affairs. *Critical Studies in Media Communication, 17* (3), 261–293.

Zimmerman, M. (2003). Erasure, imposition and crossover of Puerto Rican and Chicanos in US film and music culture. *Latino Studies, 1*(1), 115–122.

CHAPTER TWO

When Dolores Del Rio Became Latina: Latina/o Stardom IN Hollywood's Transition TO Sound

MARY BELTRÁN

Going to the local Cineplex or turning on the television with the hope of finding Latino and Latina actors featured in starring roles can be a more heartening experience these days than it was just a few decades ago. Today we might happen upon a variety of actors of Latino and Latin American descent, perhaps Benicio del Toro, Rosario Dawson, Diego Luna, or Michelle Rodriguez, playing film and television characters that are richly textured and not predicated on the old standby stereotypes. Celebrity publicity venues such as entertainment news shows and supermarket tabloids also heavily feature Latina/o icons: Jennifer Lopez, Wilmer Valderrama, and Eva Longoria, among others, make regular appearances. Slowly but surely, Latino actors and actresses are gaining more diverse opportunities and are more concertedly promoted as stars. It's a drastic change from previous decades, when Latina/o actors typically struggled with extremely limited roles and casting opportunities.

A historical survey of Latina/o participation in Hollywood film reveals that this is only the most recent wave of global stardom. There was another era, often now forgotten, in which Latino and Latina actors were hired for their perceived box office potential, viewed as especially attractive and trendy, and promoted as international stars. In the mid-to-late 1920s, known as the Golden Age of U.S. silent film, a number of actors of Latina/o descent were among the top stars at their respective studios and in the film industry more generally. This first "Latin invasion," as the film fan magazine *Photoplay* described the influx of Hispanic actors in 1927,[1] provided opportunities for a handful of actors that has only recently been matched. Actors from Mexico in particular, such as Ramon Novarro, Dolores Del Rio, Gilbert Roland, and Lupe Vélez, the popular "Latin Lovers" of this period, had a star status that is only beginning to be equaled by the most popular Latina/os in Hollywood today.

The reign of the Latin Lovers was cut short by a number of industrial and social developments, perhaps the most important among them the transition to "talkies" in the last years of the decade. This industry shift was to have a profound impact. Aside from prompting changes in popular film genres and acting styles, producers and industry executives had to make decisions regarding what the "American" accent should sound like as characters began to speak.[2] In this reimagining of cinematic story worlds, actors with Hispanic accents, even those of the most exalted status, now had an ambivalent status and were typically cast in roles that further racialized them as distinct from stars deemed white. Arguably it is no coincidence that in this decade marked by the Great Depression Mexican Americans were increasingly scapegoated and marginalized; the evolving status of Latina/os in Hollywood can be best understood as just one aspect of this process.

Exploring how Latina/o stardom shifted throughout this period thus promises to shed light not only on how Latina/os participated and were represented in Hollywood film but also on the process of cultural racialization experienced by Mexican Americans and other U.S. Latina/os in this period. What industrial and social conditions allowed Latina/o actors to become some of Hollywood's top stars in the late silent film era? And how did the transition to sound film and the rise of accent as a marker of U.S. American identity, combined with social developments of the 1930s, affect this climate and as a result, Latina/o opportunity and star images? To begin to explore these questions, I survey the opportunity experienced and climate faced by Latina/os in Hollywood and U.S. social life before, during, and immediately after the transition to sound film.

In particular, I focus on the career of Mexican-born actress Dolores Del Rio as a telling example of the opportunity and subsequent limitations that were experienced during these periods. Described as the "leader of the Latin invasion" by *Photoplay*,[3] Del Rio arguably was one of the industry's most powerful actors, as well as the most successful Latina, within a few years of her arrival in Los Angeles in 1925. At the peak of her success she starred in a number of critical and box office hits, including the silent films *What Price Glory?* (1926), *The Loves of Carmen* (1927), and *Resurrection* (1927), and the early sound film *Ramona* (1928). Dolores Del Rio was also among the top twenty money earners in Hollywood at her career peak,[4] signing a $5 million, multifilm contract with United Artists in 1928.[5] Not coincidentally, Del Rio's career subsequently underwent major changes with the industrial and social shifts of the 1930s. While she continued working, she found that the star status that she achieved in the late 1920s was not possible after the industry's conversion to sound film and notions of star appeal had shifted to privilege "all-American" stars over those of Latina/o descent.

I explore these questions through historical research, in conjunction with critical analysis of Dolores Del Rio's career and star publicity during her years in Hollywood, 1925 through the early 1940s. In my research, I analyzed Del Rio's films and star promotion materials, including publicity photographs, press books, promotional posters, and film reviews.[6] Although a number of Del Rio's early films have not been preserved, analyses of film stills, promotional materials, and film reviews allowed me to "fill in the blanks" when I was not able to view her films. In this process emphasize the years of 1928 through 1932, the period during which the U.S. film studios converted to the production and exhibition of sound films.

THE 1920S AND HOLLYWOOD'S FIRST LATIN WAVE

The 1920s were a unique period for U.S. popular culture. In this era of suffragists, flappers, and tensions over immigration, the social norms of masculinity, femininity, and whiteness were under challenge, and at times, revision. Such tensions played a role in the popularity of fashions, art forms, and performers deemed foreign, cosmopolitan, sexually transgressive, and/or culturally taboo.[7] For example, the tango, Harlem dance clubs, Italian actor Rudolph Valentino, jazz music, and new, skin-baring fashions became popular in this time period. Influenced by the influx of silent films imported from such countries as Germany and France, as well as by the relative prosperity of the times (Shindler, 1999), U.S. citizens appeared to be looking outside the country and particularly to Europe for direction in regard to sophisticated culture and lifestyle.

These national cultural trends included a romanticization of the Spanish colonial history of California and the southwest, as scholars such as Carey McWilliams (1946) and more recently Matt Garcia (2002) have described. There also was a rising interest in Latin American cultural forms in the realm of popular entertainment. Broadway had begun to turn to Latin America for inspiration with respect to narratives and music in the 1910s (Roberts, 1999), while a number of Latin music–inspired songs became popular with the general public in the next decade. The tango also came into vogue as social dancing became a popular pastime in the 1920s (Roberts, 1999; Studlar, 1996).

The growing film industry played a major role in these cultural trends. In addition to the importing of films, directors, actors, and other creative personnel from Europe and elsewhere were emigrating to the United States and taking leading roles at the major studios, becoming some of the most popular and influential players within the industry. Foreign names and faces proliferated in the Hollywood star system by the 1920s, with such actors as Pola Negri, Rudolph Valentino, and home-grown vamp Theda Bara filling the pages of *Photoplay* and other film fan magazines. In line with the sensibilities of the times, these stars typically were promoted in a manner that emphasized their wealth, glamor, and flamboyant lifestyles.

With respect to film genres, melodramas set in exotic locales and populated with passionate and romantic characters were extremely popular with U.S. moviegoers. Surveys of popular films before the conversion to sound reveal that 1920s films often capitalized on public curiosity with the foreign and the wealth and tastes of the upper class.[8] Films such as *The Mark of Zorro* (1920) and *The Sheik* (1921) were national sensations that prompted the production of similar desert romances and melodramas set in exotic locales, a trend that continued throughout much of the decade. Richard Koszarski (1990), for example, found Latin or Arabian themes in the top five films from 1923 to 1927.

The popular acting style in these Great Lover roles was broad and passionate, emphasizing the display and expressiveness of actors' bodies. As Sklar (1994) asserts, "[T]he alternative to traditional American behavior that movie audiences most clearly demanded [during the silent film era] was passionate behavior" (p. 100). The Latino actors and actresses who were successful in this era arguably were made stars by film audiences who not only appreciated their aesthetic appearance, but also were responding to their effective physical expression of emotion on the screen. It should be noted that these actors typically were not portraying Latina/o characters. As Dolores Del Rio once commented regarding her silent film career, "I tried to interest my producers in stories about Mexico. I wanted to play a Mexican. But they preferred me to play a French woman or Polynesian."[9]

Rudolph Valentino's popularity played no small part in these trends. Public passion for the Italian actor considered the first Latin Lover flowered with *The Sheik* and *The Four Horseman of the Apocalypse*, both released in 1921, and was still going strong in 1924 and 1925, when the annual *Exhibitors Herald* poll found that he and Norma Talmadge were the biggest male and female box office draws in the country.[10] The star's popularity seemed to only grow with his unexpected death in 1926, demonstrating continued public interest in a new type of romantic figure, the mysterious ethnic Other (Studlar, 1997). Actresses who fell in the Latin Lover category also were popular, at least in part because of U.S. audiences' fascination with how they "temporarily blurred the boundaries of gender, ethnicity, and race" (Bernstein, 1997, p. 6). Regardless of the reasons for their appeal, the Valentino phenomenon prompted a positive disposition toward employing actors in the

Latin Lover tradition. Erotic androgyny (on the part of men), an air of mystery, and a darkly handsome appearance became lucrative traits for actors and actresses to possess, and a number were employed expressly because of this. This group included several actors born in Mexico, including Ramon Novarro and his second cousin Dolores Del Rio, Lupe Vélez, and Gilbert Roland, all of whom secured contracts at the major studios in the 1920s. Some non-Latino actors even acquired Latino-sounding names to capitalize on the vogue, the best known example being that of Austrian Jewish actor Jacob Krantz, who changed his name to Ricardo Cortez in the early 1920s to better exploit on his Valentino-like looks.[11] Notably, it didn't matter whether these actors spoke English or spoke it well, as it was their looks and expressiveness that were key to their acting and appeal as stars.

Latinidad, which I define according to its simple translation from Spanish as "Latin-ness," was not simplistically viewed as positive within the landscape of popular culture of the period, however. This can be seen in how the promotion of successful Latina/o stars of the period typically performed a deracializing function, positioning them as acceptable ethnics. Studlar (1996), in her exploration of Spanish actor Antonio Moreno's career in the late 1910s, describes a process by which Moreno was promoted to whiteness, or at least to the status of the "right kind of ethnic" in star promotion texts (p. 178). We can infer that he, like other actors considered romantic Latin types, needed to avoid the negative connotations that might be associated with ethnic, working-class Mexican Americans in this era.

For Mexican actors Ramon Novarro and Dolores Del Rio, such negotiation also was arguably necessary because of potential negative reaction to their nationality. Outside Hollywood, tensions were beginning to mount regarding the status of Mexicans and Mexican Americans, particularly with respect to Mexicans who had emigrated to the United States to work as laborers. During this period, "nativists" argued for the superiority of Anglo-Saxons and called for English-only laws and other covenants to deny Mexican Americans full citizenship rights. In contrast, southwestern employers asserted their desire for unrestricted immigration so that they might hire Mexican laborers.[12] These tensions came to a head in debates over such topics as "Americanization" programs and the segregated schooling of Mexican American children, reflecting national ambivalence regarding the cultural citizenship of Mexican Americans in this era.

In addition, the dominance of Anglo-Saxon whiteness was still asserted in Hollywood in a manner that had a strong impact on Latino and Latina acting hopefuls. As several scholars, most notably Antonio Ríos-Bustamente (1992) and Clara E. Rodríguez (1997), have documented, the opportunities that Latina/os enjoyed in Hollywood's early decades depended greatly on whether they had fair skin and European facial features. The most successful tended to have the appearance of and to be viewed primarily as foreigners of Spanish ancestry, a dynamic of Hollywood's representation of Latinidad that continues today (Valdivia, 2005). As Alicia Rodríguez-Estrada (1997) argues in regard to the career of Mexican actress Lupe Vélez, stars who were viewed as "ethnic" might be able to maintain careers but were less likely to be cast in romantic lead roles in A-list films. Notably, these perceptions were not based strictly on skin tone. Rather, Del Rio's public image as Spanish Mexican and Vélez's as *mestiza* were based in large part on class-related associations,[13] an example of the cultural racialization that Latina/os typically experienced.

Another telling illustration of the continuing dominance of whiteness could be found in the broader popular culture of the 1920s. In early cosmetics industry promotions, for example, light-skinned Anglo women were foregrounded as the most beautiful even while images of Latinas and other nonwhite women were at times used to promote particular products, reflecting the foundational belief that "the true American face was still a white face" (Peiss, 1998, p. 149). Such discourses of Hispanic inferiority would be represented and experienced more overtly in subsequent years.

DOLORES DEL RIO: THE "FEMALE VALENTINO"

This was the historical and industrial context in which Dolores Del Rio achieved success as an actor in Hollywood. Her entrance into the star system in the mid-1920s serves as a vivid illustration of how the vogue for the foreign and exotic in U.S. popular culture created an opening for some Latina/os to establish careers, play leading roles in popular films, and become international stars, while her Hollywood career as a whole illustrates the shifts that took place over the next decade.

Given the emphasis on Dolores Del Rio's family background in her early star image, certain facts are well known. According to her first studio biography and other sources, Del Rio was born Maria Dolores Asúnsolo, in Durango, Mexico, on August 3, 1905 (Wilson, 1927). She grew up in a wealthy family of Spanish-Basque heritage; her father was a bank president and landowner. Del Rio (then Asúnsolo) attended school at the Convent of St. Joseph in Mexico City, where students reportedly were allowed to speak only French and also learned several other languages. For her own amusement she studied dance in Europe; she later became known as one of the finest tango dancers among the Mexican elite. At 15, she married wealthy Jaime Martinez del Rio; after embarking on an extended honeymoon in Europe, they settled into the privileged life in Mexico City. Known as one of the best dancers in the city, Dolores would at times perform the tango or other Latin dances at society gatherings and charity functions.

It was at such an event that del Rio (her married name, with a lower case "d" traditional to Mexico) met U.S. film director Edwin Carewe. The story has it that Carewe, in Mexico with his fiancé, saw del Rio dance at a party and was immediately impressed by her. The Carewes and del Rios struck up a friendship, and Carewe urged the Mexican couple to come to Hollywood so Dolores could try her hand at film acting and Jaime at screenwriting. ("He told me I was the female Valentino," Del Rio said in an interview published in the *San Francisco Chronicle* in 1981 [Byrne, 1981]). The del Rios finally relented in 1925; Dolores del Rio (whose last name was soon Anglicized as Del Rio) was 20 at the time. She was quoted in a Mexican newspaper as saying that she hoped to be able to present an image of the sophisticated Mexicana missing in Hollywood film at the time. "It is my dearest wish to make fans realize their [Mexicans'] real beauty, their wonder, their greatness as a people. The vast majority seem to regard Mexicans as a race of bandits, or laborers, dirty, unkempt, and uneducated. My ambition is to show the best that's in my nation" (qtd. in Carr, 1979, p. 42).

Edwin Carewe subsequently was the first and most influential shaper of Dolores Del Rio's star image in Hollywood. At the time that Del Rio consented to work with him, he had a multipicture deal with First National and was a popular director with other studios. Carewe placed Del Rio under contract and acted as her manager, as well as directing her in many of her first films. Moreover, he was often mentioned alongside Del Rio in early news items introducing the young starlet . As such he can be viewed as her patron in the public eye, an association that arguably eased Del Rio's rise to stardom, given the need to that existed to promote the Mexican starlet, like Antonio Moreno, as the right kind of ethnic and in a manner that supported popular notions of "imperial meaning making" with respect to the status of Mexicans and Mexican Americans (Pratt, 1992, p. 4). While Mary Louise Pratt (1992) utilized this phrase to describe the dynamics of early travel writing, it becomes an apt descriptor of the discursive thrust in which Del Rio's introduction to U.S. moviegoers was embedded.

Dolores Del Rio's film career began in 1925 with a bit role in Carewe's "jazz baby" romance, *Joanna*. Much of this role ended up on the cutting room floor, but roles in four more films followed in 1926. These included a small role in the society drama *High Steppers* (also directed by Carewe), the lead in the crime caper *Pals First*, and a role in a Universal Pictures comedy. Her first reviews were not so positive. In response to her role in *Pals First*, *Variety*, referring to Del Rio as a "Latin actress" and "Edwin Carewe discovery," described her performance as lackluster (August 26, 1926, p. 18). In particular, the reviewer took umbrage with Del Rio's "Latin" appearance. Critics' opinions quickly turned around with Del Rio's fourth film role in 1926, however. In Fox Film's comedic World War I tale *What Price Glory*, Del Rio portrayed Charmaine, a flirtatious French innkeeper's daughter caught in a love triangle between two American officers. The role casts Del Rio as a vivacious, free-spirited woman who can't help but share herself passionately with both men; a viewing of the film reveals its direction and the cinematography place great emphasis on her exuberance and the expressiveness of her body in the role. A critic for *Variety* predicted that the film would be a big success, based in no small part on Del Rio's perceived sex appeal: "[S]he registers like a house afire. It is no wonder she had the whole army after her!" (Fred., December 1, 1926, p. 12). The film in fact proved to be a huge hit. The song "Charmaine" also was extremely popular with audiences, who were able to buy the sheet music in theater lobbies; over a million copies were reportedly sold (Walker, 1979, p. 82).

Meanwhile, Dolores Del Rio was introduced to U.S. audiences through promotional efforts. Harry D. Wilson, Del Rio's high-profile publicist, targeted magazines and newspapers with introductory feature stories and photographs that capitalized on the more positive stereotypes of high-class Mexicans of the day and proactively avoided the landmines of negative stereotypes. While constructed as a sophisticated and fashionable lady, her Mexican nationality never ceased to figure in to this resulting publicity in interesting ways. She was typically described as a Mexican (or just as often, Spanish or Castilian) beauty; *Photoplay*, for example, dubbed Del Rio "The Daughter of the Dons," and a "perfect Latin type" in an early article (St. John, June 1926, p. 66). Her image was made more palatable, in addition, through steady mentions of her family's wealth and references to Del Rio's presumed strict morality. As Wilson (1927) trumpeted in his first biography of Del Rio, which we can surmise was disseminated widely to the press:

> This is the first time in film history that a Mexican girl has risen to the highest rung of filmdom's ladder. Mexico justly rejoices in her achievements and her tremendous success. ... Her social standing in Los Angeles and Hollywood is one of the highest and her friends cannot be counted in numbers. She is active in society and welfare work and spends many hours of her spare time in helping worthy causes. (p. 6)

Similarly, pains were taken to underscore that Del Rio had pursued acting as a leisure activity and had never needed to engage in such unseemly behavior as training or alteration of her physical appearance on the path to becoming an actress. For example, *Photoplay* offered this description of Del Rio's entree into film acting:

> She was rich. She was happily married. She had everything she wanted. Dolores Del Rio came to Hollywood seeking neither fame nor romance nor money. She went into the movies "just for fun." But the movies refuse to let her go, because she is one of the great discoveries of the year. (June 1927, p. 66)

Despite this narrative that was shared with the press, Del Rio's glamorous and fashionable image had in fact been crafted with the help of a fashion expert.

According to biographer Larry Carr (1979), upon her arrival in Hollywood, Del Rio "bore little resemblance to the acknowledged beauty of world-wide fame she was to become ... Shy and reserved, she dressed conservatively and wore almost no makeup. The film colony found her 'interesting' and 'pretty in a foreign way,' but privately some thought her 'kind of dowdy' and 'too sedate'" (p. 5). In this era in which U.S. women were challenging tradition and gender constraints through such fashion and beauty practices as bobbed hair and shorter hemlines, Del Rio's personal style fit better with an earlier era. Peggy Hamilton, a designer who had created clothes for popular film actress Gloria Swanson, was commissioned to design a high-fashion wardrobe more suitable for a young Hollywood star, according to Carr. Meanwhile, countless publicity photographs in which Del Rio is utilized as a fashion mannequin—initially in traditional Spanish garb such as lace dresses and *rebozos*, but quickly in U.S. and French couture—were disseminated to women's magazines and the fashion pages of daily newspapers, as was becoming a standard promotional practice for female stars. Hamilton also served to an extent in the capacity of what would be considered an agent or personal manager's role today, throwing large parties at which fan magazine writers and others in the press could meet Del Rio (Carr, 1979).

The result of these efforts was a rash of positive publicity for the young Dolores Del Rio, such that her name was reportedly known widely by 1927. She was even "confident enough to turn down a lead opposite Douglas Fairbanks, Snr, [sic] which gave her compatriot, Lupe Velez, her break [playing a feisty Argentinian girl] in *The Gaucho*" that year (Braun, 1972, p. 35). She instead appeared in two other films that became hits. One was a Carewe-helmed adaptation of Leo Tolstoy's *Resurrection*, a melodrama about a Russian peasant girl forced to turn to prostitution after an affair with a married man ends unhappily. *Resurrection* was quite successful, with Del Rio described as a "potent" box office draw in at least one of her reviews (*Variety*, May 18, 1927).

Reviews for her other 1927 film, the Raoul Walsh-helmed *The Loves of Carmen*, based on Bizet's famous opera, were even more positive. Del Rio received strong praise for her portrayal of the amorous Spanish siren. "Sid.," writing for *Variety*, raved that *Loves* contained "plenty of hell, sex and box office" and that Del Rio in particular made an erotic splash in the film (September 28, 1927, p. 53). *Photoplay* also praised Del Rio's beauty and sexual appeal in its critique of her portrayal of "the raven-haired, olive-skinned sinuous-limbed Carmen" (July 1927, p. 69). Several reviewers made ethnic comparisons, suggesting that Del Rio was particularly suited to play Carmen, presumably because her nationality gave her a naturally fiery temperament. Despite this early stereotyping of Del Rio by critics, her rising popularity was undeniable. Analysis of the film's promotional materials bears out that they capitalized almost solely on Del Rio's name and image; the young actress was proving to be one of Hollywood's top female box office draws.

WHEN LATIN LOVERS COULD SPEAK

The end of the window of opportunity experienced by popular Latino and Latina actors such as Dolores Del Rio was already in sight in 1927, as film studios, some quickly and others more grudgingly, began to prepare for the impending conversion to sound film. Prompting and coinciding with shifting public tastes, this change was to have far-reaching impact. Virtually overnight, an actor's voice became an integral part of his or her public image. Walker, in his survey of the transition, found that actors begin to be panned after their first talkies for a variety of complaints, for instance, for having voices considered not "robust" enough, for lacking what was deemed to be the appropriate emotional register for a particular role or their star image, or for having a voice that appeared to indicate a lack of education or class (1979, pp. 49–62). A speaking style associated with middle-class status and lack of identifiable ethnicity came to be associated with desirable notions of U.S. American whiteness. Stars who didn't speak English fluently or who had "non-American" accents were taking crash courses in English and elocution in attempt to save their careers.

Particularly important, film executives were wrestling with what a U.S. accent should sound like. Notions of race and class played no small part in this process. Interestingly, British-inflected English was initially seized on as the most desirable, in part because precise enunciation was deemed necessary with the rudimentary early microphones (Walker, 1979). While soon dropped as the ideal, this initial preference and other cultural biases in the first years of sound had a profound impact on actors' careers. For example, director William C. Demille, in describing problems that got in the way of some actors' achieving the proper U.S. American accent, stated that "the rolling Western 'r' gives the lie to an otherwise excellent 'society' characterization ..." (*Scribners* April 1929, qtd. in Crafton, 1997, p. 450).

In a related shift, audiences' tastes were quickly changing as well. The 1930s were a time when public interest in the foreign and cosmopolitan was on the wane and national tastes shifted dramatically. Marriage and family, thrift, "all-American" (typically, Anglo-Saxon and blonde) looks, chastity, and natural beauty were now privileged, in sharp contrast to the prior emphases of the flamboyant and nontraditional public tastes of the 1920s. In film, down-to-earth narratives of family life and contemporary adventure stories began to be emphasized over the exotic storylines of previous decades. In related shifts, character roles such as the gangsters played by James Cagney and musical ingénues played by Ruby Keeler were increasingly popular, while new, wise-cracking romantic leads such as those played by Clark Gable and Jean Harlow were replacing the "great lover" characters formerly in vogue (Hampton, 1970, p. 401; Mordden, 1988, p. 146). As *Photoplay*, *Motion Picture World*, and other film fan magazines began to report on sound films and the new crop of actors, it became apparent that many stars of the late silent period no longer had an obvious starring role to play.

Scholars disagree on how Latino actors and actresses were affected by these changes. It is difficult to accurately surmise, moreover, how audiences might have reacted to Spanish accents on screen. The filmographies of Latina/o actors of the period do reveal that they typically faced the end of their Hollywood careers or were relegated to roles that incorporated (and often exaggerated) their accent in the transition to talking films. The few options included taking roles in the Spanish-language versions of studio films, as *Mexicana* Lupita Tovar, Antonio Moreno, and occasionally Lupe Vélez chose to do. Other actors found work portraying singers or dancers in the Latin musicals produced in the 1930s and 1940s as Latinidad was increasingly paired with music and dance, dynamics described by Ana M. López (1991) in her discussion of the representational politics of such "Good Neighbor" films. Carmen Miranda, for example, made her living almost exclusively typecast in such roles, while Dolores Del Rio was confined to similar roles in the waning of her Hollywood career. These typically were not star-making roles to the same degree as those played by the Latin Lovers of late silent film, however. Moreover, such performances arguably reinforced the cultural racialization of Mexican Americans and other Latina/os by emphasizing the "foreign" language, accent, and music of Latina/os and Latin Americans.[14] Similarly, another of the few options for Latina/os in early Hollywood sound film was taking roles that exaggerated accents, and often exploited stereotypes, for laughs or suspense. For example, at the time of her suicide in 1944, Lupe Vélez was best known for the RKO *Mexican Spitfire* series, in which her character's fractured English played prominently for laughs. Similarly, Ramon Novarro, "to his eternal discomfort," found work in lower-tier studio Republic's film parodies of major studio films (Mordden, 1988, p. 175), while Gilbert Roland was often stuck in Latino gigolo roles such as the one in Mae West's *She Done Him Wrong* (1934).

The social preoccupations of the times played a large part in the lessening of opportunity that Latina/o actors experienced. The Great Depression (called *La Crisis* in Spanish) in particular, which resulted in unprecedented, widespread unemployment and poverty, dampened enthusiasm for foreign stars and increased the preoccupation with defining what it meant to be "American." With its onset in 1930, previously contested attitudes toward Mexican Americans turned increasingly negative. The new patriotism often defined Mexican Americans, and by extension other Latina/os, as un-American and a threat to the United States. Such sentiment was promoted, for example, by President Hoover, who denounced Mexicans "as one of the causes of the Depression," established the first border patrol, and supported the deportation of hundreds of thousands of Mexicans (and often by mistake, Mexican Americans) in the early 1930s (Sánchez, 1993, p. 213).

Hollywood was in no way left out of the crisis. In Los Angeles, by now firmly established as the nation's movie-making capital, 41.6 percent of Angelenos were reported to be unemployed (Acuña, 2000, p. 216). Mexican American neighborhoods in particular were hard hit by new barriers to employment and massive poverty that arose in relation to *La Crisis*. The Mexican American theater community, for example, was decimated by the joint devastation of the repatriation of talented actors, playwrights, and directors, and massive poverty and unemployment (Kanellos, 1990). The struggle the Mexican American community experienced in this time period arguably further obstructed them from working in a creative capacity in the film industry and served to reinforce negative stereotypes that many non-Latina/os held.

Meanwhile, the film studios were facing difficulties on two fronts. First, film attendance dipped alarmingly in the early 1930s as consumers had less money to spend on leisure pursuits (Balio, 1993). Second, various religious and civic groups, most notably the Catholic organization Legion of Decency, were calling for censorship of films because of what they deemed racy, un-American subject matter. In reaction, film producers increasingly took the safe route, both through the enforcement of the Production Code and through more informal emphasis on "Americanism" in films (Sklar, 1994, p. 175). Overall, Hollywood cinema became more conservative, patriotic, and white-centrist by the mid-1930s.

The Production Code itself also arguably played a part in the decreasing opportunities for Latino actors and actresses throughout this period. While it ostensibly banned racial defamation in the form of slurs or demeaning portrayals, it also forbid what was termed "miscegenation," or the depiction of sexual relations between people of different racial designations. These strictures left Latina/o actors and characters, defined in the United States at this time as neither black nor white, in a hazy limbo. The Code arguably had a chilling effect on Latina/o casting, particularly the casting of Latino men in romantic lead roles opposite Anglo actresses, even while light-skinned Latinas were at times paired with Anglo men, as Carlos E. Cortés (1997) asserts, reflecting a gendered ambiguity to racial and ethnic status of Latina/os in this period.

In relation to the many changes taking place in the country and in Hollywood, stars in the 1930s became what Walker (1979) terms "more 'democratic' and less 'divine,'" though the term democratic is arguably a misnomer here with respect to race and ethnicity (p. 209). Family life, "all-American" looks, and down-to-earth personalities came to be emphasized in promotional efforts over the exotic images attached to many stars in the 1920s. As Shindler (1999) argues, "[t]he stars of the 1930s were the girl or boy 'next door' types like Ginger Rogers or James Stewart" (p. 214). While this wasn't generally spelled out, the new vogue also was for actors who were fair-skinned and of Western European extraction.

Given these various developments, Latina/o stardom in the 1930s never matched the level of possibility that existed in the late silent film era. As Hispanic accents increasingly were coded as comic or threatening and always as marginal to national ideals, and the Production Code also tended to prohibit Latino actors from portraying romantic leads, Latina/o stars faced uncertainty in Hollywood; most were unable to maintain their star status over the course of the decade. As Crafton (1997) points out, sound was a major factor in the marginalization of nonwhite actors in the 1930s, even while "ethnic" music and characters were included in film narratives. As he notes, "ethnic voices and musical traditions could readily be expropriated, transformed into entertainment, while both cordoning off and erasing the source" (p. 416). This was often the case. For example, the new Latin musicals tended to confine Latina/o performers to exoticized and circumscribed roles as singers and dancers. Narratively, they typically functioned as sidekicks and romantic trophies at best, as Dolores Del Rio's career trajectory in 1930s Hollywood aptly illustrates.

DEL RIO AND THE SHIFT TO SOUND

As noted earlier, Dolores Del Rio weathered major changes in her career in relation to the conversion to talking film. Dewitt Bodeen (1976) asserts that even prior to the transitional years, Del Rio worked diligently on her English in preparation for the impending change. Her stardom was in fact still to peak. The star's Hollywood career crested in 1928 with respect to the number of film projects in which she appeared and the variety of roles she played. She starred in six films this year. Of these two were silent films and four were sound films, a few of which included songs sung by the actors. Exploration of these films and Del Rio's career in these years reveals a great deal about the evolving status of Latina/o in post-sound Hollywood.

Of Del Rio's silent films released in 1928 two were produced and released by Fox Film: the Western *Gateway of the Moon*, in which the actress plays a "half-caste" Indian woman and *No Other Woman*, a film that had almost been shelved permanently but was released after the success of *Loves of Carmen*. They received little attention; Del Rio had more success with the films with musical scores; in these she played a wide range of characters. These roles included a Jewish prospector's granddaughter in MGM's adventure film *The Trail of '98* (1928); a Russian woman who becomes a prostitute after being abandoned by her lover, the prince, in *The Red Dance* (1928); and an "untamable" Gypsy bear tamer who meets her match in Edwin Carewe's *Revenge* (1928). Del Rio also scored a resounding hit this year in the early sound film *Ramona* (1928), discussed further below.

A telling illustration of shifting public tastes can be found in reviews of Del Rio's last silent film, *Revenge,* which was released by United Artists. Publicity for the film depicts Del Rio at the height of her star status; promotional stills and film posters are dominated by her image, highlighting her physicality and dark beauty. But despite the fact that *Revenge* was of the quality of many successful silent melodramas of earlier years in many respects, the film was rated "just fair" by *Variety.*

In spite of the active year that Dolores Del Rio experienced in 1928, her status was rapidly shifting. As noted earlier, film actors were finding themselves on widely diverging paths at their studios while discussions took place among executives with respect to which were going to make the leap to talkies. It appears that for the most part these meetings were held behind closed doors and not documented for the historical record. Allen R. Ellenberger (1999), in his study of the career of Ramon Novarro, found documentation of one such meeting that took place at Novarro's studio, MGM. According to Frances Marion, a screenwriter also under contract with the studio at the time, an MGM executive had posed the all-important question regarding Novarro's prospects: "He can sing and play the guitar, but what about his accent?" (qtd. by Ellenberger, 1999, p. 182). The answer was not recorded for posterity, but Ellenberger did discern that Lewis Stone, Lionel Barrymore, and Conrad Nagel were given the go-ahead for talkies, while Novarro was not (p. 83). The distinction between different categories of sound films during the transitional period is also important to make here. Like her second cousin, Del Rio, while appearing in early "soundies" (films with musical scores but no dialogue), also was not encouraged to quickly star in films with sound dialogue, or "talkies." In fact, even while she continued to be cast in studio films, Del Rio's accent ultimately brought about the waning of her status and casting possibilities as a film actress in Hollywood as talkies became the norm.

This did not happen immediately. Another marker of Del Rio's status as one of the top stars in Hollywood before the transition was her inclusion on March 29, 1928, with the "[t]he most famous, the highest paid names in American motion pictures," a small group of successful actors under contract with United Artists, in a pioneering radio broadcast meant to "prove to millions of fans that their idols had voices ... good enough to meet the challenge of the talkies" (Walker, 1979, pp. 1 & 211). Del Rio joined Mary Pickford, Douglas Fairbanks, Charlie Chaplin, D.W. Griffith, John Barrymore, Norma Talmadge, and Gloria Swanson in this endeavor and sang a song from *Ramona* as her contribution. Rumors that she had used a voice "doubler" on the broadcast rose in the newspapers in subsequent days, but they were soon quelled as false (Walker, 1979).

Ramona was a notable role for Del Rio in several respects. First, the film, featuring a Movietone musical score, marked Del Rio's singing debut. Second, it marked a distinct shift in the ethnic marking of the roles the star began to be offered. The narrative, adapted from an 1884 novel by Helen Hunt Jackson, centers on a romance between a young Mexican (presumably Spanish, interpreted as "white," but later found to have American Indian blood) woman and an American Indian man in California of the romanticized mission era. A consistently popular story of racial mixing and misunderstanding, it had already been released in film version twice previously. It is striking that during this period in which Latina/o actors began to be considered and racialized as nonwhite, Dolores Del Rio was chosen to star in this narrative that focused heavily on racial purity and mixing. Moreover, reviewers, in praising Del Rio's acting in the role, tended to confuse "'Indianness' with 'Mexicanness,'" as Hershfield (2000) points out (p. 15). *Photoplay*, for example, asserted that "there could have been no more fitting person to impersonate the Indian-blooded Ramona than the Mexican Dolores Del Rio" (March 1928, p. 52).

Despite an accent that some found heavy,[15] *Ramona* proved to be a success. The film's songs also were quite popular, particularly the title song (Walker, 1979). Nonetheless, while the film may have solidified Del Rio's stardom, it may also have served as a symbolic marker of the Mexican-born actress's changing image in Hollywood as not sufficiently white or U.S. American.

Del Rio also starred the following year in the tearjerker *Evangeline* (1929), the last film in which she was directed by Carewe. The film, based on a poem by Henry Wadsworth Longfellow, focuses on the separation of the title character from her betrothed during the French Acadians' brutal expulsion from Novia Scotia by the British in 1755. Del Rio's accent is almost impossible to discern in the commercial DVD release of the film; most notably she sings two songs. Regarding the reception she received, the limitations that Latinas were beginning to face in an increasingly racialized Hollywood quickly are evident in publicity for the film. While the film was in production, a September 1929 *Vanity Fair* article stated that in taking the role of the "Nordic heroine," Del Rio was undertaking a "hazardous" task, "for *Evangeline* is an American tradition, but one which Senora [*sic*] Del Rio's undoubted talent should make her understand" ("Evangeline," p. 77). Reviews of Del Rio's performance in the film were mixed as well, and the film did not do well. *Film Daily* described Del Rio's voice as "small" but "charming" (August 4, 1929, p. 17). According to *Variety*, Del Rio, "[t]he paprika Latina girl ... has some good emotional sequences, but somehow doesn't seem to fit her role" (July 31, 1929, n.p.).

In the meantime, Del Rio experienced some personal difficulties and rare bad publicity. Her separation and divorce from her husband Jaime Del Rio, and his later death from illness in Berlin in December 1928, put a momentary damper on her image. According to several accounts, she had been romantically involved with Edwin Carewe, who had divorced his wife, but separated from him after the filming of *Evangeline*. In 1930, Carewe returned to his ex-wife and Del Rio married Cedric Gibbons, MGM's most successful art director.

In attempt to work her Spanish accent into a role, Del Rio's first talkie was in the role of a Spanish singer, Lita, who works at a French brothel but maintains her virtue in *The Bad One* (1930). She was not well received for her work in this picture. Ironically, Lita's awkward efforts to learn North American slang in the film can be seen as emblematic of Del Rio's struggle to be seen as a mainstream Hollywood star at the time. Her character's accent was criticized by *Variety*, which stated, "Lita's gradual efforts to simulate American slang are painfully self-conscious, rather than even suggestive of cuteness" (June 18, 1930, p. 37). It is not possible to disentangle this critique from criticism of the increasing shallowness of Del Rio's roles, or from umbrage with Del Rio's own nonnative accent.

The star broke her management contract with Edwin Carewe after this film and signed with Joseph Schenck at United Artists, then suffered what apparently was a nervous breakdown that kept her from fulfilling the contract (Braun, 1972; Reyes & Rubie, 2000). The United Artists contract was ultimately cancelled in 1931. While Del Rio never spoke directly about that time she has intimated that she was struggling with interpersonal problems (Bodeen, 1976). While she was away, further transformations were in motion in Hollywood. For one, the star system continued to evolve. Dominating the screen now were leading ladies of a different, more streetwise style, "screen ladies like Joan Crawford, Norma Shearer, Bette Davis, Ruth Chatterton and Jean Harlow, whose voices contributed so much to defining their roles as worldly women of the 1930s" (Walker, 1979, p. 203). Del Rio was no longer in vogue as a dark beauty and was pigeonholed as a Latina actress at this time when Mexican, no matter how Spanish or wealthy, no longer easily translated as glamorous and cosmopolitan.

The 1930s brought decreasing options for Dolores Del Rio, although she was able to bank on her former stardom for a time. In 1931, Del Rio negotiated a new contract, this time with RKO Radio Pictures. She found her subsequent roles and publicity increasingly limited, however. The first of her films for RKO was *Girl of the Rio* (1932). Considering that this was a remake of *The Dove* (1927), which had been boycotted by the Mexican government for what it considered negative representations of Mexican characters, Del Rio's acceptance of this role is particularly telling of the constraints she was experiencing. Her role is that of a somewhat dimwitted cantina singer in a Mexican border town; the other Mexican characters (one given the embarrassing moniker of Señor Tostado) fare far worse. Del Rio appears to be struggling in the role, either with its apparent limitations or the new, subtler talkie-style of acting, or both. Her actual accent is difficult to discern, as much of her character's dialogue calls for her to speak broken English (the character's trademark saying throughout is the awkward phrase, "You betcha your life!"). "Rush," reviewing for *Variety*, ultimately panned Del Rio for what he or she called an "indifferent performance" (January 12, 1932, p. 15).

The tactic of launching foreign actors' talkie careers in the roles of foreigners with imperfect English was in fact utilized many times in the early part of the decade. Greta Garbo's first talking role in *Anna Christie* (1930), promoted with the now-famous tag line "Garbo talks!" is a prime example, while Ellenberger (1999) argues that Ramon Novarro also was confined to playing non-Americans. This approach seems to have been more successful for Garbo than for Del Rio, Novarro, and other Latina/o actors, considering their subsequent career trajectories. Perhaps this was because Garbo was considered more easily definable as white and thus even as a foreigner, closer to the U.S. ideal.

By 1932, the industry had for the most part converted completely to talkies. Del Rio was still considered very much a star, with an image as a high-class, tasteful lady. Invitations to the parties that she and husband Cedric Gibbons threw were reportedly much vied for amongst Hollywood notables. She also continued to be lauded for her looks and figure throughout the 1930s. In just one such example, she was named the "most perfect feminine figure in Hollywood" in *Photoplay* in 1933 ("Most Perfect," p. 74). Meanwhile, Del Rio was struggling to even be considered by casting directors for A-list film roles. Her career was resuscitated somewhat by the splash she made in RKO's 1932 South Sea romance *Bird of Paradise*, in which she played the Polynesian island princess Luana. The story of Luana's forbidden love with Johnny, an U.S. American sailor, the film heavily exploits the titillation of a modern colonialist take on interracial island love. As such, Del Rio's role offered her little to do other than lust for Johnny and speak in a gibberish meant to pass for a Polynesian language. The film advertising in turn emphasized the racy storyline, potential nudity, and sexual content. (One promotional poster showed a half-naked Del Rio, a flowery lei strategically placed on her torso, in a clinch with Joel McCrea, accompanied by the copy, "glamorous drama of lovers whose worlds were a million miles apart, but whose hearts throbbed together!" and "White man … native girl … two hearts in a flowery paradise!"). Despite the praise the big-budget film received, it didn't earn enough to turn a profit.

By 1933, the star found she was now offered roles mainly in Latin musicals, her dancing ability again paying off. She acted in several musicals for RKO and had a surprise hit in her first, *Flying Down to Rio* (1933). In this film she played a Brazilian heiress, Belinha de Rezende, who falls for a U.S. American band leader. While Del Rio received positive reviews for her portrayal of the aristocratic Belinha, the role exemplified the Dark Lady motif that came to dominate her sound film career (Berg, 2002).[16] Belinha and other Dark Lady characters, while elegant and coy, also are posited as irresistible; I would argue in addition that the role type reflects and reinforces colonialist tropes of Latinas as inherently sexy and sexual, typically while functioning in the narrative role of trophies for white male lead characters to compete over. But Del Rio appears to have been optimistic about the direction her career was taking, hoping the role meant her opportunities were on an upswing. As the actress noted in later decades to *Film Weekly*, "For the first time I was to play the part of a smart modern woman with plenty of music and comedy around me. I knew it was a sign I could play a sophisticated role. I was no longer little Luana or Ramona" (July 1972, p. 456).

Del Rio's optimism did not take her far. After the release of *Flying Down to Rio*, RKO chose not to renew her contract. Del Rio instead signed with Warner Bros. in 1934 and was cast in another string of Latin musicals. Her film image came to be dominated by coolly flamboyant Latin dance costumes, whether ruffled, sequenced, or feathered. The first of these musicals and respective set of costumes for Warner Bros. was *Wonder Bar* (1934). In this film Del Rio played another Dark Lady character, in this case a Latin dancer, Inez, for whom three men—portrayed by Al Jolson, Dick Powell, and Ricardo Cortez—compete. Moreover, Inez has little agency of her own within these dynamics. A publicity still from the film of Del Rio as Inez dancing with Cortez illustrates how costuming came to overpower Del Rio's underdeveloped characters in these 1930s films. In this instance a dramatic feather boa dominates the scene.

Still attempting to salvage her career, the following year Del Rio appeared in two more musicals for Warner Bros., *In Caliente* (1935) and *I Live for Love* (1935). Del Rio garnered positive reviews, but critics' comments ultimately were far less effusive than those of years' past. Such was the case in this review for *I Live for Love* from *Variety*: "Del Rio gives a nice performance and has been well photographed" (October 23, 1935). While Warner's remake of the historical sex farce *Madame DuBarry* (1934) had provided Del Rio with a potential change, a part in which she could actually show her acting range again, it too proved a disappointment. It ultimately was cut drastically by the Hays Office because of perceived racy content, according to Del Rio (Braun, 1972).

While Del Rio continued acting in a few films in the late-1930s, her career was in noticeable decline. Audiences were looking for a radically different sort of star than had been the rage in her heyday. Dolores Del Rio herself is quoted as saying, "By the mid-1930s ... there were a new set of fresh faces, and the really plum roles were going to actresses like Bette Davis or Katherine Hepburn or Barbara Stanwyck" (Hadley-Garcia, 1990, p. 5). Following a few other films for Warner Bros. that didn't register highly with audiences, Del Rio and the studio had difficulties coming to agreement during contract negotiations in 1936. Del Rio finally chose to sign with Columbia Pictures later that year. Del Rio made just one film,

Devil's Playground, for Columbia. In this film she again played a Mexican dancer and femme fatale. Del Rio broke her contract and returned to Fox in 1937. Her films for Fox included *Ali Baba Goes to Town* (1937), in which she played herself, and roles as a nightclub singer in the World War I espionage film *Lancer Spy* (1937) and as a French singer in the adventure drama *International Settlement* (1938).

By 1938 she was not able to land lead roles, according to Del Rio. Her personal life also was increasingly unstable. She had had an affair with Hollywood upstart Orson Welles in the late-1930s and divorced Cedric Gibbons as a result of it. Because of disappointment over a collaboration with Welles, *Journey Into Fear* (1942), and the end of their relationship, Del Rio left Hollywood. She moved back to Mexico City, where she worked steadily in Mexican cinema, helping to usher in its Golden Age. Among her many accolades, she won the Mexican equivalent of an Academy Award for Best Actress, the Ariel, three times, for *Las Abandonadas* (1945), for *Doña Perfecta* (1951), and for *The Boy and the Fog* (1953). She later married for a third time, to Lewis Riley in 1959. Del Rio made a few, brief forays back to Hollywood to act in such films as *Flaming Star* in 1960 and *Cheyenne Autumn* in 1964 and was cited both as a talented actress and gracefully aging beauty. Dolores Del Rio died in Newport Beach, California, in 1983.

CONCLUSIONS

As I document in this chapter, the late silent film era of the mid-to-late 1920s provided an opening for Latino and Latina stardom that only recently is beginning to be matched. This era provided unique opportunities for a number of light-skinned Latina/o actors, whose images were shaped in a manner that promoted them as acceptably deracialized stars to the U.S. and global public. Such was the case for popular Mexican actress Dolores Del Rio. Developments in the film industry and sociopolitical landscape of the 1930s changed these opportunities and the nature of stardom possible for Del Rio and other Latina/o stars and aspiring actors.

As a part of this evolution, Latina/o casting and star images underwent a dramatic shift. Increasingly, a "racial politics of casting" designated Latino actors and actresses as nonwhite and limited their casting options in Hollywood films.[17] As noted earlier, in the prior decade Dolores Del Rio had been cast in roles that spanned a wide range of nationalities and character types. She found that the opportunity to play characters considered "white" was blocked after the transition to talking film, however, as she increasingly was cast only in Latina, Polynesian, or Spanish roles by the mid-1930s. Del Rio and other Latinas were offered more opportunities than nonwhite actresses of other ethnicities, however. In comparison, African American actress Louise Beavers was confined to maid roles, while lighter skinned African Americans Fredi Washington and Dorothy Dandridge were cast in romantic lead roles typically only in black-cast films in the 1930s and 1940s, respectively.

Latina/o actors and characters nevertheless were insistently racialized when they were inserted into white-dominant texts, ensuring that they would not threaten the status quo of studio-era Hollywood. For instance, Latina/o characters proliferated in Latin-themed musicals and other films of the "Good Neighbor" variety in the 1930s and 1940s, but these generally were not fully developed roles that would support audience appeal and rising stardom. They instead provided color to the settings in which white characters' narratives were carried out. In addition, aside from a few particularly successful actors and actresses, the Latina/o performers who inhabited these roles were not promoted as potential stars.

Within the newly imagined (and importantly, aural) racial hierarchy of the star system and story worlds of sound film, Latina/os began to occupy a liminal, shadow space between the categories of whiteness and blackness, not fully equated with blackness nor fully allowed into the privileged realm of whiteness. As an element of these dynamics, the voices and bodies even of light-skinned Latina and Latino stars came to be inscribed in a manner that set them apart from whites in Hollywood. In the case of Dolores Del Rio, these tendencies were tempered slightly, likely because of her elegant star image. She was less able to escape this Hollywood paradigm as the 1930s progressed, as this survey of her Hollywood career illustrates. For example, as can be evidenced in many of Del Rio's 1930s films, Latinas began to be set apart from white actresses in Hollywood films through their positioning as erotic others. As sexual puritanism became a prominent aspect of the construction of white femininity in Depression-era Hollywood, the Latina star body in contrast was often coded as always comparatively more seductive. Role types such as the Dark Lady figure Del Rio often portrayed increasingly were the norm for Latina actors.

Similar shifts were taking place in the sociopolitical landscape. During the years of early sound film, Olvera Street in downtown Los Angeles, once the heart of the Mexican American community, was restored to turn-of-the-century quaintness as a tourist attraction. Notably, the restoration took place in the same years that hundreds of thousands of Mexicans were forcefully deported and Mexican Americans continued to experience discrimination and segregation in the city and country at large. As Sánchez (1993) notes, "The lesson [of the restoration of Olvera Street] was clear: Mexicans were to be assigned a place in the mythic past of Los Angeles—one that could be relegated to a quaint section of a city destined to delight tourists and antiquarians. Real Mexicans were out of sight and increasingly out of mind" (p. 226). Olvera Street thus can be understood as a telling illustration of the shifting status experienced not only by actors such as Dolores Del Rio, but by all U.S. Latinoa/s in this era. Cultural exchange across U.S.-Latin American borders, if the word exchange can even be used, now typically amounted to U.S. appropriation of performers and cultural forms, even while Latino/a individuals were kept out of the sociopolitical mainstream.[18] Moreover, such movements in the realm of Hollywood film and in U.S. social life arguably lent impetus to one another. Most Latina/o actors, whether they had achieved a level of fame and were trying to establish careers, found they had become nonwhite—with all of the limitations that included—in the eyes of film producers and casting directors. As such they were confined to roles in Hollywood storyworlds that could be described as quaint at best.

NOTES

1. "The Latin Invasion" (1927, p. 59).
2. For further discussion of this transitional period in U.S. cinema, see Walker (1979) and Crafton (1997).
3. "The Latin Invasion" (1927, p. 59).
4. Hadley-Garcia (1990, p. 39).
5. United Artists press release (1928b).
6. The majority of this archival research was conducted at the Margaret Herrick Library of the Academy of Motion Picture Arts and Sciences in Beverly Hills, California, while materials were also located at the Film and Video Archive at UCLA, at the Harry Ransom Center for the Humanities at the University of Texas at Austin, and at the Wisconsin Center for Film and Television Research at the University of Wisconsin-Madison.
7. See, for example, Studlar (1996) and Koszarski (1990).
8. For further discussion, see Walker (1979); Koszarski (1990); and Sklar (1994)
9. Quoted in Ellenberger (1999, p. 70).
10. Dyer MacCann (1992).
11. See, for example, Rodríguez (2004).
12. For further information, see Sánchez (1993) and Acuña (2000).
13. These dynamics have been well documented by Alicia Rodríguez-Estrada (1997), and also observed by Charles Ramírez Berg in personal conversations that we have had about the actresses.
14. As Marez (2004) notes, accent and sound became "important ideological weapon[s]" in U.S. race relations through such dynamics in this era (p. 59).
15. According to López (1998), it was "thick and her English almost unintelligible" (p. 13).
16. See Berg (2002) for more extensive discussion of the Dark Lady stereotype and its history in Hollywood film.
17. Shohat and Stam (1994, p. 189).
18. Notably, as Coco Fusco (1995) has argued, such dynamics still aptly describe many cultural exchanges across the American borders today.

REFERENCES

Acuña, R. (2000). *Occupied America: A history of Chicanos*, 4th ed. New York: Addison Wesley Longman.
Balio, T. (1993). *Grand design: Hollywood as a modern business enterprise, 1930–1939*. New York: Charles Scribner's Sons.
Berg, C. R. (2002). *Latino images in film: Stereotypes, subversion, and resistance*. Austin: University of Texas.
Bernstein, M. (1997). Introduction. In M. Bernstein & G. Studlar (Eds.), *Visions of the East: Orientalism in film* (pp. 1–18). New Brunswick, NJ: Rutgers University.
Bodeen, D. (1976). *From Hollywood: The careers of 15 great American stars*. South Brunswick, NJ: A. S. Barnes and Company.
Braun, E. (1972, July). Queen of Mexico. *Films and filming, 18*(10), 34–37.
Byrne, B. (1981, November 20–27). Dolores Del Rio. *San Francisco Chronicle*. n.p.
Carr, L. (1979). *More fabulous faces*. Garden City, NY: Doubleday.
Cortés, C. E. (1997). Chicanas in film: History of an image. In C. E. Rodríguez (Ed.), *Latin looks: Images of Latinas and Latinos in the U.S. media* (pp. 121–141). Boulder, CO: Westview.
Crafton, D. (1997). *The talkies: American cinema's transition to sound, 1926–1931*. New York: Charles Scribner's Sons.
Dyer McCann, R. (1992). *The stars appear*. Metuchen, NJ: Scarecrow.
Ellenberger, A. R. (1999). *Ramon Novarro*. Jefferson, NC: McFarland & Company.
Fusco, C. (1995). *English is broken here: Notes on cultural fusion in the Americas*. New York: New Press.
Garcia, M. (2002). *A world of its own: Race, labor, and citrus in the making of greater Los Angeles, 1900–1970*. Chapel Hill: University of North Carolina Press.
Hadley-Garcia, G. (1990). *Hispanic Hollywood*. New York: Carol Publishing Group.
Hampton, B. B. (1970). *History of the American film industry: From its beginnings to 1931*. New York: Dover.
Hernández, T. K. (2002). The Buena Vista social club: The racial politics of nostalgia. In M. Habell-Pallán and M. Romero (Eds.), *Latino/a popular culture*. New York: New York University Press.
Hershfield, J. (2000). *The invention of Dolores Del Rio*. Minneapolis: University of Minnesota.
Kanellos, N. (1990). *A history of Hispanic theater in the United States: Origins to 1940*. Austin, University of Texas.
Koszarski, R. (1990). *An evening's entertainment: The age of the silent feature picture, 1915–1928*. New York: Scribner. The Latin invasion (1927, June). *Photoplay*, p. 59.
López, A. M. (1991). Are all Latins from Manhattan? Hollywood, ethnography, and cultural colonialism. In L. D. Friedman (Ed.), *Unspeakable images: Ethnicity and the American cinema* (pp. 404–424). Urbana: University of Illinois.
López, A. M. (1998). From Hollywood and back: Dolores Del Rio, a trans(national) star. *Studies in Latin American popular culture, 17*, 5–32.
Marez, C. (2004, Fall). Subaltern soundtracks: Mexican immigrants and the making of Hollywood cinema. *Aztlán: The journal of Chicano studies, 29*(1), pp. 57–82.
McWilliams, C. (1946). *Southern California: An island on the land*. Santa Barbara, CA: Peregrine Smith.
Mordden, E. (1988). *The Hollywood studios: House style in the golden age of the movies*. New York: Alfred A. Knopf.
Most perfect. (1933, February). *Photoplay*, p. 74.

Peiss, K. (1998). *Hope in a jar: The making of America's beauty culture*. New York: Metropolitan Books.
Pratt, M. L. (1992). *Imperial eyes: Travel writing and transculturation*. London: Routledge.
Reyes, L. & P. Rubie. (2000). *Hispanics in Hollywood: A celebration of 100 years in film and television*, 2nd ed. Hollywood, CA: Lone Eagle.
Ríos-Bustamente, A. (1992). Latino participation in the Hollywood film industry, 1911–1945. In C. Noriega (Ed.), *Chicanos and film: Representation and resistance* (pp. 18–28). Minneapolis: University of Minnesota.
Roberts, J. S. (1999). *The Latin tinge: The impact of Latin American music on the United States*, 2nd ed. New York: Oxford University.
Rodríguez-Estrada, A. I. (1997). Dolores Del Rio and Lupe Velez: Images on and off the screen, 1925–1944. In E. Jameson & S. Armitage (Eds.), *Writing the range: Race, class and culture in the women's West* (pp. 475–449). Norman: University of Oklahoma.
Rodríguez, C. E. (2004). *Heroes, lovers, and others: The story of Latinos in Hollywood*. Washington, DC: Smithsonian.
Sánchez, G. J. (1993). *Becoming Mexican American: Ethnicity, culture and identity in Chicano Los Angeles, 1900–1945*. New York: Oxford University.
Shindler, C. (1999). *Hollywood in crisis: Cinema and American society, 1929–1939*. London: Routledge.
Shohat E. & R. Stam. (1994). *Unthinking eurocentrism: Multiculturalism and the media*. New York: Routledge.
Sklar, R. (1994). *Movie-made America: A cultural history of the movies*, rev. ed. New York: Vintage Books.
St. John, I. (1926, June 27). Daughter of the dons. *Photoplay*, pp. 66–67.
Studlar, G. (1996). *This mad masquerade: Stardom and masculinity in the jazz age*. New York: Columbia University.
Studlar, G. (1997). Out Salome-ing Salome: Dance, the new woman, and fan magazine orientalism. In M. Bernstein & G. Studlar (Eds.), *Visions of the East: Orientalism in film* (pp. 99–129). New Brunswick, NJ: Rutgers University.
Valdivia, A. (2005). The location of the Spanish in Latinidad: Examples from contemporary U.S. popular culture. *Letras femininas, 31*(1), 60–78.
Walker, A. (1979). *The shattered silents: How the talkies came to stay*. New York: William Morrow and Company.

FILM REVIEWS

The Bad One [review]. (1930, June 18). *Variety*, p. 37.
Evangeline [review]. (1929, July 31). *Variety*, p. 17.
Evangeline [review]. (1929, August 4). *Film Daily*, p. 8.
Evangeline. (1929, September). *Vanity Fair*, p. 77.
Fred. (1926, December 1). *What Price Glory?* [review]. *Variety*, p. 12.
I Live for Love [review]. (1935, October 23). *Variety*, n.p.
The Loves of Carmen [review]. (1927, July). *Photoplay*, p. 69.
Pals First [review]. (1926, August 26). *Variety*, p. 18.
Ramona [review]. (1928, March). *Photoplay*, p. 52.
Resurrection [review]. (1926, December 1). *Variety*.

Rush. (1929, July 31). *Evangeline* [review]. *Variety*, p. 17.
Rush. (1932, January 12). *Girl of the Rio* [review]. *Variety*, p. 15.
Rush. (1932, September 13). *Bird of Paradise* [review]. *Variety*, p. 19.
Sid. (1927, September 28). *Loves of Carmen* [review]. *Variety*, p. 53.
Waly. (1930, July 25). *The Bad One* [review]. *Variety*, p. 37.
Waly. (1928, December 1). *Revenge* [review]. *Variety*, p. 12.

ARCHIVAL MATERIALS AND FILMS

Bacon, L. (Director). (1934). *Wonder Bar* [motion picture]. United States: First National and Warner Bros. VHS. Distributor, MGM (Warner), 1998.

Carewe, E. (n.d.) Biography file. Margaret Herrick Library, Academy of Motion Picture Arts and Sciences. Beverly Hills, CA.

Carewe, E. (Producer/Director). (1928). *Evangeline* [motion picture]. United States: United Artists. DVD Distributor, Image Entertainment, 2000.

Carewe, E. (Producer/Director). (1928). *Revenge* [motion picture]. United States: United Artists. Film print viewed at the UCLA Film and Television Archive.

Cooper, M. (Producer), & T. Freeland. (Director). (1933). *Flying Down to Rio* [motion picture]. United States: RKO Radio Pictures. VHS. Distributor, Turner Home Entertainment, 2000.

Del Rio, D. (n.d.). Biography file. Margaret Herrick Library, Academy of Motion Picture Arts and Sciences. Beverly Hills, CA.

Del Rio, D. (n.d.). Photograph file. Harry Ransom Center for the Humanities, University of Texas at Austin.

Edwin Carewe Productions & United Artists. (1928). *Revenge* promotional posters and publicity stills. *Revenge* file. Margaret Herrick Library, Academy of Motion Picture Arts and Sciences. Beverly Hills, CA.

Fox Film. (1927). *Loves of Carmen* promotional advertisements. *Loves of Carmen* file. Margaret Herrick Library, Academy of Motion Picture Arts and Sciences.

RKO Radio Pictures. (1932). *Bird of Paradise* exhibitors' press book and publicity stills. Margaret Herrick Library, Academy of Motion Picture Arts and Sciences. Beverly Hills, CA.

Sarecky, L. (Exec. Producer) & H. Brenon (Director) (1932). *Girl of the Rio* [motion picture]. United States: RKO Radio Pictures. Film print viewed at the UCLA Film and Television Archive, University of California-Los Angeles.

Selznick, D. O. (Producer) & K. Vidor (Director). (1932). *Bird of Paradise* [motion picture]. United States: RKO Radio Pictures. DVD. Distributor, Roan Group Archival Entertainment, 1999.

United Artists. (1928a). Press release, Dolores Del Rio. Margaret Herrick Library, Academy of Motion Picture Arts and Sciences. Beverly Hills, CA.

United Artists. (1928b). *Ramona* exhibitors' press book. *Ramona* (1928) film file. Margaret Herrick Library, Academy of Motion Picture Arts and Sciences. Beverly Hills, CA.

Walsh, R. (Producer/Director). (1926). *What Price Glory?* [motion picture]. United States: Fox Film. Film print viewed at the UCLA Film and Television Archive.

Wilson, H. D. (1927, May 5). Official biography of Dolores Del Rio. Dolores Del Rio file. Margaret Herrick Library, Academy of Motion Picture Arts and Sciences.

CHAPTER THREE

The Importance OF Spanish-Language AND Latino Media

MARI CASTAÑEDA

During the spring 2006 immigrant rights rallies, the importance of Spanish-language and Latino media became very evident in the mobilization of people around work stoppages and protest events (Henao, 2006). Spanish-language radio personalities and local newspaper columnists, such as Univision Radio's "El Piolin," not only informed the public, but also encouraged their audiences to participate in the rallies, which were increasingly viewed as opportunities for Latino, especially immigrant, empowerment (Williams & Farhi, 2006). In mainstream media, the role of Spanish-language radio in helping fan the fervor against the proposed immigration law and the formation of mass demonstrations was viewed as politically improper and biased (Kasindorf, 2006). Yet the Pew Hispanic Center confirms that "the vast majority of Latinos ... view the Spanish-language media as an important institution for the economic and political development of the Hispanic population" in the United States (Suro, 2004, p. 24). The 2006 immigration movement was indeed an important political, economic, and cultural moment for many Latinos, and the Spanish-language media's participation in covering and supporting the public protests demonstrated the growing importance of Latino media in helping shape the links between Latinidad, civil society, and the transcultural political economy of the Americas.

Spanish-language and Latino media are historically, and continue to be, very important in the United States, and this chapter examines how and why this is the case. It does so by exploring two questions: first, how is the Spanish-language media industry part of the dynamic relationship between immigration flows, global media, and the U.S. communications infrastructure? And second, in which ways are Spanish-language and Latino communication circuits offering new modalities of encounter, empowerment, and representation? In the past decade, it has become clear that Spanish-language and Latino media, and Latinos as a population, are challenging and transforming the broader sociocultural landscape of the United States. The edited volume by Mariela Páez and Marcelo Suárez-Orozco entitled *Latinos: Remaking America* (2005) documents how U.S. Latino populations are transforming schools, politics, migration patterns, religion, employment, language, family structures, and ultimately, notions of cultural citizenship and national identity. Consequently, this chapter aims to understand how the intersection of Spanish-language media, especially its expansion to new regions across the United States, with the dynamic demographic changes occurring within Latino communities, are producing new forms of interaction that are mediating "both the form and cultural content of life" in North America (García Canclini, 2003, p. 257). In the following sections, this chapter will discuss such transformations by examining the political economy of Spanish-language media in the United States, the correlation between new immigration patterns and the emergence of media outlets in new geographic locations, and the role of media in Latino communities today. Ultimately, the study attempts to show how Spanish-language media is intimately linked to larger societal and industrial transformations on a global scale.

THE POLITICAL ECONOMY OF SPANISH-LANGUAGE MEDIA IN THE UNITED STATES

The political economic changes of the Spanish-language media industry are not occurring in a vacuum, but are part of a larger transformation of globalization. The global market expansion of the media industry across North American borders and beyond is, according to Dan Schiller and Vincent Mosco (2001), the "*sine qua non* of a new and more comprehensive phase of corporate transnationalization in general" (p. 15). Globally branded companies in a variety of sectors such as finance, consumer products, and fast food chains, for instance, are moving into the Latin American and U.S. Latino markets, and exploiting the power of print, electronic media, and digital communication services in order to create and expand the transborder marketing and advertising campaigns of their products (Castañeda Paredes, 2001).

The changes in demographics are one of the major reasons why companies have become very interested in the Latino and Latin American consumer markets and consequently, have helped spur the growth of Spanish-language media. The 2000 US Census reported that the Latino population increased by more than 50 percent since 1990, and by 2050, Latinos will constitute nearly 25 percent of the total U.S. population (de la Cruz & Ramirez, 2003). It is also estimated that by mid-century, the population south of the U.S. border will grow beyond 950 million (Guzmán, 2001). In addition, Latinos have a purchasing power of $581 billion, and by 2012, their economic clout will surge to $926 billion (*Hispanic Fact Sheet*, 2003). For advertisers and marketers, the population boom translates into a profitable "Latin goldmine." Thus, the growth in Latina purchasing power and the changes in demographics are creating a situation in which Spanish-language and Latino media are more important than ever in the escalating transnational media environment and the quest to access global markets. The following sections examine more specifically how this context provides a key for understanding the importance of the newspaper, radio and television industries in the transnational political economy of Spanish-language media.

THE RISE OF SPANISH-LANGUAGE NEWSPAPERS

Since 1990, Spanish-language newspapers have more than tripled whereas English-language newspapers have experienced an 11 percent decline in circulation. According to the Latino Print Network, Spanish-language newspapers have grown in popularity: in 2003 there were well over 600 daily publications whereas in 1970 there were 232 publications nationwide (Mullman, 2005). In addition, there are presently thousands of weekly and monthly community oriented publications that serve local Latina/o readers in the United States, for example, *El Sol Latino, diálogo Bilingüe,* and *Elité* all serve the rural Latino communities across Western Massachusetts (Jones, 2005). One notable trend of this increased popularity is the emergence of Spanish-language versions of mainstream (English-language) newspapers. The *Dallas Morning News, Star-Telegram,* and *The Republican* launched Spanish-language newspapers, *Al Dia, La Estrella,* and *El Pueblo* in their respective markets in order to maximize their content and create synergistic links between their media holdings (Soto, 2004). The goal is to secure a share in local media markets while also creating awareness of other media products, including English-language and Spanish-language publications, local radio and television outlets. The attractiveness of the Spanish-language publications sector is deeply related to the competitiveness of the Latino media industry as whole, and the need to develop niche markets in order to attract audiences and advertisers.

In addition to the publication of Spanish-language versions of mainstream papers, another industry trend is the creation of national corporate alliances. Such developments have emerged in the wake of media deregulation, in large part inspired by the Telecommunications Act of 1996 and the removal of local ownership limits and cross-ownership restrictions, which allow a newspaper company to merge with other newspaper and/or local broadcast station owners. In January 2004, for instance, the two largest Spanish-language newspapers in the United States, *La Opinión* and *El Diario/La Prensa* joined forces to create the first nationwide Spanish-language newspaper chain in the U.S (Cardenas & Goldman, 2004). The newly formed newspaper chain, ImpreMedia, was designed to acquire a slew of weekly and daily newspapers across the country in an effort to create a "network of newspapers that serves the Latina/o community" and advertisers on a national scale (Madore, 2004). The company is characterizing itself as a quasi *USA Today*, but in Spanish.

The formation of ImpreMedia is apparently an attempt to compete with the growing group of mainstream media that are developing niche products in order to attract the Latino audience. For instance, the Tribune Company created *Hoy* in New York initially in order to compete with *El Diario-La Prensa*, and launched the same newspaper in Chicago in order to compete with the *La Raza*, the oldest Spanish-language newspaper in the Midwest. Now that Tribune is no longer affiliated with *La Opinión*, it has begun publishing *Hoy* in Los Angeles as well. In response to ever-increasing competition, the executives of ImpreMedia also hope to replicate the hugely successful "one stop shopping model" of Univisión. This model allows advertisers to gain access to audiences across media markets and media forms, which is especially beneficial for national advertisers. The present developments in the print industry thus point to the growing importance of cross-ownership in Spanish-language media and the ways in which the politics of ownership are also shaping the contours and growth across the broader industry.

THE TRANSFORMATION OF SPANISH-LANGUAGE RADIO

In addition to print, Spanish-language radio is also one of the fastest growing media sectors in the United States, and increasingly a critical feature of any company hoping to become a global media brand (Holt, Quelch, & Taylor, 2004a; Holt, Quelch, & Taylor, 2004b; Ward, 2001). Radio is important not only as a venue for cultural connection, but also as a site for capital accumulation. According to Castañeda Paredes (2003), Spanish-language radio grew nearly 1000 percent since 1980, and industry analysts predict that the sector will continue to grow well into the next decade. Although there are less than 1,000 full-power Spanish-language radio stations (compared to 12,000 English-language outlets), there are thousands more that are broadcasting as low power stations or offering extensive Spanish-language content within their programming lineup.

According to Fries (2004), Spanish-language radio is successful because Latinos listen to more radio than any other ethnic minority group in the United

States A study by Wirthlin Worldwide confirmed that Latinos surpassed African Americans as radio listeners, and comprised 95.5 percent of the audience for the 600 full-power Spanish-language radio stations in the United States. Within the radio marketing industry, Latino listeners are deemed as loyal, youthful, and "ready to spend" their disposable income (Chandler, 2005). The Pew Hispanic Center's report, "Changing Channels, Crisscrossing Cultures: A Survey of Latinos on the News Media," specifically outlines the percentage of Latinos listening to radio and watching television. According to the report, 58 percent of Latinos received their news from radio and 82 percent from local television. In terms of language preferences, 43 percent of U.S. Latinos preferred their radio news in English, 34 percent prefer Spanish, and 23 percent receive their news in both languages. Television has higher percentages with 86 percent of Latinos preferring English, 77 percent preferring Spanish, and 81 percent viewing TV in both languages.

For Latino audiences, however, radio is more than just a venue for consuming commercials. In addition to accessing news and entertainment, Ríos (2000) argues, Latinos also use Spanish-language media in order to achieve cultural maintenance in a society that is still incredibly racist and xenophobic. Mitchell (2005) argues that these cultural spaces become even more critically important in a political and educational environment that promotes English-only "racist and ethnocentric ideological perspectives and practices," and disparages linguistic-minority populations. Thus, as ethnic media research suggests, radio "is much more than simply plain entertainment. In the modern world, it has acquired important social, cultural, and even political functions through its popularity and mass consumption" (Ríos, 2000, p. 183).

In reality, these functions have always been part of Spanish-language radio. In the early days of radio, outlets located at the U.S.-Mexico border reached Mexican and Mexican American audiences residing in Texas and California. Spanish-language radio kept communities connected to Mexico and also expanded the reach and scope of these seemingly Mexican media enterprises (Crawford & Fowler, 2002). The fluidity of the airwaves in many ways encouraged the transnational character of broadcasting at the border, and with more people from Mexico and Latin America immigrating and resettling in the United States, it became increasingly evident that Spanish-language radio, and later television, could extend beyond the national boundary (Gómez-Quiñonez & Maciel, 1998).

THE EXTENSION OF SPANISH-LANGUAGE TELEVISION

The expansion of markets was one of the major reasons why Mexico's largest media conglomerate, Televisa, entered the U.S. media sector in the 1960s. For

Televisa, the largest Spanish-language media conglomerate in Latin America at the time, "the U.S. market was an obvious and potentially lucrative arena. Televisa was producing profits in Mexico; a U.S. subsidiary would redouble those profits" (Rodriguez, 1999, p. 36). As a result, the emerging transnational corporation utilized its capital and resources in order to create a Spanish-language television network that would concurrently exist within the U.S. communications infrastructure. Over time, Mexico's Televisa owned and operated a number of broadcast TV stations (largely in the west and southwest) and through them transmitted its Spanish International Network (SIN). However, in the mid-1980s Televisa was forced to divest itself of SIN and its broadcast outlets when the newly emerging U.S. based competitor, Telemundo, challenged the foreign ownership of SIN (Rodriguez, 1999). The U.S. Federal Communications Commission (2006) agreed that Televisa, as a "foreign entity," was unquestionably in violation of the Communications Act of 1934, which stipulated that the ownership of broadcast licenses by foreign owners was forbidden in the United States[1] Up until that point, the ownership structure of SIN had not been interrogated, and consequently, the foreign ownership of U.S. broadcast licenses by Televisa was overlooked for almost 25 years. Yet Televisa did not entirely abandon the U.S. television market. Although SIN was sold to Hallmark, which later renamed the network "Univisión," the Mexican media conglomerate retained a strong presence in the United States by developing long-term programming deals with Univisión's successive owners (Dávila, 2001).

Interestingly, as a result of the changes to free trade policy in North America toward the end of the twentieth century, Televisa is currently in the process of recapturing its ownership share of U.S. Spanish-language television while also building a stronger presence within the broader Spanish-language and Latino media landscape in the Americas and Caribbean. Not only is Televisa attempting to develop "American" subsidiaries, but it is also lobbying for more communications deregulation, liberalization, and privatization in countries south of its border. This would grant Televisa greater access to new media markets. Not surprisingly, Univision, the fifth largest network in the United States, is also developing similar transnational aspirations, although it already controls 90 percent of the U.S. Spanish-language television and radio market share. Univision's move into Mexico and Latin America, for instance, is an effort by its current majority owner, Jerrold Perrinchio, to create an awareness and presence of its product to the growing population of Spanish-speaking audiences outside the United States.

What is most interesting about the latest battle over the control of Spanish-language television is the fact that (1) foreign ownership continues to be a deeply contested and selective terrain within the U.S. broadcast policy framework since the context of Spanish-language media is one that is intimately linked with the transnational cultural industries of Latin America; and (2) the attempt by Televisa to reclaim its possession of Univision includes discussions with other non–United States, global media conglomerates such as Venevisión from Venezuela and Saban Entertainment from Germany. In this context where the global and the national intersect, and are intersecting further as a result of North American Free Trade Agreement (NAFTA) and Free Trade Agreement of the Americas (FTAA), it is not clear how broadcast policy in the United States will account for such important changes, which profoundly influence cultural production and civil society for Latinos in the Americas, and in the United States in particular.

Consequently, the emergence of Spanish-language media in the United States is not simply the result of what communication policymakers call the "invasion of foreign entities," but a broader process of "flexible capital" that helped foster the emergence of a transnational media environment (Yúdice, 2003). The transnationalism of Spanish-language television was encouraged by the flexibility of capitalism as well as the extension of Latin American culture into the United States that was already underway through the international division of labor. Thus, Spanish-language media helped form a "territory of meaning" for the growing Latino population in the United States and simultaneously became an important site for capital accumulation (p. 104).

NEW MEDIA OUTLETS AND THE REMAPPING OF LATINA AUDIENCES

The emergence of new media outlets in the wake of broader demographic and corporate changes and the ways in which these new venues speak to the geographical remapping of Latinos is currently reshaping the cultural and political landscape of the United States Since 2000, the Latina/o population has grown over 60 percent, and currently includes over 35 million Latinos, many of whom speak predominantly in Spanish or are bilingual (Navarro, 2003). The United States is in fact considered "the fifth largest Hispanic nation in the world" with over 7 million Hispanic households residing in the country (Richardson, 1998). According to Ramos (2005) the United States "isn't even a true foreign country ... [because] Spanish-language media continues to grow. Every major city in this country has radio, television, newspapers, and magazines in Spanish (The project for excellence in journalism, 2005). We can find Spanish programming and information in even the smallest and most remote places" (p. 110). In fact, it's the emergence of Spanish-language media in communities where it hasn't existed that is one of the most fascinating outcomes of the changing Latino demographics and the reorganization of Spanish-language media.

As immigration and employment patterns shift in the United States, cities and towns especially located in the south, sortheast, and northwest are experiencing a boom in Latino oriented local and national media. Places like Walla Walla, Washington, Portland, Oregon, Birmingham, Alabama, Atlanta, Georgia, and Charleston, North Carolina, Bangor, Maine, Essex Junction, Vermont are witnessing the (slow) emergence of a Spanish-language media industry, in large part because the Latina/o immigrant population is also growing in those areas (Turner, 2006). These new media outlets are creating new modalities of representation for Latinos who are not necessarily experiencing open arms in their new towns. Some of the workers I have interviewed in these newly emerging radio, newspaper, and television outlets are following a tradition in which ethnic media focus on relevant Latino issues, such as immigration, education, and employment that are critical for Latino, especially immigrant, populations that are not necessarily discussed in more English-language, non-Latino oriented media outlets. In many cases, the Spanish-language newspaper and radio outlet (or program) is a positive source of affirmation, particularly when the mainstream media is describing immigrants in negative terms and Latinos continue to experience blatant racism and discrimination (Flores & Yúdice, 1993).

Spanish-language media in places like the south become beacons of hope when programming or articles are able to address some of the challenges and the "pain of geopolitical displacement" that occurs for many Latinos (Habell-Pallán, 2005). For instance, the program *Tertulia* on WFCR, an NPR affiliate in Western Massachusetts, works within this model of utilizing mass media and Latin American cultural production in order to address the political, economic, and cultural realities of Latinos in the region, many of whom are from the Caribbean. *Tertulia* takes it name from the cultural practice in Spanish-speaking countries in which people come together to discuss politics, culture, and broader issues in a community setting. The success of *Tertulia* has fostered a greater openness toward Spanish-language programming on low power stations, public radio, and college campus outlets in Western Massachusetts. Although the region does not have the same levels of programming as Los Angeles or New York City, the emergence of Spanish-language media, especially nonmainstream, Latina/o oriented and community-based cultural outlets demonstrates the transformation of Latino cultural capital in the United States.

It's important to note that the geopolitical displacement also impacts media south of the border. When conducting research in Teochitlan, Mexico, a small farming town outside of Guadalajara, the mayor told me that many of the men from the town were now living in Atlanta, Georgia, most of them illegally employed in various canneries and service sector outfits. One of the men, who had recently returned from Atlanta, mentioned that he was very glad to see that there was digital cable in Teochitlan, especially since his digital cable service included the Univision channel. "Me sentí como si todavía estaba en Atlanta," he said. Mato (1998) argues that indeed companies like Univision are "simultaneously exposing U.S. Latinos to soap operas, news and other productions from Latin America and Latin American audiences to news and other programmes that allow them to learn about the lives Hispanos in the U.S." (p. 115). This sort of transborder exchange actually points to the unique positioning of Spanish-language media and its importance within the larger terrain of "identities and cultures under contemporary transnational conditions" (Lionnet & Shih, 2005, p. 21). Consequently, the material, political, and cultural conditions of the present moment are reinforcing the important role that media play in Latino communities and set the stage for new modes of representation as well as the extension of communicative cultural practices that are transforming the participation of Latinos in civil society on a broader scale.

RETHINKING THE ROLE OF MEDIA IN LATINO COMMUNITIES

Spanish-language and Latina/o media in the United States have historically been more oriented toward serving the needs and interests of the community, and at times working as an advocate on behalf of Latinos. Even in the broadest sense, Spanish-language media have helped develop a sense of identity, despite a geopolitical narrative that characterizes Latinos as both vilified immigrants and celebrated movies stars within the mainstream media and broader political environment. Rodriguez (1999) notes that although Spanish-language media have varied in terms of political content, their defining characteristic is how they work as "the public voice of [Latinos]; they defend the interest of these often-embattled peoples as they help create a common culture for their communities" (p. 15). Unlike much of the mainstream English-language media outlets, Rodriguez further argues that Spanish-language and Latino media often position themselves as mediators in the acculturation and assimilation processes of Latinos in the United States and as a result, tend to emphasize a social service orientation to journalism and entertainment that provides relevant news and information.

Yet the present movement toward more nationally syndicated programming in the commercial media sector is diminishing the number of locally produced programming, and this is especially problematic in Spanish-language media. As economies of scale become increasingly important in a highly competitive media environment, identical programming content is being repackaged and rebroadcast in a variety of venues and cities. This practice is quite common in the U.S. English-language media sector, but it is a sector that is almost ten times larger than the U.S. Spanish-language media industry. Thus economic practices such as national syndication and consolidation are reorganizing the Spanish-language radio sector in ways that minimize local community issues and concerns, and media producers and community groups fear that the potential of Spanish-language media will not be reached. Castañeda Paredes (2003) notes that as deregulation policies restructure the U.S. media landscape, the importance will be minimized in the wave of bottom-line imperatives. For some radio program producers, for instance, the narrowing selection of music also restricts the large number of creative, avant-garde, and politically oriented compositions that are produced and available in Mexico, Latin America, and the Caribbean, but seldom reach the United States.

Dávila (2001) also confirms that the growing competition within the media industry has generated a shift in the practices and culture of the Hispanic advertising and marketing industry. Whereas Latina/o creative executives in the 1970s and early 1980s worked together to develop a legitimate industry that was sensitive to the differences between Latino ethnicities as well as validate the importance of Latino audiences and consumers, the period after the 1990s was deeply affected by intensifying global competition, and as a result, "the sense of camaraderie" was diminished. Advertising agencies, including those that served Spanish-language media, emphasized "the abstract ideal of 'Hispanics' as an undifferentiated reality" in order to expand "revenues within a larger and more competitive environment" (p. 53). Homogeneity thus became an important practice for survival.

However, this broad-based approach received much criticism from scholars and community Latino media producers since it viewed and treated audiences as homogenized consumers and not engaged citizens (Levine, 2001; McChesney, 2000; Nuiry, 1996). Nonprofit Latino media have challenged the utilization of media as merely marketing tools for commercial profit, and have attempted to create media spaces that reclaim communication outlets as forms of empowerment for Latinos as a whole, and local communities in particular. Straubhaar (2006) argues that this form of reclamation often produces "a strongly localized or hybridized adaptation of what is considered current or modern in global patterns" (p. 689). Despite the pressure by market forces to imagine panethnic audiences and content, commercial systems have felt the opposition to its formulaic creation of limited programming choices and narrowly defined viewing publics. One response to the homogeneity in commercial Spanish-language media is the expansion of community oriented communication outlets as important tools for reconsidering the role of media in communities.

An excellent example discussed briefly earlier is *Tertulia*, the only Spanish-language program on WFCR. The music producer of the program, Luis Meléndez, has worked on *Tertulia* for over 20 years. The show began because in the late-1970s, Western New England lacked a Spanish-language program that addressed the growing Latino community. The show that began as *Que Tal Amigos* was later transformed into *Tertulia*, which aimed to follow the Latin American and specifically Puerto Rican tradition of community dialogue, political engagement, and cultural interchange.

According to Mr. Melendez, the role of *Tertulia* in the community became increasingly important in the 1990s when commercial Spanish-language radio stations in the region were purchased by larger commercial outfits, and stations were outfitted with national programming. Local programming thus fell to the wayside, and *Tertulia* filled in the gaps, especially with regard to news and information that pertained to Latinos in Western New England. Mr. Melendez also notes that the dearth of pertinent local programming not only transformed *Tertulia* into a program that opened its airwaves to the community, but also became a major voice in translating for the "North American audience" the relevant issues that affect Latinos in the neighborhood and abroad. Although *Tertulia* is a predominantly Spanish-language program, many of the listeners are not necessarily Latino or Spanish-speaking.[2] Thus, Mr. Melendez is well aware of the opportunity that *Tertulia* has with its ability to educate and engage Latinos as well as non-Latinos. For the programming team at *Tertulia*, the broadcast program is a political and cultural tool that has the power to play an important role in disenfranchised communities.

Yet hot button issues such as immigration have also spurred a reinterpretation of commercial media in Latino communities. The aftermath of the Immigration Rights Rallies of spring 2006 have prompted scholars and activists to consider seriously the power of Spanish-language media, especially at the local level. In spring 2006, the world witnessed some of the largest mobilizations of immigrants that the United States has ever seen. In a span of 4 months, more than 5 million people walked out of their jobs, schools, and homes and marched on major city streets and small town squares in order to rally against and protest the impending immigration laws that Congress was considering (Feagans, 2006). The particular law that infuriated the immigrant and Latino public was H.R. 4437 "Border Patrol, Antiterrorism, and Illegal Immigration Control Act of 2005," popularly known as the Sensenbrenner Law because it was masterminded by House Representative Sensenbrenner, a Republican from Wisconsin. The House of Representatives passed this legislation in fall 2005, and in spring 2006, the Senate was debating whether or not to support this law as well. A slew of grassroots organizations and NGOs across the United States began educating the public about the passage of H.R. 4437 in the House and its implications if turned into law. One of the most significant issues was the way in which the law linked terrorism with immigration and criminalized undocumented people in the United States.

Noting the extremity of the law, grassroots organizations began campaigning against the impending legislation and involved Spanish-language radio personalities, especially those who were immigrant and at one time also undocumented in the United States The recent use of Spanish-language radio to mobilize people in support of immigrant rights demonstrates the significant potential for media in the political or cultural empowerment of Latino communities in the United States In Los Angeles, deejays like "El Cucuy" (known in English as the "The Bogeyman") provided information about the national boycotts and rallies, and encouraged listeners to participate in the walkouts. Also in Los Angeles, the popular deejay "El Piolin" (known in English as the "Tweety Bird") organized other local commercial Spanish-language radio deejays in order to create a wide-ranging distribution of information about the legislation and protests in the city and across the country. Eduardo Sotelo, "El Piolin," came to the United States as an undocumented immigrant from Guatemala in 1986, so he understood and could relate to the struggles of his undocumented Latino listeners. His personal experience fueled his support of the immigration rights protests and his morning commute radio program became a venue for discussing the complexity of the immigration reform legislation, life as an immigrant in Los Angeles, and the ways in which audience members could participate in the public rallies and debate. In his program, "El Piolin" informed "people where to go, what to wear, and what signs to carry" (Balz & Fears, 2006). It's important to note, however, that "El Piolin," along with nationally syndicated Spanish-language radio deejays, are often critiqued as "shock jocks" who are just as homophobic, racist, and sexist as their English-language counterparts. Perhaps the immigration movement past spring was as aberration to the radio content that is often broadcast on commercial radio, but there is no denying that the immigration debate sparked an awareness about the emerging political power of Latinos as well as the cultural politics of Spanish-language media.

There are numerous accounts of how politically inactive Latinos, particularly in regions with new Latino populations, became nascent activists as a result of radio deejays and grassroots organizations encouraging Latino listeners to participate in the immigrant rights rallies. The usage of Spanish-language radio as a medium for mobilizing Latinos occurred not only in California, but also in other states such as Illinois (which triggered the movement), Minnesota, Tennessee, Washington, Georgia, Florida, Texas, North Carolina, Washington DC, Colorado, New York, Wisconsin, and Utah.

Organizations such as Inmigrantes Unidos de la Florida worked closely with local area radio stations such as WLCC 760 AM (La Ley) in order to distribute information. Some Spanish-language newspapers also printed regional news accounts about the rallies and conducted series of investigative reporting in order to examine how participation in the protests affected the lives of immigrants. For instance, many Latino immigrants lost their jobs as U.S. Americans counterattacked the pro-immigrant rallies and a backlash emerged. However, this didn't prevent Spanish-language media from reporting about the front lines. In Fort Myers, a group of newspaper editors and reporters working for Spanish-language newspapers in the region held various meetings about how to proceed as well as balance their roles as voices for and of the community while also adhering to professional journalistic standards (Cardenas & Deggans, 2006). At this meeting it was concluded that it was best to provide the most information as possible while also encouraging participation as a method for remaining faithful to journalistic values.

Interestingly, the notion of objectivity has been a constant point of contention for Spanish-language media. Mainstream outlets have criticized Latino media producers for often working as advocates for the community and taking a subjective perspective on stories. With such few outlets, it's imperative to connect with the public so that it may have the information it needs in order to mobilize, if necessary. In many ways, this is why commercial Spanish-language media, radio in particular, was so effective during the immigrant rights rallies, and also, so ironic. Johnson (2000) notes that ethnic media, especially nationwide commercial outlets, often fail to function as political actors because of the pressures of the bottom line. While this is historically correct on some level, the rage against immigration in recent years seems to have spurred a political and cultural transformation of Spanish-language media in the United States In 2006, as the immigrants' rights movement intensified, commercial and nonprofit Spanish-language media exerted its advocacy role in a more expanded manner, and as a result, major issues such as immigration spurred a reinterpretation of the importance of media in Latino communities. With Congress' inability to develop a bipartisan resolution to the issue, it seems unlikely that the debate will end soon, and it seems more likely that more media accounts and documentaries will emerge as Latinos attempt to tell their own stories.

CONCLUSIONS

Studying Latina/os in the media promises to illuminate the contemporary global and transnational historical moment. The uses of Spanish-language commercial and noncommercial interests and Latina/os as well as others result in the inclusion in areas that were not previously being covered. Whereas the role of ethnic media has traditionally combined news with political and cultural community formation, the contemporary situation in which Latina/os are the fastest growing minority behooves us to reexamine approaches to ethnic media. One major characteristic that has been foregrounded in this chapter is the transnational and political economic and cultural flows that inform Spanish-language and English and bilingual Latina/o media. These flows have been historically consistent, that is, ownership, production, and flows of programming as well as the mobility of people who have migrated back and forth across American borders. As such the remapping of Spanish-language media in the United States is really about the changing national imaginary and economy of an entire nation.

Ultimately, the changes occurring within the Spanish-language newspaper, radio, and television commercial and noncommercial industries point to the dynamics between Latino demographic shifts, the rise of transnational media, and the ways in which new modalities of representation are becoming increasingly important as anti-immigrant and anti-Latino sentiment rise. Latino oriented outlets of cultural production are thus able to create competing narratives of Latinidades in the United States. Certainly, these competing narratives are not without controversy or contention, especially when commercial outlets, despite opening spaces of political discourse, are still beholden to the bottom line, or entertainment content reinforce sexist, racist, and homophobic ideas. Yet hot button issues such as immigration provide the best hope of utilizing Spanish-language media outlets as community resources and hopefully, through engagement with local media producers, members will challenge problematic ideologies. Although Spanish-language media is far from perfect, it is still very important within the larger cultural and political landscape, especially when mainstream English-language media continues to misrepresent and/or erase Latina/o experiences in the United States.

NOTES

1. Many Latin American countries, such as Argentina, have similar broadcast ownership rules. In Argentina, however, the biggest broadcast owner Goar Mestre, who was originally from Cuba, was able to circumvent the rules because his wife was an Argentinian citizen.
2. According to the WFCR general manager, *Tertulia* has a large number of non-Spanish speaking listeners.

REFERENCES

Balz, D. & D. Fears. (2006). "We decided not to be invisible anymore": Pro-immigration rallies are held across the country. *Washington Post*. April 11.
Cardenas, J. & E. Deggans. (2006). Immigrant rallies born in air. *St. Petersburg Times*. April 12.
Cardenas, J. & A. Goldman. (2004). Spanish-language newspapers La Opinion, El Diario to Merge. *Los Angeles Times*. January 16.

Castañeda Paredes, M. (2001). The reorganization of Spanish-language media marketing in the United States. V. Mosco & D. Schiller (Eds.), *Continental order? Integrating North America for cybercapitalism*. Lanham, MD: Rowman and Littlefield.

Castañeda Paredes, M. (2003). The transformation of Spanish-language radio in the United States. *Journal of Radio Studies, 10*(1), 5–16.

Chandler, M. (2005). Nuevo radio: More Latinos listening. *San Jose Mercury News*. August 6.

Crawford, B. & B. Fowler. (2002). *Border radio: Quacks, yodelers, pitchmen, psychics and other amazing broadcasters of the American airwaves*. Austin: University of Texas.

Dávila, A. (2001). *Latinos, Inc.: The making and marketing of a people*. Berkeley: University of California Press.

Dell'Agnese, E. (2005). The US-Mexico border in American movies: A political geography perspective. *Geopolitics, 10*(Summer 2), 204–221.

de la Cruz, P. & R. Ramirez. (2003). *Current population reports: The Hispanic population in the United States, March 2002*. Washington, DC: U.S. Census Bureau. Also available: http://www.census.gov/prod/2003pubs/p20-545.pdf

Fries, G. (2004). Radio is the tool to tune into ethnic consumers. *DSN Retailing Today*. November 22.

García Canclini, N. (2003). From national capital to global capital: Urban change in Mexico city. In A. Appadurai (Ed.), *Globalization*. Durham, NC: Duke University Press.

Gómez-Quiñonez, J. & D. R. Maciel. (1998). "What goes around, comes around": Political practice and cultural response in the internationalization of Mexican labor, 1890–1997. In D. R. Maciel & M. Herrera-Sobek (Eds.), *Culture across border: Mexican immigration and popular culture*. Tucson: University of Arizona.

Guzmán, B. (2001). *The hispanic population census 2000 brief*. Washington, DC: U.S. Census Bureau. Also available: http://www.census.gov/prod/2001pubs/c2kbr01-3.pdf

Habell-Pallán, Michelle. (2005). *Loca motion: The travels of Chicana and Latina popular culture*. New York: NYU Press.

Henao, L. A. (2006). After the protests, Latinos start to come together politically. *Christian Science Monitor*. August 10. p. 14.

Hispanic Fact Sheet. (2003). Atlanta, GA: University of Georgia Outreach Services. January.

Holt, D. B., E. L. Quelch, & . A. Taylor. (2004a). How global brands compete. *Harvard Business Review, 82*(9). September 1.

Johnson, M. A. (2000). How ethnic are US ethnic media: The case of *Latina* magazines. *Mass Communication and Society*, Spring/Summer, 3(2&3), 229–248.

Jones, M. L. F. (2005). In other words. *Presstime*. August.

Kasindorf, M. (2006). Spanish DJs take lead role in politics. *USA Today*. p. 2A.

Levine, E. (2001). Constructing a market, constructing an ethnicity: U.S. Spanish-language media and the formation of a syncretic Latino/a identity. *Studies in Latin American Popular Culture, 20*(33), 33–51.

Lionnet, F. & S. Shih. (Eds.). (2005). Introduction: Thinking through the minor, transnationally. *Minor transnationalism*. Durham, NC: Duke University Press.

Maddore, J. T. (2004). El Diario, Calif.'s La Opinion merge. *Newsday*. January 16.

Mato, D. (1998). On the making of transnational identities in the age of globalization: The US Latina/o-"Latin" American case. *Cultural Studies, 12*(4), 598–620.

McChesney, R. (2000). *Rich media, poor democracy: Communication politics in dubious times*. New York: New Press.

Mitchell, C. (2005). English only: The creation and maintenance of an academic underclass. *Journal of Latinos & Education, 4*(4), 253–270.

Mosco, V. & D. Schiller. (Eds.). (2001). Introduction: Integrating a continent for a transnational world. *Continental order? Integrating North America for cybercapitalism.* Lanham, MD: Rowman and Littlefield.

Mullman, J. (2005). Tribune, ImpreMedia duking it out. *Crain's Chicago Business.* April 4.

Navarro, M. (2003). As Univision looks to buy into radio, a debate over how big is too big. *The New York Times.* June 23. p. C8.

Nuiry, O. E. 1996. Magazine mania: Whose media is this, anyway? *Hispanic.* December, p. 53.

Páez, M. & M. Suárez-Orozco. (2002). *Latinos: Remaking America.* Berkeley: University of California Press.

The Project for Excellence in Journalism. (2005). *The state of the news media: An annual report on American journalism.* Retrived February 4, 2006, from http://www.stateofthenewsmedia.org/2005/narrative_ethnicalternative_intro.asp?media=9

Ramos, J. (2005). *The Latino wave: How Hispanics are transforming politics in America.* New York: Rayo.

Richardson, B. (1998). Address to the League of Latin American Citizens (LULAC) on education and foreign policy. *USUN Press Release.* July 1.

Ríos, D. I. (2000). Chicana/o and Latina/o gazing; audiences of the mass media. In D. R. Maciel, I. D. Ortiz, & M. Herrera-Sobek (Eds.), *Chicano renaissance: Contemporary cultural trends.* Tucson: University of Arizona.

Rodriguez, A. (1998). Hispanic media: Media enterprises serve people of Latin American descent. In *History of mass media in the United States: An encyclopedia* (pp. 251–253). Oxford: Francis and Taylor.

Rodriguez, A. (1999). *Making Latino news: Race, language, class.* Thousand Oaks, CA: Sage Publications.

Smothers, S. (2005). Opportunities abound in ethnic markets. *Presstime.* September.

Soto, H. (2004). Now more newspapers than ever in Spanish. *The San Diego-Union Tribune.* February 22.

Straubhaar, J. (2006). (Re)asserting national television and national identity against the global, regional, and local levels of world television. In G. D. Meenakshi & D. M. Kellner (Eds.), *Media and cultural studies: Keyworks.* Oxford: Blackwell.

Suro, R. (2004). *Changing channels and crisscrossing cultures: A survey of Latinos on the media.* Washington, DC: Pew Hispanic Center.

U.S. Federal Communications Commission. (2006). *Draft report: Review of the radio industry.* Washington, DC: GPO.

Ward, D. (2001). Hispanic outlets-media roundup: Hispanic boom presents plenty of PR opportunities. *PR Week.* November 26.

Williams, K. & P. Farhi. (2006). Spanish-language radio's big voice; stations act as community center and tutor to bridge the gaps between homeland. *The Washington Post.* July 3, p. D1.

Yúdice, G. (2003). *The expediency of culture: Uses of culture in the global era.* Durham, NC: Duke University Press.

Part II. Performance and the Self

CHAPTER FOUR

Performing THE Responsible Sponsor: Everything You Never Wanted TO Know ABOUT Immigration Post-9/11

BERNADETTE MARIE CALAFELL

Ethnic profiling is now accepted behavior, official policy and "Arab-looking" people, including most Latinos and brown people have become an ongoing source of anxiety and mistrust for true "patriotic" Americans ... Because of this new racism, brown people are being forced to overstate their patriotism as a survival strategy.

(GOMEZ-PEÑA, 2005, P. 274)

To be sure, the pervasiveness and insidiousness of these recent nativist movements might well create the false impression that this is a novel idea. But, nativism is nothing new. It is as old as the republic itself and probably here to stay, even if at times it submerges beneath the surface.

(HERNÁNDEZ-TRUYOL, 1998, P. 131)

Within the realm of Latina/o Communication Studies scholars have examined the rhetoric and rhetorical strategies of Latina/o social movements, in particular the Chicano Movement (Delgado, 1995; Fernandez & Jensen, 1995; Flores & Hasian, 1997; Hammerback & Jensen, 1980, 1994, 1998; Hammerback, Jensen, & Gutierrez, 1985; Jensen & Hammerback, 1980; Sedano, 1980), Chicana feminist rhetorics (Flores, 1996; Palczewski, 1996), and Puerto Rican and Nuyorican protest rhetorics (Cordova, 2004; Enck-Wanzer, 2006). Studies of histories of protest and struggles of Latina/o communities have also encompassed critical examinations of immigration policies including Proposition 187 (Hasian & Delgado, 1998; Ono & Sloop, 2002), responses to it (Holling, 2006), and rhetorical constructions of Mexican immigrants (Flores, 2003).

Largely these and other studies within the realm of Latina/o Communication Studies have taken rhetorical or textual approaches. In this chapter I add to work on Latina/o activism and immigration; however, I diverge in my methodology by contributing to the growing body of work in Latina/o performance studies. Little work has emerged as of yet in the field of Latina/o performance, but the research that has been published has examined Chicana/o displacements and performances of home (Calafell, 2004), performative pilgrimages (Calafell, 2005; Menchaca, 2005), and performances of Latina/o identities (Willis, 1997; Moreman, 1999). The topic of immigration and expected performances of citizenship as they interact in the lives of Latina/os and other immigrant groups has yet to be undertaken. Therefore, in taking a performance-centered approach I use my experiential knowledge as an insider/outsider in the process of immigration as a third generation Mexican American married to an Egyptian citizen post-9/11 to highlight the performances required to embody a responsible sponsor and "good" citizen.

I have been involved in an ongoing relationship fraught with misunderstandings, miscommunication, disappointment, and sparse moments of joy. This is a relationship that I knowingly and naively entered in the name of love. Yes, I knew there would be complications and it would not be easy, but it was a relationship I was willing to enter. It is a relationship between me, my government, and my husband Mohamed (an Egyptian citizen). Since 2002 Mohamed and I have been involved with the U.S. Citizenship and Immigration Services' (USCIS) process of applying for permanent residency. We began this process at the end of my second year as a graduate student at the University of North Carolina and continue to this day as I am now a faculty member in Denver. I mark these shifts in my position because they also mark the way I am viewed as a sponsor for Mohamed to stay in this country. As a professor I now possess a certain level of cultural capital, yet given all the antiliberal backlash and current depictions of university professors, I am equally marked with suspicion. Therefore I need to act on these suspicions as well as on federal requirements. Though I had two more years of funding available as a graduate student I made the choice to finish my doctorate in three years because I needed to meet the minimum income requirement necessary to qualify as a responsible sponsor.[1] This was my first step in becoming and performing as a responsible sponsor.

In this chapter, autobiographical performance, an aspect of a performance ethnography perspective, is used to highlight and give voice to the experience of myself and my husband Mohamed as we have traveled through the immigration process post-9/11. This chapter gives light to several positions. First, it highlights my position of what Patricia Hill Collins (2000) terms an outsider within being superficially part of the system of citizenship but never fully enmeshed because of my Otherness. As a Chicana I have the privileges of U.S. citizenship but daily face the very real experiences of racism and increasing anti-Mexican fervor. This narrative is also tied to my familial relationship to immigration that I as a third generation Mexican American have had the privilege of not knowing firsthand, until now. Second, this chapter highlights the complexities of Latina/o identities or *Latinidad*. I want to consider how processes and issues such as immigration produce effects that make the body remember. In this particular case, my body remembers the long silenced history of Andalusian Spain and an even more complicated identity than what the term Latina/o would denote.

In engaging in autobiographical performance, I am guided by the words of Pelias (2005) who argues, "Performative writing expands the notion of what constitutes disciplinary knowledge" (p. 417). I do not use this chapter to give a history about immigration policy or rhetoric, rather I intend to ground immigration policies post-9/11 in fleshed bodies that demonstrate the consequences of the ideologies that emerge from them. I am interested in the performances that are required to satisfy these ideologies. I do not mean to let our experiences speak for all who have been in this situation; rather I use our story as a way to highlight the politics of our position that may have some shared characteristics with others who have occupied spaces similar to ours. Collins (2000) argues that we must recognize the individual and unique aspects of black women's experience, while still remaining committed to a collective politic that acknowledges shared oppression based on historical, economic, political, social, and ideological forces. I share Collins' view and use it to guide our own story as it relates to others, particularly of Middle Eastern descent and who are Muslim, who have also crossed paths with immigration post-9/11. We share what Muñoz (2000) would term an affect of Otherness that is created through a lack of identification with an official national affect. Furthermore, in writing this narrative I use the "I" as a possible space of empathy and identification, which seeks to implicate the reader (Madison, 1998; Pelias, 2005).

Specifically, in this chapter I am interested in highlighting the ways the immigration process blurs the private and the public, rewards and reinforces heterosexuality and rigid definitions of marriage, and forces those who must go through its processes to perform in ways consistent with its ideologies. This process manifests itself similar to Scott's theories of the public and hidden transcripts. Scott (1990) argues that public transcripts performed by those in positions of subordination are often or appear to be complicit with dominant ideologies, while hidden transcripts will often be at odds with these transcripts. This process is particularly significant for both Mohamed and I as we each bring our raced personal, historical, and cultural relations with immigration: I, as a third generation Mexican American who identifies as Chicana and Mohamed as an Egyptian citizen who wants to become a naturalized U.S. citizen. Generation, imaginings of home, and (im)possibilities of (im)migration shape each of our performances in this process.

AUTOBIOGRAPHICAL PERFORMANCE

Linda Martín Alcoff (1991–1992) argues that "a speaker's location is epistemically salient" (p. 7). Agreeing with Alcoff, I use my voice as someone involved in the process of immigration as testimony and as a beginning to critique these systems of power as they relate to racism, nationalism, and heteronormativity. I see this move consistent with the turn to a critical ethnography that Madison (2005) argues "begins with an ethical responsibility to address processes of unfairness or injustice within a particular *lived* domain" (p. 5, emphasis in original). As a Chicana academic I find solidarity with Enrique Murillo Jr. (2004) who writes, "My experience as an educational ethnographer, to date, can sometimes be described as traveling those blurred boundaries when Other becomes researcher, narrated becomes narrator, translated becomes translator, native becomes anthropologist, and how one emergent and intermittent identity continuously informs the other" (p. 166). Like Murillo, I acknowledge how my various subjectivities that have positioned me as Other. I speak from the power-laden space of the ethnographer/performer (Madison, 2005) as well as from the space of Otherness constructed around peoples of Mexican origin in the United States. I speak from a history of immigration in my own family (though not through the formal channels that Mohamed and I now engage) that I now come to understand even more through my embodied knowledge or theories of the flesh.

While I find subjectivity and self-reflexivity to be of central importance to my stance, it is not without critique (Madison, 2005). Madison cautions that "we take ethical responsibility for our own subjectivity and political perspective, resisting the trap of gratuitous self-centeredness" (p. 8). Madison highlights the insurgence of what I term narcissistic autoethnography that uncritically assumes the personal voice is itself political. I share Madison's concern and attempt to guard against narcissism in my narrative through critical self-reflection and a sustained critique of the self that is embedded in dialogic performance. In guarding against narcissism, I operate from the space of dialogic performance or conversation as advocated by Conquergood (1985). I account for my voice and Mohamed's voice in this story as they intersect with larger dialogues of citizenship in order to move beyond the personal to reflect upon the cultural. Madison asks that we understand "the embodied self ... a voice wedded to experience" (1998, p. 278). In addition, I turn to Alexander (2006), who though writing of a performance ethnography that takes the stage, still allows me to find many similarities with the performances I engage in daily in this process and in this autobiographical performance.

Alexander writes, "The potential resides in how participants choose to maintain or disrupt the perceptual stasis that that exists within their *habitudes and habitus* and how they *might* act toward influencing social awareness of problematic human conditions that may be revealed or explored through performance ethnography" (p. 412, emphasis in original).

In this autobiographical performance I offer my and Mohamed's participatory experience of immigration.[2] I use these narratives to flesh out our subjectivities of Egyptian and Chicana as both Mohamed and I negotiate, struggle, and fight for home in this process. I offer personal accounts and documents that trace our journey that began in 2002. These documents include photographs that demonstrate the ways we perform heteronormativity, intimacy, and domesticity.

MARCH 3, 2003

> Falling in love, the otherness of the other, is the greatest joy; and vulnerability in the face of the other is a sweet surrender, a gift rather than a sacrifice. (Oliver, 2001, p. 224)

I sit in the office of our new immigration lawyer. He is Argentinean. He is the second lawyer Mohamed has hired to help us through this process. The first took his money and never filed the paperwork. But what rights does he have as an "alien" to protest? A few days before this meeting I tell Mohamed, "If we are gonna get another lawyer she or he has to be Latino. It has to be someone who understands." Would they understand or do I assume because of the migration of my family to this country there would be a shared understanding? Am I imposing a shared theory of the flesh that would bind our experiences together as Latina/os, though it might do me well to remember that not all Latina/os have the same relationship with or any relationship to immigration?

We talk through some paper work ... copies of birth certificates, a translation of an Egyptian birth certificate, marriage license/certificate, fingerprints for background checks, medical tests, the five hundred plus fee for each application, plus the lawyer's fee (legal immigration does not come cheap or easy), copies of passports, entry visas, form I-485, application for employment authorization, form G-325A, Petition for Alien Relative, Affidavit of Support, copies of income tax returns, photographs, and a letter from UNC-CH that verifies my income. This is everything thus far, but I am sure there is more to come.

We begin discussing the upcoming special registration that INS[3] now requires of "certain" immigrant groups. Let's be honest—Arab men—they are the ones that are targeted. As Ono and Sloop (2002) write, "The production and proliferation of new enemies to blame, to oppose, and to conquer is part of a distinct contemporary culture" (p. 35). This comes as no surprise. This is just another move in a long line of racial profiling and nativism (Acuña, 1998; Carrasco 1998; Hernández-Truyol, 1998). Another move in a hate campaign that has been going on since September 11, 2001. I sit and look at the beautiful gentle Egyptian man next to me who so reminds me of my grandfather who passed away more than a year ago. I cannot bear the thought of being without him, yet it is a very real possibility. A victim of circumstance, a victim of bad timing. Post-9/11 whose rights are protected? I remember often hearing a popular quote about the Holocaust—something to the effect that if you didn't pay attention and speak against injustices committed to others, no one would be left to speak for you. How true that rings to me now as it seems that very few people give a damn about the rights of "these damn immigrants" and the citizens who happen to be married to them. "Those immigrants." Such familiar words, just a new context. Isn't this how hate campaigns begin? As self-described Chicano performance artist Guillermo Gómez-Pena (2005) writes, "Then came 9/11 and, along with several million brown men with foreign-sounding names, I became a generic 'suspect'" (p. 161). He argues, "The Other is once again perceived as seriously threatening, as 'un-American.' There's been an overnight shift of parameters and attitudes toward, say brown people. We are no longer hip, sexy, and exotic creatures on the global menu. In the world according to Bush and his evangelical cowboys, we are all 'suspicious'" (p. 272).

This lawyer speaks honestly with us. His honesty and intensity scare me. There are no smiles here, no laughs, only an overwhelming sense of sadness and even grief. There is a very real possibility that my husband will be deported. Our marriage means nothing if he is deemed a threat, though I see no just cause. If he does not have the right paper at the right time, a receipt from immigration, he could be doomed. Even if he does have this paper he could still be doomed. Our future, any certainty we have is up in the air. Where will I go? What will I do? Can I get a job at the American University in Cairo? Suddenly, this dissertation and my newly acquired job are not as important as I had once thought. Will I lose it all again? Home is an imagined thing. Home is contested. Home is not open to everyone. I theorized home as a performative space between two bodies born out of a shared affect of Otherness rather than any physical location,[4] and now I wonder what that space will become without this body.

APRIL 21, 2003

I am on pins and needles. I lay on the couch under Mohamed's blanket as I await his phone call. *He has to call me.* He has to let me know what is going on. Registration day for all men of Middle Eastern nationality in the United States has arrived and with it all my anxiety and fear. Our roles have reversed and I am no longer the strong one. He did not receive the receipt from INS yet to validate his claim that he has started his immigration paperwork, but he cannot really wait any longer; he has to go. The day before his trip to Charlotte, North Carolina, for this interview we go over everything. I give him the checkbook, our marriage license, copies of forms, and my birth certificate. He gives me his debit card and PIN as well as his phone number in Egypt. Just in case ... All night I could not sleep and as soon as the clock marks 7:30 a.m., opening hours for the INS office, I move closer to the phone: 8 o' clock, 8:30, 9. It is unbearable; 9:30 the phone rings. Instinctively I know it is him. "Everything is alright Bern. I am okay." "I was so worried, I was so scared." I would come to find out that people we knew were deported as the result of this "special registration." We feel lucky and blessed this time around.

While this experience is terrifying for us I consider the fear that exists daily in the southwest and along the border, where Mexicana/os and Chicana/os are often suspect or constructed as forever foreign. I remember a history of Mexican Repatriation. Rosales (1996) writes that "Between 1929 and 1936 at least six hundred thousand Mexican nationals and their children, many of whom were born in the U.S. returned to Mexico" (p. 49). A little more than a decade later Operation Wetback would once again target Mexicans. Shortly after World War II, in 1954 the U.S. and INS rounded up thousands of undocumented workers deporting them to Mexico (Rosales, 1996). Thus the special registration that we now face seems to be in many ways eerily similar to other special immigration acts or exclusions. Paralleled experiences decades later only the face of the Other shifts in this moment and this particular act.

JUNE 2003

Opening the mail I read,

> This refers to the Application for Employment Authorization which you filed with the Immigration and Naturalization Service on March 5, 2003.
>
> You have been scheduled for an appointment to be processed with regard to your application by an office of this Service at the location, date, and time listed below ...

I read on ... the date listed is *Wednesday, July 16, 2003*. While the news is good and it is news we have been waiting for, it is also quite frustrating. July 16, 2003 is only two days after we are supposed to arrive in our new home—Syracuse, New York ... You cannot really say no to INS. You cannot really reschedule. Weeks ago I finished a dissertation in order to meet the demands of the job I was going to be taking. Now again, I rush. Will we stay in North Carolina longer and delay the trip to New York? We make the plan to drive to Syracuse and let Mo get back on the road the next day—12 hours backs to North Carolina and then another 12 hours back to New York. We have to have some agency. We have to have some choice here. We had planned on letting INS know of our new address once we had settled, but again we never dictate the schedule and we are always in their service. I will wait in Syracuse once again for him to return. I will wait once again for him to call and let me know it is all okay.

OCTOBER 2003

> The Application for Permanent Residence you filed has been received by the office listed below for processing. Once all processing and background checks have been completed, you will be scheduled for an interview to discuss your application. The normal processing time for this type of application is 9 months.

Once again INS has dictated my schedule. I had bought my ticket to the National Communication Association convention and was to leave the morning of November 19. But as luck would have it, I must once again rearrange my life at the drop of the hat for INS. Prior to the notification of our interview we had been collecting everything in anticipation of it. You learn from other couples who have gone through the process before you to save everything. The information we share amongst ourselves is invaluable. Another couple Deborah and Ahmed, friends of ours in North Carolina, having just gone through their interview sent us copies of the documents that they were required to take with them to their interview. With this list I began compiling. The photo albums I meticulously created became our scrapbooks and were a "genre of the self" (Katriel & Farrell, 1991, p. 2). You must have proof. You must have a life performed before the camera. Introverts need not apply. All the things other couples take for granted suddenly become essential in helping you establish that indeed your marriage is "true."

I establish the proof through two lists—proof of shared financial life and proof of shared social life. Good thing I kept that receipt for the sofa we bought or the table and chairs that Mo paid for using our shared checking account. I think through and rationalize every transaction we make. Which account, who signs, what name is on the receipt. All of this is of utter importance to me. Yes, bank records, leases, insurance policies, receipts, all of these must be kept. Don't forget the receipt for his car to be fixed using your credit card, I tell myself. The flights I booked for us to Phoenix for Christmas ... I have the receipts to attest to the fact that this man has indeed become part of my family. I could include the graduation pictures with all of us together—the new family. Oh yes, the pictures of when Aunt Leila came to visit from Egypt. Certainly I would not meet his family if this were all a farce. Nothing could be more all American as the snapshots of our trip to Disneyland in July of 2003 when we attended a friend from Chapel Hill's wedding in Los Angeles. Yes, the continuity is established, there we are with James, Mufridah, Lisa, and Tarik in North Carolina, and now we are all there together in LA for James and Mufridah's wedding. Katriel and Farrell (1991) argue that scrapbooks are texts of identity that "articulate a sense of coherence and significance" (p. 2). Do our narratives and actors suggest coherency?

I perform the construction of ourselves through time with increasing intimacy. Do I have all the anniversary cards sent to us? Do I still have envelopes addressed to Mo at the address on the lease we both signed? Oh, be sure to include the pictures of us at home. The ones of him mopping the floor and me washing the dishes. Those will surely establish domesticity and perform assimilation by disrupting any racist stereotypes about the patriarchy or machismo of Arab men. I do not try to sound offensive but I know I am dealing with stereotypes and dominant ideologies of Arab and Muslim men, therefore in our scrapbooks I tell a different story. I tell a story that is counterhegemonic and puts flesh on the one-dimensional image that so pervades the national imaginary.

In putting together our materials Scott's (1990) words echo in my head, "the greater the disparity in power between dominant and subordinate and the more arbitrary it is exercised, the more the public transcript of subordinates will take on a stereotypical, ritualistic cast" (p. 3). The desire to perform assimilation and domesticity is not unwarranted given the histories of nativism and Othering in this country. Writing about the master narrative of white supremacy in California Almaguer (1998) describes the ways Asian immigrants were treated, "While they too were unambiguously deemed nonwhite, these immigrants carried the extra burden of being a 'peculiar' people who spoke a completely unintelligible eastern language, had 'abhorrent' culinary tastes, dressed 'strangely,' and practiced a form of 'pagan idolatry' clearly at odds with Judeo-Christian religious traditions. In cultural terms, Chinese and Japanese immigrants, therefore, were perceived initially as more like the uncivilized and heathen Indian population than any of the other cultural minorities in the state" (p. 166). Couldn't we as easily substitute Arab in the modern day? With this knowledge photographs are assembled that seek to make Mohamed appear less Other, less foreign, and less threatening. Post-9/11 he clearly understands the constructions that frame his identity and willingly engages in these performances of domesticity and assimilation. He names himself against dominant constructions though the affiliation is not ideal. His is a tactic[5] based on timing and possibility that allows for some agency and possibility if even small.

We have performed domesticity; now we must perform intimacy. I remembered the stories I had heard from the other couples we knew who had also been through this process. Some had even gone to the extreme of taking nude pictures with them to the interview! I refused to go to that extreme. Instead I include modest pictures of Mo in the bathtub with his head sticking out of the shower curtain. I mimic the same pose and place them side by side in the photo album. I also include the single photograph taken of our wedding day at the Durham County Courthouse in North Carolina. Bell (1999) argues that "weddings are more than rites of passage, weddings also 'make' private sexual relationships public" (p. 177). Bell elaborates on the value of control that underlies the cultural performances of weddings: "Weddings are expressions of, indeed, creations of, the need for order, control, stability. Every culture guards its couplings with implicit and explicit regulations, doles out rewards and punishments, and measures individuals by their enactments. Weddings are celebrations, ultimately, of individual complicity in the social conspiracy to control sex—the necessary channeling of the gushing stream" (p. 189). Reading Bell's words I wonder about the control performed in the photographs we choose as proof of o ur intimacy. I wonder if I act or perform as an agent of the state who has mastered control of the Other and who uses these photographs to attest to this. Is our intimacy at the service of the state who sees how my own sexuality has been controlled and tamed and is now complicit with establishing or proving the trustworthiness of an "alien applicant"?

Going through the pictures I think to myself, "This should be enough, right?" Intimacy is established ... but it might be best include some pictures of us hugging and kissing. As Bell (1999) writes, "The kiss at the end is the promissory note for sex to come, as well as the demarcation of safe passage through liminal space" (p. 177). The more you can document intimacy the better.

I prepare the lists, make copies of documents, and pack our suitcase of proof to take with us to the interview. Photo albums—check. Copies of financial documents—check. Copies of framed pictures—check. Immediately after the interview we will drive back to Syracuse and I will hop on a plane to Miami.

In preparing these documents and being given an opportunity for performance, I must acknowledge that this is an act of privilege. Though it does not feel like a privilege we must acknowledge the privilege our class status affords us in being able to hire a lawyer and pay expensive immigration fees for every form. Privilege in the sense that we have the ability to afford to go through this process of documentation, a process that is not cheap and because of this it is not privy to everyone. I consider histories of undocumented migration in my family, illegal migration to the north that now generations later affords me the luxury of a documented entry and "responsible sponsorship." All of this weighs heavily upon me.

NOVEMBER 19, 2003
UPSTATE, NEW YORK

We arrived yesterday afternoon. I did not sleep at all … I sat in the sitting room of the hotel room freaked out, scared, and contemplating all of our options. As soon as the sunlight broke we got dressed; me in my professor attire and Mo in his suit and tie. How does one dress for an interview to establish the legitimacy of their marriage? We check out of the hotel, move the car, and walk toward the federal building. Of course we had walked this route the day before, but in this second walk it seems so much more intensely unfamiliar. We walk through the metal detectors and I open our suitcase. The people laugh, joking with us that it is very clear why we are here. Should I take this joking as a good sign? Am I making this more than it has to be? We ride the elevator up and finally make our way to the office …

Officer A … which one is s/he? I watch each couple being taken back and try to gauge the look on each officer's face. That one looks friendly. "I hope that is the one we get," I whisper to Mo. That one looks scary … I hope that is not Officer A. Some of the people in the waiting room have kids with them. That surely must beat my suitcase of "proof." That must be the real proof of a successful union … does untenured, just out of school mean, and not wanting children anything when asked about the lack of reproduction in your union? Does the fact that you have developed a body of scholarship under a specific name seem like a valid reason for not changing your name to that of your husband? I can only hope. I am too nervous to sit. I walk around the office surveying the pictures of success stories, those people who had passed through these walls and now are captured forever in images of them taking the oath of citizenship. Will Mo's picture someday hang on these walls as the ideal Other who had been approved and sanctioned by the state?

Finally, our time comes as Officer A calls our name. She does not seem friendly and immediately I dread what I imagine to come the next hour. Office A is a middle-aged African American woman in a blue suit and white shirt. Is she a person? Does she feel? Does she have a family? Why does she work here? I want to humanize her, to make her real, and make her more like us. She is a woman of color like me. Does she feel the racial undertones of this situation? Certainly she must have some feeling? Who would be the ideal interviewer? Once we enter her office I am overwhelmed by the signs and the video camera. The signs to my right assure those that sit in the chairs that Mo and I now occupy that if you lie it is a crime and will be fined and prosecuted as such. The video camera hanging in the left corner of the room captures our every move and I wonder who else will watch this tape. How many times will my words be reproduced? What are the implications if I accidentally make a mistake or forget something? Will it be used against me later? The force of surveillance is so intense in this space, and I wonder if our reactions to the surveillance itself is a text that will be discussed even after we have left this space. While this surveillance is intense I think of other forms of surveillance that exist in the everyday life, particularly around the border. Certainly it seems that surveillance in this case is magnified, but for many of us who occupy spaces of Otherness in the national imaginary are we not always under some form of surveillance? Lugo (2000), for example, documents this surveillance through the pervasive nature of border inspections further commenting on the ways skin privilege, language, and citizenship inform this surveillance.

As the interview begins Officer A explains the nature of the meeting. Given her explanation I provide her with a copy of the lists I have compiled and tell her I am more than happy to walk through the documents and photo albums with her. She proceeds to look at the pictures themselves. Despite the care with which I have taken to perform a coherent and consistent narrative she reads it out of place, skipping pages, and barely even looking at the second album. I am embarrassed as she sees the pictures of me, performing "divaness" in my single days, but perhaps she reads them as honest and a testimony of what has been tamed through marriage. The interview proceeds.

> Officer A: So you met in North Carolina?
> Bernadette: Yeah. I was going to school there, but I finished my degree and we moved here.
> Officer A: So you moved here for work? What do you do?
> Bernadette: I am a professor at Syracuse University.
>
> *Suddenly, I have discursively marked and positioned myself in another class bracket in her mind, and her demeanor clearly demonstrates this. She becomes a lot friendlier. I wonder how she negotiates my ethnicity, my identity as Chicana, my own family's history of undocumented migration in this country. Or does my whiteness, both in my physical appearance and in my performance cloak this history? With the change in her demeanor I remember the words of Scott, "Subordinates offer a performance of deference and consent while attempting to discern, to read, the real intentions and mood of the potentially threatening powerholder" (p. 3). I continue to try and read her and adjust my performance accordingly.*

Officer A: So how did you meet?

I laugh nervously as I am embarrassed by the story. It is not the kind of story I like to tell, but in this situation and others like it I have been forced to retell it many times. Each time I am ashamed. Mohamed is much more composed than I am and he proceeds to tell her the story of our meeting at a club in Chapel Hill. He tells of the honest looking girl who seemed to look so out of place. He makes sure to include just enough of the right details to bring the story to life. The story is almost too cliché. In the back of my mind I discipline myself with my Mexican Catholic guilt that never stops. What kind of woman are you to meet a man in a bar and marry him two months later? Officer A is satisfied with Mohamed's telling, at least for the moment. She gets to the real issue at hand attempting to gauge Mohamed's threat level.

Officer A: So Mohamed if you have kids what religion will they be?

Mohamed: Well you know I didn't have a choice. I was born and raised Muslim. My parents are Muslim and in Egypt most people are Muslim. But Bernadette is Christian and my best friend is Christian. I am not like some of these Muslim people that hate Christian people. So I want to tell our kids about both of our religions and let them choose. It does not really matter to me because I do not really practice my religion. As long as they have God I will be happy.

As I watch Mohamed speak I am reminded of Scott's (1990) words that, "Much of what passes as normal social intercourse requires that we routinely exchange pleasantries and smile as other about whom we may harbor an estimate not in keeping with our public performance. Here we may perhaps say that the power of social forms embodying etiquette and politeness requires us often to sacrifice candor for smooth relations with our acquaintances. Our circumspect behavior may also have a strategic dimension: this person to whom we misrepresent ourselves may be able to harm or help us in some way" (p. 1). Though we are in no way in a normal situation, I cannot help but note the scripted pleasantries exchanged between the three of us and Mohamed's sincere yet strategic responses. Officer A seems pleased. She continues to perform friendliness and comfort with his answer. So comfortable in fact that she begins to critique President Bush and his invasion of Iraq. I am not smart enough to catch on to what she is doing as I too eagerly agree with her shaking my head enthusiastically. Perhaps it is because I have been away from the border and its pervasiveness for so long. Perhaps it is because, I, third generation, white-skinned Mexican American have the privilege of feeling safe. My ability to pass and perform Whiteness has afforded me the luxury to be off guard for a moment, to forget my Otherness. However, Mohamed is a lot smarter and he knows the game, perhaps it is because his body never lets him forget.

Mohamed: Well you know it is not that simple. Saddam is not innocent. He has hurt a lot of people ...

"The public transcript will typically, by its accomodationist tone, provide convincing evidence for the hegemony of dominant values, for the hegemony of dominant discourse" (Scott, 1990, p. 4).

Mo continues to defend the actions of President Bush persuasively. His performance of loyalty is convincing enough that even I start to believe him. Later he reminds me that in Egypt there is no criticism of the government, and he is wise to this trick. How different is this from World War I when Hernández-Truyol argues that Germans became the victims of nativist and nationalist fervor? Hernández-Truyol (1998) continues, "The rejection of the 'enemy within' replayed itself in World War II when thousands of Japanese were relocated from their West Coast homes to internment camps in isolated settings. The Supreme Court in Korematsu v. United States upheld this wartime order issued by President Franklin D. Roosevelt on grounds of national security" (p. 129). Given this history, it comes as no surprise that Mohamed performs a public transcript that is not positively misleading, but "is unlikely to tell the whole story about power relations" (Scott, 1990, p. 2). It is a performance that operates from the desire "to appeal to the expectations of the powerful" (p. 2). It is a performance that is required of us at this moment in time. Satisfied with Mohamed's response and in light of this history, Officer A congratulates us. But it is a victory celebrated too soon ...

Officer A: Mohamed your background check has not cleared yet. Bernadette's has. What I can do though is have you give your fingerprints for your green card and when your background check clears we will send it to you. Here is my phone number, you can call and check in with me. *I will call that number several times requesting to speak to Officer A only to be put off, ignored, and dismissed all together. This is the last time I will ever speak to Officer A who has determined the legitimacy of our marriage. Weeks later I will still wonder about Officer A. I will continue to try and humanize her. I will consider how her public transcript differed from her hidden transcript. Could I ever really know Officer A? I will wonder about my desire for racial and gendered affiliation with Officer A as a woman of color, particularly in light of the overbearing black and white dichotomy that continues to persist. I will consider the ways that the black and white dichotomy shaped our realities in North Carolina where it often seemed that Mo and I as part of Latino and Arab communities felt resentment and tension not only from white communities, but also from a place we did not expect, African American communities. I will consider how these tensions were and are shaped around histories of citizenship, rhetorics and fallacies of scarcity, and language.*

As Mo makes his fingerprints on the card that will eventually become his green card, I nervously think this is not right. This is not how it works. They do not call you for an interview unless your background check has cleared. That is what everyone has told us. This is not right. No, no, no, no. Did they need to see us first to clear us? Does someone need to watch our tape? We leave deflated not knowing how to make sense of what just happened. As we drive back to Syracuse I get on the phone with our lawyer in North Carolina who assures me that everything sounds okay. I still don't trust it and I don't feel safe about traveling to Phoenix for the holidays without a green card. I board a flight to Miami literally sick and tired.

FEBRUARY 18, 2004
"WELCOME TO THE UNITED STATES OF AMERICA"

It is with great pleasure that we welcome you to permanent resident status in the United States.

Mo's green card arrives and I read the date of issue: February 4, 2004. It is exactly three years from the date of the death of my grandfather. Looking at the card it all seems to come full circle; the death of one person who represented home and the legitimization of another who has become my home. How different were these two men? Each desired to perform and embody the mythic American Dream. Jose Muñoz, whose family originally settled in New Mexico, one minute Mexican and the next American, but always with a difference, was a man who sacrificed year after year for his *guera*. I stand looking from the picture of Mohamed holding his green card, the sign that he had made it, to the picture of tata on the altar I had constructed in his memory. He wore a plaid button-up blue and gray shirt, his thinning hair combed back, and his mustache neatly cut. My eyes in his eyes. I look closer, his skin was several shades darker than mine, but I smiled as I remembered the time that to my amazement I found out, "Tata had white legs!" Yes, his legs were as white as my arms. Years of working in construction had permanently tanned his body so that he was in a sense two-toned. How ironic. His skin color so highly valued in Mexican cultures and regarded as a symbol of status and privilege in this country, was sacrificed so that his *guera* might have a better shot at life. Yes, he must have had some hand in this …

POSTSCRIPT
JUNE 1, 2006

Since I first began documenting this process last year a great deal has changed. I do not simply mean in the course of our relationship with immigration, but with the larger climate of immigration in the United States. As a Chicana growing up in Arizona, Aztlán, I always felt the pervasiveness of the border. I left Phoenix in 2000, venturing east to Chapel Hill, and then northeast to Syracuse in 2003. In the course of these moves I have come to know firsthand the contours of Latina/o identities, shifting patterns of immigration, and an increasing rise in nativism toward Latina/os that has resulted in groups like the Minutemen "guarding," my beloved border in Arizona. As anti-Mexican sentiments have increased and I remain in this tenuous relationship with immigration, I become more fearful. Preparing to leave the northeast and return to the southwest for a new job, I wonder how it will differ. I return, I migrate, in a sense to my space, my home that is now being both ideologically and physically recolonized. I consider how different my performance might be if I were to go back now, three years later for the immigration interview. In light of the increasing anti-Mexican sentiment that continues to rise, would it be possible for me to perform the ideal sponsor?

While I ponder this question, I remain fearful and intensely feel the politics of my body, my identities, even while it seems Mohamed is finally in the clear. On May 8, 2006, our anniversary nonetheless, we excitedly drove back to the upstate office after receiving a notice just a few days earlier that Mo had been granted his new green card—his real permanent residency. There was no need for a second interview; we simply had to go to the office for fingerprints and paperwork. We were in! Even in this long desired safe space the fear remained. The body doesn't forget. Nervously we entered the office and waited to be called. Mo had told me, "Bern, don't let them take me by myself to another room. Promise you will come with me." Sitting side by side waiting for the African American officer to call Mo back after she finishes processing his paperwork, I stare at the huge replica of the Statue of Liberty. My history of immigration is not Ellis Island and Lady Liberty. My history is based in conquest, broken treaties, and lands that change names but never our connection. Lost in thought I hear Mo's name called and the officer instructs him to follow her through a door. I slowly and hesitantly follow. Fingerprints were taken, smiles were given, and in the end we left happy told to expect the green card soon.

In all of this, feelings of safety coupled with feelings of instability overcome me. I am taken back to family stories of migration, of Little Grandma 96 years old when she died, never speaking English, giving birth to my own grandmother in the small mining town of Jerome, Arizona. I think of the black and white photo that hangs in my office of my tata, José Muñoz, standing both proudly and defiantly with his friends in the desert of South Mountain in Phoenix, though in my imagination I believe he is in New Mexico. I think of my own fears of crossing the border in Arizona fearful they would not let me through. I remember the fear seeing a border patrol car in the next lane. Even the fear for Mo and I as we drove through south Texas while the border patrol waved us by. Though I am a third generation Mexican American, who is frequently not recognized as such because my appearance does not meet the stereotype of Mexican, have what some might term an irrational fear; it nonetheless exists. The body remembers and the body feels the pain and the trauma inflicted upon our people. Most of all I remember my most recent border crossing to Mexico City in search of some glimmerings of myself, my family's roots, and generally my voice as a newly married woman. The fusing of myself as a newly married Chicana with my Egyptian family, the rediscovering of an Arabic past, all came crashing down on me emotionally as I walked through the *Templo Mayor* seeing signs of Egypt everywhere. Listening to my distant voice in my recorded fieldnotes, more than three years old, I hear the fear even back then, though it seemed colored by hope.

> I've been looking for home now for quite some time. I met with a woman today named Susana when I went to go tour the *Templo Mayor*. Previous to meeting her I kept thinking about Mohamed, but when I met with her even before I said anything she drew out connections between Egyptian culture or Arab culture and Mexican culture. I've been looking for home for so long … thinking I was going to find it on a Latino body. Not even sure what home meant. I'm struck right now by the many layers I've seen today. The layers on the temple being built over and over again. Layers of religion transposed on each other. The struggle, the fight for religion. Layers of different cultures influencing one another. Layers on my body. Layers in my name. She said, "Your name is an Arabic name." My name, Spanish name, Mexican name, Arabic name, now overlaid with another Arabic name—Mansour. What do these connections mean, what do these similarities mean? What is home? I've come to Mexico City to see home. To come home, to know what that is. I came to see from a non-Chicano point of view … I see Mohamed's picture as he lies in a Mexican blanket. Again another contradiction, or is it? If I come to Mexico City and Mexico City is everything then it's nothing at the same time, you know? Mexico City is Egypt. If Mexico City is whatever, then I'm nothing … what am I, a citizen of the world?

A MORE COMPLEX *LATINIDAD*?

Years later after writing the above journal entry I have come to understand that the connections I felt in Mexico City and with Mohamed were not simply whimsical but based in our real histories and blood lines that once again demonstrated to me that *Latinidad* continues to be even more complex than we might comprehend. Our bodies never let us forget even if popular histories and understandings of identity ask us to. Menocal (2002) writes of Andalusian Spain and the coexistence of Muslim, Jewish, and Christian communities. Citing Menocal, Valdivia (2004) reminds us that Spain was a space for hybridity. Reading Mencocal's work myself I come across her description of the *khalifa*, the successors to the Prophet Muhammad. The second of these caliphs was named al-Mansur (Menocal, 2002, p. 53). Literally seeing both my and Mohamed's names or approximations of them linked together on the page, in history, in our blood lines and from my understanding of Calafell, Spain being a part of Andalusian Spain, I come to see *Latinidad* in a whole new way. Aparicio (2003) has written convincingly of the shared affects or feelings that connect Latina/o groups as an example of *Latinidad*, but through this (re)performance of citizenship post-9/11 I come to understand *Latinidad* not only on the affective level but through the body, what some might call a theory of the flesh. Anzaldúa (1987) first taught me that I was *mestiza* and led me to appreciate having a "tolerance for ambiguity." However, it was the knowledge that I gained in the everyday experience that took my understanding of identity and community to an entirely different level. Writing about the complexity of Latina/o identities Valdivia notes, "Latinas as a constructed category gain meaning by virtue of their supposed location as an in between ethnicity, not white yet not black. Yet this is not a simple process as the fact is Latinas are not uniformly brown" (p. 4). Valdivia turns to the concept of hybridity to examine Latina/o identities arguing that "hybridity also opens up the space for the study of cultural negotiations, conflicts, and struggles against the backdrop of contemporary globalization" and it is "foremost a rejection of essentialist notions, either of gender or of ethnicity and race, as well as an acknowledgement that there is no purity that can be found either at the level of culture, the body, blood, or DNA" (p. 4). She argues that we as Latinas are radical hybrids and in my experience with immigration that calls forth both my family history of migration as a Chicana and my current affective and long-ignored history with Arab and Islamic communities I come to embody this radical hybridity. The possibility of the coming together of my two worlds that are really not that separate, my hope, and my desire for wholeness all still resonate; however, after all of this I am still left with the contradictions and fears that underlie all of these experiences. How can we expect or aspire to even consider ourselves citizens of the world when in fact we are barely recognized as citizens of our own countries? I am ready for a new performance.

NOTES

1. At the time "the determination of eligibility to sponsor an immigrant will be based on an evaluation of your demonstrated ability to maintain an annual income at or above 125 percent of the Federal poverty line."

2. In this chapter, I begin with my narrative, but as this project extends I would like to include Mohamed's narrative more moving toward a dual authorship of this project that really performs the dialogue called for by Conquergood.
3. Throughout this process the name changed several times, INS, Homeland Security, BCIS, USCIS ...
4. See Calafell (2004).
5. I use tactic in the sense of Michel DeCerteau's *Practice of Everyday Life*. I do not mean to engage in a strictly DeCerteauian read of the situation but I want to point to the complexity of the situation. Mohamed's response and performance of these scripts is both oppressive and liberating in that it grants him some agency in an impossible situation. This performance is specifically enabled by this time, space, and official audience.

REFERENCES

Acuña, R. (1998). Occupied America. In R. Delgado & J. Stefancic (Eds.), *The Latino condition: A critical reader* (pp. 171–174). New York: New York University Press.

Alcoff, L. (1991–1992). The problem of speaking for others. *Cultural Critique, 20*, 5–32.

Alexander, B. K. (2006). Performance ethnography: The reenacting and inciting of culture. In N. K. Denzin & Y. S. Lincoln (Eds.), *The Sage handbook of qualitative research*, 3rd ed. (pp. 411–441). Thousand Oaks, CA: Sage.

Almaguer, T. (1998). The master narrative of white supremacy in California. In R. Delgado & J. Stefancic (Eds.), *The Latino condition: A critical reader* (pp. 165–170). New York: New York University Press.

Anzaldúa, G. (1987). *Borderlands/la frontera: The new mestiza*. San Francisco, CA: Aunt Lute.

Aparicio, F. R. (2003). Jennifer as Selena: Rethinking Latinidad in media and popular culture. *Latino Studies, 1*, 90–105.

Bell, E. (1999). Weddings and pornography: The cultural performance of sex. *Text and Performance Quarterly, 19*, 173–195.

Calafell, B. M. (2004). Disrupting the dichotomy: "Yo soy Chicana/o?" in the new Latina/o South. *The Communication Review, 7*, 175–204.

Calafell, B. M. (2005). Pro(re-)claiming loss: A performative pilgrimage in search of Malintzin Tenépal. *Text and Performance Quarterly, 25*, 45–58.

Carrasco, Gilbert Paul. (1998). Latinos in the United States: Invitation and exile. In R. Delgado & J. Stefancic (Eds.), *The Latino condition: A critical reader* (pp. 77–85). New York: New York University Press.

Collins, P. H. (2000). *Black feminist thought: Knowledge, consciousness, and the politics of empowerment*, 2nd ed. New York: Routledge.

Conquergood, D. (1985). Performing as a moral act: Ethical dimensions of the ethnography of performance. *Literature in Performance, 5*, 1–13.

Cordova, N. I. (2004). The constitutive force of the *Catecismo del Pueblo* in Puerto Rico's popular democratic party campaign of 1938–1940. *Quarterly Journal of Speech, 90*, 212–233.

Delgado, F. P. (1995). Chicano movement rhetoric: An ideographic interpretation. *Communication Quarterly, 43*, 446–455.

Enck-Wanzer, D. (2006). Trashing the system: Social movement, intersectional rhetoric, and collective agency in the Young Lords organization's garbage offensive. *Quarterly Journal of Speech, 92*, 174–201.

Fernandez, R. A. & R. J. Jensen. (1995). Reies Lopez Tijerina's "The land grant Question": Creating history through metaphors. *Howard Journal of Communications 6*, 129–145.

Flores, L. A. (1996). Creating discursive space through a rhetoric of difference: Chicana feminists craft a homeland. *Quarterly Journal of Speech, 82*, 142–156.

Flores, L. A. (2003). Constructing rhetorical borders: Peons, illegal aliens, and competing narratives of immigration. *Critical Studies in Media Communication, 20*, 362–387.

Flores, L. A. & M. A. Hasian. (1997). Returning to Aztlan and La Raza: Political communication and the vernacular construction of Chicano/a nationalism. In A. Gonzalez & D. V. Tanno (Eds.), *International and Intercultural Annual Vol. XX: Politics, Communication, and Culture* (pp. 186–203). Thousand Oaks, CA: Sage.

Gómez-Pena, G. (2005). *Ethno-techno: Writings on performance, activism, and pedagogy.* New York: Routledge.

Hammerback, J. C. & R. J. Jensen. (1980). The rhetorical worlds of César Chavez and Reijes Tijerina. *The Western Journal of Speech Communication, 44*, 166–176.

Hammerback, J. C. & R. J. Jensen. (1994). Ethnic heritage as rhetorical legacy: The Plan of Delano. *Quarterly Journal of Speech, 80*, 53–70.

Hammerback, J. C. & R. J. Jensen. (1998). *The rhetorical career of César Chavez.* College Station, TX: Texas A & M University Press.

Hammerback, J. C., R. J. Jensen, & J. A. Gutierrez. (1985). *A war of words: Chicano protest in the 1960s and 1970s.* Westport, CN: Greenwood.

Hasian, M. A. Jr. & F. P. Delgado. (1998). The trials and tribulations of critical race theory: Understanding the rhetorical ambiguities of proposition 187. *Communication Theory, 8*, 245–271.

Hernández-Truyol, B. E. (1998). Natives and newcomers. In R. Delgado & J. Stefancic (Eds.), *The Latino condition: A critical reader* (pp. 125–131). New York: New York University Press.

Holling, M. A. (2006). Forming oppositional social concord to California's proposition 187 and squelching social discord in the vernacular space of CHICLE. *Communication and Critical/ Cultural Studies, 3*, 202–222.

Jensen, R. J. & J. C. Hammerback. (1980). Radical nationalism among Chicanos: The rhetoric of Jose Angel Gutierrez. *The Western Journal of Speech Communication, 44*, 72–91.

Katriel, T. & T. Farrell. (1991). Scrapbooks as cultural texts: An American art of memory. *Text and Performance Quarterly, 11*, 1–17.

Lugo, A. (2000). Theorizing border inspections. *Cultural Dynamics, 12*(3), 353–373.

Madison, D. S. (1998). Performance, personal narratives, and the politics of possibility. In S. J. Dailey (Ed.), *The future of performance studies: Visions and revisions* (pp. 276–286). Annandale, VA: National Communication Association.

Madison, D. S. (2005). *Critical ethnography: Methods, ethics, and performance.* Thousand Oaks, CA: Sage.

Menchaca, D. (2005). Performing identities in (un)familiar territory: A pilgrim's journey home for the feast day of Our Lady of Guadalupe. *Theatre Annual: A Journal of Performance Studies, 58*, 67–121.

Menocal, M. A. (2002). *The ornament of the world: How Muslims, Jews, and Christians created a culture of tolerance in medieval Spain.* Boston, MA: Little, Brown, and Company.

Moreman, S. (1999). Chupa mi cacahuate: The terms of my Latino identity. In N. K. Denzin (Ed.), *Studies in symbolic interaction, a research annual*, Vol. 22 (pp. 65–75). Illinois: University of Illinois Press.

Muñoz, J. E. (2000). Feeling brown: Ethnicity and affect in Richard Bracho's *The sweetest hangover (and other STDS). Theatre Journal, 52*, 67–79.

Murillo, E. G. Jr. (2004). Mojado crossing along neoliberal borderlands. In G. W. Noblit, S. Y. Flores, & E. G. Murillo, Jr. (Eds.), *Postcritical ethnography: An introduction* (pp. 155–179). Cresskill, NJ: Hampton.
Oliver, K. (2001). *Witnessing: Beyond recognition.* Minneapolis, MN: University of Minnesota Press.
Ono, K. A. & J. M. Sloop. (2002). *Shifting borders: Rhetoric, immigration, and California's proposition 187.* Philadelphia, PA: Temple University Press.
Palczewski, C. H. (1996). Bodies, borders, and letters: Gloria Anzaldúa's "Speaking in tongues: A letter to 3rd world women writers." *Southern Communication Journal, 62,* 1–16.
Pelias, R. J. (2005). Performative writing as scholarship: An apology, an argument, an anecdote. *Cultural Studies and Critical Methodologies, 5,* 415–424.
Scott, J. C. (1990). *Domination and the arts of resistance: Hidden transcripts.* New Haven: Yale University Press.
Sedano, M. V. (1980). Chicanismo: A rhetorical analysis of themes and images of selected poetry from the Chicano movement. *The Western Journal of Speech Communication, 44,* 177–190.
Valdivia, A. (2004). Latinas as radical hybrid: Transnationally gendered traces in mainstream media. *Global Media Journal, 2,* 1–21.
Willis, J. L. (1997). "Latino night": Performances of Latina/o culture in northwest Ohio. *Communication Quarterly, 45,* 335–354.

CHAPTER FIVE

Hybrid Performativity, South AND North OF THE Border: *Entre la teoría y la materialidad de hibridación*

SHANE T. MOREMAN

> Ethnography is hybrid textual activity: it traverses genres and disciplines.
>
> —JAMES CLIFFORD "PARTIAL TRUTHS"

In the summer of 2002, I ventured to Mexico City to study ethnography. While I had come to one of the world's largest metropolises to improve my epistemological skills—the processes by which I might know "others"—I also came to Mexico City to discover, uncover, or even recover parts of myself. Since the time my mom disclosed that my absent biological father was/is Mexican, I have struggled to try to understand what, if anything, I could claim of Latina/o-ness and of whiteness. In my early twenties, I also began to inform the world that I am gay. Therefore, both my Latina/o and my gay identities have been braided together in an inseparable way—as discovery, as knowledge, and as material effects in the world. My own identity trajectory has been precarious because I had options (albeit unsavory) to avoid and deny their performance: my gayness versus my possibility for passing as straight, my Latina/oness versus my whiteness. While in Mexico City, I was seeking to find locate myself amidst a cosmopolitan backdrop.

Concurrent to my time in Mexico City, Paulina Rubio, a Mexican pop star, was readying to release her album, *Border Girl*. My memories of Mexico City are inseparable—not unlike my gayness and Latina/oness—from Paulina Rubio's pop culture diffusion. Her songs and her images were both backdrops and centerpieces during my time there—places and moments to remark on my own performative embodiments of ethnic hybridity as theory and materiality. The theory of Performativity has become a way to explain the constitution of the racial body in U.S. discourse, specifically the hybrid body. Judith Butler laid the groundwork for performativity in her explanations of the discursive constructs of gender. Butler (1988) argues that gender is not a radical choice, or a project for and of the individual, or imposed or inscribed by language. At the same time, she states that bodies do not preexist the cultural conventions that signify them. For Butler, gender is "a performative accomplishment compelled by social sanction and taboo. In its very character as performative resides the possibility of contesting its reified status" (p. 520).

Following Butler, scholars have begun to understand that the performativity of race can be outlined in much the same way: performing the racialized body is not a radical, individual choice, nor does language impose or inscribe ethnicity as a "blank slate." Utilizing Merleau-Ponty, Butler argues for a phenomenology of the body, particularly damning to the biological, geographical, or physical essentialisms of race and ethnicity. For Merleau-Ponty, the body's appearance is not predetermined by an interior essence, but the body's expression is the "taking up and rendering specific a set of historical possibilities." Butler weaves phenomenology of the body with Austin's performative utterance to arrive at her conclusion: "the body is a historical situation ... and is a manner of doing, dramatizing, and reproducing a historical situation" (p. 521). And the theater provides Butler's metaphor for how gendered bodies perform/how racialized bodies perform: "Actors are always already on stage, within the terms of the performance. Just as a script may be enacted in various ways, and just as the play requires both text and interpretations within the confines of already existing directives" (p. 526).

Taking Butler's work a step further, Inda (2001) proposes that, like gender, race does not refer to a pregiven body. He asserts,

> Rather, it works performatively to constitute the racial body itself, a body that only procures a naturalized effect through repeated reference to that body. [Racial performativity] is not a singular act of racial body constitution, but a reiterative practice through which discourse brings about the effect that it names. (p. 88)

Over time, the reiterations bring about a naturalized and normalized effect and a racialized body is created in U.S. discourse that actually never materially exists before or beyond the act of naming any one body in a racialized way. Inda reminds us that the racing of a body is a process: "One that must be reiterated by various authorities and in various times and places in order to sustain the naturalized effect of 'race'" (p. 88). Naturalizing the "hybrid" body, however, is complicated. How to account for multiplicity of geographies, nationalities, ethnicities, social economic statuses, and border-crossings? Racial performativity is my theoretical compass as I trek through my own identity to explore the complexity of a hybrid identity that moves south and north over the U.S./Mexico border in both physical and ideological ways.

Gloria Anzaldúa (1990) asserts that hybrid ethnic individuals, which she terms the "new *mestiza*," adjusts to the contradictions of their multiple identities by developing a tolerance for the contradictions. She says,

> She learns to be Indian in Mexican culture, to be Mexican from an Anglo point of view. She learns to juggle cultures. She has a plural personality, she operates in pluralistic mode—nothing is thrust out, the good, the bad and the ugly, nothing rejected, nothing abandoned. (p. 379)

Like Anzaldúa, my definition of hybridity is a both/and existence in which we operate within contrasts trying to hold these differences together. Holding differences together adds one more job to the "to do" list of performativity in my attempt to complicate racial binaries with hybridity.

In the current age, globalized media systems offer opportunities for audiences of all types to interact with symbols and meanings from other cultures while remaining within their own culture. Paulina Rubio stands to profit from this globalized media system as she seeks to enact herself as an interstitial being, a border girl. As James Carey (1989) explains the media become part of the understanding of and the creation of reality. For Carey, "Communication is a symbolic process whereby reality is produced, maintained, repaired and transformed" (p. 23). He further explains, "Reality is brought into existence, is produced, by communication—by, in short, the construction, apprehension and utilization of symbolic forms" (p. 25). Media systems provide particularly potent symbolic forms for us to communicate our realities.

It follows then that Paulina Rubio's entrée into this symbolic system is an act to communicatively redefine reality via a globalized media system. Globalization and hybridization inform each other as processes that are generative. Nestor García Canclini (1995) helps to explain the generative process of hybridity: "I understand for hybridization that sociocultural processes in which discrete structures and practices, that existed in separate form, combine themselves to generate new structure, objects, and practices" (p. 14). According to Canclini, the two spaces where hybridity are most intense are at the metropolis and at the borders. Rather than just thinking of metropolitan areas and borders areas as physical existences, he reminds us that globalized mass media have created metropolitan and border areas in which we exist. Thus, as identities are formed today, they are met with contradictory callings found within globalized media. Canclini says, "The study of [cultural processes] ... rather than conducing to the affirmation of self-sufficient identities, is useful in order to know about the ways of situating ourselves in the middle of heterogeneity and to understand how hybridizations are produced" (p. 18). Again, it is the processes not the staid results that are of interest in understanding hybrid identities.

Both performativity and hybridity can be viewed as theories of everyday cultural practices, as resources for self-determinacy, and as always local, material embodiments. As with all theories, they are difficult if not impossible to operationalize. And also similar to all theories, these theoretical views have their limits: in the hegemony of white U.S. culture, in the limiting and limited repertoire of performative acts available for people outside normative boundaries, and in global, mediated constructions of Latina/o. The limitations of performativity—as always already implicated in the power structures it produces—find Latina/o an increasingly precarious subject position, too easily and often marked materially as poor, illegal, uneducated—especially for women.

Similar to Cepeda's (2003) analysis of the stardom of Shakira, my analysis details how as Paulina Rubio enters U.S. Latina/o discourse she is producing and produced through Latina/o performativity. With her *Border Girl* publicity marketing, although she seeks a hybrid identity status, she is read as Latina and then considerations and values are given to her by her audiences through that reading. Dissimilar to Cepeda's work, I also include myself alongside Paulina Rubio. Rubio and I both struggle for self-definition. For example, within U.S. race discourse, I am often read as white although I always seek to be read as Latina/o and sometimes as hybrid. The ways that Rubio's and my meanings are constructed and utilized by others and ourselves provide a glimpse into how the discourse around hybridity exists and is changing. The everyday performances of Paulina Rubio map and are mapped by limits and excesses of hybrid performativity specifically through my Latin/white body and my borderland contexts. The determinate performances that we make still must be made within a discourse that is unforgiving of self-determinacy—except a self-determination that recenters white as privileged and Latina/o as ancillary to whiteness.

Through performative writing (Pollock, 1995), I write myself at the crossing of various discourses of race and ethnicity, gender, sexuality, nationhood, and class. Performativity and hybridity, too often written in high theory without "teaching" exemplars, are ripe for writing moments that attempt to capture not "reality" but how identities are enacted in real moments and how those identities have material consequences in the real word. Foregrounding my mediated relationship with Paulina Rubio, I bring the quotidian practice of pop star usage out of "the merely obscure background of social activity" (de Certeau, 1994) and into clarity as an act of significance within the mundane acts of everyday life. Paulina Rubio is a hybrid product of mass media and globalized times. For me, she is object lesson and cautionary tale to discuss how my own identity is influenced by the same forces that influence Paulina Rubio's image (re)production in the United States. In the end, for both of us the hybrid identity while theoretically important it is not always performatively possible due to the matrices of race; however, only through attempting these transcendences can change occur.

PAULINA RUBIO: ¿ERES LA PERSONA QUE TE DICES?

A composite of the twenty English-language interviews of articles about Paulina Rubio spanning from June 2001 to April/May 2004 show that she has been in the Spanish-language media for most of her life. Born June 17, 1971, she is the daughter of a famous Mexican actress Susana Dosamantes. Her parents divorced when she was a child, and she lived with her mother who traveled throughout Latin America and Europe as an entertainer. In the 1980s, Paulina Rubio started a career of her own, joining a youth singing act named *Timbiriche*. In the 1990s, she began a successful solo singing career, becoming a hit Mexican solo singer.

Then, in 2002, she began a new leg of her career with her album *Border Girl*, seeking to cross over into both the U.S. and the English-language market. The title of the album declares the intention to inhabit that liminal space of the border. The album is a compilation of songs that help to serve Rubio's hybrid identity goals by being a cross-lingual production with a mixture of different types of songs. Four of the songs have both an English-language and a Spanish-language version. Also, three of the English-language songs were previous Spanish-language hits for Paulina Rubio. Another of the English-language songs is a famous Spanish mariachi ballad. In addition, she covers a KISS hit in English. And the remaining three of the English-language songs are original to the *Border Girl* album.

Within her global marketing and interviews, Paulina Rubio lays claim to purposefully controlling her identity. One headline reads, "No Rules: Paulina Rubio Does Whatever She Wants—With Her Music" (Holsten, 2004, p. 42). Another reads, "Paulina Rubio is cool, collected, and armed with a new album that crosses every border" (Morales, 2004, p. 80). Following upon consistent themes of self-determination ("does whatever she wants") and transcendent identity formation ("new album crosses every border"), I analyze the content of the twenty articles for ways that she enacts a hybrid identity as understood through Anzaldúa (1990). Although she is often touted in the United States as a Latina artist, in practice she claims to try to do much more with her projected image and music. Her image and music become ways for her to express a hybridity of inspired content and projected self-identity.

Paulina Rubio celebrates her music as being a blend of many influences. In her CD booklet, she comments on her musical range of influences and the resulting range of her musical product. Her words are sometimes misspelled and her lines are sometimes grammatically incorrect, consciously so as these liners are heavily edited. Therefore ambiguity adds to the composite-feel of her sentiment:

> Here is my special "Miss Coctail" of dance, chill out, ambience, mex hip, hip hop, drum & bass jungle, *batacuda, ay hay mi mariachi,* why so pop?, it's be-bop glam, in the house, progressive, afrobeat, eurobeat, breakbeat! To my fans!!!!, this is f—in' great album is for you all! (Rubio, CD liner notes, 2002)

The misspellings, the misnomers, the awkward translations from Spanish to English—they all contradict her visually flawless press photos and the self-proclaimed perfectionism of her interviews. Thus, the lines stand out with intensity as being intentionally skewed toward a meaning of multiplicity. Again, it is her celebration of the many that is important here. She draws from a wide variety of sources to create a hybrid sound and feel.

In interviews she is more centered in her comments, but they still follow the same philosophy of polyglot. She refers to various ingredients in the recipes for her songs: rancheras, mariachis, dance, hip-hop, rock, and pop. She labels her new style: "It's called folklore futurista,' Rubio explains, 'and it's the power of culture with instruments: Brazil, trumpets, Mexico, flamenco guitars, Spain, accordion, Colombia'" (Martinez, 2004, p. 27). In another interview she is quoted on her musical style, "futuristic folk" (Holsten, 2004, p. 42). The singer also expresses her source of inspiration as being based upon many different cultural experiences. "'It's important that you don't forget your roots,' she says, 'but you can also draw from other cultures'" (Morales, 2004, p. 80).

Her source of self-identity, indeed, becomes just as variegated as her musical influences. Through her many firsthand experiences traveling and living abroad, Paulina Rubio has discovered the various cultural offerings from around the globe and integrated many of them into her construction and performance of self. Raised in Mexico City, Los Angeles, and Madrid and therefore privy to many cultures from her youth to her adulthood, Rubio notes, "I was born in Mexico and raised in Spain,' explaining her mix of styles in perfect English. 'It's not something prefabricated'" (Cobo, 2004, p. 58). Although raised in Spain, she travels extensively. "[S]he spent her early years traveling around with her mother to sets in Mexico, the United States, and Europe" (Morales, 2004, p. 82). In her travels, she learns other languages. "Paulina spent a great deal of time in Europe, learning Italian and French and becoming attuned to the cultural mores of European societies" (Holsten, 2004, p. 43). She assumes an identity that is nested in Europe, Latin America, and the United States. "'I've always been here and there, so you could say that I grew up comfortably in three different cultures" (Rubio as cited in Velazquez, 2004, p. 30). Her heterogeneous geographical upbringings and visits work their way into the identity of her music:

> During a Madrid promotional visit, Rubio said of the album title [*Border Girl*]: 'I want to reflect what I am—a girl who has lived in Mexico, Spain, Italy, New York, and now Los Angeles and whose music carries a fusion of all those styles. My adolescence was a contrast of cultures. (Llewellyn, 2002, p. 44)

Hence she becomes the bordergirl and creates an album that utilizes the polyvocality of her bordergirl identity.

Drawing on scholarship that warns against the tendency to over-romanticize hybridity as a "playful space (Valdivia, 2004), I apply this warning to the bordering of identities as well. We must extend the understanding of hybridity" from the notion of ethnic cross-dressing to the deployment of hybridity for commodification purposes. Certainly ethnic ambiguity, such as the one performed by Paulina, is potentially very profitable, as it appeals to different segments of the global and local audience. Paulina's border-crossings obscure border existences for those seeking entree into the United States from Mexico. For people on the Mexican side, the border is more than just a playful metaphor of reality where one tries on different ethnicities. For the vast majority of them the border represents exhaustingly lengthy lines, humiliatingly incessant harassment, and emotionally draining debates. Cynthia Wright (1998), for example, documents the complexity of the Mexican women working along the U.S./Mexico border as they try to avoid exploitation from many facets (gender, nationality, corporations, etc.). Pablo Vila (2003) points out the less-than-ideal conditions of border existences, and how these are elided by the work of such scholars as Guillermo Gomez-Peña and Gloria Anzaldúa—and I add Paulina Rubio. The lesson offered is a stern one: do not over-idealize such an identity. Vila adds, "For scholars doing border studies from the Mexican side of the line, it is difficult to see the border as mere metaphor, as the epitomized possibility of crossings, hybrids, and the like" (p. 314). For Paulina and her marketers, the border is represented and performed as just that, a hybridity and a possibility for crossing. However, like the work of Fusco (1995) and Cepeda (2003) demonstrates, those crossings are more permissible for cultural commodities than they are for cultural bodies.

IN THE BAR

At the inception of the *Border Girl* release, in a Mexico City gay disco in *La Zona Rosa*, my friend Alexandra and I are having drinks and sharing personal stories.

Men (and a few women) move onto and off of the dance floor. One particular song packs the floor, Paulina Rubio's "*Si Tu Te Vas.*"

Unlike most U.S. discos, Mexico City club goers know routines for particular songs and, particularly, for this Paulina Rubio song. The dance form is hard to describe. With the right arm, dancers make the letter S from their crotch to their chest, and then they do it again from behind their heads and into the air above them. On a big screen TV, Paulina Rubio's video seduces the club dancers in their movements. On the margins of the clubbers, I watch men mimic their diva, Paulina Rubio, moving as she moves and mouthing her words.

On the dance floor, it is hard to find a pattern of identity. There is a range of ages, masculinities, genders, and styles. As with any public spot, heterogeneity is common. However, in this gay bar, arguably most people are there to celebrate their aberrant sexuality or to at least thumb their noses at societal pressures of the heterocompulsive. As the group of (mostly) men dances, it is unclear whether the bar patrons are enjoying Paulina Rubio for her leanings toward hybridity. In this space my gayness, along with the other patrons, is not a hindrance to be hidden but a quality to be highlighted.

Rubio's utilization of hybridity speaks to the current marketability of a multiplicity of identity—especially in such a space as the gay bar. Indeed, the gay bar may be the perfect place for watching this currency enacted. Both Frederick Corey (1996) and E. Patrick Johnson (2000) speak to the gay club as a space where contradictory identities find a home together. For them, the gay club is a space where multiplicity of identity is played out against other patrons and even against the multiple identities within one's body. In speaking of an Irish gay pub, The George, at the beginning of de-illegalization of homosexual identity in Ireland, Corey points to the varying and conflicting identities of the gay patrons who perform and subscribe to opposing identities. These identities may or may not be performed outside of the club. Corey comments on the range of gay and lesbian identities based upon the patrons' self-comfort within their own personal history but also the patrons' self-comfort developed out of their place in societal history.

Similarly, of the black gay bar, Johnson shows how the seemingly contradictory secular and the spiritual merge. He writes,

> Drawing upon a longstanding tradition of blurring the sacred and the secular in African American culture, African American gay men embed their own secular traditions—house/club music, vogueing, dragging, snapping—within black sacred traditions to provide a more liberating way to express all of who they are. (p. 108)

Like those gay spaces, this particular gay bar is a site for the sexual hybridity—but there are still real limitations to that hybridity. Alexandra and I decided to descend to the basement of the bar. In the small basement, there is less room for socializing and only room for dancing. The music is much louder and personal space is minimized. To get to the basement, you can enter a separate door on the street, or you can descend down a spiral staircase at the back of the bar. I warn Alexandra, "Only men are allowed in the basement, so … So you have to act like you're a man." She has had a couple of beers. Her glassy eyes squint at me, and she agrees with an audacious smile.

We walk to the back of the bar and into the men's restroom. At the back of a hallway-like bathroom stands a bouncer. Past two stalls and a long urinal trough, he officiously postures himself in front of the descending metal stairs that lead down to the men-only basement. Alexandra and I saunter through the restroom, careful not to step in puddles of unknown liquids. Two drunk men sway at the urinal. One man has one hand on his hip and holds his penis with the other. The second man steadies himself with both palms on the wall. A mirror stretches the length of the communal urinal trough, allowing them to watch Alexandra and me pass by.

Undaunted, Alexandra follows me past the bouncer and then starts down the spiral staircase. Three steps down, the bouncer says to Alexandra, "No! No puedes pasarte." I hop up the steps to intercede. I plead, "Por favor. Ella es una hermafrodita." I am not sure that this is the correct word. I am hoping this term, like gay, lesbian, and homosexual, is a cognate that is shared by both Spanish and English. I am hoping, too, that Alexandra's body is a cognate that could be understood as either gender or both genders at the same time. Alexandra stands silent and motionless, not offering anything up that might tilt the bouncer toward disbelief. The bouncer glances up and down her body. He tells me that I can go down, but she cannot. Finally, without much pleading, I concede to the bouncer. As we walk back through the piss-scented men's room slump-shouldered and a bit embarrassed, I am more conscious of Alexandra's gender and her limitations for passing as a man or even a hybrid hermaphrodite. Valdivia (2004) asserts, "Against, or in relation to, overly celebratory approaches to the *jouissance* of the hybrid, we have to consider the tensions and pains of hybridity—the fact that it is not all fun and profits" (p. 5). It is also important to remember that part of the pain of hybridity is that its acceptance and/or recognition cannot always be conjured upon command.

MOVING AS SHE MOVES AND MOUTHING HER WORDS: HYBRID PERFORMATIVITY

My South Texas upbringing brought a musical mixture of Spanish and English. This lingual distinction of Spanish and English is often blurred in South Texas public and private contexts. For example, for New Year's Eve I went with my white grandparents to the Veterans of Foreign Wars Hall to drink vodka and bring in the New Year. A chrome and glass jukebox against wood-paneled walls is the bar's main attraction. The New Year's crowd is transitory with elderly couples and groups coming and going, but never dropping the bar's attendance below twenty people. As the different groups form and disperse, the juke box is approached by many patrons. The music, not always current, ranges in singers and songs: Willie Nelson, Pedro Infante, Freddy Fender, Patsy Cline, Juan Gabriel. The disco, pop, teeny-bopper music of Paulina Rubio would never be found here amongst these aged military men and women.

After the halfway mark is reached on the vodka bottle, my white grandfather, an old World War II navy sailor with a tattooed-right bicep leans over and asks me, "In Fresno, do they mix the music like this?"

I nod as I answer, "Yes ... well, it depends on where you go, I guess."

He sits up straight again and pours himself some more Skohl vodka while nodding his head. He begins a story about how the VFW (Veterans of Foreign War) is experiencing a divide amongst its members like he has never seen before. "The Mexicans sit at that end of the bar. The whites sit at the other end of the bar." He shakes his hand and stirs his vodka-7 with his right ring finger. "I hate to see that."

I glance around, looking for exceptions to the segregation, but I see few. After Willie Nelson sings "... blue eyes cryin' in the rain ...," a Mexican patron gets up to drop her quarters into the jukebox. Then Pedro Infante croons "... por un amor, he llorado de gotitas de sangre del corazon ..." Within the same bar and within the same jukebox, both songs are played for patrons to express their allegiance to one side of the ethnic divide.

The VFW is a context that demonstrates how the practice of ethnicity can be an act that separates groups. There are times and places when people prefer to maintain rather than transcend their ethnic differences. As Earl Shorris (1992) explains, most bilingual artists do not mix the languages. As culture is so closely tied to language, when the languages are not mixed, the cultures are not mixed either. Shorris says, "Not even in Vikki Car or Joan Baez or Linda Ronstadt—all of whom are Latinas or have a Latina/o parent—do the musical cultures marry. They sing in Spanish or English, they are Mexican or American, never Mexican-American" (p. 58). Shorris uses broad strokes to paint culture, blending language with cultural identity, but this melding is a common belief among many. As the varying bilingual abilities of U.S. Latina/os show, language does not necessarily equate to a cultural identity. Bilingual artists, be they U.S. born or international, usually do not mix the two languages, and in places like the VFW, these lingual delineations help the patrons keep their lines of ethnic differences well-marked.

On the U.S./Mexico border, my South Texas world was (and when I go home still is) a mixture of Spanish and English. This Spanglish linguistic environment is the one in which I am most comfortable. Moving in a Spanglish lingual mode puts me in a mood of clever poetics. Anzaldúa (1990) comments on a similar experience in her own life, "The way I grew up with my family was code-switching. ... So the body and the feeling parts of me come out in Spanish and the intellectual, reasoning side comes out in English" (p. 266). Similarly, for me, Spanish is a language of comfort and familiarity, while English is about correctness and formality.

Differently from Anzaldúa though, it is the performative moment of code-switching that is most exhilarating for me, not the moment of arrival to a different language, but the transitioning between the languages that gives me thrill. In those lingual moments, I am enacting a hybrid performativity, not calling reference to one racial body but trying to reference both and neither at the same time. When I move between languages, I confuse the "who" of who I am and rest in a hybrid state. Or better said, my language becomes my performative moment that contains possibilities for self and its construction in the historical moment.

With my white grandparents, I speak the only language they know, English. The president of the VFW, a Latino man in his late fifties, walks by and my grandfather stops him to announce my arrival back home. He says, "Frank, this is my grandson, Shane. He's a professor in California ... a professor!" Frank kindly and blandly shakes my hand.

My grandfather continues, "The VFW helped Shane get his start. He won the VFW's 'Voice of Democracy' scholarship contest and gave a speech about the United States Constitution right out front of here. He was just a freshman in High School and he gave that speech right under the flag pole out there." Both of my grandparents are chest-swollen with pride. I sit up straight, attempting to mirror their pride.

Frank raises his eyebrows, makes a face like he learned something new, and pats me on the back. He says, "Good job, son. Nice to see you tonight. Happy New Year." Then he moves onto another table.

Within earshot of Frank, my grandfather gruffs, "See, I don't care if you're Mexican or white. You need to treat people better. This guy is just rude."

My grandmother, with her years of experience at calming down this sailor, tries to smooth things over: "Oh, Jim. Now come on, it's New Years. Don't be that way."

I can feel the unintended but still evident racial tension in my grandfather's comment. Although my grandfather claims that Frank's identity is irrelevant to my grandfather's criticism, he still calls Frank's racial identity to the forefront. The public context makes this announcement precarious. My own Latina/o identity feels held accountable for Frank's behavior, even if my grandfather says that race is not a factor. In this context of racial tension, race is always a factor.

Both Paulina Rubio and I perform Latina/o—as gendered bodies, with scripts that require interpretations, within cultural restricted corporeal spaces, and enacting Latina/o within "already existing directives" (Butler, 1988). Hybridity enters this picture in an examination of the mundane performances of Latina/o that can be part of a "critical genealogy" of hybridity. A critical genealogy requires an expanded notion of "acts" of Latina/o constitution—as socially shared, historic, and performative. While the performative holds out possibilities of transformation, hybridity may foreclose those same possibilities.

Hybrid performativity is a way to disrupt the reality of dichotomous racial relations and a way to envision how to overcome the limits of the discourse on race. The act of self-subscribing to hybridity might not be a revolution, but it is the seed, the beginning to a new envisioning of the self both in doing and in thinking. In the VFW hall, along the borderlands in general, and within U.S. discourse, Latina/o is often defined against whiteness. Noticeably, Paulina Rubio is an absent option on the VFW juke box. She sings a style of music not honored here. Her hybridity is not necessarily geared toward this older, rural audience.

As Paulina Rubio enters U.S. discourse, she is trying to market herself as someone who transcends those dichotomies. Through marketing, she creates a fiction of herself to counter an existing fiction of race. As Inda (2001) explains,

> If "race" is a social fiction, then the meaning of race, and hence the constitution of racial bodies, is fundamentally unstable and open to all sorts of resignifications. Simply put, no project of racial domination can be predestined to hold racialized bodies in positions of subordination. (p. 75)

In marketing herself and in producing a multilingual album that draws from many sources, Paulina Rubio tries to transcend simple racial categories. However, when I look for her in my reality—on the radio, in magazines, on TV—I still find her locked into Latina/o performativity, into the existing directives that are historically, socially, and culturally operant.

GLOBALIZED MEDIA AS AN OPPORTUNITY FOR HYBRIDITY

Paulina Rubio's marketing efforts have placed her around the globe, and people are using her music in the everyday cultural production of their own lives. In my own life, Paulina Rubio follows me. In the San Antonio International Airport, I am leaving southern state after spending New Years with my grandparents. I am waiting in a terminal to board a plane for Fresno. Walking the horseshoe of gates in the terminal, I wander around, reading the different signs and symbols available.

Since this is San Antonio, Texas, the color palette of any place that tries to market itself as authentically Tex-Mex is an array of pastels: pinks, blues, greens, and yellows. On the walls are mural-like paintings of chubby Mexican-looking people dancing. In the center of the horseshoe is a "last chance" Tex-Mex airport restaurant, offering itself as the final opportunity to partake of South Texas. Remember the Alamo? Where whites may be outnumbered in this city, but they will not be defeated? The nested airport restaurant, at a real borderland of material privilege, promises an authenticity.

While I wait for my boarding call, I scan the crowd waiting with me. A range of young military types, dressed in their Air Force Blues, lounge about the terminal. There are two men, one white and one black, in dressy casual clothing talking on cell phones. A fifty-ish heterosexual couple glowers at one another. I glance over to the Mexican restaurant. There are certain places where you can always find gay men working—banks as tellers, retail department stores as sales clerks, and restaurants as waiters. The waiter at this particular restaurant has spiked up hair with dyed bangs. He is about 5′ 5″. He is Latino. The music that he is working to, piped through the tiny, tinny speakers, is Paulina Rubio. I can hear her singing—maybe with a bit too much vigor for this early in the morning—"La luna te dira que yo te quiero ver, El sol te seguira alla a donde tu estes." I smile because I recognize the CD, Paulina Rubio's *Border Girl*. I smile because I have found another gay man ... and another Latino. At this moment, I am relying on racial codes that society uses to designate the "Latina/o." As Alan Hyde (1997) posits, "Race is a claim that necessarily involves the construction of a specularized body by the privileged eye" (p. 223). As I watch him sweep, I am saddened a bit. As a 30-something light-skinned professor, I am seldom assumed to be Mexican. Although there are many that veer in other directions, he represents a group with a racial coding that also helps to structure his life path.

This moment of finding the gay Latino within the artificial staging of Mexicanness is a moment in which the ethnic individual is used to authenticate an artificial Mexican staging. The context is enhanced not only by the gay Latino but also Paulina Rubio. For the staging, it is her Spanish voice, and if anyone recognizes her, her Mexican heritage that serves to decorate the scene, creating a backdrop for airport passengers to enjoy Mexican culture one last time. Rona Halualani (2000) says we deeply comprehend ethnic identity by

> [R]e-engaging ethnic and cultural identity as the complicated interrelationship between structural forms of identity (e.g., governmental categories, official histories, legal constructions) and cultural forms of identity (e.g., the enacted expressions and speaking practices within a group, the everyday living, verbal performances, and social interactions of a group). (p. 587)

At this space in the restaurant, I see the merging of a structural form of capitalist commodification of ethnicity with the cultural identity form of a Latino man working to get paid. The two are intertwined and interdependent upon one another. And like the Latino waiter, Paulina Rubio's music is intertwined with the commodification of ethnicity. She becomes both text and context at this moment. She is part of the structure as well as the cultural form. The waiter catches me eyeing him. The flight attendant calls me to board the plane, and as I leave, Paulina's song plays as the waiter sweeps and mouths her words.

For us to understand the mediated hybrid presence of Paulina Rubio, we should see it in its material terms. Shome and Hegde (2002) argue, "Globalization as a phenomenon produces a state of culture in transnational motion—flows of people, trade, communication, ideas, technologies, finance, social movements, cross border movements, and more" (p. 174). Materially then, Rubio, her ideas, and her products move through and around national structures on this planet. Globalization happens within and through permeable and unstable national boundaries—relying on local needs and interests. Shome and Hegde explain that the fault lines of economic and cultural power shift with such speed and scale that "these lines are ... producing new forms of articulations and disarticulations, new configurations of power, and new planes of dis/empowerment that cannot be equated with any other period" (p. 174). Indeed, the local interpretations of Paulina Rubio provide opportunities for newly constructed meanings and newly provided subversions to established systems of domination. One local interpretation could easily feature the visual—how Paulina Rubio is portrayed to be seen: with the attendant cleavage, curves, costuming, and direct gaze of high fashion *and* the come-hither look of Playboy centerfold—with more clothes. This easy Mulvey-read of "to be looked-at-ness" is laminated with money: nothing about Paulina Rubio is "cheap"—the carefully coifed hair, the beautiful clothes, the diva makeup. Class—in the "old sense" of the word—is written all over her as produced by intense labor and many professional hands.

The symbolic systems that are provided through globalization and that produce Paulina Rubio are not necessarily from groups whose identity politics are liberated: the music industry has a clear investment in affirming feminine beauty and offering Paulina Rubio as a new pentacle of perfection. As a reiteration of feminine performativity, Paula Rubio images reaffirm gender norms. As a reiteration of Latina identity, however, the "read" is not so simple. For example, Valdivia (2004) warns that the Latina image stands to both deconstruct as well as reconstruct racist imagery.

Latina actresses can play a broad range of characters, including black, white, and everything in between, through providing casting directors with an easy way to foreground the few famous Latinas out there who by virtue of ambiguity slip into these roles. This presents both an employment opportunity as well as the possibility for seeing more people of color on the screen and in print. However, the second effect is that hybrid Latinas and ethnic ambiguity also provide mainstream culture with a chance to displace and replace blackness. Blackness, once more, gets pushed to the [left] margin (Valdivia, 2004, p. 15).

As Carey reminds us, the symbols themselves are not necessarily what creates our reality, but our interpretation of those symbols. Valdivia stands firm to point out that images, in this case Paulina Rubio's image, still are invested within a system that privileges her light skin color over the skin color of someone darker. Thus, within these dominant media systems, there are dominant translations of the symbols within that stand to serve some communities over others.

Stuart Hall provides a way to understand how local interpretations of globalized symbol systems might provide a way out of the current discourse of ethnicity and its dominating symbols. Hall (1997) gets us to understand if we buy into the notion of signification, then we can also buy into the notion of resignifying a signifier. Indeed, Hall feels that this resignification process is probably the best way to think through and out of oppressive meanings and their power constructs. He says, "For if signification depends upon the endless repositioning of its differential terms, meaning in any specific instance depends on the contingent and arbitrary stop, the necessary break" (p. 51). And at that break, if we can resignify or signify differently, then previously oppressive patterns might be subverted or even transformed.

Homi Bhabha (1994a) similarly believes in the liberating possibilities of resignification. Upsetting the simple binaries of good/bad, right/wrong, and us/them (and their corresponding identity terms) is a way to get around repressive structures. Bhabha sees the process of hybridity as offering that chance of resignification. For Bhabha, we are in a postcolonial time when the effects of colonialism are still be felt and recreated. All around us is the colonial discourse that has assigned meaning to our lives and kept up within certain understandings of the world. He argues that colonial discourse emphasizes fixed forms of self and therefore fixed forms of "other." He argues, "Fixity, as the sign of cultural/historical/racial difference in the discourse of colonialism, is a paradoxical mode of representation: it connotes rigidity and an unchanging order as well as disorder, degeneracy, and demonic repetition" (1994a, p. 66). Thus out of colonialism has come a range of standards in relation to ethnic and racial identity that has set up patterns of such things as justice, truth and, merit. However, Bhabha (1994b) celebrates hybridity as the area where change can happen. "[I]t is at the level of the interstices that the intersubjective and collective experiences of nationness, community interest, and cultural value are negotiated" (p. 269). Therefore, the in-between of the interstitial are key moments in identity formation and articulation for not only the development of new identity, but also the explication of how that identity came about.

Riding a globalized media wave, Paulina Rubio is a hybridized identity being that is resisting fixity in a postcolonial culture. Her album wants to reach more than the audiences who have previously known her and seeks to span into the realms of non-Spanish speaking, non-Latina/o identified audiences. To do so, her "handlers" are clearly articulating standards of beauty that affirm and "naturalize" femininity—as young, as curvaceous, as sexy. To market Paulina Rubio, as "border girl," hybridized and globalized, radical and reaffirming, resistant and revolutionary, requires that gender be articulated in very traditional ways. In short, global hybridization trumps gender performativity. She may be "border," rearticulated as wealthy, multilingual, and talented, but she is still very much a *girl*.

Indeed, the waiter in the airport restaurant might be situated in much the same way: a commodity mobilized to articulate an authenticity; a young man working for a paycheck. Paulina Rubio's "over the top beauty," her song lyrics, her diva status are appropriated by him and by me to say something different about sexuality, desire, the "to be looked-at-ness" of gay cruising. Or are we back in the same old articulations? Remember the Alamo? I seek to be a hybridized individual who can be more than white and more than Latina/o. I am seeking out spaces and media that allow and encourage such a hybridized identity. During this time of globalized media and possibilities of hybridity, both Paulina and I must have audiences and communities ready to recognize and accept.

A HYBRID IDENTITY FORECLOSED

Paulina Rubio postures herself as someone of hybrid identity, an identity that recognizes many ethnic and national sides, claims all of those sides, and is free to move from one side to another. Her hybridity resists, in U.S. dominant discourse on race and ethnicity, the labeling of Latina/o. She does not shun a Latina identity; however, she adopts a more cosmopolitan and globalized persona. Yet her attempts to position herself as more than Latina fail. The reasons for this failure lie in a complex set of intersectional structures that include the popular utilization of Latina/o media by U.S. Latina/os; the construction of a Latina/o category by market and government forces; the prevalence of identity categories that function as if independently from each other; and the marginalization and devaluation of racialized minorities. Thus Paulina does not have complete agency in determining how she is positioned within U.S. popular culture. Her efforts to represent and perform a cosmopolitan hybridity are thwarted by a number of forces attesting, in part, to the lack of permeability of the nation-state even as capital seeks borderless transnational movement.

Latina/os do not have a common biological descent; nor do they all claim a common national descent. This lack of common claim throws a generalized Latina/o identity into a state of ineffable identity status. While some (Fox, 1996) suggest that the media replace geography and history thus facilitating new identities, Paulina's case study embodies the endurance of location and specificity. Paulina Rubio grew up in the spotlight of transnational Latin American/Mexican media.

A U.S. comparison to her might be Janet Jackson or Drew Barrymore. As she crosses to the United States, she is not a new star because she has been a media star for years. However, crossover narratives that deploy the myth of discovery represent her as a new star (Cepeda, 2000). Thus, as she tries to create herself anew, some of her audience still remembers who she was before *Border Girl* much as Shakira's Colombian audience remembers her before her crossover (Cepeda, 2003).

In addition, even though she is entering the United States, the border she crosses shifts and moves. Geographic locales are not necessarily defined by the national structures that claim them. Just because a person lives in the United States, does not necessarily mean that the person's citizenship or national identity rests with the country's larger identity. Latina/os, like Rubio, possess complicated transnational identities that cloud the issues of us-versus-them that the nation-state identity claims need for self-sustaining authenticity claims. Valdivia (1999) reminds us, like Rosaldo and Anzaldúa, that "Latina/os who live in the United States could have been here for centuries … Other Latina/os may come from Puerto Rico which is, but also is not, part of the United States. … Then you have the whole Central American and South American migratory patterns. … How can you maintain an us-versus-them terminology? How do the media, popular culture, music, and dance fit into this schema? (p. 483) Therefore, Paulina Rubio, while in the United States proper, is associated with a group, "brought into the domain of language and kinship through the interpellation of" ethnicity (Butler, 1993, p. 7), that is not only well-acquainted with her, but their movement is just as varied as hers—and now they are in the United States as Latina/os.

Paulina Rubio is trying to be a star during a time when the Latina/o identity is still forming and reforming. Within U.S. discourse, Latina/o is one ethnic label separate from other ethnic labels—and an ethnic identity still being formed and explained. Fernando Delgado (1988) finds possibility in the ambiguity of the Latina/o identity, marking this lack of definition as valuable rather than crisis-causing: "I reject the need to categorize, control or construct what Latina/o identity terms might be. Instead, I demonstrate that Latina/os can be many different things when, as subjects, they put identity terms into their everyday communication practices" (p. 424). Delgado, attempting to contextualize ethnic identity, acknowledges and honors the multioptional discourse labels of Latina/o identity. At the same time, he asserts that Latina/os do not become lost identities in a vernacular jungle, but they still find ways to identify with one another and with cultural icons at large. With a globalized Latina/o identity, and decaying nation-state boundaries, Paulina Rubio becomes one of those Latina/o icons that attracts and maintains the Latina/o audience.

Both Paulina Rubio and I are asking for the United States to see itself spilling out of the boundaries of its current self-understandings. As Roman De la Campa (2001) adds, "It becomes crucial to remember that the invention of

America [the United States] has always been an arbitrary exercise in location, a site not far from the lines of utopia and nostalgia" (p. 1). We both ask the United States to revamp the utopia and nostalgia to include more than the melting pot and the Spirit of '76 but also *la raza cósmica* and *Cinco de Mayo* and possibilities yet unforeseen.

Race, ethnicity, gender, sexual preference—these are all socially performed and materially constructed meanings that exist in human discourse. Moreover, and most importantly for this chapter, they are performed. They are arbitrary and contestable and their significance is dependent upon the context. At the same time, Butler (1993) argues, we are "compelled" to live in a world where these theoretical claims are adamantly contradicted in the "real world," where commonsense holds that gender, ethnicity, race, and sexual preference are stable, polar, discrete, and intractable. The success of theorizing globalized media systems and calls for hybridity remains to be seen—especially in my life.

POSTSCRIPT

In the winter 2003, I leave a closing gay bar with my friend Carlos. The crowd is mostly Latina/o with a smattering of white, black, or Asian clientele. All night I have been speaking English, Spanish, and Spanglish. All night I have been listening and dancing to Spanish music, English music, and music mixing both Spanish and English. Riding shotgun in Carlos' gold '97 Thunderbird, I play DJ on the car stereo. Flipping through the stations, I find "*Sexi* Dance" by Paulina Rubio. The English version goes, "Don't stop me now. Surrender to the beat. Just you and me. Just like it used to be. Set your heart free, when we're together." The Spanish version goes, "No pares no …"

As Carlos pulls away from the bar, we begin singing her song. Both of us are mocking her "S" dance. As the song is concluding, I turn down the music to ask Carlos a question. Suddenly we realize that we are singing different versions of the song. He is singing the Spanish version; I am singing the English version. Both of us laughing, I ask, "Is she singing in Spanish or English?" In my drunken stupor, I try to turn the song up again but accidentally change the station. I cannot locate and recapture the station with her song on it. I insist, "Carlos she was singing in English." He responds, "No *mijo*, YOU were singing in English, she and I were singing in Spanish. Your *bolillo* side got the best of you." (*Bolillo* is Mexican slang for "white person.")

Just then a beer bottle explodes against the side panel of the Thunderbird, flung from a car in a parallel lane. Carlos' license plate frame reads "Who's your Papi now?" and above that frame is a [gay] rainbow flag sticker. He decided to decorate his car this way four years ago when he could no longer hide his gay identity. I have always chastised him for using his car to advertise his gayness. At this moment, I wonder if that's why we got pegged.

Someone from the other car screams "*jotos*" (Mexican slang for "faggot") and speeds away. I quickly survey our surroundings. Most of the gay bars in Fresno are located on the Mexican side of town. We've just left the gay bar, an area that lacks street lights. Visibly angry, Carlos floors the gas petal and races to follow the car.

"Carlos," I plead, "What are you going to do if you catch them? Come on. Let them go." He refuses with a shake of his head and continues to run lights and round curves.

I think to myself, "If we stop, and he gets out, I'm taking the chance of being a white gay guy on the Mexican side of town. This could be bad." Then I begin to rehearse my plan, "Well, I'll just talk Spanish and butch myself up and play up my Mexican side. I won't let my gay *bolillo* side get the best of me."

Finally, we stop at a red light. They keep going. Carlos is breathing hard. We watch as their tail lights grow smaller in the distance. He turns to me and says, "If *you* hadn't been with me, *I* would have fought them."

"Well," I maintained, "If the cops would have come, *I* would have done all the talking." We both laugh at the differences we are demarcating. Our laughter also marks our successful escape from potential violence and rage: the ever present material danger of our sexualities in white and Latina/o, heteronormative U.S. discourse.

Paulina Rubio's music enters the United States at a volatile time for Latina/o identity. Young Latina/os find her as a mediated pop star that they can perform in various venues. We can sing like her in our cars, we can dance like her in our clubs, we can dress like her in daily life. The moment that her performance becomes part of the performative of Latina/os is the moment when she is no longer the cosmopolitan, self-determining, polyglot.

Here in the United States, Paulina Rubio becomes part of the performativity that hides its own genesis, reinstates racial and ethnic essentialisms, and punishes individuals for performing race, gender, or sexuality incorrectly. The material realities of a celebration of Latina/o identity are dangerously at odds with white culture. As she crosses the border hoping to be the next Latina superstar, she has the freedom to cross back and forth playing a game of semantics that benefits her most. However she does not exercise total control in terms of how she is marketed and consumed. She is symbolically contained, domesticated, and categorized. Similarly, the material and physical containment of the Latina/o population … wherever you draw the line … gets stuck in long lines waiting to cross to the United States or on the side of town that is less desirable. Maybe one day the Latina/o image will become as Paulina Rubio wants to be portrayed—polyvocal, self-determining—but until then both sides of the border are not quite ideal, either for Paulina or other border crossers.

For Paulina Rubio and myself, both south and north of the border, a hybrid identity really rests at a global and theoretical level. The identity is cast from a mixture of identities and a vision for how those identities can be played against each other, as a denial of each other, or even in combination with one another. However, the local, not the global, is where the hybrid identity loses its efficacy and is not as easily enacted. My car, my speech, my friends, my grandparents—these are contexts and enactments of my identities that are privileged by dominant ideology and are performed on a thin line between danger and pleasure, between agency and structure. Depending on our closeness to whiteness, both Paulina and I can pass for mainstream subjects sometimes. However this depends on location and situation. We both also face symbolic and physical border inspections (Lugo, 2000) that negate or, at least challenge, celebratory approaches to hybridity For Paulina Rubio and myself, the enactment of multiple identities may not always be a choice but is still something to be questioned, explored, and pursued in a more just future utopia.

ACKNOWLEDGMENT

This chapter was derived from the author's dissertation: "Performativity and Latino-White Hybrid Ethnic Identity: Performing the Textual Self," University of South Florida, 2005 (Director, Elizabeth E. Bell). A version of this chapter was presented at the 2004 WSCA conference in Albuquerque, New Mexico. Also, this chapter of the dissertation was presented at the 2004 Doctoral Honors Seminar, Mediated Communication division. For their insight and encouragement, the author would like to thank his writing group at California State University, Fresno: Diane Blair, Kevin Ayotte and Sally Tannenbaum.

REFERENCES

Anzaldúa, G. (Ed.). (1990). *Making face, making soul, Haciendo Caras: Creative and critical perspectives by women of color*. San Francisco: Aunt Lute Books.
Bhabha, H. K. (1994a). Frontlines/borderposts. In A. Bammer (Ed.), *Displacements: Cultural identities in question*, Vol. 15 (pp. 269–272). Bloomington: Indiana University Press.
Bhabha, H. K. (1994b). *The location of culture*. New York: Routledge.
Butler, J. (1988). Performative acts and gender constitution: An essay in phenomenology and feminist theory. *Theatre Journal, 40*(4), 519–531.
Butler, J. (1993). *Bodies that matter: On the discursive limits of "sex."* New York: Routledge.
Carey, J. (1989). *Communication as culture: Essays in media and society*. Boston: Unwin Hyman.
Cepeda, M. E. (2000). Mucho loco for Ricky Martin; or the politics of chronology, crossover, and language within the Latin(o) music "boom." *Popular Music and Society, 24*(1), 3.
Cepeda, M. E. (2003). Shakira as the idealized, transnational citizen: A case study of *Colombianidad* in transition. *Latino Studies Journal, 1*, 211–232.

Cobo, L. (2004, June 22). Paulina Rubio: Border girl. *Billboard, 114*, 18.
Corey, F. C. (1996). Performing sexualities in an Irish pub. *Text and Performance Quarterly, 16*(2), 161–171.
Delgado, F. P. (1998). When the silenced speak: The textualization and complications of Latina/o identity. *Western Journal of Communication, 62*(4), 420–438.
de Certeau, M. (1994). The practice of everyday life. In J. Storey (Ed.), *Cultural theory and popular culture: A reader* (pp. 474–485). New York: Harvester Wheatsheaf.
de la Campa, R. (2001). Latin, Latino, American: Split states and global imaginaries. *Comparative Literature, 53*(4), 373–388.
Fox, G. (1996). *Hispanic nation: Culture, politics, and the constructing of identity*. Tucson: University of Arizona Press.
Fusco, C. (1995). *English is broken here: Notes on cultural fusion in the Americas*. New York: New Press.
García Canclini, N. (1995). *Hybrid cultures : Strategies for entering and leaving modernity*, In C. L. Chiappari & S. L. López (Trans.). Minneapolis: University of Minnesota Press.
Hall, S. (1997). Old and new identities, old and new ethnicities. In A. D. King (Ed.), *Culture, globalization and the world-system* (pp. 41–68). Minneapolis: University of Minnesota Press.
Halualani, R. T. (2000). Rethinking "ethnicity" as structural-cultural project(s): Notes on the interface between cultural studies and intercultural communication. *International Journal of Intercultural Relations, 24*, 579–602.
Holsten, M. (2004, April). No rules—Paulina Rubio does whatever she wants—with her music. *Hispanic*, 42–45.
Hyde, A. (1997). *Bodies of law*. Princeton, NJ: Princeton University Press.
Inda, J. X. (2001). Performativity, materiality, and the racial body. *Latino Studies Journal, 11*(3), 74–99.
Johnson, E. P. (2000). Feeling the spirit in the dark: Expanding notions of sacred in the African American gay community. In D. Constantine-Simms (Ed.), *The greatest taboo: Homosexuality in black communities* (pp. 88–109). Los Angeles: Alyson Books.
Llewellyn, H. (2002, June 13). Universal's Rubio aims to cross "border." *Billboard, 114*, 44.
Lugo, A. (2000). Theorizing border inspections. *Cultural Dynamics, 12*(3), 353–373.
Martinez, J. (2004). Paulina Rubio: The golden girl's powerful punch. *Latin Style: The Latin Arts and Entertainment Magazine, 50*, 26–28.
Morales, J. (2004, April). Ready to rock: After an almost two-year hiatus, Paulina Rubio is cool, collected, and armed with a new album that crosses every border. *Latina*, 80–82.
Pollock, D. (1995). Performativity. In C. N. Davidson & L. Wagner-Martin (Eds.), *The Oxford companion to women's writing in the United States* (pp. 657–658). New York: Oxford University Press.
Rubio, P. (2002). *Border girl*. [CD liner notes] USA: Universal Records.
Shome, R. & R. S. Hegde. (2002). Culture, communication, and the challenge of globalization. *Critical Studies in Media Communication, 19*(2), 172–189.
Shorris, E. (1992). *Latinos: A biography of the people*. New York: W. W. Norton Company.
Valdivia, A. (1999). La Vida es Loca Latina/o. *Critical Studies in Media Communication, 16*(4), 482–484.
Valdivia, A. N. (2004). Latinas as radical hybrid: Transnationally gendered traces in mainstream media. *Global Media Journal, 2*(4). 17 pars.
Velazquez, G. (2004, April/May). A border girl: Living on the edge. *Latino Leaders, 5*, 30–34.
Vila, P. (Ed.). (2003). *Ethnography at the border*. Minneapolis: University of Minnesota Press.
Wright, C. (1998). "Maquiladora Mestiza" and a feminist border politics: Revisiting Anazaldua. *Hypatia, 13*(3), 114–132.

Part III. Contextually Representing the Heterogeneity

CHAPTER SIX

Policing THE Latina/o Other: Latinidad IN Prime-Time News Coverage OF THE Elián González Story

ISABEL MOLINA GUZMÁN

Although U.S. Latinas/Latinos remain generally invisible in the mainstream news, there continue to circulate those exceptional stories (Méndez-Méndez & Alverio, 2001, 2002; Subervi-Veléz, 2005)—recent raids on undocumented immigrants, the 2006 immigration rights marches and the 1999–2000 custody battle over Cuban refugee Elián González. In this chapter I specifically focus attention on the Elián case in order to provide a broader theoretical framework for studying the symbolic dimensions and ideological repercussions of mainstream television news coverage of Cuban identity and Latinidad. The Elián case is particularly important because it remains one of the most covered stories in television news history, second only to the O. J. Simpson trial (Center for Media and Public Affairs, 2000). Indeed, the four major U.S. television news networks (ABC, CBS, NBC, and CNN) devoted 36.5 hours or 5 percent of their overall programming time to coverage of the conflict between conservative U.S Cubans and the U.S. federal government (Méndez-Méndez & Alverio, 2001). In addition to the high amounts of television news coverage, the case was also followed with interest by a large majority, 78 percent, of the U.S. population (Gillepsie, 2000). The unprecedented public interest along with the extraordinary level of news coverage surrounding the Elián story makes it an iconic case in U.S. Latina/o Media Studies.

The unprecedented and troubling attention to Elián and the Miami Cuban community inevitably contributes to a marginalized construction of Cuban identity and Latinidad that is both gendered and raced. Sasha Torres (1998a) argues that television as a medium is increasingly dependent on the construction of racialized difference to produce its daily set of images and narratives. As television networks undergo institutional changes within the industry and its programming cycles to better target the growing numbers of ethnic and racial minority viewers (Gandy, 1998; Torres S., 1998a), television news plays an increasingly integral role in mediating contemporary notions of ethnic and racial identity. Whether it be news representations of black women (Reeves, 1998), the 1992 beating of Rodney King and ensuing Los Angeles riots (Gray, 1995, Torres S., 1998b) or news coverage of U.S. Cubans and the Elián custody dispute (Molina Guzmán, 2005, 2006),[1] the scholarship suggests that televisual news mediations of ethnic and racial minorities contribute to the formation of public policy and public opinion about those groups.

In this chapter I explore how the mainstream discursive practices of national television news coverage of Elián symbolically colonize the U.S. Cuban community by producing a homogenized gendered and racialized narrative of Cuban identity ultimately defined against the subtext/context of the performance of patriarchal whiteness.[2] Symbolic colonization theorizes that the mainstream media play a significant role in the hegemonic incorporation and exclusion of ethnic minority populations that potentially challenge the boundaries of the imagined nation. Like the cultivation theory of symbolic annihilation (Gerbner et al., 1994), which argues that the media erasure of particular demographic groups, such as the elderly or ethnic and racial minorities, affirm negative public attitudes and beliefs about those groups in turn influencing public policy, the theory of symbolic colonization proposes that the absence of complex narratives in mainstream news coverage of ethnic and racial minorities polices existing hierarchies of difference with potentially discriminatory consequences. In other words, symbolic practices affirm material practices that produce, reproduce, and maintain inequality. Thus, the practices of mainstream television journalists reproduce symbolically colonizing narratives of marginalization that maintain the hegemonic power-knowledge nexus by eliding multiplicity within ethnic communities and privileging an ethnic homogeneity inscribed by gendered and racialized signifiers. My use of the term multiplicity builds on Lisa Lowe's (1996) definition of ethnic heterogeneity as "the existence of differences and differential relationship within a bounded category" (p. 67). Prime-time news coverage of the Elián case erased the multiplicity within and among U.S. Cuban and Latina/o communities.

PRIME-TIME NEWS AS CULTURAL DISCOURSE

Barbie Zelizer (2004) suggests that a cultural studies approach to analyzing journalistic texts and practices is one that "considers the meanings, symbols and symbolic systems, ideologies, rituals and conventions by which journalists maintain their cultural authority as spokespeople for events in the public domain" (p. 101). Such an approach recognizes that journalists are involved in the production of culture and ideology as it is connected to the audiences they serve and "make sense of the news in ways that reflect their own identity politics" (p. 102). The circulation of messages through prime-time news plays a critical role in the reproduction of social and political inequality and the social construction of knowledge, identity, and a group's social status, specifically around issues of race, ethnicity, and gender (Allen, 1998; Bell & Garret, 1998; Bird & Dardenne, 1988; Fairclough, 1995; Thorburn, 1988; van Dijk, 1998; Zelizer, 1990).

Like others forms of popular communication, contemporary television news coverage functions as a hybrid source of entertainment and information contributing to public understandings about Latinidad (Bell & Garret, 1998). Such a discursive analysis of prime-time news in this sense is concerned with how media representations help produce meaning; mediate the relationship between meaning and the social formation of power; and inform the construction of identity and subjectivities (Hall, 1997). Ethnic media scholars are calling for the increased use of qualitative methods to compliment the quantitative cataloging of positive and negative stereotypes (Subervi-Veléz, 1999). Toward that end, this chapter engages in a qualitative discourse analysis grounded in a cultural studies framework that examines how the meanings embedded in prime-time evening news of the Elián case produce narratives of ethnic and racial difference.[3]

My analysis focuses on the production of *gendered* and *racialized* discourses that contribute to the symbolic colonization of U.S. Cubans. While gendered news discourse is defined as a set of journalistic practices that foreground gender to frame the public understanding about a particular news event, issue, or figure, a racialized news discourse highlights race and racial difference (Vargas, 2000). An analysis of gendered discourses examines the semiotics of "woman as sign" as well as the characteristics of femininity and masculinity used to tell the story. Vargas argues mainstream news coverage about Latinas/os is often located within the realm of the feminine by encoding the lives of Latinas/os within the domestic sphere of home and family and ascribing to Latinas/os stereotypically feminine characteristics, such as powerlessness, dependency, irrationality, and emotionality. Racialized news discourses are defined by the use of stereotypic media images to mark a group of people as outside the norms of whiteness. Because Latinidad is often ascribed with problematic hyperfeminine and hypermasculine attributes and nonwhite characteristics, news representations of Latinas/os are both gendered and racialized. The Elián case study illustrates how the gendered and racialized discourses of mainstream television news contribute to the symbolic colonization of the U.S. Cuban community specifically and Latinas/os more generally.

CONTEXTUALIZING POPULAR REPRESENTATIONS OF U.S. CUBANS

Prior to the Elián controversy, the U.S. Cuban exile community occupied a privileged, albeit problematic, space within the imaginary of national U.S. popular culture, in part due to the representational dominance of personalities like Desi Arnaz, Gloria Estéfan, and Andy Garcia (Peréz-Firmat, 1994). Historically, popular representations of Cuban immigrants have not proven as problematic as that of other Latina/o populations. For instance, while contemporary representations of Puerto Ricans remain confined within the urban terrain of poverty, crime, and hypersexuality, dominant constructions of Cubans are located within narratives of prosperity and conservative sexual and social politics. Unlike Dominicans, Mexicans and other Latin American immigrants who are inscribed by the popular rhetoric of illegal immigration and migrant poverty, the representation of Cuban migration was until the 1980s deracialized and indeed politically romanticized (Kanellos, 1994; Ono & Sloop, 2002; Santa Ana, 2002).

In relation to popular representations of other Latinas/os U.S. Cubans exist within the double-edged discourse of the "exceptional" model Latina/o minority–olitically and socially conservative capitalist entrepreneurs. Although U.S. Cubans are coded as ethnic and racial outsiders, they are simultaneously privileged through popular narratives of *Cubanidad* that inscribes them as "honorary whites" (Fusco, 1995). For example, despite ongoing changes in the racial composition and political positions of the U.S. Cuban community, popular representations about Cubans remain grounded in homogenizing stereotypes of the exile community as politically conservative, law abiding, religious, predominantly white and middle to upper class, and staunchly anti-Castro, such as the U.S. Cuban character of Angie Lopez (Constance Marie) on *The George Lopez Show*.

Beginning with the first wave of immigration by mostly pro-Batista supporters to Florida during the height of the Cold War in the late-1950s and early 1960s, Cuban exiles played a pivotal role in defining cultural representations of Latinidad in the United States. This first wave of Cuban refugees was madeup of mostly white, upper-middle class professionals with preexisting ties to Miami (Pedraza-Bailey, 1985; Stepick, Grenier, Castro, & Dunn, 2003). Unlike other immigrants from the Caribbean and Latin America, Cuban immigration was encouraged and supported by the U.S. federal government throughout the 1960s and 1970s (Pedraza-Bailey, 1985; Rumbaut, 1994; Torres, 2002). Cuban immigrants were represented as political refugees appreciative of the United States but eager to return to their Cuban homes. The federal government created special programs for Cuban exiles (such as the Cuban Adjustment Act of 1966 and the Cuban Refugee Program) that provided Cubans with economic assistance and bypassed standard immigration procedures (Pedraza-Bailey, 1985). These programs allowed Cubans an unprecedented level of economic and political success further cementing popular notions of Cubans as exceptional and different from other Latina/o, ethnic, racial, and immigrant groups (Stepick et al., 2003). For the United States, the romantic image of Cubans leaving their beautiful island homes, professional careers, and extended families for the protection of U.S. capitalism and democracy provided symbolic proof of communism's lack of moral legitimacy and Fidel Castro's disintegrating support and inevitable political demise (M. Torres, 1998).

The intergenerational, political, racial, and economic multiplicity that defines the contemporary U.S. Cuban community are often erased from national entertainment and news texts. As one U.S. Cuban observed in the wake of the Elián González coverage,

> Long before the shipwreck survivor landed in America, cigars, music, and antique cars in Havana got more ink than the innumerable human rights abuses of Cuba's repressive government. Coverage of Cuban exiles, meanwhile, would lead you to believe that we are all rich entrepreneurs and fire breathing right-wingers. (Barciela, 2000, p. 128)

Within the U.S. cultural landscape, Cubans are often represented as more educated, wealthier, and industrious than African Americans and other Latina/o groups, an image often propagated by Cubans themselves (Soruco, 1996). Although Cubans are more likely to complete high school, attend some college, and earn higher income than other Latina/o groups, the demographic data demonstrate that a higher percentage of the Cuban population compared to Mexican, Central, and South American populations is currently living in poverty (U.S. Census Reports, 2000). Indeed, the Pew Hispanic Project reports that the income differential between Cubans and other Latina/o groups is much smaller than income differences between Cubans and the white population (Brodie et al., 2002). This means that there is less of an income difference between Cubans and other Latina/o groups and a larger income disparity between Cubans and the white population. In other words, the demographics of the Cuban community are aligning more closely with those of other Latina/o groups.

Over the past 20 years, Cuban immigration has shifted from educated professionals to working-class Afro-Cuban laborers, who often face discrimination within Miami's black community, Cuban community, and the community at large (Pedraza-Bailey, 1985; Portes & Stepick, 1985). Recent Cuban immigrants have a much tougher time finding work and are less likely to benefit economically from the privileges of Miami's Cuban ethnic enclave (Stepick et al., 2003). Cuban Studies scholars have extensively documented how changes in Cuban demographics have correlated with shifts in the racial privileged afforded to exiled Cubans.

For example, the negative media representation and political backlash surrounding the April-October 1980 Mariel boatlift that brought 125,000 Cubans to Miami and the Balseros of the early 1990s. While most of the Mariel refugees were working-class laborers, some of them with family ties to Miami, the mainstream media coverage focused attention on Afro-Cubans, homosexual Cubans, and the small percentage of refugees with criminal records (Mirabal, 2003; Rumbaut, 1994).[4]

Nevertheless, the cultural status of Cuban immigrants as temporary political exiles in the U.S. war against communism continued to situate U.S. Cubans in a position of privilege compared to other Latin American and Caribbean groups. As such, Cuban immigrants' strong ties to their native culture, religion, language, and political opposition to Fidel Castro is celebrated and, until recently, relatively unchallenged by the U.S. media. Thus, U.S. audiences' media exposure to Cubans is as informed by Cold War tainted news coverage of Cuban exceptionalism as it is by the highly visible "white" bodies of entertainment personalities like, Desi Arnaz, Gloria Estéfan, and Andy Garcia. It is against this long-standing popular narrative of Cuban identity or *Cubanidad* that the gendered and racialized signification surrounding prime-time news coverage of the Elián story must be contextualized.

SYMBOLIC COLONIZATION: FROM ONE OF "US" TO ONE OF THE "THEM"

Given that the majority of national journalists, visual and print, are predominantly white and the majority of editors predominantly white and male, the production of mainstream prime-time news narratives is implicitly informed by racialized and gendered hierarchies of power (Rakow & Kranich, 1991; Rodríguez, 1999; Vargas, 2000). News about Latina/os remains unnewsworthy unless the issue is sensationalistic enough to be entertaining or an event is perceived as a symbolic threat to the established social order. Therefore, it is not coincidental that most national coverage about Latina/os focuses on illegal immigration, sexual reproduction statistics, poverty, and crime (Ruíz, 2002; Vargas, 2000). In the Elián case study, there is third driving force in the journalistic coverage—the ideological threat of Latinidad to established mythologies about the imagined nation. Building on the concept of symbolic colonization, the chapter's analysis focuses on three narrative strategies within prime-time news: (1) the homogenization of intra-ethnic differences within the U.S. Cuban community; (2) the feminized infantilization of the U.S. Cuban community; (3) the positioning of U.S. Cuban identity outside of socially acceptable performances of whiteness. Together these three narrative strategies work to symbolically colonize and ideologically police the U.S. Cuban community by shifting the representational frame from exceptional political exiles to ethnic exiles defined by the gendered and racialized discourses of tropicalization.

Homogenizing the Ethnic Other

According to the US Census 2000, close to 750,000 U.S. Cubans live in Miami, Florida, making up approximately 35 percent of the city's total population. The Miami Cuban community has created a nation within a nation—as economically, politically, and socially diverse as any other community in the United States. By celebrating the old country and the new, U.S. Cubans have formed hybrid cultural practices and ways of speaking and performing Cuban identity. Furthermore, the predominantly white anti-Castro exiles of the 1960s have been joined throughout the 1980s and 1990s by Cubans of African descent as well as more politically progressive Cubans, adding yet more layers of multiplicity and complexity to the diverse nature of this Latina/o community. Today the Afro-Cuban faces of deceased chanteuse Celia Cruz and baseball pitcher Orlando "El Duque" Hernandez are as familiar to mainstream U.S. audiences as Gloria Estéfan and Andy Garcia.

Nevertheless, because of their historical position as the racially white "model minority" among Latina/o communities, U.S. Cubans occupy a unique space within the dominant imaginary of U.S. popular culture (Pérez-Firmat, 1994). Miami's contemporary Latina/o community is better defined by its political, racial, ethnic, and economic differences, but the U.S. media have until recently remained invested in mythologizing the U.S. Cuban community as Havana, and the historically foreground identity narratives of exile Cuban identity as conservative, anticommunists/anti-Castro and pro-Republican.

One early example of this type of journalistic narrative is an *ABC World News Tonight* segment aired on December 10, 1999:

> It is all the talk here. Most of it, "Keep Elián in America." Felt most strongly among Cuban expatriates, in this city, united and politically powerful. In fact, many reporters expected them to hold huge demonstrations here, but that has not happened. So far, only a tiny smattering of protest.
>
> This is, it turns out, complicated. It seems Cuban Americans loathing of Fidel Castro is competing with their equally strong love of family, making it difficult for some to support a cause that would keep a father from his son.

The use of language like "united and politically powerful" resonates with the traditional news coverage of U.S. Cubans as political elites (DeSipio & Henson, 1997). Mainstream journalistic assumptions about the identity and expected behavior of U.S. Cubans are further revealed throughout the report, such as "In fact, many reporters expected them to hold huge demonstrations here, but that has not happened. So far, only a tiny smattering of protest." This statement interestingly reveals that the newsworthiness of the story is the unexpected outcome—mainstream journalists expected to witness Miami Cubans virulently protesting Castro, but that set of actions did not initially occur. Similar to the findings by Stuart Hall, Charles Critcher, Tony Jefferson, John Clarke, and Brian Robert in *Policing the Crisis* (1978) regarding mainstream British newspaper coverage of alleged urban violence and black British youth, violent protests by Miami Cubans did not materialize. The absence of chaos and disorder within Miami's exile community became the significant news story. It is the racist expectation of ethnic violence and racial disorder rather than the actual actions of ethnic minority communities that drive mainstream television news coverage (Torres M., 1998b).

The anomaly created by the orderly and rational circulation of United States. Cuban discourses about the Elián case is explained within the ABC news story by proposing another homogenizing construction of the U.S. Cuban community, the dominant notion that U.S. Cubans are equally as profamily as they are anti-Castro. In the end, the ABC news report maintains the problematic and false construction that all Miami Cubans are both anti-Castro and profamily and that those two identities cannot be reconciled. The underlying journalistic assumptions about U.S. Cuban identity embedded in the early news coverage are made visible in later news coverage in several ways. First, by the end of the story in May 2000, anti-Castro Miami Cubans do protest en masse under the banner of anticommunist and profamily values illustrating that both identity positions are reconcilable. Second, moderate and progressive U.S. Cubans who support an open relationship with Castro and Cuba would make their voices heard throughout the conflict destabilizing the homogenous constructions that all U.S. Cubans are anticommunist. And third, citizens and journalists in Cuba would eventually successfully circulate the oppositional news frame that U.S. anti-Castro protestors do not exclusively occupy the profamily values position. Together these three ensuing events point to the diversity of identity positions and relationships within the U.S. Cuban community revealing stereotypic journalistic assumptions. Like other early news stories about Elián, the ABC segment's use of stereotypical visuals, such as older men working in cigar rolling shops, gathering in coffee shops, and playing dominos, reify the popular nostalgic iconography associated with Cuba and U.S. Cubans exiles. The implicit ideological message underlying such journalistic texts is that most U.S. Cubans live in Miami, think alike, act alike and share the same political values.

Another segment by *CNN Worldview Tonight* aired on January 6, 2000 further illustrates how this homogenizing frame is circulated throughout the network news coverage. Mark Potter, the on-air reporter, identifies all the Miami demonstrators as U.S. Cubans, although it is nearly impossible to visibly differentiate Cubans from other Latina/os (or non-Latino U.S. participants for that matter). Despite comments by at least one on-air source that the demonstration was multiethnic, the ethnicity of the activists is repeatedly referenced as "Cuban American." Not only is the ethnic, racial, and economic diversity among the demonstrators elided, the group identity is objectified and dehumanized through the use of descriptors like "dozens" and "the crowd" to describe the event. The visible diversity of the participants is reduced to one ethnic label, which is further reduced to images and language descriptive of an uncontrollable mass:

> Shortly afterward, *the crowd began to surge forward* through the barricades, through the police officers on horseback *who could not hold them back*. Moments later, the *whole group was moving* east through downtown traffic, the police *struggling to keep ahead of the crowd*, sealing off streets along the way. (emphasis mine)

Similar to the type of language and metaphors used to describe undocumented workers during news coverage of California's Proposition 187 (Santa Ana, 2000), the participants of this protests are linguistically and visually framed as uncontrollable, destructive, and unrelenting tides. They are eventually reduced from the insider status of U.S. Cuban citizens to the outsider status of "Them/Other" through the news story's on-camera interview of Miami police officer Nelda Fonticella who is quoted as saying, "We will not allow them to shut down the city." U.S. Cubans are thus positioned within the news coverage as both homogenous mass and threatening outsiders.

Feminizing the Ethnic Other

A key element of the narrative strategy of ethnic homogenization is the gendered foregrounding of hysteria, hyperemotionality, and religiosity, characteristics stereotypically associated with feminine powerlessness and irrationality. In approximately 22 percent of the news coverage collected for this study, reporters used language and images that emphasized the emotional and irrational nature of the U.S. Cuban community. Phrases like the "volatile majority" (*World News Tonight*, January 9, 2000); "full of fervor and outright passionately determined" (*World News Tonight*, April 4, 2000); and "prayers, tears and denunciations of the government's action, fueled the crowd's emotion" (*World News Tonight*, April 22, 2000) emphasized the emotional characterization of the Cuban community, characteristics that are associated both with women and Latinas/os. Not only is this type of gendered language feminizing, but it also reinforces the news construction that the U.S. Cuban community is outside of the borders of social acceptability, outside the borders of the imagined nation.

As is true of the narratives about Latina immigration elsewhere (Ruiz, 2002), the symbolism of mothers and motherhood plays an important role in the feminization and consequent infantilization of the Miami Cuban community (Molina Guzmán, 2007). Not surprisingly Elisabet Brotons, Elián's deceased biological mother, played a subtle yet key role within the prime-time television news coverage. Although Elisabet is rarely the explicit focus of the news coverage, her multiple and competing identities as Elián's mother, Cuban citizen, prospective U.S. Cuban exile, and undocumented Latina immigrant places her at the story's core. Her actions provide the news coverage's raison d'être. In other words, her relationship to Elián and her death at sea frame the story's melodramatic emotional narrative as well as the story's journalistic "uniqueness." Elisabet functions simultaneously within the symbolic terrain of ethnic-specific Cuban identity and panethnic Latinidad. She moves between journalistic constructions that position her within the preexisting discourses of antidemocratic Cuba, U.S. Cuban exceptionalism, and panethnic Latina, albeit white, motherhood.

However, despite the narrative importance of Elisabet, she is rarely given subjectivity within the journalistic coverage. In the 166 television news segments examined, not one story mentions Elisabet by name, although most reference her by using Elisabet's action as a descriptor for Elián's identity.[5] For example, in four stories aired on November 28, 1999 and December 6–8, 1999 on *ABC World News Tonight* the only reference to Elisabet is made during the anchor's lead-in to the segments, which describes Elián as the 6-year-old "whose mother died at sea as she was bringing him to Florida." This pattern is also found in news segments aired on CBS, CNN, and NBC. Elisabet's actions frame the narrative of the story even as she remains nameless, identified only by her death and biological relation to Elián (Tapia, 2001).

Invoking Elisabet as the nameless mother who sacrifices herself to bring her son to the United States provides a journalistically unique and emotional narrative that in part explains the sensationalized flurry of national news coverage. The journalistic emphasis on Elisabet's illegal and dangerous journey affirms familiar popular and panethnic narratives about Latinas. Her social status as a mother and the tragic events surrounding her death locate Elisabet within long-standing U.S. archetypes of Latina immigrant femininity and domesticity, that of the self-sacrificing almost-virginal always-religious ethnic mother who gives up her own happiness, in this instance her own life, so that her child may obtain the "American Dream." This is an archetype reified for the U.S. public through Hollywood films such as *Mi Familia* [My Family] and television programs such as PBS's "American Family." Not coincidentally, one of the few images of Brotons circulated through the news media is a family photo of her smiling into the camera as she hugs a young Elián. Because Brotons is deceased and unable to represent herself, the visual replication of this scarce image contributes to the construction of Elisabet as a loving mother whose identity is only significant in terms of her relationship to her son Elián.

Elisabet's journalistic construction as the good self-sacrificing mother is embraced and rearticulated by the Miami Cuban community in the mainstream media through narratives of religiosity. For instance, in one of the first national television stories, a November 26, 1999 *CBS Evening News* segment filmed outside of Elián's hospital, Marisleysis González, Elián's second-cousin and surrogate mother in the United States, is interviewed on-camera: "The first thing that came to my mind: How did he survive by himself when he's only five? And I'm still thinking about it. And the only thing I can probably say is that it's just a miracle. God wanted him here for freedom." Similar to this news excerpt, U.S. Cuban men and women interviewed by journalists often described the events surrounding Elián's rescue through religious imagery and language. Indeed, as coverage of the news story progresses, Elisabet and Elián are increasingly mythologized through predominantly Catholic iconography in turn contributing to the panethnic construction of Elisabet as the sacred and self-sacrificing Latina mother. Elisabet is grounded in a story of love and sacrifice in which the young mother places the son she struggled to give birth to after years of miscarriages in the sole remaining inner-tube with her only bottle of water. Not knowing how to swim she drowns during the night, but an exhausted and dehydrated Elián is guided to safety through shark-infested waters by a pair of dolphins sent to him by a guardian angel.

Associated Press (AP) photographs and television news coverage retell Elisabet's legend to mainstream audiences reaffirming the religious character of the Miami Cuban community. For instance, in an AP photograph of a mural painted in Little Havana, Elian's inner-tube is depicted being guided by dolphins sent to protect him by *La Virgen de la Caridad del Cobre* [Our Lady of Charity, Cuba's patron saint]. In the photograph's background are the scales of justice with Pope John Paul II and President Bill Clinton hanging in balance, the Statue of Liberty, a pair of archangels, and Jesus Christ. Elisabet Brotons gently smiles as she watches over Elián's "divine" rescue.

Photographs and news footage of the mural appeared in two *ABC World News Tonight* segments about the intermingling of Cuban exile politics and religion broadcasted on January 23 and March 31, 2000. These stories aired two months apart use the same file footage, the same sources, and almost identical reporting. Both implicitly present a feminized image of the Miami family and Cuban community. The initial story begins with a visual montage of mostly older men and women hugging, kissing, and touching the young Elián. Dramatic images are accompanied by equally dramatic yet still homogenizing language with U.S. Cuban sources quoted on-air using hyperreligious and emotional language.

Images of Elián are juxtaposed against Catholic paintings of holy saints, and the voices and images of the U.S. Cuban sources are eventually contrasted against the sole voice of U.S. Cuban dissent and rationality, a politically moderate academic news expert.

Although the ABC network coverage demonstrates the most sensationalistic use of gendered discourses, similar visuals and language can be found throughout all four networks. Together the surreal emotional images of adults, in particular adult men, weeping at the sight of the child along with images of prayer circles and close-ups of rosary beads contribute to the gendered construction of this community as hyperreligious, superemotional and thus ethnically different and marginal. U.S. Cubans, once unquestionably embraced as temporary members of the imagined nation, are reinevitably incorporated into marginalizing representations of Latinidad. They occupy an ideological space in-between—not quite American and no longer Cuban—caught between two cultures and claimed by neither.

Elisabet's, Elián's, and the U.S. Cuban community's exceptionalism is eventually policed and ideologically contained through the gendered discourses of the news coverage. As the Miami family and the Cuban American community become increasingly represented through a feminized frame, the U.S. federal government is invited into the narrative in often paternalistic tones that further codes the U.S. Cuban community as infantile:

- Today, another congressman, trying to skirt the current law, wants to make the boy a permanent resident alien. The attorney general, however, is *standing firm*. (*World News Tonight*, January 12, 2000)
- *In language even a 6-year-old might understand*, the Justice Department made clear today what the law says about who controls the fate of Elián González. (*World News Tonight*, January 12, 2000)
- The attorney general is now telling everyone once again *'simmer down,'* this case belongs in the federal court. (*World News Tonight*, January 13, 2000)
- It's already been an extraordinary two months, and this afternoon it took the U.S. government and a Catholic nun for the grandmothers of Elián González to sit down in private with their grandson, which means *it took a stern warning* from the Justice Department before Elián's Cuban American relatives backed off. (*World News Tonight*, January 26, 2000) (emphasis mine)

Standing firm, giving stern warnings, telling the U.S. Cuban exile to simmer down—this type of language constructs the U.S. federal government as maintaining institutional and patriarchal authority and simultaneously places the U.S.

Cuban community in the gendered role of a recalcitrant but powerless child. The gendered discourse moves from feminization to infantilization and signals the progressive loss of U.S. Cuban political agency. With U.S. public opinion turning against the Miami family, the U.S. Cuban community and the U.S. Cuban embargo, the journalistic coverage reinforces the authority of the U.S. federal government and its courts and the marginal political status of an ethnic minority community that is increasingly read as an immigrant outsider.

Racializing the Ethnic Other

By the time the conflict over Elián reaches its climax in April, the U.S. Cuban community has been journalistically framed as political outsiders and racialized ethnic Others. News coverage of actual U.S. Cuban protests and the always imminent threat of protests in Miami construct the community as hotheaded and lawless, characteristics associated with tropical Latino masculinity. Miami becomes a disorderly tropicalized space south of the U.S. border, and its Cuban inhabitants are marked as racialized Others outside the norms of U.S. citizenship.

Narrative tropes of tropicalism and tropicalization have a long history in U.S. mainstream culture. Aparicio and Chavéz-Silverman (1997) define tropicalism as the "system of ideological fictions with which the dominant (Anglo-European) cultures trope Latin American and U.S. Latino/a identities and culture" (p. 1). Tropicalism as a trope erases specificity and lumps all that is Latin and Latina/o into one homogeneous heap (López, 1991; Perez-Firmat, 1994). Attributes such as brown or olive skin, religiosity, emotionality, and metaphors of heat and instability comprise some of the most enduring tropical stereotypes about Latinas/os. Together with journalistic practices that homogenize and gender U.S. Cubans, racialized tropicalism works to symbolically colonize the Cuban ethnic enclave.

Toward the end of the conflict, the mainstream news coverage privileges Elián's Cuban family by foregrounding the father's custodial rights and simultaneously shifts the focus on the Miami Cuban community away from family values toward unruly racialized excess. Marisleysis becomes one of the primary visual and textual mechanisms through which the process of racialized tropicalization occurs. Unlike Elisabet, who is always present in the news coverage through her absence, Marisleysis ultimately circulates in the news coverage through her symbolic excess. After the U.S. federal government withdraws its support for Elián's asylum claim in late December and U.S. public sentiment turns against the Miami family in early January, Marisleysis' image is increasingly juxtaposed in the news coverage with the matronly and stoic images of Elián's Cuban grandmothers.

For instance, the grandmothers' reserved yet outraged response to claims that they sexually abused Elián during their brief U.S. visit is edited in news reports next to Marisleysis' saucy threats against the grandmothers. The consequence is that Marisleysis and the Miami Cuban community she represents are subsumed by her hyperemotional behavior. Her fragile and overdetermined femininity becomes the object of the news story. Eventually, Marisleysis is transformed from a credible spokeswoman into a racialized hyperfeminine Latina spectacle. Rather than performing the role of the exceptional middle-class, "white" conservative Cuban spokeswoman, Marisleysis is characterized by her erratic behavior, tempestuous temper, and classed-signifiers of Latina femininity.

Marisleysis and the Miami Cuban community are thus presented within the news coverage as cultural outsiders, as different, as ethnic and racial Others. Access to discourses of exceptionalism afforded to the U.S. Cuban exile community as a result of Cold War politics is foreclosed by the racialized rhetoric surrounding the contemporary politics of Latina/o immigration (Stack & Warren, 1990). Not surprisingly, Marisleysis is more often associated with her emotional breakdowns and anxiety attacks regarding her maternal desire for Elián than she is with her role as political advocate for the conservative politics of Miami's Cuban community. Her emotional instability, indeed apparent neurosis or hysteria about Elián's welfare, eventually becomes the focus of the coverage undercutting her symbolic power as surrogate mother and community spokeswoman.

Throughout the final two months of news coverage, Marisleysis' instability is framed as extreme and at times inappropriate. For example, an April 4, 2000 *CBS Evening News* segment that provides an update of the ongoing negotiations regarding Elián's custody between the Miami family and the U.S. government devotes significant time to a discussion of Marisleysis' most recent hospitalization: "*Yesterday she spoke with fear and defiance*: 'If you send Elián back to Cuba, he will be tortured. Is that what the American people are going to allow?'" (Ron Claiborne reporting). The segment's editor could have selected to paraphrase Marisleysis and avoid showing her emotional plea. However, given the sensationalistic nature of contemporary U.S. television news, it is precisely these hyperbolized displays of emotions that are central to the visual narrative of Marisleysis and by association the Miami Cuban community. Like the O. J. Simpson trial, the Elián story has all the peculiar elements of those stories that tend to make good visual news: innocent children, beautiful women, interfamily conflict, a polarized public and an unexpected, violent death.

Because the audience is only privy to a few seconds of what was probably a lengthy news conference, the selected sound bite becomes ideologically significant. Marisleysis' on-camera statement subtly positions the U.S. Cuban community as political outsiders by suggesting that despite the U.S. government and U.S. public opinion, the U.S. Cuban community is not going to allow Elián to be sent back to Cuba. By emphasizing the community's intention to oppose the

U.S. government, the representation of the Miami Cuban exile community breaks with the traditional constructions of law abiding, politically conservative, socially acceptable, exceptional Cubans. Instead, the news coverage focuses on scenes featuring the community's emotional outbursts or violent protests. The narrative of emotionality contradicts the discourse of Cuban exceptionalism and reinforces already-existing dominant stereotypes about Latinidad. In the hands of the Cuban community, Miami is framed as a south-of-the-border tropics and the childless Marisleysis is reincorporated into the news coverage as a threat to the established racial and patriarchal order.

Marisleysis becomes a stand-in for U.S. Cubans as the racialized ethnic Other, as an outsider permeating the U.S. border. In contrast to the legalistic response by government sources ensconced within performances of white rationality, the widely circulated photograph and news footage of Marisleysis accusing the U.S. government of child abuse after the federal raid on her family's Little Havana home emphasize the community's loss of credibility and political agency. Marisleysis is seen sobbing wide-mouthed, at the loss of her surrogate child. The weight she has gained throughout the ordeal highlight her ill-fitting clothes. Close-ups of her face foreground her heavy makeup, rouge lipstick, and faux red nails and together act as stereotypical markers of working-class Latina femininity. The popular image of a loud-mouthed and tearful Marisleysis evokes familiar classed and racialized images of panethnic Latinas circulated throughout mainstream popular texts, such as some of the roles played by Rosie Perez and Salma Hayek. No longer the middle-class, professional, appropriately feminine, exceptional Cuban woman, Marisleysis is the uncontrollable Latina mother without a child, without a nation.

The racialization of Marisleysis also signals the marginalization of the U.S. Cuban community within prime-time news coverage. One of the best examples of the racialized reframing of the U.S. Cuban community can be found within a *CBS Evening News* aired on March 29, 2000. The images, selected on-air quotes, and journalist texts construct the Miami Cuban community as boiling over with heat, hostility and violence. Beginning with a lead-in by Dan Rather foregrounding Miami's Cuban mayor "not-so-veiled threat of noncooperation," the specter of U.S. Cuban violence is used as the story's primary frame. The news story's language and accompanying visuals describe the protestors as "circling the neighborhood with trucks and a human chain" and actively "preparing for a confrontation." A sense of impending volatility and disorder is reinforced through the selective use of on-air interviews: "*How far are you willing to go, sir?* Do you remember Waco, Texas? *Yes, sir.* You got my answer. *Angry words with a proven history*" (Byron Pitts interviewing Armando Sotolongo). Not-so-veiled-threats, references to Waco, images of demonstrators burning tires and overturning police barricades, the news report depicts a south-of-the-border Miami in the violent hands of brown masculine Cuban bodies.

The violence and disorder surrounding journalistic coverage of brown masculine bodies is contrasted against the production of whiteness through journalistic practices rooted in objectivity. Journalistic white objectivity remains the uninterrogated norm against which the tropicalization of the Latinidad is policed and symbolically disciplined. The multiplicity of ethnic minority difference can be tamed only through contrast with that which it is not—in this instance, the journalistic reproduction of whiteness enabled through the practices of objectivity and patriarchal voices of legal, academic, and political news experts. A reliance on expert sources, who are predominately male and white; government sources, who are predominately white, non-U.S. Cuban and mostly female; and public documents grounded in the legal discourse of rationality, results in a contemporary journalistic text that reifies Western notions of objectivity and facticity (Schudson, 2001; Tuchman, 1972) and unconsciously reproduces what Ruth Frankenberg (1993) calls, "the colonial construction of whiteness as an 'empty' cultural space" (p. 243). Performances of whiteness informed by notions of rationality and objectivity are the uninterrogated ground by which ethnic minority groups are ultimately evaluated and disciplined by the court of public opinion and mainstream news.

With the exception of a few politically moderate U.S. Cuban sources, the majority of Elián legal experts, who are usually pooled from think tanks, institutions or universities, were male and white. Unlike the Miami demonstrators, who were almost always interviewed outdoors in street clothes and often wearing colorful paraphernalia, these experts were garbed in professional attire and interviewed predominately inside the respectable spaces of private offices filled with academic and legal texts or in conference rooms behind podiums with official government seals. Interestingly enough although all of the government sources interviewed on-air were white, most of them were women. Ironically, it is the voice and bodies of white women who become the mechanism through which the patriarchal rule of law is reestablished through the return of the son to the father.

The authority of the white experts and government sources carries over to the journalist themselves. Most of the journalists that appeared in these stories are white, but many like Ron Claiborne, Byron Pitts, Lucia Newman, Elizabeth Vargas, and others are not. Yet even the journalists of color have gained the right to appear on national television by perfecting their use of standard English and appropriately professional attire, in other words through the normative performance of whiteness. Thus, in contrast to the tropicalized bodies of U.S. Cubans interviewed on the streets of Little Havana, wearing casual clothing, speaking in an accented or broken English filled with emotionality, the journalistic and expert voices of intellectual and/or legal authority speak eloquent standard English free from emotive expression. The homogenized gendered and racialized Cuban body is the text upon which the story is written; whereas the experts, government sources, and journalists through their performance of whiteness become the background against which the Latino Other is contrasted and ultimately judged.

CONCLUSION: POLICING THE LATINA/O OTHER

The story of Elián González climaxes on April 22, 2000 when federal marshals penetrate the shield of Cuban activists and the home of Elián's Miami relatives in order to capture Elián and return him to his Cuban father. And the political consequences of Elián's forced return to his father are many. Elián's "rescue" restores the diplomatic relationship between Cuba and the United States helping to keep the informal immigration agreements that control the flow of Cuban exiles in place. The political power of the Cuban American National Foundation is weakened resulting in the 2001 relaxation of the U.S. embargo on Cuba.[6] After months of protests, the Miami Cuban community is left at odds with itself, with other Latina/o groups and with the U.S. population at large. Finally, the dominant racial ideology that places whiteness at the top is recuperated in the mainstream news coverage through the homogenizing, gendered and racialized process of symbolic colonization that moves exceptional *Cubanindad* into the terrain of brown Latinidad.

By dynamically shifting the status of U.S. Cubans from exceptional whiteness to criminalized brownness, the contemporary symbolic position of U.S. Cubans is marginalized. Unlike the protests against the Balseros and Marielitos, the public outcry against the U.S. Cuban community during the Elián case spanned across class, gender, and racial markers. All U.S. Cubans were read as brown, liminal noncitizens. The symbolic colonization of the U.S. Cuban community in the prime-time news must be contextualized within the ongoing nativist backlash against immigration and globalization. While Latina/o and other ethnic news outlets used the Elián case to contest the special immigration privileges provided to Cubans, mainstream newspaper readers in Miami and other global cities used the Elián case to speak out against the browning of their cities, growth of immigrant communities, and loss of native-born citizens' economic mobility. As Stepick et al. (2003) argue the conflict over Elián tapped into long-existing simmering ethnic and racial anxieties. Resonant with news coverage about California's anti-Latino immigration legislation Proposition 187, mainstream news texts about Elián play a central role in the maintenance of power and racial hierarchies during a historical moment when the complex multiplicity of U.S. Latina/o communities might be viewed as a threat to political and economic elites (Inda, 2002).

The prime-time news coverage about Elián and U.S. Cubans construct a consensus narrative about the boundaries of national identity at a point when the mythologized borders of the imagined nation are being contested by first and second generation immigrants from the Caribbean, Latin America, Mexico, and Asia. Consensus narratives "articulate the culture's central mythology, in a widely accessible 'language,' an inheritance of shared stories, plots, character types, cultural symbols, narrative conventions" (Thorburn, 1988, p. 57). The symbolic colonization of U.S. Cubans in prime times news of the Elián case affirm a consensus narrative that polices the differences between law and order and chaos and disorder, white and brown, English and Spanish, masculine and feminine, citizen and alien. Circulating these dichotomies through prime-time news, restores the national boundaries of U.S. Citizenship defined by the values and norms of whiteness and white identity. As such prime-time news coverage of the Elián case is stuff of myth and folklore, a cultural lesson in the ideological disciplining that occurs when the subaltern dares to challenge the dominant (Bird & Dardenne, 1988, p. 70). Television in general and broadcast news in particular reproduce an ideological vision of the nation, a framework for making sense of the world around us, that ultimately works in the interest of the elite (Fiske, 1991; Hallin, 1986). Elian may have gone back to Cuba, but the racializing effects of his short stay in the U.S. moved U.S. Cubans from exceptionalism into the overflowing category of brown, eternally foreign, Latino aliens.

NOTES

1. This chapter is not a reprint, it is a more complex intellectual extension of previous works. (For earlier versions see Molina Guzmán, 2005, 2007).
2. For an in-depth discussion of symbolic colonization as it functions and fails across fiction and nonfiction media texts, please see my forthcoming book, tentatively titled *Consuming Latina Bodies: Global Media Representations of Latinidad*, with New York University Press.
3. I define "discourse" as the use of spoken and written language, visual images, and other forms of communication found within the production of mainstream television news. A total of 166 news segments or approximately 6.5 hours of news coverage aired on the national evening news networks (ABC, CBS, CNN, NBC) from November 1999 to June 2000 were collected.
4. For in-depth discussion of the political and economic impact of the Mariel exiles, see Portes and Jensen (1989); Portes and Stepick (1985); Pedraza-Bailey (1985a); and Stepick, Grenier, Castro, and Dunn (2003).
5. Elisabet Brotons' subjectivity was so erased from the English-language news coverage that finding her name and the correct spelling of her name has proved difficult. This article uses the spelling of her name most commonly circulated in English and Spanish-language news print stories and television transcripts.
6. The embargo would be again tightened in 2004 with the election of Republican President George W. Bush.

REFERENCES

Allan, S. (1998). News from Nowhere: Televisual news discourses and the construction of hegemony. In A. Bell & P. Garrett (Eds.), *Approaches to media discourse* (pp. 105–141). London: Blackwell.
Aparicio, F. & S. Chavéz-Silverman. (1997). *Tropicalizations: Transcultural Representations of Latinidad.* Hanover, CT: University Press of New England.
Barciela, S. (2000). Bashing the Cubans: The Elián saga prompted open season on exiles. *Hispanic* (July–August), 128.
Bell, A. & P. Garrett. (Eds.). (1998). *Approaches to media discourse.* London: Blackwell.
Bird, E. & R. Dardenne. (1988). Myth, chronicle and story: Exploring the narrative qualities of news. In J. Carey (Ed.), *Media, myths and narratives: Television and the press* (pp. 67–86). Newbury, NJ: Sage.
Brodie, M., R. Suro, A. Steffenson, J. Valdez & R. Levin. (2002). The 2002 national survey of Latinos. A report by The Kaiser Family Foundation and The Pew Hispanic Center, Washington, D.C.
Center for Media and Public Affairs. (2000). Elián story makes the biggest splash. Report by the center for media and public affairs, June 2.
DeSipio, L. & J. R. Henson. (1997). Cuban Americans, Latinos, and the print media: Shaping ethnic identities. *Press/Politics, 2,* 2–70.
Fairclough, N. (1995). *Media discourse.* London: Edward Arnold.
Fiske, J. (1991). Postmodernism and television. In J. Curran & M. Gurevitch (Eds.), *Mass media and society* (pp. 55–67). London: Edward Arnold.
Fusco, C. (1995). *English is broken here: Notes on cultural fusion in the Americas.* New York: New Press.
Gandy, Oscar (1998). *Communication and race: A structural perspective* (pp. 1–34). New York: Arnold Press.
Gerbner, G. et al. (1994). Growing up with television: The cultivation perspective. In Jennings Bryant & Dolf Zillman (Eds.), *Media effects: Advances in theory and research* (pp. 17–42). Hillsdale, NJ: Lawrence Erlbraum.
Gillepsie, M. (2000) Americans support resumption of diplomatic relations with Cuba. *Gallup Poll Reports,* May, p. 33.
Gray, H. (1989). Television, black Americans, and the American dream. *Critical Studies in Mass Communication, 6*(4), 376–386.
Hall, S. (Eds.). (1997). *Representation: Cultural representations and signifying practices.* London: Sage.
Hall, S., C. Critcher, T. Jefferson, J. Clarke, & B. Robert. (1978). *Policing the crisis: Mugging, the state, and law and order.* New York: Holmes & Meier Publisher.
Hallin, D. (1986). We keep America on top of the world. In T. Gitlin (Ed.), *Watching television* (pp. 9–41). New York: Pantheon.
Inda, J. (2002). Biopower, reproduction, and the migrant woman's body. In A. Aldama (Ed.), *Decolonial voices: Chicana and Chicano cultural studies in the 21st century* (pp. 98–112). Bloomington, IN: Indiana University Press.
Kanellos, N. (1994). *The Hispanic Almanac: From Columbus to corporate America.* Visible Ink: Detroit.
Lowe, L. (1996). *Immigrant acts.* Durham, NC: Duke University Press.
Méndez-Méndez, S. & D. Alverio. (2001). Network brownout 2001: The portrayal of Latinos in network television news, 2000. Report prepared for the National Association of Hispanic Journalist, Washington, DC.

Méndez-Méndez, S. & D. Alverio. (2002). Network brownout 2001: The Portrayal of Latinos in Network Television News, 2000. Report prepared for the National Association of Hispanic Journalists, Washington, DC.

Mirabal, N. R. (2003) "Ser De Aqui": Beyond the Cuban exile model. *Latino Studies, 1,* 366–382.

Molina Guzmán, I. (2005). "Gendering Latinidad through the Elian news discourse about Cuban women," *Latino Studies, 1,* 1–26.

Molina Guzmán, I. (2006). Covering ethnic conflicts: Tracing the discourses of race, ethnicity and difference in the local press. *Journalism: Theory, Practice, Criticism, 7,* 262–280.

Molina Guzmán, I. (2007). Disorderly bodies and discourses of latinidad in the Elián González story. In M. Mendible (Ed.) *Bananas to buttocks: The Latina body in popular film and culture* (pp. 221–243). Austin: University of Texas Press, 221–243.

Ono, K. & J. M. Sloop. (2002). *Shifting borders: Rhetoric, immigration, and California's proposition, 187.* Philadelphia, PA: Temple University Press.

Pedraza-Bailey, S. (1985). Cuba's exile: Portrait of a refugee migration. *International Migration Review, 19,* 4–34.

Pérez-Firmat, G. (1994). *Life on the hyphen: The Cuban-American way.* Austin, TX: University of Texas Press.

Portes, A. & A. Stepick. (1985). Unwelcome immigrants: The labor market experience of 1980 (Mariel) Cuban and Haitian refugees in South Florida. *American Sociological Review, 50,* 493–514.

Rakow, L. & K. Kranich. (1991). Woman as sign. *Journal of Communication, 41,* 8–23.

Reeves, J. 1998. Re-covering racism: Crack mothers, Reaganism and the network news. In S. Torres (Ed.), *Living color: Race and television in the United States* (pp. 97–117). Durham, NC: Duke University Press.

Rodríguez, C. (Ed.). (1997). *Latin looks: Images of Latinas and Latinos in the US media.* Boulder, CO: Westview.

Ruiz, M. (2002). Border narratives, HIV/AIDS, and Latina/o health in the United States: A cultural analysis. *Feminist Media Studies, 2,* 81–96.

Rumbaut, R. (1994). Origins and destinies: Immigration to the United States since World War II. *Sociological Forum, 9,* 583–617.

Santa Ana, O. (2002). *Brown tide rising: Metaphors of Latinos in contemporary American public discourse.* Austin, TX: University of Texas Press.

Schudson, M. (2001). The objectivity norm in American journalism. *Journalism: Theory, Practice and Criticism, 2*(2), 149–170.

Soruco, G. (1996). *Cubans and the mass media in South Florida.* Gainsville: University Press of Florida.

Stack, J. F. & C. L. Warren. (1990). Ethnicity and the politics of symbolism in Miami's Cuban Community. *Cuban Studies, 20,* 11–28.

Stepick, A., G. Grenier, M. Castro, & M. Dunn. (2003). *This land is our land: Immigrants and power in Miami.* Berkeley: University of California Press.

Subervi-Vélez, F. (1999). The mass media and latinos: Policy and research agendas for the next century. *Aztlan, 24*(2), 131–147.

Subervi-Vélez, F. (2005). Network brownout 2004: The portrayal of Latinos in network television news, 1999. Report prepared for the National Association of Hispanic Journalists, Washington, DC.

Tapia, R. (2001). Un(di)ing legacies: White matters of memory in portraits of our princess cultural values. *Cultural Values, 5*(2), 261–287.

Thorburn, D. (1988). Television as an aesthetic medium. In J. Carey (Ed.), *Media, myths and narratives: Television and the press* (pp. 48–66). Newbury Park, NJ: Sage.

Torres, M. (1998). Encuentros y encontronazos: Homeland in the politics and identity of the Cuban diaspora. In A. Darder & R. D. Torres (Eds.), *The Latino studies reader: Culture, economy & society* (pp. 43–62). London: Blackwell.

Torres, M. (2002). *In the Land of Mirrors: Cuban Exile Politics in the United States*. Ann Arbor: University of Michigan Press.

Torres, S. (1998a). Introduction. In S. Torres (Ed.), *Living color: Race and television in the United States* (pp. 1–11). Durham, NC: Duke University Press.

Torres, S. (1998b). King TV. In S. Torres (Ed.), *Living color: Race and television in the United States* (pp. 140–160). Durham, NC: Duke University Press.

Tuchman, G. (1972). Objectivity as strategic ritual: An examination of newsmen's notions of objectivity. *American Journal of Sociology, 77,* 660–679.

U.S. Census Bureau. (2000). Census 2000 redistricting data. Retrieved June 15, 2001, from http://www.uscensus.gov.

Van Dijk, T. (1998). *News as discourse.* Hillsdale, NJ: Lawrence Erlbraum.

Vargas, L. (2000). Genderizing Latino news: An analysis of a local newspaper's coverage of Latino current affairs. *Critical Studies in Media Communication, 17*(3), 261–293.

Zelizer, B. (1990). Achieving journalistic authority through narrative. *Critical Studies in Mass Communication, 7,* 336–376.

Zelizer, B. (2004). When facts, truth and reality are god-terms: On journalism's uneasy place in cultural studies. *Communication and Critical/Cultural Studies, 1,* 109–119.

CHAPTER SEVEN

Real Women AND Their Curves: Letters TO THE Editor AND A Magazine's Celebration OF THE "Latina Body"

KATYNKA Z. MARTÍNEZ

Latina magazine, a bilingual Spanish/English women's magazine targeting acculturated college-educated Latinas between the ages of 18 and 45, celebrated its 10-year anniversary in October of 2006 by featuring Jennifer Lopez on its cover. Lopez had graced the cover of the magazine's premiere issue in 1996—predating the successful Selena biopic, the green Versace dress, and the three-letter moniker "J. Lo." In short, before Lopez became the highest paid Latina performer in Hollywood. Over the years Lopez has been featured on the cover of the magazine eight times, the most for any celebrity. Lopez's rise to stardom and subsequent notoriety has been tracked not only by *Latina* magazine but also by the mainstream U.S. popular press. Latina/o Studies scholars have also addressed the ways in which Lopez has been marked as a racialized, excessive, and classed subject and how her body has both challenged and conformed to hegemonic notions of beauty (see Aparicio, 2003; Beltrán, 2002; Negrón-Muntaner, 2004; R.Z. Rivera, 2003). This chapter enters this conversation by taking Lopez's song "I'm real" as a provocative starting point. The remix of this song featuring Ja Rule suggests a certain authenticity. Lopez claims to be "real" and the rapper responds to this assertion by referring to "the way you talk […] the way you look, your style, your hair" (Lewis et al., 2002). This song may be read as Lopez's attempt to move away from her diva image and a response to people who are "lovin' me and hatin' me, treatin' me ungratefully." The song's lyrics and the accompanying video, in which she has her hair pulled back in a ponytail (with baby hair visible around the edge of her forehead) and dances on a basketball court while wearing a velour tracksuit, can also be viewed as an attempt to position Lopez as similar to the everyday Latina.

Taking a cue from Aparicio who encourages critics to look "at sites where Latinidad is constituted," this chapter focuses on how *Latina* magazine reasserts Lopez's Latinidad by presenting her as "real" (Aparicio, 2003, p. 90) in relation to the voices and curves of "real women" in its letters to the editor and fashion spreads. By doing so I explore the tensions between commodified stardom and quotidian Latina experiences in the construction of Latina femininity as it is showcased on the pages of the magazine. The letters to the editor and the magazine's articles on the Latina body constantly engage in a type of direct address that presents both "real women" and presupposes a connection among Latinas. An imagined community of Latinas is originally created through the letters to the editor and furthered by the editorial decision to use "real *mujeres*," as opposed to models, in fashion spreads. Letters are often written in response to Latinas' outsider status in relation to mainstream media outlets. Other times the readers and *Latina* editorial staff attempt to establish a connection based on a common struggle within Anglo-dominated towns or professions. And at other times the connection is solely based on a celebration of curvaceous bodies—a celebration that began with Jennifer Lopez's Latina star body and was pushed along by the success of the film, *Real Women Have Curves*. Central to these discussions and the entire orientation of the magazine is a celebration of curves and the construction of Lopez as the touchstone for Latina identity insofar as entertainment industry role models and conventionally curvaceous Latinas are concerned. Together these tensions document the difficult line between agency and structure that "real Latinas," Jennifer Lopez, and the magazine editors must walk in creating and sustaining a Latina space of identity.

"OUR ORIGINAL COVER GIRL"

The October 2006 issue of *Latina* refers to Jennifer Lopez as "Our original cover girl." It is an understatement to say that Jennifer Lopez's career has taken off since the Nuyorican actress/singer/entertainer first appeared on the cover of *Latina* magazine in 1996. For example, film representations of Lopez have included a Native American (*U Turn*, 1997), an Italian American (*The Wedding Planner*, 2001), a Mexican (*Mi Familia*, 1995), an ethnically ambiguous working-class woman (*Enough*, 2002), an ethnically ambiguous professional psychiatrist (*The Cell*, 2000), and an ant named Azteca (*Antz*, 1998). Lopez has played characters with such ethnically diverse names as Grace Santiago (*Money Train*, 1995), Grace McKenna (*U Turn*, 1997), Miss Marquez (*Jack*, 1996), Terri Flores (*Anaconda*, 1997), Karen Sisco (*Out of Sight*, 1998), Catherine Deane (*The Cell*), Sharon Pogue (*Angel Eyes*, 2001), Mary Fiore (*The Wedding Planner*, 2001), and Marisa Ventura (*Maid in Manhattan*, 2002). This range of characters and ethnicities is impressive in light of the fact that Latina/o actors are usually relegated to playing a generic "Hispanic" character of low economic status with limited plot functions (Ramirez-Berg, 2002; Rodriguez, 1998).

Latino stardom within a U.S. context has largely been a function of the extent to which a Latino celebrity can embody the ideals of whiteness while simultaneously leaving her/himself subject to the white gaze (Beltrán, 2002). This said, Lopez's vulnerability to the white gaze and self-tropicalization has been predicated on what Negrón-Muntaner (2004) refers to as her "big Latin butt" that serves as "an open air invitation to pleasures construed as illicit by WASP ideologies, heteronormativity, and the medical establishment through the three deadly vectors of miscegenation, sodomy, and a high-fat diet" (p. 237). Although Lopez refutes claims that she partakes in a high-fat diet and is mum on the subject of sodomy, she has pointed to miscegenation by saying, "I guess I'm a little hippy. Latinas and black women have a certain body type. We're curvy" (Beltrán, 2002, p. 84). Lopez's public persona revels in challenging WASP ideologies by emphasizing her corporal commonalities with black women. Still many women, curvy and not, cannot help but question the extent to which she has truly challenged Eurocentric standards of beauty. Positioning Lopez within the context of color-caste hierarchies of hip-hop music, Raquel Z. Rivera (2003) questions what it means that a "very light-skinned, straight-haired—white, by Lain American standards—woman is the icon celebrated for her so-called black ass" (p. 133). Lopez, with her light skin, straight hair, and big butt is just ethnic enough to "meet Hollywood's desire for the commodified exotic other" (Molina Guzmán & Valdivia, 2004, p. 215). Her film repertoire has clearly benefited from this but early on many Mexican Americans were less than willing to accept her performance as the commodified Tejana other when she was cast for the lead role in the biopic, *Selena* (1997). Open casting calls for the roles of a preteen and adult Selena were held in Los Angeles, Miami, Chicago, and San Antonio, and thousands of girls came out for the chance to portray the singer. After cross-country auditions, the roles for the biopic went to Becky Lee Meza, a 10-year-old Mexican American from Harlingen, Texas with no professional acting experience, and Jennifer Lopez, a Puerto Rican actress from the Bronx. Press accounts during the filming of Selena made reference to the uncanny similarities between the two women's bodies. While Selena's seamstress was elated to learn that the Tejana's original gowns would fit Lopez, Latina feminists such as Aparicio (2003) emphasized that "both bodies were public enactments and physical embodiments of simultaneous colonial desire and subaltern resistance" (p. 99). Regardless of any of these similarities, initial reaction to the casting news was mixed. Many fans were proud to see their favorite singer's life story come closer to the big screen. Others, many of whom auditioned for the film with hopes that a role would launch their own career, admitted to feelings of betrayal and began to view the "open" casting call as a publicity stunt. Many were critical of what they feared to be an inauthentic representation of the Tejana. For example, the Brown Berets and the Chicano Cultural Coalition voiced organized opposition against Lopez playing the role of Selena because she is Puerto Rican (KFWB, 1996; KNBC, 1996). Such groups failed to recognize that Selena herself had collaborated with Nuyoricans. Her duet and touring plans with the hip-hop group the Barrio Boyz are just two examples of how she actively engaged in the process of translocating Tejano music (Vargas, 2002). The controversy surrounding the casting for *Selena* seems like ancient history and is rarely addressed in contemporary celebrations of the "Latin explosion" as it relates to music, film, and other sites of popular culture. For example, the second *Latina* issue featuring Lopez coincided with the release of the film *Selena* yet does not mention the casting controversy. Nonetheless, many corporate enterprises found a way to capitalize on the tragedy. The paperback biography *Selena!* was published two months after the singer's death. The book came in a unique bilingual format that allowed readers to read the book in English or flip it over and upside down to read the Spanish-language translation. The book reached the number one spot on the *New York Times* best-seller list for nonfiction paperbacks on May 21, 1995 (Tabor, 1995). *People* magazine found similar success with their Selena tribute issue. Two million copies of this magazine were sold, making it the best-selling tribute issue the magazine had ever published and generating the creation of *People en Español* (Jones, 1995).

LATINA AND THE BURDEN OF REPRESENTATION

In 1995 a young Latina Stanford law graduate, Christy Haubegger, used government and marketing surveys, consumer analysis, and census statistics to put together a business plan for the creation of *Latina* magazine. Her research revealed that most Spanish-language literature was produced outside of the United States and had very little to do with the lives of Latinas raised or born in the United States. Haubegger argued that this pointed to the need for a bilingual magazine produced by Latinas and for Latinas. She set out to do just this but found she had to fight an uphill battle to convince potential funders of the existence of a bilingual, middle-class audience of Latinas. Haubegger's project was eventually funded in 1996 through a joint venture between her own company, Alegre Enterprises, and another minority media company, Essence Communications. *Latina* magazine was created during a historical moment in which mass media had shifted from mass audience marketing to audience segmentation. Thus, the magazine's successful trajectory became a function of both late-twentieth-century audience segmentation and the recognition of the sheer size and purchasing power of the "Hispanic market." By presenting their audience as slightly different than the consumers of other mainstream women's magazines, the creators of *Latina* reinforced the idea of difference that lies at the backbone of audience segmentation (Barnes & Thomson, 1994; Maisel, 1973; Turow, 1997).

The original staff working on *Latina* magazine in 1996 was very small yet drew on members of their family to assist in promoting the magazine. Lilliam Rivera (2003), one of the original *Latina* staff members, recalls the first year *Latina* participated in the New York Puerto Rican parade and remembers the endeavor being very grassroots oriented. Former *Latina* editor, Sylvia Martínez also invokes the dedication of the magazine's staff, suggesting that the personal investment that writers have in *Latina* sets the magazine apart from other publications:

> I think our main emphasis is that we talk to the Latina about the space that we occupy both as Americans and having, in some cases, even if you're born here, having some roots or ties to whatever your Latin American country may be. And how we kind of occupy that unique space in this country. [And] that's great, that's okay, that's who we are and we wouldn't change it for anything. We can eat apple pie and *flan*, or hamburgers and *arroz con pollo* or whatever ... and I think there's a certain pride inherent that comes with that and that's kind of what we appeal to. And I think Latinas come to us for that cultural fix. Because you can get the stories in other mainstream publications but you don't have something that speaks to you directly about *familia* and whatever the subject may be that's unique to Latinos. And you know, the whole issue of moving away from home and being independent—à la *Real Women Have Curves* storyline. This is a place where so many of the people who work here have been in that situation and we know it, we understand it, and we write about it. (S. Martínez, personal communication, April 23, 2003)

In the above quote, Martínez invokes what has almost become a clichéd way of speaking of cultural diversity and multiculturalism. Food metaphors are often used to describe bicultural identities and to speak of the United States as a melting pot. However, Martínez also relates the bicultural experience of Latinas to the recent film written and directed by Latinas, *Real Women Have Curves* (2003), based on a play that was written by Josefina Lopez when the young Chicana playwright was in her teens. The screen adaptation of Lopez's play presents the story of Ana, a working-class Chicana and recent high school graduate, who challenges her mother's traditional perspectives on gender, body, and sexuality. By referring to the film, Martínez situates *Latina* magazine within a realm of cultural productions that speak to and are informed by the experiences of bicultural Latinas living in the United States. *Latina* was launched in June 1996 with 100 pages of content and an initial press run of 175,000. The magazine was originally distributed in thirty-five U.S. cities that were identified as holding 95 percent of the Hispanic population (Beam, 1996; Gremillion, 1996). The magazine increased its distribution frequency from quarterly to monthly in July 1997, six months ahead of schedule (Calvacca, 1999). In November of 2000 Solera Capital, an all women private equity partnership, made a $20 million investment in Latina Publications. Latina Publications was renamed Latina Media Ventures (LLC) to reflect a new orientation toward creating an integrated media brand. *Latina*'s monthly circulation in 2001 was 225,000. In addition, it is believed that the magazine's high pass-along rate of four readers caused the monthly readership to reach nearly 1,000,000 during this year (Latina Media Ventures, 2001). By 2005 Latina was the second highest ranked Hispanic magazine with an estimated ad revenue of $15,328,272 ("Publishing in the Hispanic Market," 2005). Haubegger explains that the magazine's readers are "living between two cultures" and adds that, because of this, they seek out things like *Latina* magazine and "low-fat enchiladas" (Coleman, 1996, p. 71). The majority of the women in Latina's target audience are believed to be bilingual and employed full time. The household income of 46 percent of readers is over $50,000, 38 percent of readers have a household income of $75,000, and the median household income is $46,262 (I Am Latina, 2007; Reach, 2007).

Initially convincing advertisers of the existence of Latinas earning over $50,000 during the mid-1990s was a difficult task Haubegger tackled in creative ways (Martínez, 2004). Recently Latina Media Ventures has collaborated with the Jones Apparel group in 2005 to market a Sears apparel line called Latina Life (Rozhon, 2005) and has also established a presence online. During the five months following the relaunch of the *Latina* website in March 2006, 75,000 visitors signed up to receive the magazine's online newsletter (Wentz, 2006). Despite these current marketing successes, Haubegger sought to present marketers with an image of Latinas as consumers of high-end products that are sold in major department stores. Haubegger reflected on her early efforts to promote the magazine and said, "I've had great information on buying power for years. But when people close their eyes and picture Hispanic women, they picture someone who cleans their office at night. We don't get to do a sales job in this market, we do an education job" (Weissman, 1999, p. 39). Haubegger's comment points to the burden of representation that rests on the shoulders of people of color who attempt to present their communities as cultural consumers. The fact that magazines for women of color have to contend with this burden of representation since the earliest stages of the promotion of their publication has resulted in final products that are quite different than most mainstream white women's magazines. This is something that is addressed in readers' letters to the editor.

"AS THE DAUGHTER OF DOMINICAN IMMIGRANTS ..."

Business periodicals have credited an individualistic drive and ambition for the success of *Latina*. While most case studies of *Latina* focus on the Haubegger success story, she redirects attention to the *Latina* audience, often invoking a feeling of familial identification and support when describing the relationship between the magazine and its audience. "Some [readers] live with their mothers who don't speak English, others have kids who don't speak Spanish. These readers are caught between the two worlds," says Haubegger. "They're trying to navigate those worlds, and every now and then they'd love to have some kind of road map that says we're here to support you, to affirm you" (Quintanilla, 1997, p. E1).

Benedict Anderson (1983), writing about the nation as a symbolic economy, argues for the universality of nationhood in so far as it is a function of the nation's promise of recognition and feelings of belonging. I draw from Anderson's conception of the nation not because *Latina* or Haubegger make a claim for nationalism but because the magazine constantly references an imagined community of Latina readers and promises to provide this community with the recognition they do not receive in mainstream media and the world at large. This is done by referring both to a Latina's country of origin and to her natural connection to other Latinas regardless of their subethnic background.

The letters to the editor section of the magazine provides examples of readers creating an imagined community of panethnic Latinas in two seemingly contradictory manners. On the one hand, they begin letters by drawing attention to their national heritage. However, the writers then go on to support the panethnic identity-building project of the magazine by suggesting that commonalities exist among all Latinas regardless of their national heritage. By doing so the writers create an "interlatino knowledge" that "itself represents an alternative discourse given the silenced knowledge about each other that has been our educational legacy" (Aparicio, 2003, p. 94).[1]

According to Anderson, two key characteristics of nationhood set the nation apart from the more universal nature of religion. First, the nation is always particular. Belonging to a nation means that you belong to a specific territory and that this nation is linguistically specific.[2] Second, the nation demands reciprocal recognition among citizens and among nations. The vernacular language used in creole newspapers was the main factor that facilitated nationalism because it connected all creoles to the metropole. Anderson stresses that it was not a particular language that built nationalism. Rather, it was the vernacular print language that generated imagined communities and built solidarities that were not dependent on and did not privilege old sacred languages. Newspapers allowed communities to emerge not as a function of blood or kinship but as a function of imagined proximity. Thus, "the newspaper reader, observing exact replicas of his own paper being consumed by his subway, barbershop, or residential neighbors, is continually reassured that the imagined world is visibly rooted in everyday life" (Anderson, 1983, pp. 35–36).

Although the *Latina* reader may not observe her neighbors reading the magazine, the letters to the editor section of the magazine serve to reassure her that other Latinas are indeed reading the magazine. According to research on the letters-to-the-editor column, most editors believe that the journalistic culture that organizes these letters has created a well-established forum for public debate and community formation. A 1990 survey of all daily U.S. newspapers with a circulation of over 100,000 found that the majority of the editorial page editors believe that letters to the editor "help readers feel represented at the newspaper" and also serve to "identify public concerns and issues" (Hynds, 1991, p. 127). The editors responding to this survey were confident that their readers enjoy the letters section. More than three-fourths of the respondents said that the letters column ranked either first or second in readership on the editorial pages.

Unfortunately, little research has been done on the letters to the editor of women's magazines. Most studies that address letter writing in women's magazines focus on the advice pages. In her empirical study of the readers of *Jackie* and *Just Seventeen*, Angela McRobbie (1991) argues that the advice page connects women to each other by informing them that they are experiencing the same set of problems.[3] Both the advice pages and the letters to the editor introduce readers to an imagined community of women that share similar experiences. However, the *Latina* letters to the editor engage in the celebration of *Latinidad* rather than the consoling of broken hearts that is carried out elsewhere in the magazine in a column entitled "Dolores Dice/Dolores Says." The letters to the editor reveal that identity construction via *Latina* magazine is more complex than the loss, pain, or suffering found on the advice page.

Four prominent themes can be identified within *Latina*'s letters to the editor. First, many readers identify their country of origin. Second, letters to the editor are written in a vernacular language that is informed by readers' exposure to both Spanish and English. Third, readers do not simply reference an imagined community but an imagined *family*. Fourth, some readers challenge the cultural-political type of panethnic Latino identity that is constructed in the magazine.

The constant identification of the reader's country of origin was the most reoccurring feature of the letters during the first three years of the magazine.

For example: "I am a 25 year-old Latina born of Mexican and Bolivian parents" (Alvarez, 1996, p. 8); "As the daughter of Dominican immigrants …" (Ramirez, 1997, p. 12); "I'm a Guatemalan living in South Central Los Angeles" (Miranda, 1998, p. 10); "My side of the family is originally from El Salvador" (Vásquez, 1999, p. 12).

Readers' specificity when referring to their Latin American heritage was less common by 2001 when women began engaging in a system of self-identification that relied on the term "Latina." For example: "I am a 19-year-old Latina virgin" (Joseph-Perez, 2001, p. 30); "As a Latina professional, I find your magazine thoroughly fulfilling" (Cordero, 2002/2003, p. 30). The timing of this shift in the readers' practices of self-identification coincides with the publication of Achy Obejas' argument (2001) that nationalism had become an obsolete idea for U.S. Latinos. By June 2004, *Latina* published the results of their website poll in which 60 percent of respondents preferred the identifier "Latina" or "Hispanic" over more specific terms such as "Chicana," "Colombian-American," and "Dominican" (*Latina*, 2004b, p. 26). Ironically, the Latinas who wrote letters to the editor in this issue of the magazine all referenced their country of origin.

Regardless of how a reader chooses to self-identify in a letter to the editor, she will usually use vernacular language that draws from both Spanish and English. Instances of code-switching include "I feel it is important not to forget our roots and our *costumbres*" (Ramirez, 1996, p. 8); "I eagerly await the next issue to discuss its articles with *mis amigas y hermanas*" (Bowles, 2001, p. 30); "We need more Latinas like *la maestra* Sonia Marie De León de Vega" (Franco, 2005, p. 28). The Spanish used in letters is also often indicative of a regional specificity. For example, a reader used both the English language and a Spanish term for "cool" within one sentence: "I sometimes buy the editors' pick in *Notas de Belleza*; so far all the products I've tried are really *chévere*" (Rivera, 1997, p. 14). Another reader exclaims, "*Que buena onda!* My sister and I love *Latina*" (Calderon & Calderon, 1997, p. 12). Though both readers use regional speech phrases, it is safe to assume that they will understand each other's enthusiasm for the magazine. *Latina's* conscious use of multiple regional dialects of the Spanish language within English articles ensures that readers gain an exposure to types of Spanish that are not limited to their country of origin.

A 2003 *Latina* article focusing on the diversity of regional dialects within the Spanish language entitled "Cross-cultural Love," recognizes that miscommunication often occurs among Latinos who speak the same language. The article presents humorous examples of a Cuban American who asks a non-Cuban Latino, "*¿Donde se coge la guagua para ir al* downtown?" The Cuban American author explains that this question is met with laughter when spoken in the company of Latinos who don't use the word "*guagua*" to mean "bus" but do use the verb "*coger*" to refer to the act of having sex. Through this lighthearted example the article points to additional differences among Latinos that are more deeply ideological than word choice. The author states, "Now, I realize that politics, love, and culture are all separate matters, but consider this: Politics are why many of us are here in the first place. Our grandparents and parents came to this country seeking better lives. The bottom line: Politics, to many Latinos, are deeply personal" (Cavallo, 2003, p. 100). He continues to explain why, after only four weeks of dating, his relationship with a Peruvian came to an abrupt end. The couple's numerous debates regarding U.S. foreign policy toward Cuba had taken a toll on the relationship.

The fact that *Latina* touches on inter-Latino miscommunications and ideological diversity suggests that the magazine is offering a more nuanced view of cultural diversity than what is usually referred to in most contemporary discourses of multiculturalism. In this sense, *Latina's* approach to creating a panethnic experience for their audience is quite different than the strategy employed on the Univision newscast organized around a commitment to use a version of the Spanish language that does not include country-specific accents or diction. This nationality neutral version of Spanish is commonly referred to as "Walter Cronkite Spanish" (Rodriguez, 1999).

In contrast *Latina* articles and letters to the editor use English, multiple regional Spanishes and Spanglish. In her article, "Tongues-twisting," *Latina* senior contributing editor Dolores Prida (2003) directly addresses the reader by saying, "Spanglish, Slanglish, Ingleñol—whatever you call it, we talk the talk *y somos lo que hablamos*. It's fun *y*, *además*, very *creativo*" (p. 60). The article includes a list of Spanglish words and phrases such as "all that and a can of *frijoles*." Prida asks readers to share their own favorite Spanglish phrases by contacting *Latina's* editor via email hoping to assemble "the first edition of the Real Diccionario of the Spanglish Academia" (p. 60). The title of this "dictionary," the idea that such a tome would even exist, and the invocation of the Real Academia, located in Madrid, challenge the privileging of "proper" Spanish and English over the lived forms of Latino expression as an authoritative voice of Spanish.

The illustration accompanying this article also engages in this challenge, presenting a cross-eyed Don Quijote holding a shield with the word "Castellano" printed across it. Near Don Quijote is a windmill with Spanglish words and phrases such as "*Bueno*, bye" and "Eh'cuse me, *pero* no!" printed on its blades. The silliness of the image, with direct reference to the paradigmatic Spanish novel, *Don Quijote de la Mancha*, complements the tongue-in-cheek article that nonetheless asserts a space for hybrid Spanishes.

While some readers criticize the magazine's simultaneous use of Spanish and English, many more readers write their letters to the editor in the two languages and defend such use of the languages. One reader responded to a teacher who sent a letter to the editor insisting on Spanish and English not coexisting in the same article: "... but she must understand that sprinkled Spanish in an English paragraph is what makes us stand out. White magazines don't do this, and black magazines certainly don't. I think the sprinkled Spanish is good. Most of us talk like that, anyway. This is part of what makes us Latinas" (Torres, 1997, p. 10). In her letter, Torres suggests that the mix of the Spanish and English languages sets *Latina* apart from other magazines and also brings *Latina* readers together. Another reader draws attention to the fact that not all Latinos had the opportunity to be raised in environments that valued bilingualism or fluency in Spanish: "My parents, for example, spoke Spanish at home but encouraged my sisters and me to speak English" (Huizar, 1999, p. 10).

The above letters suggest that *Latina* readers have identified a Latino continuum of the Spanish language. Although only short phrases or single Spanish words are included within letters to the editor that are written predominantly in English, these words and phrases are presented as normal and matter of fact. The *Latina* readers quoted above engage in a written form of code-switching that is usually only studied in spoken form. The print form of Spanish/English code-switching reflects the fact that Latinos' complex social and linguistic relations affect not only speech patterns but forms of written communication as well as a sense of identity.

The letters submitted by *Latina's* readers emphasize that juggling two languages and cultures is "what makes us Latinas." The fact that the letters to the editor are written in the same manner as the authors speak suggests that the women are including *Latina* in their community and honoring the social and communicative norms of that community. In this sense, the practice of sprinkling Spanish in an otherwise English-language text is very different than what Dávila (2000) encountered in her study of Telemundo's programming for English-dominant Latinos whose bilingualism had a tendency to feature English "only in the form of Spanglish, which is selectively used as a 'condiment,' and mostly limited to comedy shows" (p. 87). Instead, *Latina* readers' use of Spanish emphasizes the fact that their manners of expressing themselves may be English-language dominant but their experiences are bicultural.[4] In addition, the fact that the magazine prints readers' diverse regional Spanishes suggests that the coexistence of multiple dialects within a "bilingual" magazine may be pointing toward a merging of Latino identities.[5]

The imagined community created by readers is not solely based on their use of a vernacular language that welcomes both English and Spanish but also created through visions of family and home. For example, a woman writes, "... the articles were like a warm security blanket I had lost along the career ladder. There are so many ideals, values, and traditions inherent in our culture that get shunted in the professional world. *Latina* brought me home again" (Del Rio, 1997, p. 10). Another woman writes, "I am a 26-year-old mother of three, living in a very small rural town in the Midwest. Several months ago I spotted *Latina* at a local store—you can't imagine my amazement, being the only Mexican American in town. This magazine brings me a little closer to home" (Wells, 1998, p. 10). More recently a woman writes, "I am stationed in Baghdad [...] I appreciate all that you do; you help me feel a little closer to *mi casa. Gracias!*" (Alba, 2004, p. 18). The testimonials of these three very different women point to the community-building function of *Latina*. Although different experiences have led them away from their geographical "home," all three women feel the magazine has allowed them to reestablish their ties with a new family and a new sense of belonging. This family emerges through print media and can be understood as an imagined Latina community.

"MY HIPS, LIPS, AND HAIR":
THE IMAGINED LATINA COMMUNITY

The December 1998 editor's letter suggests the existence of an imagined Latina community. In her letter, the editor describes a day at the office: "Just for fun, I went around the office asking the staff what makes them Latina. The answers ranged from 'my hips, lips, and hair' to 'my music, my language, my parents' to 'my ability to eat a jalapeño without crying'" (Guzmán, 1998, p. 12). These answers are eerily similar to the markers that make J. Lo "real"—"the way you talk [...] the way you look, your style, your hair." The survey is insightful for how *Latina* envisions their imagined Latina community and connects to Padilla's study (1985) of Latino politics in Chicago. Focusing on the ways in which Mexican American and Puerto Rican community organizations created opportunities for panethnic Latino identity formation, Padilla made important distinctions between two types of Latino group identities. The cultural-political type of Latino identity references the Spanish language and Catholic religion as the bonds that bring and hold Latinos together through a strategy of bringing Latinos into the national and local political scene by introducing them as a linguistic group. In contrast, the sociopolitical type of Latino group identity applies only to those Latinos who actively participate in antiracist projects and pursue the elimination of labor exploitation. *Latina*'s reference to jalapeños, music, and hips foregrounds a cultural-political type of Latino identity.

Readers, with their multiple experiences of home, language, and community, often challenge *Latina*'s promotion of a cultural-political type of panethnic

Latino identity based on factors such as spicy food and bright lipstick. A Central American woman reminds *Latina* of the differences among Latino cultures, "Sé que nuestras culturas son muy similares, pero también tienen diferencias. Asimismo, como revista que representa a las latinoamericanas, sería magnifico que publicaran datos sobre la inmigración" (Parker, 1998, p. 10).[6] Other readers are more politically forthright. For example, one woman writes:

> Subjects like Daisy Fuentes do me no good. There is more to us than pretty faces and curvy bodies. I think it is a shame that we are so rarely exposed to the true heroes of our Latino past. Let's focus instead on people who have really contributed to *la raza*—people like Pedro Albizu Campos, the Puerto Rican revolutionary of the 1930s; Dr. Ramón Emeterio Betances, a key figure in the Grito de Lares uprising of 1868; or Lolita Lebrón, who brought attention to the cries of Puerto Rico during the 1950s. (Gonzalez, 1999, p. 16)

While the above reader strongly asserts that the magazine should pursue more political matters than Latina celebrities, other readers wholeheartedly thank the editor for *Latina*'s articles on "curvy bodies":

> I was really excited to read "My Cuban Body" [November]. I am an 18-year old *boricua* whose *curvas* have been developed since the age of 15. I have a 24-inch waist with a 36-inch bust and hips. Until now, I always felt shame and embarrassment about *mi cuerpazo*. Now I realize that my body is who I am, and nothing can change that. Thank you, *Latina*, for inspiring me to be proud of my *boricua* body. (Padilla, 1999, p. 14)

The author of this letter references a *Latina* article written by a woman who straightened her hair, dieted, and wore platform shoes all in an attempt to draw attention away from her short, curvaceous frame and wavy hair. Padilla names her subethnic group but the presentation of her heritage is not aimed at distinguishing herself from other Latinas. Padilla identifies with the author and finds strength in the story's message of embracing one's body regardless of its shape and size. Although Padilla mentions that she is Puerto Rican, she finds no inconsistency in the fact that an article titled "My Cuban Body" enabled her to accept and celebrate her "*boricua* body." Rather, panethnic bonds are created between Cuban and Puerto Rican women based on their similar body image experiences or at least their shared experience of difference in a culture where the normative female body is Anglo-centrically thin and straight.

References to Latin American countries of origin were a standard staple of letters to the editor during the first three years of *Latina*'s existence and one of the key ways in which the imagined Latina community was presented as having roots in the lives, language, and experiences of its readers. However, by 1999 the letters to the editor including references to national heritage were not as frequent as before. For example, the 1999 issue in which Padilla's letter appeared only included one reference to a Latin American home country in the letters to the editor section of the magazine. The 2002 issue that was published exactly three years later did not include any such references among the letters to the editor. As references to countries of origin began to diminish within the letters to the editor section of the magazine, they started to appear more frequently in fashion spreads.

"REAL WOMEN WITH REAL CURVES"

In July 2002, Latina launched a new section of its magazine titled "Latina Fashion: Real *modas* for the real *mujer*"[7] featuring Latinas who, although not models by profession, modeled the latest clothing styles. For the first installment of this section the magazine presented Latinas living in Houston, Texas identified by name, age, and occupation; country of origin was also referenced through text like, "'I'm not that comfortable wearing shorts,' this *cubana* initially said" (Almonte, 2002b, p. 36). By September 2002, all of the women were being identified not only by name, age, and profession but also by country of origin. The women are identified through the following format: "NASHELLY MESSINA Events coordinator for L'Oréal, 26, dominicana" (Almonte, 2002a, p. 55). This information comes before the text that describes the clothes the women are modeling. Immediately following this information are quotes from the women in which they allude to their style preferences and describe their body type. These quotes range from "I'm not afraid to show off my *caderas*" (p. 56) to "I usually shy away from anything fitted" (58). The bodies of the women are always complimented through comments such as "*Mujer*, your *figura* is too nice to hide!" (Almonte, 2002a, p. 58).

The idea of shame and hiding one's nonwaif-like body was a central theme in the Chicana play and film *Real Women Have Curves* released in January 2002. The overwhelming use of the words "curves" or "*curvas*" on the cover of Latina began that same month. Eleven issues of the magazine are printed every year. During 2002, four issues of the magazine made use of the words "curves" or "*curvas*" on the cover. The number for 2003 was six, followed by five in 2004, four in 2005, and six in 2006. The use of these words ranged from articles that offered "Jeans that fit our *real* curves!" and other stories that encouraged women to "Love your *curvas*."

J. Robyn Goodman's (2002) audience study with Latina and Anglo readers of women's magazines found that Latinas enjoy seeing "thicker" women reflected in the pages of *Latina* magazines. This notwithstanding, *Latina* letters to the editor suggest readers are not always placated by the celebration of curves that occurs on the cover of the magazine. In 2003 a reader wrote, "I live in Iowa and reading *Latina* is so refreshing. But I'd appreciate seeing women in your fashion pages who are more 'curvy' (meaning size 16 or larger). I am a size 18 and it is hard to picture some of the outfits on myself. If you don't have any models, let me know. I'll sign up" (Ojeda, 2003, p. 24). Another reader suggested that *Latina*'s editorial and advertising practices coupled with their history of employing thin models revealed a hypocrisy that upholds hegemonic standards of beauty: "While I love *Latina*, there is one thing that concerns me: Your magazine mentions that we should celebrate our curves, yet none of your advertisers, or the models, have as many curves (if any) as your 'average' Latina. It would be nice to see you show us that you mean what you say" (Rivera, 2004, p. 24). The editorial staff responded by directing the reader to the issue's fashion spread: "That's why, every month, we make it a point to invite 'average' Latinas—real women with real curves—to appear in our fashion pages. In this issue, be sure to check out page 57 to see how bold colors can work on any *figura*" (*Latina*, 2004a, p. 26).

In March 2006 *Latina* launched two new sections of the magazine called "For Every Curve" and "Real Mujeres." Although the titles of these sections of the magazine appear to be clear references to *Real Women Have Curves*, the magazine's actual engagement with the themes of the film and play seem to be missing. María P. Figueroa's (2003) detailed analysis of the play, *Real Women Have Curves*, illustrates the ways in which the characters in Josefina Lopez's play engage in a discussion of "fatness" that enables a resistance to hegemonic values surrounding women's bodies. Moreover, she draws attention to the fact that in the introductory notes of the play, the characters are described in the following terms: "The sisters, Ana and Estela are both 'plump'; Doña Carmen, their mother, is short and fat; while Pancha is 'huge' and Rosali is only a 'bit plump'" (p. 274). Though "real mujeres" that are "a bit plump" and "plump" have occasionally served as models within the pages of *Latina*, the readers receive a mixed message when they see articles encouraging them to change their eating habits.

Malkin, Wornian, and Chrisler (1999) reviewed the covers of women's magazines to see how often they included the following themes: (1) a diet message; (2) an exercise message; (3) a message regarding cosmetic surgery to change the size of the body; and (4) a general message about weight loss with no specifications about how to lose the weight. Of the twelve magazines most frequently read by women, fifty-four of the sixty-nine covers (78 percent) contained some message about bodily appearance. *Latina* does not engage in such continuous discussions of weight loss but it does often print articles on how women can eat healthier Latino dishes.

Some articles are a bit sensationalistic with titles like "Comida Latina: Can It Kill You?" (September 2003). However, the magazine has also taken a more instructive tone by including recipes for low-fat versions of traditional Latino meals: "Caribbean Cuisine Goes Low-Fat" (April 1999), "Our Comfort Comidas—Minus the Fat!" (October 2001), and "Low-Fat Faves: If You Think All Latin Food Is Loaded with Calories, Dip Again" (April 2002). A common approach used in *Latina*'s articles on food is to include the names of specific Latino dishes within the titles of the articles. For example, "Can you Eat Flan *and* Lose Weight?" (March 2003), "Eat Frijoles, Skip Aerobics—And Lose Weight!" (July 2003), and "Latin Food Made Healthy (Enchiladas Included!)" (April 2004). These articles speak to the importance of food as a component of identity.

> The article, "The Lowdown on Latin Food" begins with a direct address to the reader: Close your eyes and imagine life without sweet plantains, tasty tamales, and cheesy *buñuelos*. Impossible, huh? And yet with nearly two out of every three Latinas overweight or obese, it's time to find a way to satisfy those cravings for our *comida tan rica* without packing on the pounds. That's why we compiled this guide to traditional favorites from each Latin American region, which not only highlights the foods that are okay to indulge in, but also those you need to look at more closely. (Condo, 2004, p. 94)

The article includes a section on the food of Cuba, Puerto Rico, and the Dominican Republic, another on Mexico, and a third on South American cuisine. This approach to food and identity emphasizes the magazine's commitment to maintaining a cultural-political type of Latino identity without flattening difference across the Latina diaspora. The article suggests that a high-fat diet can be found in all areas of Latin America but that Latinas can still celebrate in the fact that their traditional dishes also include such foods as red snapper and *nopales*, which Western medical associations have stamped with their seal of approval. The magazine's scientific discussions of *buñuelos* and *nopales* serve to medicalize the reader's bodily pleasure of consuming such prototypical Latina foods. This technology of the self is one that uses medicine to "propose, in the form of a regime, a voluntary and rational structure of conduct" (Foucault, 1990, p. 100). By bringing together Latino origin foods and Western discourses of nutrition *Latina* magazine serves to create a hybrid food and simultaneously assures Latinas that their eating habits are not that irrational after all. This type of hybridity is essential to the orientation of the magazine, which celebrates a type of Latina femininity that does not go outside the bounds of appropriate curves. These bounds exclude a geopolitical critique that would question why these diets do not result in obesity in the countries of origin. The reader is encouraged to stay true to her roots by cooking traditional dishes but she is also instructed to alter the ingredients in order to be a "real woman" with conventionally Latina curves. Furthermore, the reader is not encouraged to explore historical and cultural components of nutritional regimes.

MAKING J. LO "REAL"

Though *Latina* magazine modifies traditional Latino recipes to create low-fat dishes, the meals in the play *Real Women Have Curves* are served in all their caloric glory. The garment workers' day begins with them sharing *pan dulce* and continues with the women ordering tacos and a *burrito de chicharron* purchased from the *lonchera* parked outside their tiny sewing factory. These women do not share *mole* and *pan dulce* with each other in an effort to emphasize their *Latinidad*. Rather, the food is consumed in such a way as to build community and challenge the dominant ideals of thinness (Figueroa, 2003). Attempts have been made to present food in a similar manner in the film *Selena* and in the theatrical musical, *Selena Forever*. Both narrative accounts of Selena's life have included references to her choice to consume greasy fast food without considering its effects on her physique. In the film, Selena eats pizza with her boyfriend and comments that she never diets. The musical re-creates this same story with a song titled "Pizza and Coke" (Aparicio, 2003; Paredez, 2002).

Jennifer Lopez's cinematic performance of *Selena* encourages the "real women" viewing the film to believe that her curvaceous frame may also be the result of enjoying pizza, coke, and perhaps *mofongo* as well. However, in interviews Lopez has been quoted as saying, "I think it's so funny that people look at me and say, 'Oh, bigger bodies are okay. I can eat now,' because I watch my diet and exercise an hour and a half every day" (Barrera, 2002, p. 414). Those who have followed the careers of Selena and Jennifer López are faced with the dilemma of knowing that both women have altered their bodies to emulate white notions of beauty: "Selena had liposuction and Jennifer López has significantly transformed her body and her hair since the movie" (Aparicio, 2003, p. 99).

One need not look further than the covers of *Latina* magazine to see Lopez's transformation. Of the eight *Latina* Jennifer Lopez cover stories, only the first two (1996 and 1997) present Lopez with dark brown hair devoid of blonde highlights. The 1999 article showcases a thinner Lopez with a photo that emphasizes her slimmed-down legs. This transformation is not unlike the one that Shakira engaged in upon entering the U.S. mainstream. Writing about the Colombian pop star and Christina Aguilera, Maria Elena Cepeda (2003) wonders whether hair dye and weight loss are tools in the Latina stars' efforts to "mitigate their respective receptions within the US mainstream conscience, in essence manipulating the visual in a way that renders them more 'user friendly' to non-Latinos" (p. 221). Drawing from Bordo's (1993) work on cultural attitudes toward fat and the body, I would add that losing weight is part of these women's effort to assert that they do, in fact, possess those "'managerial' abilities that, according to the dominant ideology, confer upward mobility" whether it be within the realm of a traditional economic class structure or within the realm of the transnational music industry (p. 195).

During the period between the first and fourth publication of *Latina's* cover stories Jennifer Lopez took part in both types of upward mobility and the magazine gleefully tracked the rapid escalation in the popularity of the performer. While the 1996 article that introduced Lopez to *Latina's* readers may not have promised them that she would never pick up a bottle of peroxide or hire a world-renowned personal trainer, it did declare that "This young, talented actress from the Bronx may be destined for stardom but, as she assures [interviewer] Peter Castro, she's still one of us" (Castro, 1996). Presenting Lopez as "one of us" may have become more difficult over the years. Lopez has drawn in $13 million per movie, purchased a $9.5 million mansion, flaunted a pink diamond ring estimated at costing $3.5 million, and made *Fortune* magazine's list of the richest people under 40 (Bartolomeo, 2002; Tyrangiel, 2005). Jennifer Lopez's female fans may not have par-amours that can afford to purchase jewelry in the range of $3.5 million, however these women can engage in other acts of consumption that make them feel like they are taking on part of the star's identity and making it their own. By purchasing clothing similar to that worn by Lopez, fans can recreate the image of femininity that the star projects in films, videos, and in the tabloid press (Stacey, 1994).

Lopez's fashion lines and perfumes have definitely aided in the commodification of her image and over the years *Latina* has encouraged its readers to take on part of the star's identity by stylizing themselves and imitating what Lopez flaunts in videos and on red carpets. In 2002 Lopez's hairstylist and colorist started being featured in a regular beauty advice column. In addition, a recent cover promised: "Jennifer Lopez Answers Your Beauty Questions" (February 2006). *Latina* has also remained committed to presenting Lopez as "one of us" regardless of how extravagant her lifestyle becomes. References to family are one editorial device used to make Lopez more familiar.

The 1996 Jennifer Lopez cover story in the first issue of *Latina* made references to directors, such as Gregory Nava and Francis Ford Coppola, who had worked with Lopez on feature films. The article also included quotes from Lopez's mother on topics ranging from sex and marriage to parenting (Castro, 1996). All but one of the seven Lopez cover stories published since then have included references to the family of the singer/actress. Lopez's sister, Lynda, was invited to write the December 2002/January 2003 cover story. Rather than focus on upcoming career plans, Lynda asks Jennifer about family Christmas traditions, embarrassing holiday moments, and the similarities between the Lopez sisters and their mother (Colón, 2002/2003). The article is laid out like a family scrapbook, accompanied by the requisite full-page glamor photograph of Lopez but also includes five snapshots of a young Jennifer Lopez and her two sisters.

The text accompanying these photos asks, "Isn't It Amazing How All Latino Family Albums Look Alike?" (Colón, 2002/2003, p. 85).

Lopez once again references family—her mother, grandmother, and aunt—in the 2006 *Latina* cover story. However, this time she is confiding in the Puerto Rican author Esmeralda Santiago. Santiago (2006) references Lopez's body at the beginning of the article: "Shoulders back head high, Jennifer Lopez walks like a Latina. Her famous *pompis* swaying unabashedly …" (p. 142). The author then quickly moves on to discussing Lopez's family life, referring to her mother as "Doña Lupe." The six-page article includes an interview with Lopez, a full page listing of her production and retail enterprises, thumbnail images of her *Latina* cover stories (a.k.a. "Jennifer's Hall of Fame"), and a timeline titled "Before There Was J. Lo" that chronicles Lopez's career from 1987 to 1995. This approach to the standard celebrity profile mixes family matters with the logistics of running a media empire.

In her letter to readers, the editorial director of *Latina* magazine explains how she made the decision to present Lopez as the cover girl for the magazine's 10-year anniversary issue: "The interesting thing is that Jennifer grew up as a woman and as an artist in the very same 10 years that we at *Latina* also grew up" (Cortina, 2006, p. 32). The editor lays claim to a strong association between the magazine and Lopez's development as an artist and woman. This type of association is not uncommon within the pages of the magazine—*Latina* promotes a strong celebrity-to-reader association through its celebrity profiles and promotional ads for the magazine (Martínez, 2004). Such approaches serve to position Latina celebrities as women the reader can relate to and learn from rather than unapproachable starlets disconnected from Latina quotidian experiences. Esmeralda Santiago told the *Latina* editorial staff that she hoped her interview with Lopez would show "the side of her that is quintessentially Puerto Rican" (Cortina, 2006, p. 32). She grounds her idea of Puerto Rican-ness in the concepts of being *humilde* and displaying *respeto*. Although both of these concepts are welcome steps away from rooting one's identity in her hips, lips, and hair, they remain vague markers. What is even odder is the manner in which Santiago supports the *Latina* editor's assertion that Lopez "grew up as a woman and as an artist in the very same 10 years that we at *Latina* also grew up." Santiago adds that "Learning Spanish has been part of her process of maturing as a Latina" (p. 148). This bit of information resonates with the magazine's upwardly mobile construction of *Latinidad* wherein English dominant readers, and Lopez, make the decision to learn Spanish for cultural reasons. Yet the magazine's advertisements for MTV3, *Desperate Housewives*, and *Ugly Betty* point to a media landscape that reflects a type of *Latinidad* that is not linguistically determined or rooted in broad concepts like *respeto*.

One can only hope that as *Latina* "grew up" over the past 10 years, the editors were mindful of their readers' feedback. One wonders whether a reader's article on Jennifer Lopez would look a lot different than the one written by Santiago. Perhaps a young Nuyorican would not be as easily enthralled by what Santiago refers to as "inflections of the Bronx and staccato rhythm of the street" (p. 144). There is also the possibility that many Latinas would question Lopez's decision to dramatize the horrific Juarez murders through her upcoming Nuyorican Productions film, *Bordertown*. Such conversations would add texture and politics to *Latina's* 10-year anniversary party. Real women do not only have curves but they have courage. While their courageous ideas may not always be discussed in *Latina*, multiple tensions are present in the pages of the magazine: those between a sociopolitical and a cultural-political type of Latino identity; those between Lopez's efforts to assert a Latina agency versus mainstream culture's and the magazine's efforts to commodify her; those between nation-specific discourses and efforts at panethnic alliances; and those between the normative female body and the "Latina body." These tensions come to light when "rural" Latinas speak in tension with Jennifer Lopez and the magazine. *Latina* may not be the most radical location of gendered identity discourse struggle, but its 10-year history allows us to witness the tensions that *Latinidad*, femininity, and popular culture generate as Latinas assert their/our right to speak out and be represented.

NOTES

1. I am aware of the impossibility of verifying the legitimacy of the letters to the editor. However, I believe that the letters, whatever their origins, are symbolic of a community that is being imagined by both readers and producers of the magazine. Here my approach is informed by Ien Ang's study that draws from viewers' letters regarding *Dallas*. Ang (1982) explains that "We cannot let the letters speak for themselves, but that they should be read 'symptomatically': we must search for what is behind the explicitly written, for the presuppositions and accepted attitudes concealed within them" (p. 11).
2. Either physical or imaginary borders may mark the territory. Aztlan, the name Chicanos use to describe the southwestern states taken from Mexico as a result of the Mexican American War, is an example of an imaginary territory.
3. See also Ferguson, *Forever Feminine* and Currie, *Girl Talk*.
4. A one-year survey of the letters to the editor featured in the January 1999–December 1999 issue of the magazine reveals that of eighty-eight letters, only four were written completely in Spanish. None of the 2005 letters to the editor were written completely in Spanish.
5. The linguists Ana Celia Zentella and Ricardo Otheguy are currently studying the use and nonuse of subject pronouns among Puerto Rican, Dominican, Mexican, Cuban, Ecuadorian, and Colombian communities in New York City. They aim to uncover whether the regional dialects of these communities are merging to create a panethnic form of Spanish or whether the members of national groups maintain their regional dialect to distinguish themselves from others. The results of their

study will provide insight into whether the panethnic bilingualism presented in *Latina* also exists as a lived reality in New York City.
6. "I know that our cultures are very similar, but they also have differences. Likewise, it would be great if you, as a magazine that represents Latin American women, would publish information concerning immigration" (translation is mine).
7. "Latina fashion: Real fashion for the real woman."

REFERENCES

Alba, A. (2004, February). Latinas speak up! *Latina*, p. 18.
Almonte, Y. (2002a, September). Que viva la tradición. *Latina*, pp. 55–58.
Almonte, Y. (2002b, July). Shorts and sweet. *Latina*, pp. 35–38.
Alvarez, R. (1996, Fall). Cartas/letters [Letter to the editor]. *Latina*, p. 8.
Anderson, B. (1983). *Imagined communities*. London: Verso.
Ang, I. (1982). *Watching Dallas: Soap opera and the melodramatic imagination*. London: Methuen.
Aparicio, F. R. (2003). Jennifer as Selena: Rethinking Latinidad in media and popular culture. *Latino Studies*, 1(1), 90–105.
Barnes, B. E. & L. M. Thomson. (1994). Power to the people (meter): Audience measurement technology and media specialization. In J. S. Ettema & D. C. Whitney (Eds.), *Audiencemaking: How the media create the audience* (pp. 75–94). Thousand Oaks: Sage.
Bartolomeo, J. (2002, November 4). Hot! Hot! Hot! *Us Weekly*, pp. 38–43.
Beam, C. (1996, September 1). The Latina link in two languages. *Folio: The Magazine for Magazine Management*, p. 12.
Beltrán, M. C. (2002). The Hollywood Latina body as site of social struggle: Media constructions of stardom and Jennifer Lopez's "cross-over butt." *Quarterly Review of Film and Video*, 19, 71–86.
Bowles, A. (2001, June). Your letters/Tus Cartas [Letter to the editor]. *Latina*, p. 30.
Calderon, S. & B. Calderon. (1997, December). Cartas/letters [Letter to the editor]. *Latina*, p. 12.
Calvacca, L. (1999, April 15). Christy Haubegger. *Folio: The Magazine for Magazine Management*, p. 54.
Castro, P. (1996, Summer). Jennifer Lopez: Hollywood meets the Bronx. *Latina*, pp. 40–44.
Cavallo, J. (2003, May). Cross-cultural love. *Latina*, pp. 98–101.
Cepeda, M. E. (2003). Shakira as the idealized, transnational citizen: A case study of Colombianidad in transition. *Latino Studies*, 1(2), 211–232.
Coleman, S. (1996, June 12). The essence of Latinas. *Boston Globe*, p. 71.
Colón, S. (2002/2003, December/January). The J. Lo. you don't know. *Latina*, pp. 82–85.
Condo, M. (2004, April). The lowdown on Latin food. *Latina*, pp. 94–96.
Cordero, R. (2002/2003, December/January). Your letters/Tus Cartas. *Latina*, p. 30.
Cortina, B. (2006, October). ¡Bienvenidas! *Latina*, p. 32.
Dávila, A. (2000). Mapping Latinidad: Language and culture in the Spanish TV battlefront. *Television and New Media*, 1(1), 75–94.
Del Rio, P. (1997, July). Cartas/letters [Letters to the editor]. *Latina*, p. 10.
Figueroa, M. P. (2003). Resisting "beauty" and real women have curves. In A. Gaspar de Alba (Ed.), *Velvet barrios: Popular culture and Chicana/o sexualities* (pp. 265–282). New York: Palgrave Macmillan.

Foucault, M. (1990). *This history of sexuality: Volume three, the care of the self.* Harmondsworth: Penguin.
Franco, A. (2005, February). Latinas speak up! *Latina*, p. 18.
Gonzalez, M. (1999, August). Cartas/letters [Letter to the editor]. *Latina*, p. 16.
Goodman, J. R. (2002). Flabless is fabulous: How Latina and Anglo women read and incorporate the excessively thin body ideal into everyday experience. *Journalism and Mass Communication Quarterly, 79*(3), 712–727.
Gremillion, J. (1996, June 10). Young, gifted and "Latina." *Mediaweek*, p. 34.
Guzmán, S. (1998, December). Gifts of a culture. *Latina*, p. 12.
Huizar, C. (1999, May). Cartas/letters [Letter to the editor]. *Latina*, p. 10.
Hynds, E. C. (1991). Editorial page editors discuss use of letters. *Newspaper Research Journal 13*(1), 124–136.
Jones, K. (1995, November 20). Some new English-language magazines are aimed at Hispanic readers earning more than $30,000. *New York Times*, p. C9.
Joseph-Perez, J. (2001, June). Your letters/Tus Cartas [Letter to the editor]. *Latina*, p. 30.
KFWB. (1996, June 27). *News 98* [Radio broadcast].
KNBC. (1996, June 27). *Channel 4 news* [Television broadcast].
Latina. (2004a, March 26).
Latina. (2004b, June 26).
Latina Media Ventures, LLC. (2001, January 24). Latina media ventures names Betty Cortina editorial director. *PR Newswire.*
Lewis, L., C. Rooney, J. Lopez, T. Oliver, I. Gotti, J. Atkins, & R. James. (2002). I'm real [Recorded by Jennifer Lopez and Ja Rule]. On *J to tha L-O!* [CD]. New York: Sony.
Maisel, R. (1973). The decline of mass media. *Public Opinion Quarterly, 37*, 159–170.
Malkin, A. R., K. Wornian, & J. C. Chrisler. (1999). Women and weight: Gendered messages on magazine covers. *Sex Roles, 40*(7–8), 647–655.
Martínez, K. Z. (2004). *Latina* magazine and the invocation of a panethnic family: Latino identity as it is informed by celebrities and papis chulos. *The Communication Review, 7*(2), 155–174.
Martínez, S. (2003, April 23). Personal communication.
McRobbie, A. (1991). *Feminism and youth culture: From "Jackie" to "just seventeen."* Basingstoke: Macmillan.
Miranda, C. (1998, February). Cartas/letters [Letters to the editor]. *Latina*, p. 10.
Molina Guzmán, I. & A. N. Valdivia. (2004) Brain, brow, and booty: Latina iconicity in U.S. popular culture. *The Communication Review, 7*(2), 205–221.
Monsivais, P. M. (1996, March 28). Selena search: Thousands vie for role os Tijano star. *Chicago Sun-Times*, p. 31.
Negrón-Muntaner, F. (2004). *Boricua pop: Puerto Ricans and the Latinization of American culture.* New York: New York University Press.
Obejas, A. A. (2001, September 21). Carving out a new American identity: Nationalism is an obsolete idea as Latinos outgrow labels. *Chicago Tribune*, pp. 1, 6.
Ojeda, A. A. (2003, October). Latinas speak up! *Latina*, p. 24.
Padilla, F. M. (1985). *Latino ethnic consciousness: The case of Mexican Americans and Puerto Ricans in Chicago.* Notre Dame: University of Notre Dame Press.
Padilla, L. (1999, January). Cartas/letters [Letter to the editor]. *Latina*, p. 14.
Paredez, D. (2002). Remembering Selena, re-membering Latinidad. *Theatre Journal, 54*, 63–84.
Parker, B. (1998, April). Cartas/letters [Letter to the editor]. *Latina*, p. 10.
Prida, D. (2003, March). Tongues-twisting. *Latina*, pp. 60–62.

Publishing in the Hispanic Market. (2005, October). *Folio, 34*(10), 54.
Puig, C. (1996, March 18). Audition for Selena roles turns into celebration. *Los Angeles Times,* p. B1.
Quintanilla, M. (1997, August 7). With Latina, Christy Haubegger aims for women like her—bilingual, bicultural and underrated. *Los Angeles Times,* p. E1.
Ramirez, A. (1996, Fall). Cartas/letters [Letter to the editor]. *Latina,* p. 8.
Ramirez, J. (1997, November). Cartas/letters [Letter to the editor]. *Latina,* p. 12.
Ramirez-Berg, C. (2002). *Latino Images in film.* Austin: University of Texas Press.
Rivera, L. (2003, February 17). Personal communication.
Rivera, R. (2004, March). Latinas speak up! *Latina,* p. 24.
Rivera, R. Z. (2003). *New York Ricans from the hip hop zone.* New York: Palgrave Macmillan.
Rivera, V. (1997, October). Cartas/letters [Letter to the editor]. *Latina,* p. 14.
Rodriguez, A. (1999). *Making Latino News: Race, Language, Class.* Thousand Oaks: Sage Publications.
Rodriguez, C. & H. Cordero-Guzman. (1992). Placing race in context. *Ethnic and Racial Studies 15*(4), 523–542.
Rodríguez, C. E. (1998). *Latin Looks: Images of Latinas and Latinos in the U.S. Media.* Boulder: Westview Press.
Rozhon, T. (2005, April 19). Sears plans a fall line that focuses on Hispanics. *New York Times,* p. C16.
Santiago, E. (2006, October). La Vida Lopez. *Latina,* pp. 140–150.
Stacey, J. (1994). *Star gazing: Hollywood cinema and female spectatorship.* London: Routledge.
Tabor, M. B. W. (1995, May 10). Dos for the price of Uno. *New York Times,* p. C20.
Toledo, K. (2006, October). Latinas speak up! *Latina,* p. 36.
Torres, J. (1997, July). Cartas/letters [Letter to the editor]. *Latina,* p. 10.
Turow, J. (1997). *Breaking up America: Advertisers and the new media world.* Chicago: University of Chicago Press.
Tyrangiel, J. (2005, August 22). The diva from the block. *Time,* p. 45.
Vargas, D. R. (2002). Bidi bidi bom bom: Selena and Tejano music in the making of Tejas. In M. Habell-Pallan & M. Romero (Eds.), *Latino/a popular culture* (pp. 117–126). New York: New York University Press.
Vásquez, M. E. (1999, March). Cartas/letters [Letter to the editor]. *Latina* 12.
Weissman, R. X. (1999). Los niños go shopping. *American Demographics, 21*(5), 37–39.
Wells, R. (1998, May). Cartas/letters [Letter to the editor]. *Latina,* p. 10.
Wentz, L. (2006, September 4). Latino mags prove they can serve niche online. *Advertising Age, 77*(36), 36.
Wynter, L. E. (1997, June 4). *Latina* magazine goes monthly ahead of plan. *Wall Street Journal,* p. B1.

CHAPTER EIGHT

A Morning Dose OF Latino Masculinity: U.S. Spanish-language Radio AND THE Politics OF Gender

DOLORES INÉS CASILLAS

¡Son las 5 con 4 minutos, ahora compas! ¡Arriba, arriba, arriba, arriba! ¡A trabajar hombres! ¡Eso es porque cruzamos la frontera, porque llegamos a los Estados Unidos, por el billete!

It's now 5:04 am, now compas! Get up, up, up, up! Off to work, men! After all, that's why we crossed the border, why we're here in the United States, for the [dollar] bill![1]

—EL CUCUY'S SIGNATURE MORNING LINE

¿Lo que busca un hombre [en una mujer]? ... que tiene piel de color canela, ojos verdes, una cascada de cabello ... mujeres grandes [Risas], que se rasuran, yo no me fijo en los cerritos (...) más que nada que no sea metiche o demasiado dramática [Risas].

What a man looks for [in a woman]? That she has ... cinnamon-colored skin, green eyes, cascading hair ... big women [Laugh Track], that they shave, I don't pay attention to breasts (...) above all that she's not nosy or overly dramatic [Laugh Track].

—EL CUCUY, POPULAR RADIO SHOW HOST

Men tune into El Cucuy so they can *feel* like men before going to work, to wash dishes.

—JOSÉ, SPANISH-LANGUAGE RADIO LISTENER

Broadcasting from the number one radio market in the United States and 47 percent Latino occupied region of Los Angeles, California (Arbitron, 2006; U.S.

Census Bureau, 2005),[2] Spanish-language radio host El Cucuy poses as part sex therapist, spiritual advisor, pop-psychologist, and yes, political advocate.[3] El Cucuy ("The Bogeyman") is the leading personality of a lucrative morning genre on U.S. Spanish-language radio that include New York and Miami's El Vacilón ("The Jokester"), Chicago's two boisterous hosts El Chokolate ("The Chocolate"), and El Pistolero ("The Shooter") as well as Los Angeles-based rival El Piolín ("Tweety Bird"). These hosts share numerous discursive characteristics that frame them as working-class male personalities: mainly their dialectic use of slang, occasional use of profanity, consistently misogynistic remarks, and homophobic innuendos (de la Fuente, 2005; Navarro, 2001).[4]

El Cucuy's morning programming, like that of his on-air competitors, limit music play to one to three songs an hour. Instead, morning shows are largely dedicated to live conversation with callers, guests, and comedy skits accompanied by canned sound effects and applause tracks. The impressive firstplace ratings garnered by this talk-centered genre on Spanish-language radio in each of the five largest radio markets—Los Angeles, New York, Miami, Chicago, and San Francisco—attest to its loyal following (Arbitron, 2006). Since 1998, El Cucuy's Los Angeles commuter region alone has attracted, at times, twice as many listeners as leading English-language radio personality Howard Stern (Campo-Flores, 2000).[5] In fact, El Cucuy's fall 1999 record of capturing 11.3 percent of the Los Angeles traffic-ridden listenership remains unmatched today ("Almendarez-Coello Dominates," 2000; Bachman, 2004; Szalai, 2004).

Aside from satellite dish services that specialize in Spanish-language television programming or the influx of Latino-tailored websites, such as "AOL Latino," U.S. Latinos rely on broadcast radio—much more than their Anglo counterparts—as a source of news and entertainment (Castañeda Paredes, 2003).[6] To place El Cucuy's popularity within an economic perspective, Merrill Lynch analyst Keith Fawcett claimed that "Finding (El Cucuy) is better than finding Aztec gold" (Szalai, 2004). Fawcett's use of a clichéd and racialized analogy of discovery and conquest stresses El Cucuy's reputed U.S. market value.

In the mainstream English-language press, these particular radio hosts are often superficially referred to as the Hispanic equivalents of English-language radio personalities Rush Limbaugh and Howard Stern because of their racy discussions (Baker, 2004; Calvo, 2000; Campo-Flores, 2000). Monday through Friday, Spanish-language radio listeners tune into male radio hosts engaging in sexually laden exchanges with female callers and offering advice on troubled (heterosexual) relationships (Reyes Bonilla, 2005). Contrary to Limbaugh and Stern, El Cucuy incorporates a transnational perspective evident in his routine endorsements of on-air campaigns to send money to troubled "home" countries and vigilant public updates on key Latino and immigrant-related legislation.[7]

Recognized as community leaders, Spanish-language radio hosts also use the airways to rally on behalf of their Latino listenership (Gutiérrez & Schement, 1979). For instance, their political role as on-air organizers was made most apparent in the spring of 2006, when millions of listeners attended record-breaking pro-immigrant rallies across the nation (Flaccus, 2006; Johnson & Spice, 2006; Mitchell & Espinoza, 2006; Newman, 2006; Stein, 2006).[8] These mass mobilizations, organized by grassroots organizations, served as powerful responses to a series of disconcerting anti-immigrant legislation.[9] Yet a central component of these radio hosts' gendered, politicized, on-air posturing relies on a sexist form of speech that scripts political efforts as male and works to further marginalize and silence women.

For many, these two differing on-air personifications of El Cucuy (as sexist stud *and* political rally leader) may appear as a political contradiction. I argue, however, that they both foreground the complex interplay of gender, labor, and globalization. In this article I focus more on El Cucuy's sexual-risqué nature, while discuss elsewhere the particular implications of globalization and immigration reform on the growth and character of U.S. Spanish-language radio (Casillas, 2006). Influenced by the U.S. labor market's turn to the service sector, many working-class Latino men experience what Saskia Sassen (2000a, 2000b) has called the "feminization of labor." Broadly, this chapter addresses how changes in the global economy affect not only immigrants' labor and gender roles but also their media practices. Specifically, I structure my analysis of El Cucuy and his projected relationship with predominantly Mexican and Central American audiences within both the post-9/11 political moment and the talk radio format.[10] In this context, El Cucuy provides an arena where men are not scorned for speaking Spanish, for being undocumented, or for instance, for working as dishwashers. As José succinctly states in the epigraph, El Cucuy attracts a male listenership wrought with gender anxieties, yearning to "*feel* like men."

TRANSNATIONALIZING THEORIES OF TALK RADIO

Characterized by shifts in the global economy and the mounting emphasis on protecting national borders, the post-9/11 political moment has heralded not only an increased demand for immigrant labor, but also a concomitant increase in the legal vulnerability of undocumented peoples. Following the U.S.-waged "war on terror," public discourse on immigration reform, interlaced with that of national security, has produced a profound anti-immigrant backlash. Sociological studies, particularly those rich with a feminist focus, have documented how increased migration rates, propelled by economic practices of globalization, reconfigure immigrants' labor and gender roles in newfound residences (Espiritu, 1999; Hondagneu-Sotelo & Messner, 2001; Mahler & Rodriguez, 2001; Parreñas, 2001; Rodriguez & Mahler, 1999; Schaeffer-Grabiel, 2006). As Michael Kimmel (2003) argues, "globalization changes masculinities—reshaping the arena in which local and national masculinities are articulated and transforming the lives of men" (p. 603). Given this unsettling political climate, El Cucuy's consistent early morning encouragement, to an immigrant-based listenership, to "get up, up, up … to work" for the dollar bill reaffirms the place, labor, and value of Latino immigrants. By relegating women to the status of linguistic puns on male-led programming, listeners are refashioned as "antigirly men." Similar to Cynthia Enloe's (1989) theory that corporations and governments "depend not only on capital and weaponry, but also on the control of women as symbols … emotional comforters" (p. xi) in retaining male power and authority, in many respects, this emerging brand of Spanish-language radio hosts function as transnational actors, a product of globalization's gendered order.

Radio scholars Murray Levin (1987) and Susan J. Douglas (1999) contend that the interactive and intimate format of talk radio targets politically disempowered listeners who crave a place within the larger U.S. public sphere. While these theories convincingly speak to the disenfranchised location of many Latinos in the U.S. public sphere, El Cucuy's transnational audience and radio themes also point to the fact that nation-bound and English-language specific theories have to be expanded in the contemporary situation of globalization.

Media scholars theorize on how broadcasting serves as a nostalgic substitute for traditional "town hall" forums, where citizens gathered and deliberated in political discussions (Douglas, 1999; Loviglio, 2005; Martín-Barbero, 1993; Morley, 2000; Scannel, 1996). Instead of physically congregating, people gather around media outlets or consume similar news and information, taking part in what Benedict Anderson (1991) calls an "imagined community" across geographical distances (e.g., Loviglio, 2005; Vaillant, 2002). Talk radio's practice of welcoming guests to voice jests and opinions within a mass-mediated and (relatively) unimposing forum attracts socially and politically isolated listeners. Murray Levin (1987) notes that talk radio's origins are found in the political disillusionment of the 1960s and 1970s. He draws compelling associations between the public's waning trust in national institutions and the escalating popularity of talk radio. The revival of talk radio in the 1980s capitalized on listeners' growing "isolation that came from overwork and the privatization of American life and the huge gap between themselves [listeners] and those who run the country" (Douglas, 2002, p. 487). The on-air "camaraderie" between disgruntled radio hosts and listeners reaffirmed contemptuous antigovernment attitudes as it grew in popularity. A mere 53 radio stations carried the talk format in 1984; today more than 1,000 radio stations feature a talk-centered radio program, ranging from Christian and sports to liberal and right-wing programs (Heath, 1998).

In a similar vein, Susan J. Douglas (1999, 2002) argues that social and gender anxieties in particular often manifest themselves on talk radio. In her article, "Letting Boys Be Boys ...," she convincingly points to the rise of white male radio hosts during the 1980s and 1990s as indicative of women's social and economic advances and white men's threatened sense of masculinity as well as racial and class privilege. Douglas (2002) positions the growing hysteria behind Rush Limbaugh, Don Imus, and Howard Stern and their antifeminist-speak as vain attempts to reclaim masculine roles. With Spanish-language radio's male-dominant lineup, morning talk radio has drawn an attentive male Latino listenership perhaps disillusioned with newfound gender and social roles. According to (im)migration scholars (Goldring, 2001, 2003; Hondagneu-Sotelo, 1994a, 1994b; Mahler & Rodriguez, 2001; Rodriguez & Mahler, 1999), many immigrant men "for the first time in their lives occupy subordinate positions in class, racial, and citizen hierarchies," that in turn provoke labor, racial and gender anxieties (Hondagneu-Sotelo, 2003, p. 8).

Despite numbering nearly 35 million, many Latinos are often treated and portrayed as "invisible" laborers, absent within larger discussions of U.S. politics and political institutions (Chang, 2000; Romero, 1992; Rothenberg, 1998; Sassen, 1999). This sizeable group are referred as the new labor of "brown-collar" occupations where "immigrant Latinos are over represented, largely in low-level service, construction, agricultural, and manufacturing jobs, including waiters' assistants [busboys], and painters" (Catanzarite, 2003). In urban metropoli such as Chicago, Los Angeles, New York City, and San Diego, immigrant Latinos constitute 40–70 percent of these workers (Catanzarite, 2003). Indeed, a 2004 policy report released by the Pew Hispanic Center correlated the revitalization of the U.S. economy with Latino employment numbers. During the 2004 election year, as presidential campaigns continuously espoused promises and spouted statistics, more than a quarter of the total increase in employment gains came from U.S. residents ineligible to vote (Kochhar, 2004). Ironically, while Latinos' bodies are instrumental to the U.S. political economy, they are frequently scorned by U.S. public opinion and isolated from U.S. public life (Chavez, 2001; Hondaganeu-Sotelo, 1996).

Scholars of transnational and gender studies such as Luin Goldring (2003) have effectively argued that this "sense of loss" is often converted into monetary remittances returned to home countries. A growing number of "hometown associations" or male-comprised groups organize to send money to home communities abroad and to decide how these funds are spent. Therefore, sending money home becomes a means of maintaining power and masculine authority via decision-making and political processes. Although immigrant women participate in fundraisers, they are denied the same social capital and enhancement of power afforded to immigrant men, who often work in tandem with male-led government coffers abroad (Goldring, 2001).

Pierrette Hondagneu-Sotelo (1994a, 1994b, 2003), Sarah Mahler (2001), and Patricia Pessar (1996) also suggest that such gendered activities have influenced immigrant women to envision more long-term and permanent stays in the U.S., while immigrant men adopt a transnational perspective reflective of their nostalgic desire to return home. Just as wiring money abroad is seen as a method for securing a sense of masculine order on the transnational plane, I argue that these gender anxieties are manifested through El Cucuy's male-led morning radio program, in which he and his (male) listeners reinscribe a sense of hypermasculinity to an invisible and feminized caste of male laborers. With differing gendered experiences in the U.S., immigrant men sustain and perpetuate patriarchal ideals through radio programming.

Significantly, Spanish-language talk radio has experienced what I refer to as an institutional and programming "transnational makeover." Shifts in both immigration and communications policies have affected audience composition, widened the broadcasting reach of networks, as well as sophisticated radio programming (Aufderheide, 1999; Castañeda Paredes, 2003). Spanish-language radio's institutional growth and greater national signals, together with its programmatic engagement with matters directly pertinent to Latin America, reflect the transnational moment. As a result, Spanish-language morning radio has rendered Latinos' angst over newfound gender roles public.

Cynthia Enloe (1989) encourages "making men visible as men" in an effort "to explore differences in the politics of masculinity between countries—and between ethnic groups in the same country" (p. 13). Since ideals of masculinity are not defined or practiced "identical[ally] across generations or cultural boundaries," talk theories that engage with wounded white male egos and their disillusionment with U.S. politics are not entirely applicable to immigrant Mexican and Central American men. Struggling to define themselves in relation to both immigrant women's social advances as well as ideals of white masculinity, listeners can tune into personalities like those of El Cucuy to engage in sonic acts of public (heterosexual) male posturing.

TRANSNATIONAL EXEMPLAR: EL CUCUY DE LA MAÑANA

El Cucuy's presence on stations that feature "Mexican Regional" music highlights the working-class character of his audience. Mexican regional music accounts for over half of all U.S. Spanish-language record sales and many top-rated U.S. Spanish-language radio stations are devoted to this musical genre (Clemens,

2005). Cultural critic Ben Quiñones (2005) explains that over half of Mexican regional music consumers possess less than a high school education and earn an annual income of less than $25,000.[11] El Cucuy capitalizes on his working-class base by consistently reminding listeners, quite frankly, that the wealth of the U.S. is owed to Latinos. He offers morning salutations to taxistas (taxi drivers), those making hotel beds, flipping burgers, washing dishes, and working beneath the sun. Aware of his listenership, he literally and figuratively foregrounds a collective immigration and working-class experience through his morning show.

Moreover on the radio, the voice becomes the only physical trait "available to listeners as a basis for making assessments of the speaker" (Scannel, 1996, p. 36). Accent, tone, pitch, and word use are acoustic cues that help listeners identify a speaker's gender, race, class, and educational level based on listeners' own socially learned correlations between sound and personal qualities. El Cucuy's ability to skillfully vacillate between a Honduran accent and Mexican slang thus reflects his primarily Mexican and Central American listenership. His show depicts itself as raza-focused, addressing mestizo/a Latinos that privilege their indigenous descent. Frequent sound bites from listeners and callers remark on El Cucuy's commitment to helping raza (El Cucuy siempre ayuda a la raza) and his iconic status among Central Americans and Mexicans (El Cucuy es raza).

El Cucuy's personal traits shared on the air match and resonate with those of his targeted listenership. For instance, if guest speakers rattle off numbers or percentages, El Cucuy often admits that math is not his strength with such disclaimers: "mira, como no fui a la escuela/hey, I didn't go to school." He insists that guests explain their points in "real terms" through colorful adjectives. As a native Spanish speaker, El Cucuy repeatedly states that he already knows the two most essential English words: Home Depot and Coke. The reference to Home Depot in particular alludes to the familiar meeting place for Latino day laborers who congregate outside hardware stores for short-term hires by contractors (Greenhouse, 2005; Valenzuela, Kawachi, & Marr, 2002). Because both Home Depot and Coke are universal brand names and not necessarily English words, his specification of the two symbolically critiques English-only policies. In an interview with *The New Yorker*, El Cucuy offered a much more poignant example of his English skills. He explained that "yo oprimo el numero dos/I press number two" (Baum, 2006, p. 43), a reference to the growing availability of Spanish-spoken instructions by pressing an alternate, often number two, when contacting businesses and government offices by telephone. By broadcasting El Cucuy's personal qualities as an undocumented immigrant and limited English speaker, he validates those of his listeners. His well-known life narrative from undocumented immigrant to celebrity offers his fans "proof" of the rewards of hard work and frequent prayer; his struggles as an undocumented immigrant are seen as heroic for leaving the beauty of home to toil in the U.S. labor market. In these instances, however, El Cucuy's affirmation displays a conservative immigrant work ethic and false notion of the American Dream, where hard work automatically reaps social and economic rewards. Oddly, his discernment of the American Dream lacks the usual considerations he gives to race, class, and linguistic prejudices experienced by Latinos, topics frequented on his show.

El Cucuy's public praises relayed on-air to immigrants on the U.S. side of the border joins a larger transnational discourse, with its undercurrents of money and labor, championed by Mexico's former president Vicente Fox and echoed by U.S. president George W. Bush. President Fox's well-documented public thanks to Mexican-origin laborers in the U.S. for their monetary remittances sent to Mexico are instrumental in the rebuilding of a viable Mexico that Mexican laborers can, one day, return to.[12] Likewise, President Bush has expressed public appreciation toward Mexican laborers for working in positions considered far too unattractive for U.S. (non-Latino) Americans. El Cucuy's radio persona underscores those larger international sentiments posed by male politicians.

THE SOUND EFFECT OF GENDER

As the opening quote of this chapter conveys, El Cucuy's disquieting gender politics are clearly heard through his on-air reference to women. El Cucuy restores a sense of male agency by positioning Latinas in a traditional and voiceless space. Women are used as linguistic props and strategically bear the brunt of the joke, as the object(s) of "funny" silences and misunderstandings. Humor, for El Cucuy, works to demarcate gender roles over the airwaves by assigning often weak, treacherous qualities to women and strong, gallant characteristics to men. Accompanying El Cucuy's actual spoken discourse, studio sound effects and canned laugh tracks guide audiences, by directing listeners to laugh at specific moments. Together, the use of laugh and applause tracks with studio sound effects "normalizes" El Cucuy's troubling gender sentiments.

In particular, El Cucuy's strategic deployment of "picardía," a Latin American mode of humor based on wordplays and phrases of doble sentido [double meaning], linguistically polices who can listen in. Regarded as a "low brow" sense of humor for its reliance on cunning craftiness, picardía, popularly referred to in Mexican Spanish as "pelados" for its crude nature, relies on a male-figured storyteller who linguistically mocks others using classed, gendered, and vulgar insinuations (Peña, 1991). As host, of course, El Cucuy represents the licensed and authoritative male raconteur. On the radio, picardía forces listeners to pay close attention to the subtleties of word choice in order to "get" the joke, often at the expense of women. This mode of humor relies on popular vernaculars of Spanish and functions in code, thereby limiting its use and understanding almost exclusively to native Spanish speakers. In doing so, El Cucuy's practice of picardía prohibits non-Latinos from listening or taking part in the program thereby inversing the U.S. ethno-linguistic tendency to privilege English. The on-air dialect requirement, in many ways, creates a public space where a gendered form of Spanish becomes the official language. This dynamic is further entrenched as dialects of Spanish are reinvented and resignified over time. El Cucuy's riddles and jokes favor the male migrant familiar with Spanish-language pronunciations and accents of English-language phrases. Tactically, El Cucuy often employs English-language acronyms as stand-ins for Spanish words within his joke telling. For instance, in order to understand his interchange of the noun DVD (the media unit) and the verb dividir [to divide] within his jokes, listeners need to be familiar with the English-language pronunciation of the acronym DVD as well as the Spanish-language verb "dividir."

El Cucuy's linguistic slapstick, reinforced by a host of bizarre sound effects, serve as audible and often gendered cues for listeners. Reminiscent of the early days of radio comedy, the routine sounds of horns, buzzers, water dripping, zippers, pages flipping, heavy sighs, and applause tracks help audiences imagine El Cucuy's aural staging. Water dripping often signifies a slow-paced segment of a story or emphasizes silence over the air; heavy sighs display signs of exasperation; and although the sound of zippers acoustically set up sexually tinged scenes, it only implies when a man is "ready," not a woman. The sound effect of the zipper communicates a masculine sexuality through the notion of pants in at least two ways. First, women are often fashioned through the gendered ideal of dresses, not the more masculine wear of pants. Second, figuratively speaking, women do not wear the pants in the relationship meaning they hold limited decision-making power. The absence of a comparable acoustic prompt for women reflects their lack of sexual agency over the air.

Paddy Scannel (1996) notes that the laugh track in particular "not only serves as a function to legitimate what the host says (however problematic it may be), it also changes from a private to a public conversation" (p. 34). The host-caller conversation provokes a false sense of intimacy, while the laugh track serves as a greater reminder that the private conversation is actually public as well as an acoustic cue for when the moment of "listening" transitions from being "voyeuristic" to "entertaining." Most importantly, the laugh track validates El Cucuy's pelados and reifies the gendered power differentials that characterize the relationship between El Cucuy and his callers and guests, since they do not have the capability to "laugh track" back.

Overall, El Cucuy maintains a double standard in his approach of women. Though he praises his own mother (and mothers in general) with saint-like devotion, many female callers and guests are treated as potential love interests or inherent heart breakers, and mostly with overall suspicion. El Cucuy's perpetuation of "marianismo," the ideal that women should model the mothering nature of the Virgin Mary, functions as the ultimate counterpoint to his exaggerated masculine-machismo character.[13] The concept of marianismo relies on the feminization of the informal, domestic sector so that women focus their energy and identity toward household and familial responsibilities (Chaney, 1979; Mayo & Resnick, 1996; Stevens, 1973). Machismo, traditionally defined by breadwinner and protector roles, depends on the male, public sector of labor and the formal economy. As mentioned, changes in the global economy have forced immigrant men to work within feminized positions of labor, for instance, within hotel and restaurant industries. More so, the increasing legal vulnerability of immigrants' rights also constructs more feminized perceptions of immigrant men, as racial profiling limits their public mobility. El Cucuy's upholding of marianismo ideals strengthens machista attitudes in an attempt to reclaim more masculine, public roles. Instead, El Cucuy, part of a larger genre of male-led morning programming, constructs and perpetuates an idealized brown, hypermasculine, public space over the airwaves.

One skit in particular from El Cucuy's 1999 compact disc compilation of work entitled "Gringo en la Luna de Miel/ Gringo on His Honeymoon" exemplifies how women, although silent, still represent the underlying "funny" side of the joke. This example also unveils the underlying tensions of masculinity between white U.S. men (gringos) and those of color (Mexican). In this track, El Cucuy explains that a gringo and a mexicana marry and decide to spend their honeymoon in Cancún amidst the beauty of the local beaches and hotels. To add to the acoustic scenery of a hotel on the beach, the background noise consists of birds squawking, the sound of waves crashing into the beach, the low humming of conversation chatter, and the clatter of dishes and silverware. El Cucuy acts as narrator, hotel manager, husband/gringo, and wife/mexicana by adopting a different vocal style for each character.

> Narrador: Se quedan en una suite nupcial ahí preciosa. Se avientan dos o tres dias sin salir ni a comer, como al tercer día bajan al lobby para comer algo. Y cuando estan sentados ahí en el lobby el gerente del hotel ve y se aproxima al gringo y le dice:
>
> Gerente: [En inglés con acento] Excuse me, Mr. Smith?
>
> gringo: Yeah, I am John Smith.
>
> Gerente: [En inglés] Oh Mr. Smith, me da muchísimo gusto [en español] (...) a saludarlo, soy el gerente del hotel, y para mí es un placer de veras atenderlo personalmente y darle la bienvenida porque usted escogió el mejor hotel para venir a pasar su

luna de miel acá a Cancún. ¿Cómo le han tratado Mr. Smith? ¿Cómo se le ha tratado aquí en el hotel?

gringo: [lentamente y en español con acento] O, de maravilla, excelente. Yo en la mañana me aviento a la terraza, a mediodía me tiro a la terraza, en la tarde me aviento a la terraza, y a la noche me tiro a la terraza.

Narrador: Ella se voltea y le dice:

mexicana: Me llamo Te-re-sa, imbécil. [Risas]

Narrator: They stay in a beautiful suite for newlyweds. After three days of not leaving their room, they [gringo and mexicana] descend to the hotel lobby for dinner. There the hotel manager approaches them and asks.

Hotel Manager: [In an accented English] Excuse me, Mr. Smith?

gringo: Yeah, I am John Smith.

Hotel Manager: [In English] Oh hello, Mr. Smith, I am very happy to meet you. [In Spanish] I'm the hotel manager; it's a pleasure to personally serve you. I wanted to thank you for choosing to spend your honeymoon at the best hotel in Cancun. How is everything? How has the hotel treated you?

gringo: [Slowly in an exaggerated Spanish accent] Oh marvelous. Excellent. In the morning, I throw myself on the terraza. In the afternoon, I throw myself on the terraza. In the evening, I throw myself on the terraza. And at night, I throw myself on the terraza.

Narrator: The wife then replies:

mexicana: My name is Te-re-sa, you idiot. [Laugh Track]

While the gringo draws attention to his accented Spanish with the added effect of speaking slowly as if choosing his words wisely, the hotel manager approaches him in English but inconspicuously switches to Spanish. The transition is discreet, alluding listeners to believe that the hotel manager may be fluent in both languages, as detected by the equal pace of the words in both. In contrast, the gringo's slow-paced speech alone linguistically marks him as monolingual, intellectually dim and not as adept as the hotel manager. Both verbs "tirar" and "avientar," conjugated in the Spanish past tense as "tiro" and "aviento" entails to throw, hurl, cast, or project. Given the speaker, his admission that me tiro [I throw myself] literally means that the gringo-husband threw himself down on his mexicana-wife and/or figuratively that he threw her down, both seemingly aggressive gestures. Although the gringo's exaggerated articulations in Spanish serve as the repetitive "funny" element of the joke, the punch line really arrives with his wife. Despite being rendered voiceless throughout the exchange, the joke is "on her," as cued by the laugh track. It is not seen as humorous that a man would openly discuss his sexual activities with the male hotel manager, but not knowing how to pronounce his wife's name ("terraza") with an "authentic" Spanish pronunciation ("Te-re-sa") is deemed as truly funny.[14]

Wordplays and linguistic puns showcased on radio are coded as "struggles over power, pecking order, and masculine authority" (Douglas, 1999, p. 101). Specifically, "who says what to whom and how speaks volumes about who has power, who doesn't, and how that power is both challenged and maintained" (p. 104). In the hotel example above, the use of a Mexican hotel manager versus "John Smith," whose generic name alone signifies narratives of conquest as well as popular couplings with "native" women (e.g., Pocahontas) together with a Cancún setting with its own U.S. tourist associations, depicts an aural scenario steeped in nationalist, racial, and masculine struggles. Even sociolinguists, Susan J. Douglas argues, admit "ritual insulting—insults as part of a game, done for laughs—occur most frequently during times of cultural stress" (p. 104). The hotel manager, although waiting on the gringo and his mexicana-wife, is the only one who remains comically unscathed and keeps intact both his clout as the hotel manager and dignity as a male Mexican citizen.

On the radio, linguistic slapstick compensates for the absence of the visual as silent films attempted to visually compensate for the voice (Douglas, 1999). Here, the "visual" manifests itself in multilayered fashion; as a Central American radio host in an English-language radio field, El Cucuy's presence is significant, particularly to the growing Central American population residing in Los Angeles. Public relations campaigns with photos of El Cucuy confirm listeners' acoustically constructed visions of El Cucuy's working-class background. Specifically, his indigenous facial features, dark-skinned complexion, short stature, occasionally "mullet" hairstyle, and sizeable gold crucifix match his on-air persona. El Cucuy's billboard charisma transports images of working-class labor from the back of the restaurant to busy highway interstates and boulevards. His popularity has produced a mainstream visibility for working-class Mexican and Central American men, as evident by El Cucuy's positive press in *The Los Angeles Times, Newsweek, New York Times,* and *The New Yorker* (Baum, 2006; Calvo, 2000; Campo-Flores, 2004).

EL CUCUY AS POLITICAL ALLY

Even as El Cucuy adopts a "low brow" mode of humor, he vocally advocates for the rights and livelihood of immigrants and U.S. Latinos. From speaking out on state-specific initiatives to rallying against national legislation to lamenting the low voter turnout in both U.S. and Latin American elections, the airways constitute his podium. El Cucuy welcomes listeners to call if their political position differs, though these invitations usually turn into male linguistic dueling matches, with El Cucuy reigning as "victor." Infrequent attempts to reel women into political discussions on El Cucuy's show undermines their contributions, authority, and relegates women to the status of trivial political actors. In doing so, he reiterates Western discourse's centrality of the male subject as political actor (Fraser, 1992).

For instance, in September 2003, California's Senate considered granting drivers' licenses to undocumented immigrants. This bill, spearheaded by Senator Gil Cedillo, proposed that immigrants be given the opportunity to obtain legal permission to drive regardless of their legal status (Glendhill, 2004). Framed in the media as a Latino-specific issue, the controversial initiative occupied headlines and op-ed pages for weeks (Cedillo, 2003; Hansen, 2003; Leslie, 2003). In an effort to garner more support for the initiative, two female attorneys appeared on El Cucuy's thenafternoon radio show. The attorneys were introduced once by their first names and thereafter referred as abogadas/lawyers. As observed over the years, female radio guests often remain nameless and assigned nicknames according to their profession (doctora/doctor) or gender (mujer/woman). Perhaps worse, El Cucuy, in attempts to convey a trusting relationship with women guests, will infantalize their first names: "María" becomes Mariquita, "Dolores" is referred to as Lolita, and "Teresa" is recast as Teresita. Made more apparent by El Cucuy's consistent naming of male guests, the oversight trivializes the contributions made by women professionals to serious on-air discussions. By choosing their "names" for them, he robs them of any symbolic agency.

In the midst of the attorneys' legal explanation of where the bill stood in the Senate's pipeline, El Cucuy injected his own one-liners, loosely asking: "¿y que, piensan que nosotros no manejamos? Nos montamos en un solo carro ... como si era carpool" [What, they don't think we drive ... we all pile in like a carpool]. The two attorneys giggled nervously along as El Cucuy took command of the conversation:

> Mira [baja su voz] que seamos francos aquí, frente frente, dime ... ¿hay un peligro ... realmente, en serio, nos van a remandar? ¿Entonces, a quien le toca nuestro lugar en los files, eh? Ellos, pos no. [suspira] [levanta su voz] Pero si necesitan pararse cada hora a aplicarse su bloque del sol [Risas] tú sabes, los blanquitos se queman, se ponen doraditos, colorados [Risas] ... Es más, llevan sus botellas de plástico de agua por todos lados [Risas; abogadas se ríen]. Piden su break cada diez minutos [Risas] ... Nos morimos de hambre en California [Risas; abogadas se ríen].
>
> Look, [lowering voice] let's be frank, face to face here, tell me ... are we in danger ... really, can you see [them] telling us to leave? Who will take our place in the fields then? They can't [sigh]. [raising voice] They'd have to stop every hour to apply sunblock [Laugh Track] You know, white people, they burn, they get all red [Laugh Track] ... they drag their plastic water bottles everywhere [Laugh Track; attorneys laughing]. They take a break every ten minutes [Laugh Track] ... We'd all starve in California [Laugh Track; attorneys laughing].

El Cucuy's request to speak "frente frente/face to face" and assurances that his guests be "francos/frank" signifies a common tactic used among radio hosts, to linguistically craft an intimate or personal setting (Montgomery, 1986; Scannel, 1996). Although his use of the word "peligro/danger" could be interpreted as somewhat excessive since the issue simply involved drivers' licenses, the stupendous attention afforded to the bill was indeed laced with anti-immigrant rhetoric. Proponents of the bill argued that in the aftermath of the terrorist attacks of September 11, 2001, this documentation would open the floodgates to (terrorist) immigrants. The description of "danger" aptly captured the anti-immigrant sentiment of the moment and El Cucuy's possible empathy with audiences. In other words, while from the outset the controversy may have appeared to be about drivers' licenses, in actuality the debate unearthed issues concerning immigrants, and the subsequent economic, social, and security "threat" of potential permanent residency. Arguably, larger fears of inverted racial, social order as well as miscegenation accompanied the cursory concerns of legality and immigrants. Perhaps believing that the attorneys' somewhat lengthy explanation was not making an impact on his audiences, or simply wanting to keep the show entertaining, El Cucuy began to quip on the possibility of blanquitos (white people) working in the state's agricultural fields.[15] His use of "nosotros/us" and "ellos/they" along with different work ethics and tanning capabilities, favored the labor and value of farm workers, all presumed to be of Latino origin. El Cucuy reifies social boundaries with his insinuation that Latinos are farm workers, yet his speculation that "nos morimos de hambre/we'd starve" affirms that "nosotros/us" does more for "ellos/they" than vice versa. While El Cucuy himself perhaps did not know the particulars regarding a bill's process in the Senate, in true El Cucuy fashion, the conversation ended soon afterward with him having the last word. Although California's then governor Grey Davis defended the bill, the provision to allow undocumented immigrants the right to drivers' licenses ultimately lacked Senate and public support.

Two years later, with Governor Arnold Schwarzenegger, the political issue of granting drivers' licenses to undocumented immigrants resurrected. This time, El Cucuy's show went a step further and sent the "Cucuy-mobile" eight hours north of their Los Angeles studios to report on the anticipated signing of the bill to law by Governor Schwarzenegger. Parked across the street from the steps of California's capital in Sacramento, the Cucuy-mobile (a van caricatured with El Cucuy's face and the phrase "raza") served as the show's portable eyes and ears, reporting back via phone to El Cucuy. Alma, a female reporter with El Cucuy's San Francisco affiliate radio station, was dispatched to Sacramento to report on location. Conveying optimism, El Cucuy remarked:

> Claro que nosotros necesitamos licencias de manejar hombre, para transportar nuestra familias e hijos a la esuela, para llevar nuestros enfermos al hospital, y también para nosotros mismos a llegar al trabajo, esto es porque llegamos a los EE.UU., ¿ayudamos

también a *ellos*, verdad? Hay que ver cuando el Gobernador Schwarzenegger firma el 60, nuestro Cucuy-móvil se va quedar estacionado allí mismo afuera del capital [énfasis puesto].

Of course man, we need [drivers'] licenses to transport our family and children to school, to take sick ones to hospitals, and ourselves to work, that's why we came to the United States, after all; this benefits *them*, am I right? Let's find out when Governor Schwarzenegger is expected to sign it [Senate Bill 60], our Cucuy-mobile will be stationed there outside the California capitol until then [emphasis added].

El Cucuy downplayed the controversy surrounding undocumented immigrant drivers' licenses by reframing the issue as a matter of mutual benefit between undocumented immigrants and "ellos/them," or non-Latino employers. As expected by political observers, even with bipartisan support from politicians and the perceived irony of the governor himself (though rich and white) identifying as an immigrant, Governor Schwarzenegger vetoed the bill.

Although many English-language talk-centered radio programs do not leave the confinements of their recording studios, morning radio shows are more accustomed to broadcasting from local grand openings, festivals, and charity-sponsored events. Because morning radio slots attract the largest number of listeners, and hence, garner the highest rates of advertising revenue, local businesses and organizations, for instance, opt to feature grand openings or sales over the morning airwaves to reach as many listeners and potential customers as possible. Spanning the two varieties, Spanish-language morning talk radio (in addition to grand openings, festivals, and fundraisers) often broadcast from advocacy organizations, Immigration Naturalization Service (INS) buildings, health fairs, and health clinics. In this case, the Cucuy-mobile's travels to the state capitol and play-by-play coverage point to El Cucuy's open lobbying on behalf of his constituents. Nonetheless, El Cucuy's political lobbying and on-air advocacy, by all accounts sincere gestures, generate an attentive listenership in which El Cucuy himself also financially profits from.

Despite the political orientation of the three morning shows leading up to Governor Schwarzenegger's anticipated signing, El Cucuy managed to weave sexual innuendos into his political commentary. Alma's morning salutations were often met with some type of risqué remark:

Alma: Aquí estamos puestos y listos pero como que Sacramento le gusta dormir Cucuy, porque ya son las 6 y pico y todavía no vemos tanta gente en la calle. Pero estamos aquí, listos a platicar y a charlar con nuestra raza.

El Cucuy: ¿Eso es típico de nosotros, no? Raza siempre se despiertan tempranito, listos ... somos trabajadores hombre. Alma, me imagino en que la gente ya están trabajando o todavía en la cama, haciendo un poco de, tu sabes. [Risas]

Alma: Claro, también, es la verdad.

Alma: We're parked here and ready but it looks like Sacramento likes to sleep, because it's a bit after 6 and we don't see a lot of folks out on the street. But we're ready to talk with our raza.

El Cucuy: That's typical of us, right? Raza wake up early, they're ready ... man, that's why we're such good workers. Alma, I think folks are either already at work or you know, still in bed, doing a bit of you-know-what. [Laugh Track]

Alma: Well, of course, that's true.

Aside from California and national-specific matters, El Cucuy laments the low number of U.S. Latino votes cast in both U.S. and Latin American elections. He publicly stated, "[W]e Hispanics do everything in this country. We clean the buildings. We clean the roads. We pick the crops. The only thing we don't do is vote" (Baum, 2006, p. 43). In the summer of 2006, he kicked off a "Votos por América" eleven city voter registration tour via bus where he broadcast live outside Latino supermercados (supermarkets) in an effort to boost the number of Latino registered voters. One of the tour's routine slogans included "If you're a citizen, register to vote! If not, find out how to become a citizen!" (Hendricks, 2006). Reflecting many of the arguments present in contemporary scholarship on immigration and gender, El Cucuy also encourages listeners to participate politically on a transnational scale. Linking monetary remittances (la remesa) with political efficacy, El Cucuy promotes the practice of absentee voting by U.S. Latinos as a means of strengthening their role in political matters abroad.

HUMANITARIAN VOICE-OVERS

For El Cucuy, humanitarian acts and community service are rescripted as inherently masculine through his monetary donations and subsequent political influence. El Cucuy has translated his celebrity fame into numerous humanitarian efforts showcased on both his radio show, as well as on his websites. His "El Cucuy Foundation" has generated millions of dollars toward local U.S. Latino communities as well as rebuilding efforts in Central America and social causes in Mexico. For instance, while the English-language media raised relief funds in 2005 for the aftermath of Hurricane Katrina, El Cucuy dedicated airtime toward raising money and awareness to areas of Mexico hit two months later by the lesser known Hurricane Wilma. El Cucuy's involvement with both U.S. and Latin American charity events has propelled a fame that transcends geographical borders, from Central America and Mexico to the U.S.

Dozens of pictures of El Cucuy posted on his two websites (www.cucuy.org or www.cucuy.com) showcase his participation in community-related efforts, often posing with celebrity artists and/or politicians. One finds pictures of El Cucuy in

Central America handing out toys to children, walking with the president of El Salvador, with the First Lady of Honduras, as well as acting as Grand Marshall of Mexican festivals in Chicago, San Francisco, Los Angeles, and Dallas. His foundation website details the opening of the "El Cucuy Help Center," a health clinic and resource center for Latinos in the Los Angeles area; lists different locations for obtaining free diabetes screenings; and highlights the unveiling of new homes built in Honduras, all courtesy of El Cucuy's Foundation. A community in Honduras even went so far as to rename their small pueblo after his legal name (Renán Almendarez Coello), despite the fact that there is no radio station in Honduras that carries El Cucuy's show. His fame underscores that transnational activity extends beyond the physical movement of bodies to how the airwaves serve as another route of mobility. Specifically, El Cucuy's celebrity status is indicative of the migration of cultural icons and symbols that occur with the migration of people, but perhaps more significantly, their money. He represents the exemplar of a transnational masculine image: an immigrant that navigated two borders and now sends money home to Central America, Mexico, and local U.S. Latino communities. These pictures showcasing El Cucuy's humanitarian acts "endorse" his on-air character and work to "voice over" his patriarchal narrative. They offer a visual perception that conflicts and superimposes his masculine spoken character.

For El Cucuy, notions of masculinity are shaped by the marginalization of women and the radio banter of white men who are either linguistically teased or altogether absent. His masculine expressions are those of a larger transnational order, a linguistic mouthpiece of a reconfigured state of gender, labor, and social norms mimicked on Spanish-language radio and validated through his political pandering with presidents and politicians. While El Cucuy champions for working-class immigrants, his privileging of men strengthens male-identified forms of political participation. The popular and lucrative genre of morning talk radio speaks to the legion of U.S. male listeners absent within the larger U.S. public sphere yet popular on Spanish-language dials. If El Cucuy, a discursive example of the predominantly masculinist genre of morning radio, reflects the transnational acoustic moment, women are relegated to the silent pause at the end of the show.

ACKNOWLEDGMENT

Mil gracias a María Elena Cepeda whose generosity never ceases to amaze me. Cepeda provided close critical readings on multiple drafts of this chapter. The following colegas offered valuable insights and assistance throughout different stages: Rosa Linda Fregoso, Susan J. Douglas, Frances R. Aparicio, Catherine Benamou, Robin Li, Nicholas Syrett, Larisa Casillas, and Angharad Valdivia. Finally, this chapter benefited from resources granted by the UC President's Postdoctoral

Fellowship and the department of Latin American and Latino Studies at the University of California, Santa Cruz.

NOTES

1. Translation note: I offer English-language translations of Spanish-language broadcasts rather than word for word transcriptions. I have chosen not to italicize or differentiate any of the Spanish since by doing so I would be marking Spanish, normalizing the English text, and sustaining U.S.-based class and racial hierarchies. For an elaborate discussion on the politics of language and translation, see the work of Sánchez (1983), Anzaldúa (1987) especially Chapter 5, Zentella (1997), Aparicio (1998b), and Hill (2003).
2. U.S. Latinos refers to persons of any Latin American origin living within the geographical boundaries of the United States. I also interchange "U.S. Latino" with "Latino" and only use the label "Hispanic" when referencing a source that has done so. For a general understanding of Latino and other ethnic labels, see Oboler (1993).
3. El Cucuy's real name is Renán Almendarez Coello. Popular legend describes a "Cucuy" as a male cross between a human and animal with glowing red eyes that hides in closets or under the bed. Used primarily in Mexico and in the southwest United States, this mythical figure is used to police children out of dangerous, dark places. For a folkloric explanation see Garza (2004).
4. Public controversy over homophobic satires has, in particular, surrounded New York City's top-rated show, El Vacilón de la Mañana (Navarro, 2001). For instance, according to de la Fuente (2005) in 1994, a coalition of three lesbian organizations, Las Buenas Amigas, African Ancestral Lesbians United for Societal Change, and The Lesbian Avengers, waged a four-month protest campaign against the radio show, its radio station WKSQ-FM, and its parent company, Spanish Broadcasting System (SBS). As a result, El Vacilón de la Mañana quietly retired some of the show's "gay" scripted characters on a temporary basis. A feature-length film, aptly titled "El Vacilón—The Movie" based on the popularity of the radio show, debuted in thirty Hispanic-identified media markets with box office success.
5. Despite his ratings success over Howard Stern, El Cucuy does not rake in comparable revenues. Ben Fong-Torres (2005) highlights this distinction with a compelling quote from El Cucuy: "People will always compare us based on our popularity, but he is the one who has made millions, while my ratings have always been higher."
6. Latinos account for 10 percent of all U.S. radio listening and listen to radio an average of three hours a week longer, see the special issue dedicated to "Hispanic Radio" by the trade magazine *Radio Ink* (2002) as well as Arbitron-issued research reports (2005, 2006).
7. I use quotations around "home" to indicate that it does not necessarily "signify a physical entity fixed in a particular place, but rather a mobile symbolic habitat, a performative way of life and of doing things in which one makes one's home while in movement" (p. 47); see David Morley's (2000) insightful text.
8. These rallies took place in both Latino and non-Latino identified metropolis, from Miami, Florida; Charlotte, North Carolina; Milwaukee, Wisconsin; Chicago, Illinois; Nashville, Tennessee; Dallas and Houston, Texas; San Francisco and San Diego to Los Angeles, California.
9. Two controversial pieces of legislation were passed in December 2005 (House of Representatives) and May 2006 (Senate). The former, HR4437 known as "The Border Protection, Anti-terrorism, and Illegal Immigration Control Act," asked, among other things, (1) that a 700 mile

wall be constructed along the U.S.-Mexico border; (2) that state and local enforcement be authorized to enforce federal immigration law; (3) changes in law so that individuals, organizations, and religious factions be criminally penalized for assisting undocumented immigrants; and (4) that felon penalties be imposed on immigrants for residing in the United States as undocumented. The latter, S2611, was largely a modified version of HR4437. A detailed trajectory of the bill's route to passage can be found at http://www.govtrack.us/congress/bill.xpd?bill=h109-4437, retrieved November 1, 2006.

10. Methodologically, I taped four five-day sessions of El Cucuy's shows approximately a year a part: October 2002, September 2003, October 2004, and October 2005. Occasionally, audio clips of El Cucuy's morning show are available on his www.cucuy.com website. None of his archived shows are available for public use. I have also been an intermittent morning listener for nearly four years, read his autobiography, and purchased compact disc compilations of his work. In public, I frequently engage male listeners such as construction workers and painters that I observe listening to his show.
11. Ben Quiñones makes the following comment about the nature of Mexican regional music: "[t]his is not Gloria Estefan or salsa; this is rancho music, straight working-class." Quiñones' comment alludes to the racial and class distinctions between Mexican and Central American communities in the United States and those of Cuban descent, considered a more affluent segment of the U.S. Latino community. His comment, however, neglects the history of salsa and its ties to working-class Latinos of color both within and outside the United States. See the work of Frances R. Aparicio (1998a).
12. The male partnership between politicos and immigrant men create a transnational process, wherein Latin American elites encourage immigrant men to send money home. In actuality, remesas (remittances), cloaked in the interest of public service, serve as economic safeties that benefit local elites. See María Elena Cepeda's (2003) explanation of this conundrum within a Colombian context.
13. As the counter component to marianismo, the "malinche" ideal refers to an indigenous or mestizo woman who carries whore and traitor qualities. The tale of the malinche has undergone its own feminist revisions courtesy of Chicana feminists who argue that the dichotomy of marianismo/malinche not only mirrors the predicament of Chicana feminists who advocate for both racial and gender-specific issues but it also limits Chicanas within two unproductive ideals (Alarcon, 1989; Fregoso, 2005, Chap. 2; Segura & Pesquera, 1988–1990; Zavella, 2003).
14. The rest of the compact disc follows a similar suit of sexually laden humor, offering skits where couples miscommunicate while having sexual intercourse, a mother advises her daughter not to "turn around" during sex with her newlywed husband, and a doctor examines a patient's finger by asking him to undress completely, among others.
15. The pejorative term "blanquito" refers to one as both white (blanco) and small (as indicated by the addition of "ito").

REFERENCES

Alarcon, N. (1989). Traddutora, Traditora: A paradigmatic figure of Chicana feminism. *Cultural Critique, 13*, 57–87.
"Almendarez-Coello dominates just-released Arbitron radio rankings." (2000, October 17). [Electronic version]. Business Wire.
Almendarez Coello, R. (1999). *Disco del Cucuy* [CD]. New York: RCA International.

Anderson, B. (1991) *Imagined communities: Reflections on the origin and spread of nationalism.* New York: Verso Books.
Anzaldúa, G. (1987). *Borderlands: The new mestiza.* San Francisco: Spinsters/Aunt Lude.
Aparicio. F. (1998a). *Listening to salsa: Gender, Latin popular music, and Puerto Rican cultures.* Hanover & London: Wesleyan University Press/University Press of New England.
Aparicio, F. (1998b, Spring). Whose Spanish? Whose language? Whose power?: Testifying to differential bilingualism. *Indiana Journal of Hispanic Literatures, 12*(Spring), 5–25.
Arbitron. (1996, Fall). *Arbitron radio market rankings.* Retrieved November 1, 2006, from http://www.arbitron.com/home/mm001050.asp
Arbitron. (2005a). *Ethnic time spent listening.* Retrieved February 1, 2007, from http://www.arbitron.com/home/hispaniclistening.htm
Arbitron. (2005b). *Hispanic radio today 2005 edition: How America listens to radio.* Retrieved October 10, 2006, from http://www.arbitron.com/downloads/hispanicradiotoday05.pdf
Arbitron. (2006). *Hispanic radio today 2006 edition: How America listens to radio.* Retrieved October 10, 2006, from http://www.arbitron.com/home/hispaniclistening.htm
Aufderheide, P. A. (1999). *Communications policy and the public interest: The telecommunications act of 1996.* New York: Guilford Press.
Bachman, K. (2004, March 17). Univision radio parts with top host El Cucuy. [Electronic version]. *Mediaweek.*
Baker, C. (2004, May 4). FCC overlooks Spanish radio stations in crackdown. [Electronic version]. *The Washington Times.*
Baum, D. (2006, October 23). On the air, Arriba! Getting out the Latino vote. *The New Yorker,* pp. 36–43.
Calvo, D. (2000, January 27). Radio around the dial, keep'em laughing: Renan Almendarez Coello. [Electronic version]. *The Los Angeles Times.*
Campo-Flores, A. (2000, July 24). The bogeyman will get you. *Newsweek, 136*(4), 49.
Casillas, D. I. (2006). *Sounds of belonging: A cultural history of Spanish-language radio in the United States, 1922–2004.* Unpublished doctoral dissertation, University of Michigan, Ann Arbor.
Castañeda Paredes, M. (2003). The transformation of Spanish-language radio in the United States. *Journal of Radio Studies, 10*(1), 5–16.
Catanzarite, L. (2003, September). Wage penalties in brown-collar occupations. In *Latino Policy and Issues Brief, 8.* University of California, LA: Chicano Research Center.
Cedillo, G. (2003, September 18). Drivers' licenses for all will protect public safety for all. [Op-ed]. *The San Francisco Chronicle,* p. A–23.
Cepeda, M. A. (2003). Shakira as the idealized, transnational citizen: A case study of *Colombianidad* in transition. *Latino Studies Journal, 1,* 211–232.
Chaney, E. (1979). *Supermadre: Women and politics in Latin America.* Austin: University of Texas Press.
Chang, G. (2000). *Disposable domestics: Immigrant women workers in the global economy.* Cambridge, MA: South End Press.
Chavez, L. R. (2001). *Covering immigration: Popular images and the politics of the nation.* Berkeley, CA: University of California.
Clemens, L. (2005, December 1). The sound that sells. [Electronic version]. *Marketing y Medios.*
de la Fuente, A. (2005, November 14–20). Hispanic shock Jock Boffo at B. O. *Variety, 400*(13), 16.
Douglas, S. (1999). *Listening in: Radio and the American imagination.* New York: Times Books.
Douglas, S. (2002). Letting boys be boys: Talk radio, male hysteria, and the political discourse of the 1980s. In M. Hilmes & J. Loviglio (Eds.), *Radio reader: Essays in the cultural history of radio* (pp. 485–504). New York: Routledge.

Enloe, C. (1989). *Bananas, beaches, and bases: Making feminist sense of international politics.* Berkeley, CA: University of California.
Espiritu, Y. (1999). Gender and labor in Asian immigrant families. *American Behavioral Scientist,* 42(4), 628–647.
Flaccus, G. (2006, March 29). Spanish-language media credited on pro-immigrant rallies. [Electronic version]. *The Boston Globe.*
Fong-Torres, B. (2005, July 10). Radio waves. [Electronic version]. *San Francisco Chronicle,* p. PK–45.
Fraser, N. (1992). Rethinking the public sphere: A contribution to the critique of actually existing democracy. In C. Calhoun (Ed.), *Habermas and the public sphere* (pp. 109–142). Cambridge, MA: MIT Press.
Fregoso, R. L. (2005). *Mexicana encounters: The making of social identities on the borderlands.* Berkeley, CA: University of California.
Garza, X. (2004). *Creepy creatures and other Cucuys.* Houston TX: Arté Público Press.
Glendhill, L. (2004, May 26). Latinos demand law on licenses. [Electronic version]. *San Francisco Chronicle,* p. B–4.
Goldring, L. (2001). The gender & geography of citizenship in Mexico-U.S. transnational spaces. *Identities: Global Studies in Culture and Power,* 7(4), 501–537.
Goldring, L. (2003). Gender, status, and the state of transnational spaces: The gendering of political participation and Mexican hometown associations. In P. Hondagneu-Sotelo (Ed.), *Gender and U.S. immigration, contemporary trends* (pp. 341–354). Berkeley: University of California.
Greenhouse, S. (2005, October 10). Front line in day laborer battle runs right outside home depot. [Electronic version]. *The New York Times.*
Gutiérrez F. & R. Schement. (1979). *Spanish language radio in the southwestern United States.* Austin: Center for Mexican American Studies, University of Texas.
Hansen, V. (2003, September 18). Time for frank talk about illegal immigration. [Op-ed]. *The San Francisco Chronicle,* p. A–23.
Heath, R. (1998, February). Tuning into talk. [Electronic version]. *American Demographics,* pp. 48–53.
Hendricks, T. (2006, August 1). Popular DJ takes registration drive to Latino voters. *San Francisco Chronicle,* p. A–4.
Hill, J. (2003). Mock Spanish, covert racism, and the (leaky) boundary between public and private. In B. Rampton (Ed.), *The language, ethnicity, and race reader* (pp. 199–211). New York: Routledge.
Hilmes, M. & J. Loviglio. (Eds.). (2002). *Radio reader: Essays in the cultural history of* radio. New York: Routledge."Hispanic Radio." (2002, May 27). *Radio Ink,* 17(10).
Hondagneu-Sotelo, P. (1994a). *Gendered transitions: Mexican experiences of immigration.* Berkeley: University of California.
Hondagneu-Sotelo, P. (1994b). Overcoming patriarchal constraints: The reconstruction of gender relations among Mexican immigrant women and Men. *Gender & Society,* 6(3), 393–415.
Hondagneu-Sotelo, P. & M. Messner. (2001). Gender displays and men's power: The "new man" and the Mexican immigrant man. In H. Bord & M. Kauffman (Eds.), *Theorizing masculinites* (pp. 200–218). Thousand Oaks, CA: Sage Publications.
Hondagneu-Sotelo. P . (2003). *Gender and U.S. Immigration: Contemporary Trends.* Berkeley: University of California Press.
Johnson, M. & L. Spice. (2006, March 23). Thousands marched for immigrants. [Electronic version]. *Milwaukee Journal Sentinel.*

Kimmel, M. (2003). Globalization and its mal(e)contents: The gendered moral and political economy of terrorism. *International Sociology, 18*(3), 603–620.

Kochhar, R. (2004, June). *Latino labor report, first quarter 2004: Wage growth lags gains in employment.* PEW Hispanic Center.

Leslie, T. (2003, September 18). California's system of issuing IDs is dangerous and getting worse. [Op-ed]. *The San Francisco Chronicle*, p. A–23.

Levin, M. (1987). *Talk radio and the American dream.* Lexington, MA: Lexington Books.

Loviglio, J. (2005). *Radio's intimate public: Network broadcasting and mass-mediated democracy.* Minneapolis: University of Minnesota Press.

Mahler, S. J. & P. Pessar. (2001). Gendered geographies of power: Analyzing gender across transnational spaces. *Identities: Global Studies in Culture and Power, 7,* 441–459.

Martín-Barbero, J. (1993). *Communication, culture, and hegemony: From the media to mediations.* Newbury Park, CA: SAGE.

Mitchell K. & A. Espinoza. (2006, March 25). Tens of thousands protest bill. [Electronic version]. *The Denver Post.*

Montgomery, M. (1986). DJ talk. *Media, Culture & Society, 8*(4), 421–440.

Morley, D. (2000). *Home territories: Media, mobility, and identity.* New York: Routledge.

Navarro, M. (2001, August 13). Latino radio gaining popularity and scrutiny. [Electronic version]. *New York Times.*

Newman, M. (2006, April 10). Immigration advocates rally around U.S. [Electronic version]. *New York Times.*

Oboler, S. (1993). *Ethnic labels, Latino lives: Identity and the politics of (re)presentation in the United States.* Minneapolis: University of Minnesota.

Parreñas, R. S. (2001). *Servants of globalization: Women, migration, and domestic work.* Stanford: Stanford University Press.

Peña, M. (1991). Class, gender, and machismo: The "treacherous" woman of Mexican folklore. *Gender & Society, 5*(1), 30–46.

Pessar, P. (1996). Toward a feminist analytics of the global economy. *Indiana Journal of Global Legal Studies, 4,* 7–41.

Quiñones, B. (2005, March 24). "¡Despiertese, Despiertese! starting the day with Piolín." [Electronic version]. *LA Weekly.*

Quiñones Mayo, Y. & P. Perla Resnick. (1996). The impact of machismo on Hispanic women. *Affilia, 11*(3), 257–277.

Reyes Bonilla, D. (2005, Winter). Let's talk about sexo: Spanish-language radio beats Howard Stern and takes over the airwaves. [Electronic version]. *Colorlines, 8*(4), 1–4.

Rodriguez, A., P. & S. J. Mahler. (1999). Engendering transnational migration: The case of salvadorans. *American Behavioral Scientist, 42*(4), 690–719.

Romero, M. (1992). *Maid in the U.S.A.* New York: Routledge.

Rothenberg, D. (1998). *With these hands: The hidden world of migrant farmworkers.* New York: Harcourt Brace.

Sánchez, R. (1983). *Chicano discourse: Socio-historical perspective.* Rawley, MA: Bergin and Garvey.

Sassen, S. (1999). *Guests and aliens.* New York: New Press.

Sassen, S. (2000a). *Cities in a world economy.* Thousand Oaks, CA: Pine Forge Press.

Sassen, S. (2000b). Women's burden: Counter-geographies of globalization and the feminization of survival. *Journal of International Affairs, 53*(2), 503–524.

Scannell, P. (1996). *Radio, television, and modern life.* Cambridge, MA: Blackwell Publishers.

Schaeffer-Grabiel, F. (2006). Planet-Love.com: Cyberbrides in the Americas and the transnational routes of U.S. masculinity. *SIGNS: Journal of Women in Culture and Society, 31*, 331–356.

Segura, D. A. & B. M. Pesquera. (1988–1990). Beyond indifference and antipathy: The Chicano movement and Chicana feminist discourse. *Aztlán: Journal of Chicano Studies, 19*(2), 69–92.

Stein, J. (2006, March 28). 500,000 and no one invited me? [Electronic version]. *TIME.*

Stevens, E. P. (1973). Marianismo: The other face of machismo. In A. Pescatello (Ed.), *Female and male in Latin America* (pp. 90–111). Pittsburg: University of Pittsburg Press.

Szalai, G. (2004, March 19). El Cucuy tunes in higher ratings for SBS. [Electronic version]. *Hollywood Reporter.*

U.S. Census Bureau. (2005). American community survey. Retrieved August 15, 2006, from http://factfinder.census.gov/servlet/ACSSAFFFacts?_event=Search&geo_id=&_geo Context=&_street=&_county=los+angeles&_cityTown=los+angeles&_state=04000US06&_ zip=&_lang=en&_sse=on&pctxt=fph&pgsl=010

Vaillant, D. (2002). Sounds of whiteness: Local radio, racial formation, and public culture in Chicago, 1921–1935. *American Quarterly, 54*(1), 25–65.

Valenzuela, A., J. A. Kawachi, & M. D. Marr. (2002). Seeking work daily: Supply, demand, and spatial dimensions of day labor in two global cities. *International Journal of Comparative Sociology, 43*(2), 192–219.

Zavella, P. (2003). Talkin sex: Chicanas and Mexicanas theorize about silences and sexual pleasures. In G. Arredondo, A. Hurtado, N. Klahn, O. Nájera-Ramírez, & P. Zavella, (Eds.), *Chicana feminisms: A critical reader* (pp. 228–253). Durham, NC: Duke University Press.

Zentella, A. C. (1997). *Growing up bilingual: Puerto Rican children in New York.* Oxford: Blackwell Publishers.

Part IV. Latina Women as Cultural Readers

CHAPTER NINE

Media Practices AND Gendered Identity AMONG Transnational Latina Teens

LUCILA VARGAS

Numerous qualitative studies have shown that people use media texts, practices, and technologies to express and reaffirm their identities, especially their gendered identities (e.g., Hobson, 1982; Morley, 1986; Radway, 1987; Seiter, Borchers, Kreutzner, & Warth, 1989), yet the scholarship on how transnational youth use media for performing a hybrid gendered identity is in its infancy. The germinal ethnography of Marie Gillespie (1995) on the use of television among teens of Punjabi descent living in London initiated an approach that I find to be the most appropriate for the research on working-class, transnational Latina teens that I present here. This approach views "immigrant" teens as part of transnational formations. I frame the chapter with Judith Butler's (1990, 1993) notion of identity as *performativity*, which posits that when performing an action, we are not only expressing and reaffirming our identity, but that, at the same time, we are "doing" identity. In other words, we constitute our identities by repetitive acts, by everyday practices. The possibilities that working-class transnational Latinas have for "doing" gender are restricted by the identity as "Latinas" that is ascribed to them in the United States. In their daily lives, "cultural" and class distinctions oftentimes take precedence over gender difference. Living in the margins, these teens cannot ignore powerful axes of difference that the theory of *performativity* neglects. Thus, I also draw on the contrapuntal approach to hybridity proposed by Marwan M. Kraidy (2005). The musical term counterpoint refers to a polyphonic quality of sound, or texture, in which distinct melodies play "against" one another. Transnational teens (re)construct their gendered selves against the backdrop of contrasting representations of Latina femininity (Cortés, 1997; Dávila, 2002; Fregoso, 1995; Rodríguez,

1997; Rojas, 2004). Also, to "do" identity they actively use media texts created by institutions anchored in different cultures. My aim is to cast light on the relationship between mediated popular culture and hybrid gendered identity formation processes by examining how a small group of working-class, transnational Latina teens who live in the U.S. South talk about themselves and their media practices. What I am doing here differs from most qualitative research on audiences because I am seeking to explain how Latina teens' hybrid gendered identities are constituted *in and through* their media practices and *in and through* their talk about media and popular culture. I am interested in the particular ways in which they talk about their media and popular culture memories, and their present practices and desires to simultaneously express and "do" a hybrid gendered identity.

The chapter is part of a larger *action-research* project that I carried out with the help of grassroots organizations serving Latina/o youth. I begin by summarizing the methodology of the larger project. Then, I present the notion of gendered identity as *performativity*, and subsequently discuss the specific meaning that Kraidy attaches to the elusive trope of hybridity. To ground the analysis on the teens' cultural milieu, I then talk about the limited options for producing a gendered identity that are available in Latin American as well as in U.S. Latino communities. After that I move on to describe and interpret the findings. Because the analysis foregrounds the data collected through *Who I Am Collages,* a method that I describe below, the discussion is organized according to the five techniques used by the teens to compose a gendered identity in these visual narratives of self. Accordingly, I first introduce the five techniques, and briefly discuss two of them, which are encoding femininity through images of girls and young women and using few or no signs of masculinity in their collages. Then I talk about how the teens alluded in their collages to media practices that they viewed as either feminine or gender-neutral, while at the same time shying away from practices clearly gendered as masculine, such as video game playing. Next I dedicate entire sections to the remaining techniques including references to romantic heterosexual relations, and encoding a desire to beautify themselves through fashion and beauty product imagery. Finally, to illustrate how media and popular culture are implicated in the construction of individual, unique gender configurations, in the last part of the chapter I present three cases that show differing degrees of defiance and accommodation to the often-conflicting regulatory frameworks that coexist in the transnational Latina/o milieu. I use the term *transnational Latina teens* to talk about both first- and second-generation immigrant young women of Caribbean and Latin American descent. Rather than referring to them as "immigrant," I use "transnational" to stress the fact that the milieu in which they relate to media and popular culture crisscrosses national borders. Crossing borders back and forth, or *circular migration* (Rouse, 1995), is as common in their social networks as is code-switching between linguistic and popular culture codes. The teens who participated in my project ranged widely in developmental stages, levels of bilingualism, national origin, family situation, and immigration experience. Such diversity brought in a fascinating variety of ways of using media and popular culture for identity construction.

METHODOLOGY

Action-research comprises a host of methodological approaches that seek, simultaneously, social change (action) and understanding (research). I followed the Southern Cross University approach because it offers guidance while at the same time leaving room for methodological imagination. Action-research's major tenets uphold that research is a spiral, iterative, and emergent process. It calls for the researcher to keep "refining methods, data and interpretation in the light of the understanding developed in earlier cycles" (Southern Cross University, 2001). My project included two after school programs that aimed to facilitate the learning of critical media literacy skills among a small group of teens. I taught a semester-long course (12, 90-minute sessions) in Durham, North Carolina, in 2002 and a summer course (5, 90-minute sessions) near Carrboro in 2004. These programs were the "sites" of my fieldwork. Located in the U.S. South, Durham (pop. 187,035) and Carrboro (pop. 16,784) did not have Latina/o residents until the 1990s. At the time of the fieldwork, Durham had a small Latina/o population (8.6 percent) and an unusually large black population (43.8 percent, whites were 45.5 percent). By contrast, most Carrboro residents were white (72.7 percent) and there were similar numbers of blacks (13 percent) and Latina/os (12.3 percent) (U.S. Census Bureau, 2000). My initial intention was to implement only the Durham program, but the early findings led me to implement the Carrboro program too. To a great extent, I chose Durham and Carrboro because I was quite familiar with the local scene and had access to community organizations. Yet these settings offered me the opportunity to study a new and poorly understood social formation: U.S. Southern Latina/os. The relatively large numbers of Latina/os who came to the region in the past two decades meant a major demographic change in the U.S. South (U.S. Census Bureau, 2000). It is estimated that, at the time of the fieldwork, more than half a million Latina/os resided in North Carolina (El Pueblo Inc., 2003). This number includes both first- and second-generation immigrant and other U.S.-born Latina/os.[1]

In addition to my interest in women's lives and the fact that it is easier for me, as a woman, to work with young women than with young men, I chose to work only with the former because I wanted to investigate intra-group differences rather than differences between the sexes. Out of the seventeen teens (ages 12–20) seven had been born in Mexico,[2] two in El Salvador,[3] one in Venezuela,[4] one in Honduras,[5] one in Colombia,[6] one in Puerto Rico,[7] and four in the continental United States to Salvadoran immigrants.[8] In Pierre Bourdieu's terms, with the exception of Gabriela,[9] who had been middle-class in her home country, the teens had a working-class *habitus;* their tastes and dispositions corresponded to those of the urban working poor of the Caribbean and Latin America. They attended public schools, lived in modest neighborhoods, and their parents performed blue-collar or "unskilled" work. They were *mestizas* and they mirrored the diversity of Latinas' bodies. The foreign-born were dealing with issues of racialization for the first time. They talked about themselves as different from Black, Anglo, and Asian American youth. Sometimes they used the terms *Latina* and *Hispanic* to identify themselves, but even U.S.-born teens talked about themselves by referring to their country of origin or descent too. Importantly, ten were the children of "new *braceras,*" a term used by Pierrette Honfagneu-Sotelo (2002) to refer to the increasing number of single women who migrate on their own or with their children.

As most action-researchers do, I relied on naturalistic methods, especially in-depth interviewing (Spradley, 1979, 1980). I took fieldnotes, collected materials produced by the teens for the class, and audiotaped and transcribed the seventeen (90-minute) group sessions and the fourteen (30–45 minute) individual interviews. In addition, I collected what I call *media narratives of self* through two methods that I transferred from anthropology and sociology (Vargas, 2004, May). One is the *life media calendar,* which draws on the life history method used by sociologists and seeks to elicit media and popular culture memories and thus to understand participants' media practices through time. The second method is the *Who I Am Collages,* which was inspired by Wendy Lutrell's (2003) anthropological study with pregnant teens.[10] This method is particularly useful for research with teens because, by encouraging them to produce a visual narrative of self, it enables them to articulate feelings and ideas that they might not have been able to put into words. All seventeen teens turned in calendars and fourteen explained their calendar to me during individual interviews. In addition, sixteen teens turned in collages, with fifteen teens presenting their collage to the class and one explaining it to me in private.

Because the collage method specifically asks participants to compose a visual narrative of self, combined with data gathered by other instruments, the collages provided rich material for analyzing the teens' ways of constructing their identities. A large part of my data are self-reports on media preferences and behavior that I gathered within the context of media literacy programs; I interpret these data in light of this context. I see the collage-making, the talk about media and popular culture, and the talk about the collages as *performative*. As signifying practices, collage-making and media and popular culture talk are means through which the teens "did" gender for their peers and for me, in the particular context of my project. In addition, I have looked, and have not found, evidence in the data indicating that the media experience reported by the teens might be significantly different from that of other working-class, transnational Latina teens that I have observed in my 12 years of living in the area. To interpret the collages, I draw on feminist scholarship (Jones, 2003) and other literature on visual culture and representation (Pieterse, 1992; Sturken & Cartwright, 2001), and on the use of images in qualitative research (Prosser, 1998; Rose, 2001). But, most of all, my interpretation hinges on the teens' explanations of their own work and in other data that I collected throughout the project. Naturally, my interpretation is shaped by my own lived experience as a Mexican immigrant.

Working within the framework of after school programs in which attendance was not mandatory meant that I faced the constraints typical of such programs, such as participant self-selection and high attrition and absenteeism rates (Cooper, Charlton, Valentine, & Muhlenbruck, 2000). In Durham, six teens attended between eight and eleven sessions, and the other six attended only about half of the program's class time (two quit after the midterm and four were often absent or late). In Carrboro, three teens attended between four and five sessions, but the other two attended only three sessions. Finally, I present the talk as it was uttered, but I include my English translation too. Before discussing how the teens perform gender through their media and popular culture talk, I introduce Butler's notion of *performativity*.

GENDERED IDENTITY AS *PERFORMATIVITY*

Blending ideas coming from feminist, poststructuralist, and psychoanalytic theories, queer theorist Judith Butler has delved into the problematic related to the constitution of the subject, the emergence of subjectivity, and the formation of gendered and sexed identities. Important for my use of Butler's insights in this research, is, first, her understanding of identity as signification, constructed in and through language and discourse—and thus fluid and in need of constant reproduction; and, second, her Foucauldian claim that sex and gender are the effects (rather than the cause, as essentialist theories assume) of institutions, discourses, and practices. In *Gender Trouble* (1990), Butler conducts a genealogical analysis of the notion of identity. She begins with Simone de Beauvoir, one of the existentialist philosophers who posited that the self is a becoming and that it is constituted through its deeds. Beauvoir encapsulated her ideas of gendered identity in her legendary claim "one is not born a woman, but rather becomes one." Her processual view of gendered identity laid the foundation for feminist challenges to essentialist notions of gender as something stable and existing prior to culture. Butler (1990), however, goes beyond existentialist claims:

> My argument is that there need not be a "doer behind the deed," but that the "doer" is variably constructed in and through the deed. This is not a return to an existential theory of the self as constituted through its acts, for the existential theory maintains a prediscursive structure for both the self and its acts. It is precisely the discursively variable construction of each in and through the other that has interested me here. (p. 181)

What she argues is that nothing exists outside of discourse because "doer" and "deed" construct each other within discourse, and by means of signification. There is no actor prior to the performance, as the metaphor of gender as theater suggests. Butler's concept of gender as *performativity* builds on Jacques Derrida's critique and elaboration of John Langshaw Austin's speech act theory. In *How to Do Things with Words* (1975), Austin distinguished between those statements that are merely descriptive such as "this ship is the Queen Elizabeth," and those utterances that actually do what they talk about. Austin argued that utterances like "I name this ship the Queen Elizabeth" or "I promise," actually enact the actions that they talk about. He called these statements "performative utterances," and maintained that their constitutive power depends on the speaker's intention ("serious" speech) and the conditions under which they were spoken (uttered in a public and ritualized mannered, in the presence of an authority, etc.). Derrida (1982) pointed out that the performative power of a sign relies on *iterability* and *citationality* rather than on the speaker's intention because performatives are always a repetition of highly conventional practices. The speaker is therefore citing norms, regulations, and authorities. He argued that any sign/utterance can be lifted from its context, "put between quotation marks," and repeated again, even with totally different intentions, breaking, in this way, the connection between the sign and its referent, and opening up the possibility for inauthentic (not "serious") repetitions. Using this reasoning to question essentialist notions of identity, Butler puts forward that gendered identity is "done," constituted, through the iterative citation of conventions in everyday practices.

Embracing Monique Witting's critique of the distinction between sex and gender, which maintains that gendered identity is constructed in culture and discourse, but sex is a biological given, Butler posits that both sexed and gendered identities are discursively produced, that they are "done" by signifying practices. In *Bodies That Matter,* Butler argues that individuals are "sexed" when they are interpellated (in the Althuserian sense of "hailing") as either a "she" or a "he." Butler talks about the first moment in which an infant is "girled" by someone who declares that the infant—who up until that point was an "it"—is a "girl." By means of the statement "it is a girl" the previously unsexed infant is thus allocated into a category based on gender. This "sexing" of the infant, points out Butler (1993), would be reinforced, or contested, by various authorities throughout her life (pp. 7–8).

Butler views sex and gender as hierarchical systems created by society to group individuals into political categories. "Man" and "woman" are political terms because whether one is classified as one or the other determines the claims to power that one can make. Sexed and gendered categories are "in fact the effects of institutions, practices, discourses with multiple and diffused points of origin," claims Butler (1990, p. XXIX). Here she both relies and elaborates on Foucault's analysis of power, which contends that power is not only repressive, but also productive. In the *History of Sexuality* (1978), Foucault reasons that, in addition to repressing individuals by prohibiting, limiting, and regulating their actions, juridical systems of power also define who is under their control and, by so doing, these institutions actually constitute the subjects that they claim to regulate (i.e., one becomes a "criminal" or a "law-abiding citizen"). The subject, argues Foucault, is an effect of institutions, constituted in and by their discursive structures.

Butler's (1990) assertion that gender is a "repeated stylization of the body, a set of repeated acts within a highly rigid regulatory frame" (p. 44) seemingly implies that her theory of gender as *performativity* leaves little room for individual agency. However, Butler makes an argument against gender determination based on these three points. First, given that identity is a signifying practice that requires repetition, it is likely that variation, and indeed failure on that repetition would occur. Second, because the rules governing signification are not only restrictive mechanisms, but also enabling tools for creating novel meanings, it is possible for some individuals to perform modalities of gender that, as Butler says, "contest the rigid signs of hierarchical binarisms" (p. 185). And third, because individuals have to "cite," all at once, the different rules and conventions that regulate each of their various roles, there is a "possibility of a complex reconfiguration and redeployment" of gender (p. 185). The last two points present an opening for incorporating class, "race," and other differences that Butler's theory ignores into the theory of *performativity*.

HYBRIDITY

As insightful as Butler's theorizing is, it is insufficient to make sense of media practices because it fails to account for the intersectionality of multiple axes of identity. Feminists of color have pointed out that race, class, and nation play central roles in the particular way in which a woman experiences herself. Indeed, this blindness has been the focus of harsh criticisms to Butler's work (Salih, 2002). The possibilities for producing identity that women from different cultures and classes have vary widely. To account for the complexity of transnational, working-class Latina teens' identities, I combine Butler's theory with the cultural theorizing on the trope of hybridity and other related concepts that highlight the saliency of cultural mixtures in the constitution of identity under conditions of globalization (Appadurai, 1996, 2001; Bhabha, 1994; Hall & du Gay, 1996).

Syncretism and *mestizaje* have been pivotal ideas in Latin American philosophy (Vasconcellos, 1976), literature (Paz, 1959), and cultural theory (Garcìa Canclini, 1989; Martìn Barbero, 1987, 2002). Likewise, in the United States, numerous authors have theorized the hybridity of U.S. Latina/o cultures and identities (Mato, 2003). There is important ethnographic work focusing on music and dance, such as Juan Flores's (2000) book about the hybridity of New York Latina/os, and Angharad Valdivia's (2006) essay describing how *salsa* becomes a means to construct ethnic identity. However, empirically grounded research on the way in which Latina/o youth use media and popular culture to produce a gendered ethnicity is still very scarce. Vicky Mayer's work (2003a, 2003b) with Mexican American teens is the most substantial contribution and there are a handful of other briefer studies on the topic (e.g., Moran, 2003; Subervi-Vélez & Colsant, 1993; Valdivia, 2000).

Marwan M. Kraidy's (2005) elaboration of previous theorizing on cultural hybridity is a promising avenue for the analysis of media reception practices of transnational youth. Kraidy borrows Edward Said's (1994) contrapuntal reading method to develop his contrapuntal approach to hybridity. "Counterpoint" describes a particular texture, or quality of sound, in a piece of music. Kraidy quotes Said to explain that in the counterpoint, "various themes play off one another, with only a provisional privilege being given to any particular one; yet in the resulting polyphony there is concert and order, an organized interplay that derives from the themes, not from rigorous melodic or formal principles outside the work" (Said, p. 51 quoted by Kraidy, 2005). This musical metaphor is helpful in describing the character of transnational identities because it alludes to the way in which the movement of various flows results in an "organized interplay." It is precisely the dialogue among the various melodies, the relations among them, that constitute the texture of contrapuntal music. In his research on the media reception practices of young Maronites in Lebanon, Kraidy (2005) found that they talked about themselves by bringing into play two competing discourses, "the West" and "the Arabs." Kraidy argues that these discourses "functioned not as a dichotomy, but rather as dialogical counterpoints, a notion ... [that refers] to discursive variations that create a space where the central theme is elaborated"

(p. 127). As I show below, the teens drew on the traditional discourse to talk about themselves and their media practices. But they also drew on the alternative, "modern" discourse articulated by the women's movement. Because this discourse is far less vibrant in Latin America than in the United States, these competing discourses become associated with cultural geographies.

GENDER IN LATIN AMERICAN AND U.S. LATINO PATRIARCHIES

Most research on gender in Latin America and U.S. Latino communities has relied on the notions of m*achismo* and its counterpart, *marianismo*.[11] Likewise, the dichotomous categories of "virgin/madonna" and "whore" have guided much theorizing on *mestiza's* sexuality (Chant & Craske, 2003, pp. 134–138). The essentialism implied in these notions has been challenged by authors who argue that each particular locale develops its own distinct form of patriarchy. Moreover, increasing numbers of Latin American women are now attending school, joining the labor market, having fewer children, taking up political positions, and living in nontraditional household arrangements. These changes suggest that conventional gender constructions are being shattered and that the possibilities for producing gendered identities are widening (Chant & Craske, 2003). Although gender has become a highly contested terrain, the time-honored discourse on femininity is quite alive and the variegated forms of patriarchy in Latin America are still very oppressive. The brutality of the mechanisms deployed to police women is evident in the region's levels and modes of gender violence and sexual harassment; the hundreds of feminicides that go unpunished along the U.S.-Mexico border are emblematic of the viciousness of this policing.

One of the most influential feminist scholars in Latin America, anthropologist Marcela Lagarde (1993), has put forward a typology of gendered identities available to Mexican women that includes five basic types: *madresposa, monja, puta, presa,* and *loca* [motherwife, nun, whore, prisoner, and madwoman]. In her extensive fieldwork with women in Mexico, Lagarde (1993) found that they are hard-pressed to construct their gendered and sexual identities within the boundaries of the house, the convent, the brothel, the prison, and the asylum (p. 40). She argues that all Mexican women perform, at least partially, one or two of the stereotypical identities of these figurative spaces; those who reject the house and the convent most forcefully are perceived as "bad women, sick, incapable, weird, madwoman" (Lagarde, 1993, p. 41; translation mine). Rooted on Catholicism, manifest in the folklore of working-class male migrants (Peña, 1991), and constantly reproduced by media texts like *telenovelas* (Rojas, 2004), the traditional Latin American discourse on gender and sexuality permeates working-class Latino settings (Crenshaw, 2003;

González López, 2005). The frequent contact that women migrants have with relatives back home reinforces its internalization.[12] Therefore, despite the change in gender relations that migrant families undergo (Hirsh, 1999), the limited choices for producing identity that are available to Mexican women find their way into *El norte*. As Vicky L. Ruìz (1996) talking about Chicanas says, women have been expected to be the "guardians of 'traditional culture'" (p. 132). For Chicanas, says poet Gloria Anzaldúa (1987/1999), their culture is a *cultura que traiciona* [culture that betrays], a culture that subjects women to the enduring mandates of a "cultural tyranny" that puts the burden of "tradition" on their shoulders:

> The culture expects women to show greater acceptance of, and commitment to the value system than men. The culture and the Church insist that women are subservient to males. If a woman rebels she is a *mujer mala*, If a woman doesn't renounce herself in favor of the male, she is selfish. If a woman remains a *virgen* until she marries, she is a good woman. For a woman of my culture, there used to be only three directions she could turn: to the Church as a nun, to the streets as a prostitute, or to the home as a mother. Today some of us have a fourth choice: entering the world by way of education and career and becoming a self-autonomous person. A very few of us. (p. 39)

The teens in my project aspired to pursue that fourth choice; they wanted to further their education and to have a career, but many complained about extreme policing from their mothers; at least for Carmen and Lidia, traditional beliefs about women's sexuality—especially virginity until marriage—were the cause of much conflict at home. As I describe in the remaining part of the chapter, all teens "did" gender against the backdrop of *culturas que traicionan*.

"DOING" GENDER THROUGH COLLAGE-MAKING AND MEDIA AND POPULAR CULTURE TALK

Making and talking about *Who I Am Collages* demand intense "doing" of gender. Each of the teens constructed an identity that reflected a unique gender configuration, yet it is possible to identify a few general patterns in the sixteen collages. The five main techniques that the teens employed to produce a gendered visual narrative of self include the following: (1) encoding femininity by pasting images of feminine-looking girls and young women; (2) using few or no signs of masculinity; (3) alluding to media practices that they viewed as either feminine or gender-neutral, while at the same time staying away from practices clearly gendered as masculine; (4) including references to romantic heterosexual relations; and (5) encoding a desire to beautify themselves through fashion and beauty product imagery. The first technique uses both indexical and iconic signs.[13] Three teens pasted photographs of themselves, and most pasted signifiers that in some way resemble the collage-maker. The technique was used in thirteen of the sixteen collages. Only Alex, Sabrina, and Carmen did not include representations alluding to girls and women, and Carmen was the only teen to use a picture of a young man to stand for herself—in this case, for her desire to graduate. The nearly ubiquitous presence of imagery representing girls and young women was also a means to signify their belonging to girls' groups. This technique is the most obvious way of (re)producing a gendered self in and through discourse, that is to say, in and through the signifying images and words used in the collage to compose a narrative. By pasting cutouts of girls laughing with their mouths wide open and wearing makeup and sexy attires, they were "citing" media conventions and constituting their own identities according to "the highly regulatory framework" that governs gender performances and pervades teens' media.

The second technique, using few or no signs of masculinity, complements the first one. As many other feminist authors do, Butler argues that the structures and institutions that regulate gender are grounded on a conceptual episteme (or paradigm) based on the male-female binarism. Hence, performing a feminine identity entails putting the double act of appearing feminine while at the same time not appearing masculine. In the collages, while representations of girls and women are either indexical or iconic signs of femininity, representations of boys and men are not signs of masculinity, but rather symbolic signs of heterosexual romance. Most often, the teens alluded to the objects of their desires rather than to actual romantic relationships. For example, Lidia superimposed the word "love" to a picture of pop star Enrique Iglesias and Paty drew a red heart around the picture of soccer celebrity David Beckam. Many of the collages contain a handful of signs of masculinity that have been contested by the women's movement, and therefore they are now ambiguous; for instance, Paty's collage has references to sports, Daniela's has references to competence, and Sabrina has references to career, but, as I discuss later in the chapter, only in Isabel's collage do traditional signs of masculinity take a unequivocal masculine meaning. The remaining three techniques require a more elaborate discussion than the first two, thus I dedicate a section below to each of them.

PRODUCING FEMININE SELVES THROUGH THE SIGNIFICATION OF MEDIA PRACTICES

In the collages, the teens included signs of media texts, practices, and artifacts to construct a gendered identity. I discuss this third technique in this section, but before I do that, let me talk about an in-class exercise that casts light onto the gender meaning that the teens attached to signs of media. The exercise asked students to color-code media artifacts using pink for women's media and blue for men's media.[14] When I asked about the telephone, the nine teens who worked on the activity said "pink!" But when I asked them about the videocassette recorder, no one said "pink." Three said that they had used both colors, and six said that they had used blue.[15] In the following conversation they are explaining their answers regarding the VCR:

> Lucila: Masculino, ¿por qué es masculino?
>
> Jennifer: Girls will be watching *novelas* and boys will be watching the movie.
>
> Sabrina: The movie.
>
> Daniela: It requires some work.
>
> Susana: Yo puse los dos.
>
> Isabel: Me too.
>
> Daniela: Most VCRs don't work, properly [...]
>
> Lidia: Yo lo puse masculino pero yo, yo no sé en mi casa, en mi casa tambie n lo ocupamos los dos pero el que tiene más la iniciativa siempre es mi hermano, yo por eso le puse masculino.
>
> Daniela: En mi casa, no sé porque el único hombre es mi hermanito, pero en [la] sociedad es el hombre porque, like most, yo tengo como casi todas las cosas que necesitan un poco de trabajo, or programming or some type of function, como que lo arregla mi hermanito, como que él puede programar el VCR, él puede, you know, connect the stereo, TV, go together, and he plays the Nintendo and ...
>
> Lucila: ¿Y cuántos años tiene tu hermanito?
>
> Daniela: Tiene once y ya desde chiquito empezó ha travezear con eso.

> [Lucila: Masculine, why is it masculine?
>
> Jennifer: Girls will be watching *novelas* and boys will be watching the movie.
>
> Sabrina: The movie.
>
> Daniela: It requires some work.
>
> Susana: I put both.
>
> Isabel: Me too.
>
> Daniela: Most VCRs don't work, properly [...]
>
> Lidia: I put masculine but I, I don't know, at my home, at my home we both use it, but the one who has more initiative is always my brother, that's why I put masculine [...]
>
> Daniela: In my home I don't know, because the only man is my little brother, but in society it's men because like most, I have, like almost all things that need a little work, or programming or some type of function, like it's my little brother who sets them,

like he can program the VCR, he can, you know, connect the stereo, TV, go together, and he plays Nintendo and …

Lucila: And how old is your little brother?

Daniela: He's eleven, and he began to mess up with that when he was very little.]

Both Lidia's and Daniela's comments about their brothers' ingenuity regarding media technology that "requires some work" echo a truism in media studies and shows that the teens perceived media technologies in gendered ways. The excerpt also helps to interpret their use of imagery of media technology and practices to "do" gender through collage-making. None of the collages has images of VCR or DVD hardware.[16] Other media that require great technical competence, music instruments, were conspicuously absent from both the collages and the teens' memories and desires. The persistent references to music in the collages reflected the centrality that music had for (re)constructing their ethnicity; there were twenty-nine signs of music in the collages and only Isabel's collage has no signs of music. Yet only Beatriz's collage has an image of an instrument (a guitar), and she was the only teen who talked about her desire to play an instrument. Therefore, nearly all references to music "cite" practices that observe the gender norms articulated by the dominant discourse on femininity, which limits the possibilities that women have for performing music. The signifying absence of music instruments is even more important when one considers that for the local Latina/o youth, ethnicized practices around Latin American music were rituals that help sustain the local Latina/o subculture.[17] The persistent references to music signs in the collages reflects the centrality that music had for (re)constructing ethnicity at the local level, but it also illustrates the way in which the teens "did" a gendered ethnicity.

Another practice that has been clearly gendered—and marketed—as masculine, video game playing, was conspicuously absent in the collages and in the data gathered by other instruments. Alex and Leticia reported owning a Nintendo, but only Leticia included an iconic sign of video gaming in her collage. In addition, Anabel noted in her life media calendar that Nintendo was her favorite toy at the time of the fieldwork, yet she said that she used her brother's player. What is remarkable about this signifying absence is that in the two exercises that specifically asked the teens to compose a narrative of self, only the youngest teens (Leticia and Anabel) chose to include video games. Further, eight of the nine teens who participated in the color-coding exercise identified Nintendo as a man's technology; even Leticia colored the Nintendo blue.[18] Susana said. "Yo le puse el hombre porque … mi hermano juega Nintendo y siempre trae a los amigos a jugar con él, siempre puros amigos … y las amigas, I mean, las hermanas de los amigos siempre andan jugando, viendo, caricaturas" [I put man because, men, because, my brother plays Nintendo, and always, he brings his friends home to play with him, always only boyfriends, and the girlfriends, I mean his friends' sisters always playing, watching cartoons].

This certainty, however, does not mean that video game playing was not among their practices. Even Gabriela, who often articulated socially desirable answers to my questions, admitted to playing video games "sometimes." During other sessions, Stephany admitted to playing "a lot," and Sabrina and Susana disclosed that they did play at school: "In Yahoo the messenger, it's the messenger, like you could get in and play games," said Sabrina. And Susana added, "While you are talking to people. That's the only way to talk to people [at school]." Merging video games with new technologies for interpersonal communication, computer applications such as Yahoo the messenger may be degendering video game playing, but still the teens clearly identified it as a men's activity and did not use signs of video games in their visual narratives of self.

Sabrina's and Susana's comments also offer clues for interpreting the gender meaning of other computer technologies for the teens. In the exercise, seven teens designated the computer as gender-neutral; Daniela indicated that it was feminine, but only Carla coded it as masculine. In the collages, the number of signs of computer practices (sixteen) is only surpassed by the number of music listening signs (twenty-nine). Traditional women's practices such as letter writing and telephone talking have been transformed by the internet, and they, in turn, may have contributed to the degendering of the computer, which a few years ago was seen as a men's technology. The teens made no clear-cut distinction between computers and the internet and ten collages contain signs of computer/internet practices. Such high incidence is remarkable when compared to the number of signs alluding to practices traditionally seen as women's; there are only two collages with signs of telephone talking (Paty's and Jennifer's), two with signs of magazine reading (Anabel's and Beatriz's), and one with signs of both practices (Susana's).

They had mixed opinions about movie and television watching. They saw specific genres, texts, and the practice of attending to them as gendered. Alex and Anabel, for instance, pasted in their collages cutouts of advertisements for the contemporary release of *Sleep Over*, a Hollywood film about the slumber party of four Anglo teenage girls. In the color-coding exercise, six teens coded the television set as gender-neutral, but Susana, Daniela, and Carla coded it as feminine. Lidia articulated the majority view: "Porque las mujeres son muy telenoveleras y los hombres son, les gusta ser deportistas" [Because women are very telenoveleras and men are, they like sports], she said. The minority argued that the television set was feminine because "la mujer pasa más [tiempo] en casa que, que el hombre, el hombre siempre pasa, trabajando, o afuera con los amigos" [women spend more time at home than, than men, men always are working, or outside with friends], said Susana. Note how Susana, despite the fact that her mother was an independent working woman, articulates the traditional discourse that confines women to the house. Other comments suggest that the traditional Latin American discourse on femininity was at odds with the teens' lived experience (at the time of the fieldwork ten teens were living in female-headed households, a situation not uncommon in Latina/o immigrant communities). During a conversation about cars, Lidia made a telling remark about her mother: "Yo a veces le digo a mi mamá, 'tú eres la, la muy moderna,' porque mi mamá maneja de todo, maneja de carreras porque mi hermano tiene un carro de carreras" [Sometimes I tell my mother "you're very modern," because my mother drives everything, she drives racing cars because my brother has a racing car]. Lidia's choice of the word "moderna" to describe her mother hints at the teens' awareness that "new *braceras*" were challenging Latin American traditions.

DESIRE FOR BEAUTIFICATION AND COMMODITIES

The teens talked about the desire for beautification as it is presented in advertising and teens' magazines: as universal and natural among young women (Johnson, 2000; McRobbie, 1991). Fourteen collages contain signs of this desire in references to fashion and beauty practices. When Sabrina presented her collage to the class, she said,

> Sabrina: Ok, umm, I have shampoo. I don't know. Because, I put it because you know it makes your hair smell good.
>
> Stephany: Girls like to smell good. Girls like to smell good. All of them do.
>
> Sabrina: And girls like to smell good. [...] I put got curl, because you know I got curly hair. My favorite time of the year is spring so I wrote 'spring'. I'm skilled. I love Fridays. Umm, I am sort of like an adventurous. My favorite shampoo is Pantene Pro V. I am a student. Mmm, I like getting shoes. I like taking pictures, and I like putting on make up!

Sabrina and Stephany seem to be "citing" the—apparently—natural law that mandates that "girls like to smell good." Other data suggest that perfume was the single most-desired beauty product by the teens (e.g., some carried perfume bottles in their purses; Carmen's, Leticia's, and Leticia's collages had images of perfume; and Leticia's also had the brand name Adidas Moves). In and through her narrative, Sabrina produces a feminine identity in accordance with conventional regulations of the female body. She says that she likes wearing makeup and mentions her favorite shampoo. Hair and hair products are recurrent elements in the collages. Like Sabrina, Gabriela pasted a cutout of Pantene Pro V shampoo; Stephany pasted an image of a girl blow-drying her hair; Beatriz and Paty pasted cutouts of hair, Paty put a tiny box of L'Oreal hair coloring product; and Natalia said that she had pasted a prominent image of a girl pulling her hair because she was always "fighting" with her hair. Finally, Sabrina states that she likes shoes—a feminine artifact with fetish status in many cultures. Cutouts of shoes figured in Leticia's, Anabel's, and Alex's collages too. Other teens also indicated a similar compliance with customary gender rules by including images of clothes and jewelry, and words such as "beauty," "fashion," and "looks." Femininity, thus, was encoded in most collages by cutouts of commodities, and in the case of some teens, by unmistakably branded commodities. On describing her collage, Alex underlined that New Balance was her favorite brand of tennis shoes, and that she wanted a pair of Rainbow sandals. Similarly, when Isabel asked Sabrina to clarify the meaning of a cutout of a tennis shoe pasted on her collage, Sabrina replied: "Because I like Nike shoes. And I like Nike, Nike, Nike! Nike is the best!" Her candor confirms both the impact of branding and advertising, as well as the significance of commodities in the construction of youth gendered identities, two points that have been repeatedly made in research with other youth.

THE HETEROSEXUAL MATRIX

Another technique employed by the teens to construct their identities was to include references to romantic love[19] in their collages. Once again, rather than signifying their actual experiences, most teens signified their desires. Apart from Paty and Gabriela, who pasted pictures signifying actual relationships, what they expressed most often was a desire for romantic love. In eight of the thirteen collages using this technique, such desire was clearly presented as heteroerotic.[20] The ties between media and their desires for romantic love were apparent in many collages: four teens pasted pictures of male celebrities that were the object of their romantic desire (Gabriela pasted the picture of singer Luis Miguel, Carmen pasted the picture of Luis Alfonsìn, Paty pasted pictures of actor Ewan McGregor and soccer celebrity David Beckham, and Lidia also pasted the picture of Beckman plus the picture of pop teen artist Enrique Iglesias), Anabel pasted a description of the contemporary movie release of *A Cinderella Story*, Alex pasted the lyrics of a song that unambiguously talks about heterosexual relations,[21] and Natalia pasted a cartoon portraying a boy coming out of a computer screen to offer a flower to a delighted girl.

Like Natalia, Gabriela and Paty included iconic signs of heterosexual couples. But surprisingly, only Gabriela encoded her desire for heteroerotic relationships through marriage imagery. In responding to my question about the picture of a bride and a groom in her collage, she said: "Oh, porque, no sé, yo como mujer, me gusta, me, como siempre he tenido la ilusión de tener una familia, de casarme, pero eso va a ser mucho después" [Oh, because, I don't know, I as a woman, I like, I, I have always dreamed of having a family, of getting married, but that is going to be much later]. Gabriela talks of her dream of having a family as a natural desire emanating from her womaness, "yo como mujer," she says. In this way, she "cites" the injunction of the *madresposa*, which expects women to fulfill themselves through marriage and family. However, she adds that "eso va a ser mucho después," (that is going to be much later) postponing, thus, the duty to comply with the mandate. In the following sections, I present three cases that illustrate, more specifically, the way in which media and popular culture are implicated in the construction of unique gender configurations.

"ALL AMERICAN" LATINA IDENTITY AND SUBJECTIVITY

Jennifer was one of the four teens who had been born in the United States. Her collage, which is shown in Figure 1, reveals the centrality that race and nation had for these teens' construction of gendered identities. It has recurrent signs of Anglo, middle-class girlhood, including lively but sugary colors; words such as "sweet," "angel," "happy," and "romantic," and cutouts of two cell phones, which

Figure 1. Who I Am Collage by Jennifer (Age 14)

signify the indispensable girly practice of phone talking. And Jennifer was unambiguous regarding her love of commodities and shopping. In addition to cutouts of feminine-looking pants and a sports suit prominently displaying the brand Nike, she carefully composed the word "shopping" by altering a cutout of another word with a marker. When I probed the teens' understanding of the gendered nature of shopping by asking them if men like shopping, they responded with an emphatic "No!" and Sabrina added, "A guy shopping is real weird, you see a guy shopping, you go, ok!"

Jennifer constructed her femininity as that of a U.S. young woman. At the center of the collage, she pasted a U.S. flag and, and at the top right side, she put an iconic sign of Anglo girlhood: the picture of a blonde teenage girl laughing with an open mouth. Nonetheless, she acknowledged her ancestry by the phrase "Latin American gURL." She went to some trouble to compose the word "Latin" by cutting and pasting letters; but, within the overpowering Anglo girlishness of her visual narrative, the word's small size hints at the peripheral nature of her *Latinidad*. The sisters later talked about their struggle to define themselves at school as both Americans and *not* Mexicans. Like in other regions of the United States, in North Carolina "Mexican" is not only a signifier of nation, but also a term that connotes race and working-class status.[22] Jennifer's collage thus shows how gendered identity concerns were inextricably linked to an anxiety about being racialized.

CAUTIOUS DEFIANCE OF CONVENTIONAL FEMININITY

Susana's collage, which is shown in Figure 2, is remarkable because its motif is a gender configuration that differs from the more conventional one represented in Jennifer's. At the center of the collage, there is a large cutout of the familiar sign for "women" with the word *"femenina"* superimposed and written with a red marker. In addition, there are seven different images of women, plus references to fashion and beauty. At the time of the fieldwork, Susana had been in the United States for 3 years, and she impressed me as being very mature and well adjusted. She was one of the best students in my class and she had taken leadership roles at school. Despite her pleasant personality and feminine appearance and demeanor, her collage and her media memories and practices suggest that she was caught between the traditional injunctions of her native Honduran culture and her desire to perform an alternative femininity. In describing her collage to the class, she said,

> Ok, me describo femenina, con mucho poder, me gusta trabajar en muchas fotos, por eso puse la cámara aquì, me gusta ir a la playa, escuchar música, ir de compras, y el reloj porque siempre ando de prisa, siempre a veces llego tarde y […] me gusta

hablar por teléfono, y hacer ejercicio y siempre estar en, en forma, me gusta leer, por eso la revista aquí, me gusta el deporte, me gusta el *soccer*.

[Ok, I describe myself as feminine, with a lot of power, I like working on many photos, that's why I put the camera here, I like to go the beach, listen to music, go shopping, and the clock because I'm always in a hurry, always, sometimes I arrive late and (...) I like to talk on the phone, and exercise and always be in, in shape, I like to read, that's why the magazine here, I like sports, I like soccer.]

As she does in the collage, in this narrative Susana encodes a conventional femininity while at the same time asserting her power. She refers to practices unambiguously associated with women, such as listening to music, going shopping, talking on the phone, and reading magazines.[23] But her references to power, sports, and being in shape allude to a resistant stance regarding traditional Latin American gender norms. Underneath her feminist concerns and her compelling claim to femininity seems to lie an apprehensive awareness of gender transgression. Susana constructed a femininity that challenged the submissive femininity of the *madresposa*, and it looks as if she knew that she had to do so very prudently to avoid being labeled as *loca*. In the collage she conveyed her interest in fashion by a cutout with the words "fashion consultant" and a picture of a young woman. The picture insinuates that, for her, shopping for the right garments is a serious matter. The young woman in the picture is sexy, but looks professional; she wears a tightened jacket, no jewelry,

Figure 2. Who I Am Collage by Susana (Age 16)

and a reserved ponytale. She has a pensive posture, plus a notebook and a pen in her hand. She is not just shopping for fashionable clothes. Is she carefully considering what would be the best attire to create a credible performance of femininity that does not require her to forfeit desires for power and independence?

Susana's collage also shows other ways in which media and popular culture are implicated in the performance of her different femininity. Note that she pasted the cover of the magazine *Shape* between the word "sport" and a large cutout of a young woman lifting weights. Her concern with beautification, which is evident in the collage in the phrases "a beautiful" and "lose weight" is inextricably tied to her desire for power and independence: it is a desire for a femininity that embraces physical prowess. She chose a women's magazine, but *Shape* does not adhere to traditional ideals of beauty. What is remarkable about the collage's cautious defiance of traditional femininity is that such a wary challenge seemed a characteristic trait of Susana's media practices. In her calendar, for example, she wrote *novelas* [soaps] as her favorite television show at the time of the fieldwork, and she said that her favorite movies included the romantic tale *Titanic*, the story of the ultimate girl hero *Cinderella*, and the romantic comedy *Mr. Deeds*. Her preference for *telenovelas* and romantic stories matches those of most other teens. Yet Susana was the only one stating that police dramas were among her favorite media texts. Susana said that she liked to watch "a series about the FBI" and *Expedientes Secretos [The X Files]*, and added, "Desde que yo estaba, desde Honduras, yo la he venido viendo" [I've been watching it since I was in Honduras]. Watching police dramas—a rather masculine practice—was one of her television rituals. Also, in her calendar Susana did not put Barbie as her favorite toy as many of the teens did. The following excerpt comes from the individual interview with her, in which I inquired about her memories of Barbie:

> Lucila: ¿No jugaste con Barbies?
>
> Susana: Sì, jugué con Barbies, pero no sé, más me gustaba, ¿qué era? Jugué con Barbies con mis hermanas. Pero, no sé.
>
> Lucila: ¿No era tu [juguete] favorito?
>
> Susana: No, no era mi favorito, de Barbie.
>
> Lucila: Y luego, the television show, tienes los *Power Rangers* ... ¿los veías en Honduras?
>
> Susana: Sì, se me olvidó poner *Gybon* que me gustaba más que los *Power Rangers*.
>
> Lucila: ¿Qué era *Gybon*?
>
> Susana: *Gybon* era un robote, que era como policìa, sì, es que a mì me gustaba, hoy estoy, agarré unas clases de police explorer.
>
> Lucila: También.

Susana: También. Me ha gustado siempre lo de la ley, la ley siempre me ha gustado. Quería ser abogada y despues detective.

Lucila: Sì, habìas dicho que querìas ser detective.

Susana: Detective, y me ha gustado siempre, pistolas y todo esto.

[Lucila: Didn't you play with Barbies?

Susana: Yes, I played with Barbies, but I don't know, I liked more … What was it? I played Barbies with my sisters but I don't know.

Lucila: It wasn't your favorite (toy)?

Susana: No, Barbie wasn't my favorite.

Lucila: And later you have the *Power Rangers* … did you watch it in Honduras?

Susana: Yes, I forgot to put that I liked *Gybon* more than I liked *Power Rangers*.

Lucila: What was *Gybon*?

Susana: *Gybon* was a robot that was like a police officer, yes and I liked it, and today I am taking some police explorer classes.

Lucila: Also.

Susana: Also. I have always liked things having to do with the law, I have always liked the law. I wanted to be a lawyer and then a detective.

Lucila: Yes, you had told me that you wanted to be a detective.

Susana: Detective, and I always like guns and all that.]

The characteristic trait of Susana's media practices is illustrated by this dialogue. She replies that she did play with Barbies as a child because of her sisters, but that what she has always liked are *pistolas y todo eso*. Her favorite cartoons matched her desire to have a career in the traditionally male-dominated area of law enforcement. As in her favorite television series *The X Files*, in the cartoon *Power Rangers* some of the main characters are attractive and intelligent police women. It is not easy for a 16-year-old Latina like Susana to perform the femininity embodied by *The X Files*' protagonist Special Agent Dana Scully, played by Gillian Anderson. Scully personifies an alternative femininity that is distinctively Anglo, yet Susana seems to have bridged the contradiction between, on the one hand, her Catholic upbringing and Honduran origin, which come with injunctions banning women from entering many fields, and, on the other hand, her desire to become a detective and her admiration for characters like Scully.

In her collage there are no signs of nation and the women represent various ethnicities, including Latina, Anglo, and Asian American. Susana performs a femininity that seems to transcend nationality and ethnicity, and to be related to a nearly universal struggle for women's rights. Near the middle of the term, I asked the teens to bring a magazine article to analyze in class. Susana brought a well-researched feature about women's status titled "*¿Mandan las mujeres?*"

[Do women rule?]. Moreover, in a different class when the conversation shifted into issues of sexual harassment, she said, "¡Imagínense si no cambiamos, imagínense la siguiente generación como va a ser! ¿Cómo? Ser peor. Van a decir que nosotros somos como los de antes. ¿Se imaginan?" [Imagine if we don't change, imagine how the next generation is going to be! How? It'll be worse. They're going to say that we're like those who came before us]. Susana's indignant comment hints at some sort of personal experience with the issue. Perhaps the experience of seeing the struggle of women like her mother, who achieve more independence after migrating to the United States.[24] In the awareness of women's oppression that her choice of article shows, as well as in the indignation expressed in her comment regarding the possibility that teens like them may keep reproducing the status quo, Susana reveals a way of being a transnational young woman who cautiously, but assertively, crosses many borders. Like Susana, most other teens aspired to take the fourth option that Anzaldúa says is now available to Latinas, that is to say, to gain independence through education; yet it seems that they did so aware of the popular proverb that, as writer Rosario Castellanos pointed out, sums up the indictment that hangs over woman who dare to enter into forbidden spaces: "Mujer que sabe Latin, ni encuentra marido ni tiene buen fin" [woman who knows Latin, neither finds a husband nor has a good end]. (Castellanos, 1973).

MARGINAL, TRANSGRESSIVE FEMININITY

"Yo soy una mujer y yo soy bien tough" [I'm a woman and I'm very tough] said Isabel, who constructed her identity in a decisively transgressive fashion for a 20-year-old transnational Latina. At the time of the fieldwork, she had been in the United States for over 5 years, was living with a foster family, and working as a carpenter and electrician. She also said that she had left home at 15 and had been on her own since then. Although she was the oldest of the group, she was attending the last year of high school.[25] Her demeanor was rough and her behavior sometimes rude. She often wore baggy pants and t-shirts, and twice she attended classes wearing a soccer uniform. As Natalia said, she "tried to look different." She had a tattoo and throughout the semester she changed her hair color from bleached, to bleached with blue streaks, and then to green. In Lagarde's typology, Isabel would fit the profile of the *loca* who is at risk of becoming a *presa*. Some of her comments suggest that her uncompromising performance of an alternative gendered identity has not been well received at school, where, she said, she had been ostracized by peers and penalized by teachers and administrators. Her arresting collage, which is shown in Figure 3, shows her transgressive identity. In explaining it to the class, she said,

MEDIA PRACTICES AND GENDERED IDENTITY AMONG LATINA TEENS | 209

Figure 3. Who I Am Collage by Isabel (Age 20)

¡Ay, que feo! Lo mío no es, demasiado, pero esto más o menos me representa a mì, no que andara asì, eso que andar en la calle asi allá en México, y, más que nada cuando ya me salì de la casa de mis papases, ¡ah! y luego aquí es cuando, cuando estaba con toda mi familia allá en México, y fuimos a Puetro Peñasco, al mar de Puerto Peñasco […] y, esto porque siempre he querido comprar un carro de esos y, y, aquì [apuntando a Chucky] a pesar de que he pasado por muchas cosas malas no le tengo miedo a las cosas […] Chucky, es una persona que asusta a la gente, representa mucho miedo […] entonces, a pesar de que he pasado por muchas cosas, ah, no tengo miedo, y, y aquí porque estoy contenta, aquí porque es como, cuando llegué a la casa de la señora con la que vivo ahorita y la casa está muy grande […] Y esto, porque antes cuando llegué aquì no tenìa nada de dinero y ahorita como voy trabajando y sacando dinero y lo he puesto en el banco. […] Y ésta, [pelota] porque es mi juego favorito, es mi adoración, el fútbol, y luego el volibol, porque es el segundo lugar de fútbol.

[Oh how ugly! Mine isn't too much, but this more or less represents me, not that I would be like that, to be on the street like that over there in Mexico, and above all when I've left my parents' house, ah! And then here it was when, when I was with all my family over there in Mexico, and we went to Puerto Peñasco, the beach at

Puerto Peñasco (...) and this because I always wanted to buy one of those cars and, and, here, (pointing to the Chucky doll) in spite of having gone through a lot of bad things I am not afraid of anything (...) Chucky is a person who frightens people, he represents a lot of fear (...) so, in spite of having gone through many things, ah, I am not afraid, and here because I am happy, here because it's like, when I arrived at the home of the lady I live with now and the house is very big (...) And this, because when I arrived here I had no money, and right now because I'm working and making money and I've put it in the bank.(...) And this (ball) because it's my favorite game, it's my adoration, soccer, and then volleyball, because it's in second place to soccer.]

When presenting her collage Isabel seemed to realize the striking power of the grotesque imagery that she had chosen, and thus she gave a somewhat apologetic explanation. Hers is a tale of survival. First she recounts the difficult childhood that made her like Chucky, unafraid and frightening-looking, but then she goes on to state that she is happy now. Also, Isabel explains that the picture of a man and three children at the beach stand for the cherished memory of a trip that she took with her family. In the collage Isabel defies acceptable expressions of Latina femininity by both including imagery that clearly evokes masculinity and by having signifying absences of femininity. The collage has no signs of beauty or fashion, no signs of feminine media practices, no signs of romantic love, and no signs of body (e.g., there are no sensual lips, eyes, or buttocks as in other collages). The gender of the child with the pacifier is somewhat ambiguous, and Chucky is a male doll. The collage has other traditional signs of masculinity: money, sports, and a Range Rover SUV. Further, does the absence of a woman in the picture that she chose to represent the memory of her family hint at a rejection of what Monique Wittig (1986) calls "compulsory heterosexuality"?

Isabel's media and popular culture memories and preferences reveal her identification with characters that go through painful situations like her own (e.g., loosing her parents, struggling at school). She shared some of the other teens' preferences, especially their *gusto* for traditional Latin American music and dance, but many of Isabel's preferences seemed more typical of boys than of girls. For example, when we were talking about reading, she said "I like to read mystery things, like, ah! Scary things!" Also, the heavy rock band *Metallica* was her second choice for top three artists, and among the films that she brought out were *Blood In Blood Out* (a Hollywood thriller gangster melodrama about three East Los Angeles Chicano boys) and *The Mummy Returns* (a Hollywood horror film catering to adolescent boys). She repeatedly said that she did not watch television at all; in one occasion when I asked the teens to fill up a log sheet of the weekly television watching, Isabel refused to do so. She did, however, have some familiarity with *telenovelas* and admitted to watch the Tasmanian Devil too: "Ya no miro mucho, solamente, a Tasmanian" [I don't watch much anymore, only, Tasmanian].

The Tasmanian Devil, from the Warner Brothers' series *Looney Tunes*, seemed to have a especial significance for her. It was one of the few characters that she could remember watching as a child, and rather than putting Barbie as her favorite toy in her calendar, Isabel wrote "Tasmanian."

The alternative gender configuration suggested by Isabel's collage and some of her media memories and present practices match her defiant stance regarding statements about appropriate feminine behavior made by other teens. For example, during a class when the conversation went into issues of appearance, Natalia was arguing that, as young women, they were coquettish and liked to be seen as pretty. Isabel interrupted her with a question: "¿Coqueta yo? ¡No!" [Me, coquettish? No!]. Likewise, when in another class, Jennifer said, "Like the boys will always be active and the girls will be just ..." Isabel jumped to say, "Not always!" And, more significantly, when we were talking about gender norms that oppress women, Isabel underlined the complicity of some women with such norms. "Pero muchas mujeres quieren pensar así" [But many women want to think that way], she argued. Isabel's frequent argumentative stance is evident in the following excerpt. The conversation was triggered by my questions about the extremely sexualized representation of women in the clip of the telenovela *Salomé* that we had just watched:

Susana: La forma de vestirse también tiene que ver mucho en la persona.

Lucila: ¿Por qué?

Susana: Porque, digamos así como ellas [en la telenovela], que se dice, con vestido corto, pasa por la calle, por supuesto que cualquier hombre la volteará a ver y va a querer hacer, intentar hacer algo.

Isabel: Pero es que por eso somos libres de hacer cualquier, de vestirnos como queramos. Susana: Sì, pero ...

Natalia: Pero es lo que estamos causando, es lo que nosotros causamos, si queremos hacer ...

Carla: Sì pero en el mero momento ...

Natalia: Lo que estamos causando. ¿Y para qué nos vestimos lindas? ¿Para qué nos vestimos así? ¡Para que nos miren! ¿Para qué otra cosa te vistes así?

Carla: Para que nos estén echando el ojo.

Isabel: ¡Pero no para que te violen!

Carla: Sì, pero tú los estas provocando.

Natalia: Los provocamos.

Carla: Nosotros los provocamos.

Isabel: ¡Ellos se provocan solos! Porque no les estamos [diciendo], no les estamos, así: "Ven tócame aquí" ¡Ay! Y luego al ratito, ¡pásatelas!

[Susana: The way you dress yourself has a lot to do with a person.

Lucila: Why?

Susana: Because let's say like the women (in the soap operas), let's say, with a short dress, walks down the street, almost certainly any man would turn around and stare, and would intend to do something to her.

Isabel: But that's why we are free to do whatever, to dress like anyway we want.

Susana: Yes but …

Natalia: But this is what we are provoking, this is what we provoke, if we want to do it …

Carla: Yes, but in that very moment …

Natalia: What we are provoking. And why do we dress pretty? Why do we dress that way? So they look at us! Why else would you dress that way?

Carla: So that they stare at us.

Isabel: But not so that they can rape you!

Carla: Yes, but you are provoking them.

Natalia: We provoke them.

Carla: We provoke them.

Isabel: They provoke themselves! Because we are not (saying), we're not like, "Hey come over and touch me here" Oh! And later after a little while, quit that!]

In her characteristic blunt manner, Isabel first unabashedly asserts a woman's right to play with her own style, "We're free to do any, to dress anyway we want," she says. Then she makes a case against sexist assumptions that justify sexual harassment. Though Natalia and Carla repeat the patriarchal argument that women provoke men when they dress revealingly, Isabel refutes the argument claiming that men decide by themselves how to respond to the assumed provocation. Also quite telling in the excerpt is the muted voice of Susana, who timidly agrees with Isabel that women are free to choose their attires, but does not voice further opinions. She seems to be more aware than Isabel of the highly regulatory structure that governs gender in the transnational Latina/o milieu—and of the dreaded consequences of defying it.

CONCLUSION

So, in what ways are media and popular culture implicated in the dynamics of producing a gendered ethnicity among working-class, transnational Latina teens living in the U.S. South? First, using Butler's notion of *performativity*, I argue that the teens' collages as well as their media talk are *performative;* they are acts in and through which the teens constitute their identities. In other words, when "talking" about themselves and their media memories, actual practices, and desires, the teens were in fact "doing" gender. Second, drawing on Kraidy's approach to hybridity, I posit that their gendered identities have a contrapuntual texture. As in contrapuntual music, in the teens' identities and subjectivities there is no dominant melodic voice, but rather contesting gender discourses that continuously play against one another. Belonging to marginalized communities, the teens could not overlook the centrality of axes of difference other than gender. They composed gendered and classed ethnicities in the space produced in and through the dialogue of two discourses, in a way similar to the young Maronites interviewed by Kraidy. And third, I argue that the dialogical counterpoints that created the space in which the teens composed their gendered identities were the dominant Latin American gender discourse, which permeates the transnational, working-class milieu, and the alternative discourse that the teens encountered in Anglo media representations such as Dana Scully, in the U.S. schools in which girls excel, and in the daring acts that *new braceras* perform in their everyday lives. Again, this is not to say that the two discourses do not exist in both sides of the border, but rather that they correspond to different cultural geographies.

As the previous analysis showed, various degrees of resistance to dominant gender norms are discernible in the teens' talk. Most constructed gendered identities that, while observing conventional definitions of femininity and heterosexual relations, also incorporated elements of the alternative discourse of femininity. In the cases of Susana and Isabel, concerns about cultural identity seemed buried under concerns about gender and sexuality, which brings to mind the centrality of gender in identity construction processes that Butler claims. But in the case of Jennifer, the anxieties about cultural identity overshadowed gender concerns. Because Jennifer was born in the United States, but Susana and Isabel were not, one may think that their contrasting anxieties have to do with immigrant generation. Though there is some merit to such an explanation, the fact that cultural identity was also a prominent concern of first-generation teens such as Lidia, Carmen, Gabriela, Alex, and Anabel shows that factors other than immigrant generation operate in this complicated dynamic. Jennifer's manner of incorporating Anglo femininity reminds me of Franz Fannon's "white mask," the narcissistic identification with the colonizer that constitutes the colonized subject. However, following Butler I have assumed that there is "no doer behind the deed," thus there is no "black skin" behind the mask. The partial incorporation of alternative Anglo femininity that Jennifer's collage suggests, opens up complex and fascinating questions of mimicry, passing, and colonial desire that ask for further research. At times the invocation to the alternative gender discourse seems to be a strategy to challenge the gender oppression that characterizes Latin American and Caribbean societies and pervades the transnational Latina/o milieu. Such incorporation of alternative femininity resembles the concept of mimicry proposed by Homi Bhabha (1994), who posits that mimicry is "the sign of a double articulation, a complex strategy of reform, regulation and discipline, which 'appropriates' the Other as it visualizes power" (p. 86). Thus a Latina teen constructing her identity in the interstices of two cultures may find it empowering to mimic a femininity associated with the dominant Anglo culture to resist the gender oppression of the societies that converge in the transnational Latina/o milieu.

As a final point, I would like to stress the conspicuous absence of imagery of motherhood in the collages as well as the dearth of expressions of desire to become a mother in the teens' talk. Within the oppressive framework of the conventional Latin American gender discourse, the mother enjoys a special status that women have brought into play to assert their authority and make personal and political claims. This status affords to women the possibility of challenging authoritarian structures. The best documented struggle is that of the *madres de la plaza de mayo* who took to the streets to denounce the atrocities of Argentinean military under conditions of state terrorism that prevented men from taking far less dissenting actions (Kaiser, 2005). Only the most mature teen, Gabriela, expressed her desire to become a *madresposa*. Age may explain this prominent silence in the case of younger teens, but it does not in the case of older ones. At least four other factors seem to be playing a crucial part in their apparent rejection of the *madresposa:* one, many of the teens were the children of *new braceras*, women who have challenged the gender mandates of their home countries; two, the teens' school culture emphasized education as a means of personal fulfillment; three, they participated in Anglo media and popular culture, which incorporates alternative ways of producing a gendered identity; and four, Gabriela's family had enjoyed solid middle-class status in their home country, which clearly points to the significance of class ideologies and opens up opportunities for further comparative research with teens from different social classes.

ACKNOWLEDGEMENTS

I would like to acknowledge the support of many people. Kellie Toon was my research assistant during part of the fieldwork, Jennifer Drolet edited the manuscript, and Galileo Velarde transcribed many tapes for me. My project benefited greatly from conversations with Jane D. Brown, Wendy Lutrell, and other colleagues. I am also grateful for criticism and suggestions for this chapter offerd by Angharad Valdivia. My research was supported by a Chapman Family fellowship (Institute for the Arts and Humanities, University of North Carolina at Chapel Hill) and by grants from the School of Journalism and Mass Communication at the University of North Carolina at Chapel Hill. Finally, I own an enormous debt to the wonderful seventeen young women who shared their memories and desires with me.

NOTES

1. The term "second-generation immigrant' is quite problematic. However, I use it for the sake of clarity.
2. Carla (age 13), Lidia (age 14), Paty (age 15), Yvet (age 16), Carmen (age 17), Beatriz (age 18), and Isabel (age 20).
3. Nancy (age 12) and Alex (age 14).
4. Gabriela (age 19).
5. Susana (age 16).
6. Natalia (age 16).
7. Leticia (age 12).
8. Daniela (15) and the sisters Jennifer (age 14), Stephany (age 14), and Sabrina (15).
9. Gariela (age 19).
10. Lutrell's book was published in 2003, but I was fortunate enough to hear her talk about her research years before.
11. *Machismo* and *marianismo* refer to Mexican conventional gender roles. While the former is characterized by hypervirility, aggression, and self-centeredness, the latter is distinguished by the "virtues" of the Virgin Mary, especially virginity and self-sacrifice. For a critique of these notions see Chant (2003).
12. Latin American women migrants tend to visit their home countries and keep in touch with relatives there more than men do. Also, women migrants all over the world sent a larger share of their income home than men (Chant & Craske, 2003, p. 252).
13. I am referring here to classic distinctions introduced by semiotician Charles Pierce: An iconic sign is perceived as resembling in some way the object it represents, for example a photograph of a child is iconic. An indexic sign has a direct connection to its object, for example, the fingerprints of the child are indexic signs of her. By contrast, the relation between the word "child" and the child is totally arbitrary, and thus the former is a symbolic sign, a convention (Sturken & Cartwright, 2001, p. 140).
14. For this activity, I used a handout copyrighted by the Center for Media and Values (1990). The handout does not acknowledge the author.
15. Carla, Lidia, Jennifer, Sabrina, and Daniela.
16. Only Leticia (12), pasted a cutout with eight DVD recordings; these recordings, however, featured films by Mary-Kate and Ashley Olsen—two popular culture icons of Anglo girlhood who were seldom mentioned by other teens.
17. See Vargas (2005) for a discussion of the teens' use of music to create a local youth subculture.
18. Nintendo: Blue: Susana, Daniela, Sabrina, Gabriela, Jennifer, Leticia, Natalia Lidia, Carla. Both: Carmen. Pink: None.
19. The teens expressed their desires as heteroerotic, which was the socially acceptable way to present themselves within the context of the project. Although Butler theorizes gender and sexuality together, I limit my comments about erotism and sexuality because, in part, I do not have enough data to venture into interpretations of the teens' sexual identities, and, in part, because I feel that

the teens would not have liked me to write about aspects of their identities that they inadvertently disclosed to me.
20. The four teens who did not include references to romantic love in their collages were Isabel, Leticia, Daniela, and Yvet.
21. Confessions Part II by R&B singer Usher.
22. See Valdivia (2006) for a discussion on the politics of salsa and identity among Latinos in the U.S. Midwest.
23. I have not commented on images of photo cameras because I told the teens that they were going to receive disposable cameras as part of the course's materials. Hence, they may have been primed to include such images.
24. The literature on migration suggests that gender roles are reworked upon migration in ways that favor expanded freedoms for women (Hirsh, 1999; Hondagneu-Sotelo, 2002).
25. The pacifier of the child in Isabel's collage suggests that the child is not only materially, but affectively deprived.

REFERENCES

Anzaldúa, G. (1987/1999). *Borderlands: The new mestiza = La frontera,* 2nd ed. San Francisco, CA: Aunt Lute Books.
Appadurai, A. (1996). *Modernity at large.* Minneapolis: University of Minnesota Press.
Appadurai, A. (Ed.). (2001). *Globalization.* Durham, NC: Duke University Press.
Austin, J. L. (1975). *How to do things with words.* Cambridge, MA: Harvard University Press.
Bhabha, H. K. (1994). *The location of culture.* New York: Routledge.
Butler, J. (1990). *Gender trouble: Feminism and the subversion of identity.* New York: Routledge.
Butler, J. (1993). *Bodies that matter: On the discursive limits of "sex."* New York: Routledge.
Castellanos, R. (1973). *Mujer que sabe latin.* Mexico: SepSetentas.
Chant, S. (2003). Introduction. In S. Chant & N. Craske (Eds.), *Gender in Latin America* (pp. 1–18). New Brunswick, NJ: Rutgers University Press.
Chant, S. & N. Craske. (Eds.). (2003). *Gender in Latin America.* New Brunswick, NJ: Rutgers University Press.
Cooper, H., K. Charlton, J. C. Valentine, & L. Muhlenbruck. (2000). Making the most of summer school: A meta-analysis and narrative review. *Monographs of the Society for Research and Child Development, 65*(1), 1–117.
Cortés, C. E. (1997). Chicanas in films: History of an image. In C. E. Rodríguez (Ed.), *Latin looks. Images of Latinas and Latinos in the U.S. media* (pp. 121–141). Boulder, CO: Westview.
Crenshaw, K. (2003). Mapping the margins: Intersectionality, identity politics, and violence against women of color. In L. M. Alcoff & E. Mendieta (Eds.), *Identities: Race, class, gender, and nationality.* Malden, MA: Blackwell.
Dávila, A. (2002). Talking back. Latino media and U.S. Latinidad. In Habell-Pallán & M. Romero (Eds.), *Latino/a popular culture* (pp. 25–37). New York: New York University Press.
Derrida, J. (1982). Signature event context. In A. Bass (Ed.), *Margins of philosophy* (pp. 309–330). Chicago: Chicago University Press.
El Pueblo Inc. (2003). *N.C. Latino community.* Retrieved March 16, 2004, from El Pueblo Inc. website, from http://www.elpueblo.org/
Flores, J. (2000). *From bomba to hip-hop.* New York: Columbia University Press.

Foucault, M. (1978). *The history of sexuality, volume I: An introduction*. New York: Vintage Books.
Fregoso, R. L. (1995). Homegirls, cholas, and pachucas in cinema: Taking over the public sphere. *California History, 74*(3), 316–327.
Garcìa Canclini, N. (1989). *Culturas hibridas: Estrategias para entrar y salir de la modernidad*. Mexico City: Grijalbo.
Gillespie, M. (1995). *Television, ethnicity and cultural change*. New York: Routledge.
González Loópez, G. (2005). *Erotic journeys. Mexican immigrants and their sex lives*. Berkeley/Los Angeles: University of California Press.
Hall, S. & P. du Gay (Eds.). (1996). *Questions of cultural identity*. Thousand Oaks: Sage.
Hirsh, J. S. (1999). *En el norte la mujer manda:* Gender, generation and geography in a Mexican transnational community. *American Behavioral Scientist, 42*(9), 1332–1349.
Hobson, D. (1982). *Crossroads: The drama of a soap opera*. London: Methuen.
Hondagneu-Sotelo, P. (2002). Families in the frontier: From braceros in the fields to braceras in the home. In M. M. Suárez-Orozco & M. M Páez (Eds.), *Latinos remaking America* (pp. 259–263). Berkeley: University of California Press.
Johnson, M. A. (2000). How ethnic are U.S. ethnic media: The case of Latina magazines. *Mass Communication & Society, 3*(2&3), 229–248.
Jones, A. (Ed.). (2003). *The feminism and visual culture reader*. New York: Routledge.
Kaiser, S. (2005). *Postmemories of terror*. New York: Palgrave Macmillan.
Kraidy, M. M. (2005). *Hybridity or the cultural logic of globalization*. Philadelphia, PA: Temple University Press.
Lagarde, M. (1993). *Los cautiverios de las mujeres: madresposas, presas, putas y locas*. México: Universidad Nacional Autónoma de México.
Lugo, A. (2000). Theorizing border inspections. *Cultural Dynamics, 12*(3), 353–373.
Lutrell, W. (2003). *Pregnant bodies, fertile minds*. New York: Routledge.
Martìn Barbero, J. (1987). *De los medios a las mediaciones: Comunicación, cultura y hegemonìa*. México: Gustavo Gili.
Martìn Barbero, J. (2002). Identities: Traditions and new communities. *Media, Culture, and Society, 24*(5), 621–642.
Mato, D. (2003). On the making of transnational identities in the age of globalization: The US Latina/o-"Latin" American case. In M. Alcoff & E. Mendieta (Eds.), *Identities: Race, class, gender, and nationality* (pp. 281–294). Malden, MA: Blackwell.
Mayer, V. (2003a). Living telenovelas/telenovelizing life: Mexican American girls' identities and transnational telenovelas. *Journal of Communication, 53*(3), 479–495.
Mayer, V. (2003b). *Producing dreams, consuming youth: Mexican Americans and mass media*. Piscataway, NJ: Rutgers University Press.
McRobbie, A. (1991). *Feminism and youth culture: From Jackie to just seventeen*. London: Macmillan Education.
Morley, D. (1986). *Family television: Cultural power and domestic leisure*. London: Comedia.
Paz, O. (1959). *El laberinto de la soledad*. México: Fondo de Cultura Económica.
Peña, M. (1991). Class, gender and machismo: "Treacherous woman" folklore of Mexican male workers. *Gender and Society, 5*(1), 30–46.
Pieterse, J. N. (1992). *White on black: Images of Africa and blacks in Western popular culture*. New Heaven, CT: Yale University Press.
Prosser, J. (Ed.). (1998). *Image-based research: A sourcebook for qualitative researchers*. London: Routledge Falmer.

Radway, J. (1987). *Reading the romance: Women, patriarchy and popular literature.* London: Verso.

Rodríguez, C. E. (1997). *Latin looks. Images of Latinas and Latinos in the U.S. media.* Boulder, CO: Westview.

Rojas, V. (2004). The gender of Latinidad: Latinas speak about Hispanic television. *The Communication Review, 7,* 125–153.

Rose, G. (2001). *Visual methodologies.* London: Sage.

Rouse, R. (1995). Thinking through transnationalism: Notes on the cultural politics of class relations in the contemporary United States. *Public Culture, 7,* 353–402.

Ruíz, V. L. (1996). "Star struck": Acculturation, adolescence, and the Mexican-American woman. In D. Gutiérrez (Ed.), *Between two worlds. Mexican immigrants in the United States* (pp. 125–148). Wilmington, DE: Scholarly Resources.

Said, E. (1994). *Culture and imperialism.* New York: Knopf.

Salih, S. (2002). *Judith Butler.* London: Routledge.

Seiter, E., H. Borchers, G. Kreutzner, & E.-M. Warth. (Eds.). (1989). *Remote control: Television, audiences and cultural power.* London: Routledge.

Southern Cross University. (2001). *Action research resources.* Retrieved October 4, 2001, from Southern Cross University, Graduate College of Management Website, from http://www.scu.edu.au/schools/gcm/ar/arhome.html

Spradley, J. P. (1979). *The ethnographic interview.* New York: Holt, Rinehart, and Winston.

Spradley, J. P. (1980). *Participant observation.* New York: Holt, Rinehart, and Winston.

Sturken, M. & L. Cartwright. (2001). *Practices of looking. An introduction to visual culture.* Oxford: Oxford University Press.

U.S. Census Bureau. (2000). *2000 Census of the population: General population characteristics. United States summary.* Washington, DC: U.S. Government Printing Office.

U.S. Census Bureau. (2000). *Census data for the state of North Carolina.* Retrieved from http://www.census.gov/census2000/states/nc.html

Valdivia, A. N. (2006). Salsa as popular culture: Ethnic audiences constructing an identity. In A. N. Valdivia (Ed.), *A companion to media studies* (pp. 399–418). Malden, MA: Blackwell.

Vargas, L. (2004, May). *Use of projective methods in an action-research project with transnational Latina young women.* Paper presented at the 54th Annual Meeting of the International Communication Association New Orleans, LA.

Vargas, L. (2005). Media and racialization among working-class Latina immigrant young women. In J. Peacock, H. Watson, & C. A. Matthews (Eds.), *The American South in a global world* (pp. 39–58). Chapel Hill: University of North Carolina Press.

Vasconcellos, J. (1976). *La raza cósmica.* México: Espasa-Calpe.

Wittig, M. (1986). *The lesbian body.* Boston: Beacon.

CHAPTER TEN

Watching Over THE Border: A Case Study OF THE Mexico-U.S. Television AND Youth Audience

DAVID GONZÁLEZ HERNÁNDEZ

INTRODUCTION

In the city of Tijuana the youth audience experiences a *particular* view of television. The condition of the border implies, among other dimensions, the existence of processes of sociocultural transformation that are structured by different modalities: historical, economic, political, and transnational. In view of these considerations, the development of mass communication and their impact in the region represent a complex set of broad implications in cross-border cultural transformation. These circumstances present numerous gaps of knowledge in the study of televised programming and reception in Mexico.

This border media situation has provoked, partly, two results. On the one hand, there is ongoing discussion about diverse approaches in the studies of international flow of communication messages and reception (Lozano, 2000). On the other hand, there is a need to transcend traditional categories in the study of agenda setting and reception in order to understand the magnitude of the global phenomena. In the case of the Mexico-U.S. border, I explore two aspects that are particularly relevant to my concerns. First, in studies of flow of television programs, there is insufficient data that accounts for a wide range of variables such as hours of transmission, number of channels, and amount and origin of programming. Language, quality, and quantity of audiovisual material raise issues that coincide with the cultural "proximities" and "separations" hypothesis—that is, contemporary transnational production of television with global capital as well as the inclusion of some programs with "Mexican flavor" but of foreign content, respectively.[1] A second aspect that informs my research is the need to elaborate on the relationship between television and its audience in a way that goes beyond the *centrality* of the category of "ideological reproduction"; an intellectual tradition that still predominates in the studies on the foreign content in television, but that is insufficient to explain under what circumstances a certain audience located in the border produces oppositional decoding on the television of Mexico (mainly) and the United States.

This case study examines the television agenda in the border and the reception of young viewers in Tijuana by means of the exploration of their subjectivity and interpretive schemes. It is based on a two-pronged analysis. First, I conducted an empirical study of over-the-air television channels available in Tijuana, and then used focus group discussion to understand the cross-border mediated interaction between the youth audience and television programs, emphasizing the legitimizing role of U.S. entertainment in the configuration of border culture.

CROSS-BORDER MEDIATED INTERACTION
BETWEEN U.S. TELEVISION AND MEXICAN YOUTH AUDIENCE

I use the term "border-crossing" or "transfronterizo" (which literally means "transborder") that suggests flow more than division because, although they are concepts from a variety of fields, they describe important and particular processes that refer to and give account of certain economic-social dynamics that bind Tijuana with a growth related to an external logic, mostly that of the state of California. These processes include (1) the importance of territory and geography; (2) the origin and destiny of cultural and human flows in both directions; (3) the intensity of such flows; (4) the frequency of the flows; and (5) the people or objects involved in the border-crossing processes (Alegría, 1992).

This asymmetric border-crossing bond cannot be understood by focusing only on the two economies in interaction. I raise this Mexico-U.S. heuristic component as a way to help study the dynamic of those relations and to emphasize the main idea that the "interaction" of the border region is a necessary but nonsufficient concept, where the differences between Tijuana and San Diego do not introduce a rupture but a stratified continuity of the binational social structure (Bustamante, 1989, p. 41). Thus, we could understand in a certain level that Tijuana is defined by transnational and border-crossing macroprocesses, at least in certain socioeconomic levels, due to its character of border town and location that, in the last instance, reveals the internationality of life in this region.

At first glance, the daily commercial and cultural interchanges can be translated as *U.S. cultural influence*. García Canclini (1990) has written about the intensity whereupon the *Tijuanenses*[2] live the inequality of the border, having a less idealized image than the people who consume televised messages in the country's interior (e.g., people who live in Mexico City, Guadalajara, and so on). This allows us to think about the acts of the border crosser as a set of asymmetrical points of social interaction.

In this sense, Valenzuela (1993) has reflected on the symbolic consumption by *Tijuanense* youth. Following the sociologist Agnes Heller, Valenzuela differentiates three levels of experience that influence the configuration of the social relations: everyday lived experience and context (the close relationships between subjects who daily confront their subjectivity by means of their ethnic, class, and genre condition), an imaginary context (the wide relations of recognition, generic networks of meaning that influence their collective action, whose meanings are put in circulation, frequently by the mass media), and a cross-border environment. I focus on this last category because it strongly refers to the border condition and, particularly, to the city of Tijuana.

The border territory of Tijuana, south of San Diego, California, bears out the "specificity of the interactions that are present" (Bustamante, 1989, p. 387), like the experience of the previously mentioned inequality (García Canclini), and also, the assimilations to and yearnings for *the American way of life*. However, these processes do not imply an automatic transfer of acculturation because within cultural exchange and interaction there are always forces of resistance and conflict (Valenzuela, 1993). Thus, the cross-border context recognizes, in first instance, the everyday lived experience constructed by networks that comprise a variety of concepts, images, and meanings by the population of both sides of the border. The frequent and intense interaction and participation of networks of symbolic consumption are facilitated by mass media such as radio or television that are not equally accessed by all inhabitants of the region.

According to Valenzuela, many young *Tijuanense* people incorporate San Diego or the south region of the United States in their daily condition of interaction expressing knowledge and an adhesion to networks of meaning defined by the cross-border condition of cultural differences including languages, prejudices, stereotypes, racism, and imaginary allegiances. Also, with the increasing deployment and consumption of mass media, in particular television, these conditions have intensified in a region constituted by complex processes of meaning that incorporate Mexican and U.S. codes (and constant and dynamic recoding by social groups). In sum, the mediated transmission in Tijuana and/or San Diego refers to a border-crossing environment where U.S. and Mexican television programming converges in both sides of the border.

TELEVISION PROGRAMMING ON THE MEXICO-U.S. BORDER

Contemporary Mexican scholars pay special attention to the persistence of uneven communication flows between Mexico and the United States, even, or especially in, the post–NAFTA (North American Free Trade Agreement) period. First, scholars point to a *cultural malaise* because Mexico receives a significant volume of U.S. produced content. The United States is clearly one of the main media exporters in the world and dominates certain kinds of production. These imports have long been blamed for effects such consequences such as the erosion of values, customs, and world visions of the inhabitants of receiving nations (McAnany & Wilkinson, 1997). Second, scholars pursue a *political and economic preoccupation* that take up the debate of sovereignty and national integrity (Lull, 1995), like the efforts for the establishment of NWICO (New World Information and Communication Order) in the mid-1980s. Many components of this debate continue to be very pertinent in this neoliberal contemporary era, which circulate commercial negotiations as modernity (Giddens, 1991), Placed in the framework of the NAFTA agreements between the United States, Canada, and Mexico, this academic and intellectual focus extends beyond the notion of cultural imperialism to the "new" character of global integration as form of dependency. In the case of the Mexican-U.S. audiovisual space, scholars find the situation to be highly "interdependent" (Sánchez, 1996; Straubhaar, 1991).

One way of evaluating the possible impact of these asymmetrical flows has been the analysis of foreign television content (Lozano, 2000). According to Giddens (1986), television programming contributes to the structure of meaning as an important part of regional culture. If so, the presence of U.S. television programs in Tijuana is much more than a communication process, but part of a cultural and economic force that generate an infinity of "interests of all types of groups and the commercialization of companies that produce audiovisual programming" (Ibarra, 1998, p. 142).

CONTENT CASE STUDY

In 2002 I studied the proportions of various kinds of programming in open-air TV stations (González, 2006) in Mexico (channel 2, XHGC; channel 5, Galavisión de Televisa; and channel 7 and 13 of Aztec TV, all of them privately owned), particularly for U.S. content. The percentage of U.S. programs transmitted during one week added up to a total of 43.1 percent. The percentage increased if I added other categories to the programs, for example, when the *original format patented* was U.S. origin (the case of "Family Feud" as original format and "Cien

Mexicanos Dijeron," as adapted format, but produced by Mexican Fremantle Media). The percentage increased to 52.6 when I included the audiovisual products category or, better said, programs whose *audiovisual material* was from the United States, as was the case of "Picante y caliente," "¡Ay, caramba!" and "Riesgo Total," as representative samples.

Many investigators have reached similar conclusions as far as percentage of foreign programming transmitted by Mexican over-the-air television. In general, there is an enormous difference in the proportion of what is produced and what is imported—the latter is mostly composed of entertainment, specially cartoons, and sitcoms (Crovi, 1995; Lozano, 1995/1996; Sánchez, 1995). For example, there was little national programming on Mexican channel 5 (XHGC); the 81.1 percent of U.S. content describes the function of the channel as mostly transmitter.

In the Tijuana-San Diego border the percentages of television programming changed substantially. In the 2002 study I located the presence of television production in Mexico, with the categories of *origin* and *amount* of programming as analysis axes. In November of 2003, I analyzed the transmitted television programming in the urban zone of Tijuana. The approach included other analytical elements: the hours of transmission (González, 2007b). The sample was one week of November and the source was from *TV Guide and Tele Guía* magazines, as well as from the online pages of each television station.

The unit of analysis of the televised transmission was over-the-air television channels. By their technical and socioeconomic characteristics these are within reach of a wide segment of population. Moreover, they transmitted when most of the young people had the possibility of watching television, that is to say, from 6.00 a.m. to midnight; since then fourteen of the fifteen channels transmit 24 hours daily, yet another indicator of globalizing trends in television (see appendix, Table 1).

During the studied week, the total of hours transmitted in over-the-air signal of the channels was a total of 2.646 hours (158.760 minutes). From that total we observed, between 6:00 a.m. and midnight, 1.884 hours (113.04 minutes). Of that total, more of 60 percent (1139 hours) was produced in the United States. The general profile of border programming is very varied, since it combines different genres, from situation comedies to sensationalist programs, news, magazines, and movies. Appendix, Table 2 offers a panoramic view of the three main programmatic profiles that each channel offers.

Appendix, Table 2 shows, fundamentally, the logic of programming by each channel seen in the city of Tijuana. The classification of the televised genres had minimum considerations, partly because the categories vary in the programming diagnoses. Each category designates programs with well-known formats identified by its narrative structure or content. Here I limit myself to indicate some televise genres in wide terms; I don't discuss them in depth due to the deflection that can present the study perspective: the distribution of the televise offer in the border. However, two explanations are pertinent for the classification of genres. First it refers to the genre of humor. In this study I elaborate two general distinctions: (1) the sitcoms: these programs are characterized by being produced in serial form, consecutive histories, in most cases, that place the same characters in absurd situations; and (2) Mexican programs that base their humor on the actors by means of the production of dialogue and jokes that use double meaning or banter, mostly in a sexual way.

Language is a second major issue. The question of the *origin of the programming* is inextricably linked to the language it is produced in and transmitted, at least in the border, because both Univision and Telemundo (U.S. companies) use Spanish in their programming. Thus, when speaking of U.S. programming, necessarily we must refer to the *language that it uses* if we consider the audience and its *cultural proximity* (Wilkinson, 1995). One can observe a version of this strategy in this region of the world as being part of a cultural-linguistic border market. For example, in border television programs, 10 percent is composed of soap operas (see appendix, Table 3): soap operas (telenovelas) dominate the prime time of the most important channels in Mexico. Of those 10 percent, almost 75 percent are of Mexican or Latin American origin (that is to say, 15 percent of the soap operas in the border are from the United States). Nevertheless, of the 75 percent of the soap operas in Spanish 33 percent percent are jointly produced with the Univision and Telemundo networks.

All the televised genres have a share of time on the air, nevertheless, the news predominates as first profile of the channels that they transmit in the border (Table 2 and 3). The genre of sitcoms predominates in channel 6 of Fox as first place (46 hours a week), and in channel 69 of Warner Brothers as second (35 hours and a half); and channel 21 of Aztec TV is the third ranked programming of (7 seven hours and a half). However, sitcoms occupy the sixth ranked programming offered in the border in the global percentage (see Table 3).

Table 3 represents the global overview of programming in the border. In principle it emphasizes the fact that no televised genre exceeds 15 percent of the total, which indicates that although there are a considerable variety of options, the distance between one and another televised type of programming is minimal. Also, Table 3 shows the percentage of Mexican and U.S. production. When language is separated we can see more precisely how Univision and Telemundo networks contribute to total television programming at the border. Moreover news as a type of programming predominates in the border with 14.8 percent of the total (278 hours and half a week), of which almost 60 percent (164 hours) are of U.S. origin. This is significant if we consider that almost

95 percent of the locally produced programming is also news. The local production represents 7.9 percent (150 hours and a half) of total programming in the border. Of that percentage only 10 percent (16 hours) is of Mexican/Tijuana origin. Channel 12, Televisa, produces almost 60 percent of the local total, which implies that the function of Mexican local television stations is to retransmit centrally produced shows. This explains why movies occupied the fifth place, with the 9.6 percent of the total. Local channels in Spanish offered 83 percent of that portion.

As I have indicated, the genre of situation comedies occupied sixth place, totaling 7.1 percent (135 hours: 8.100 minutes). It must be noted that 14 percent (18.5 hours) were dubbed into Spanish. In summary, the study suggests that over-the-air channels seen in Tijuana contain a varied proportion of situation comedies depending on the youth composition of the North American, Hispanic, or Mexican audience. The percentage fragmentation by televised genre points to both the variety of programming at the border and, in turn, the relative legitimacy among the youth audience of different types of programming, as I discuss in the next section.

INTERPRETATIVE SCHEMES OF YOUTH: GAME OF OPPOSITIONS

Given the programming data in the previous section, I seek to connect it to the interpretive strategies used by *Tijuanense* youth who are avid television viewers. Analysis of interpretive schemes is better if we consider them as repertoires of the audience. The interpretive repertoires, intelligible by means of discursive representations, reveal how people give account of themselves and the primary or secondary social group to which they belong as youth. I use the concept instead of "interpretive communities" because it allows the flow between definitions of communities to repertoires. Klaus B. Jensen (1987) complicates this schema by considering other criteria—in addition to socioeconomic or demographic—namely the construction of meaning (more than the adhesion or membership to a social segment or style of life). This construction of meaning refers to a cognitive component Jensen denominates as the "analytic factors" that consider the capacity of expression and perception of the specific configurations of the audience, of its search for gratifications, and its personal experiences and tastes.

For this part, I present results of a discussion group with young people (18–23 years), natives of Tijuana and of middle-class status. The purpose of this study was to have access to a discourse that could give account, with greater detail, of the forms of predominant interpretive strategies and identity construction of a young generation that has lived its entire life on the Tijuana-San Diego border. This means a greater exposure to U.S. television and an accumulation of information on the individual interactions with the U.S. south region, thanks to the possibilities and access offered by the ability to cross the border.

A semiotic methodology was used to analyze the group discussion. This allowed me to approach the discussion as a text, with several semiotic systems that come together in the "formalization of sense" (Reguillo, 1995, p. 66) or the "simulacrum of the generation of sense" (Juárez, 1992, p. 49). The analytical organizing framework was the semiotic square developed by European semiologist A. J. Greimas.[3] An important assumption of the analysis takes up the North Mexican border as a place with intense oppositions within its own social-cultural conditions: between Mexican and U.S. television, between Mexico and Tijuana, between Tijuana and the United States, between native *Tijuanenses* and immigrated *Tijuanenses*, and so on—in sum, as a place of multiple "different differences."

There are five types of oppositional relations in the discourse: young versus adult *Tijuanenses*, young viewer versus nonviewer, U.S. versus Mexican television, U.S. versus Mexican television humor, Mexican versus U.S. television news format. The fragments of dialogue between the young people illustrate the wide margin of opposition that characterizes their relation with U.S. television programs.

YOUNG VERSUS ADULT TIJUANENSES

The young *Tijuanenses* assume that adults who live in Tijuana are probably from the country's interior (central Mexico) and that they bring with them rigid beliefs. In addition, young people combine their know-how about "growing up" with a projection toward identity construction. Young *Tijuanenses* hold these values in direct opposition to those of adults, in terms of their implicit and explicit relation with the United States. They wish to take the best from the United States so as to obtain another type of quality of life in the cultural sense. Taking the best from another country forms a pragmatic vision that shapes culturally what is useful from the United States for the *Tijuanenses*. The number of values that youth associate with adults does not favor them much as it opposes that which they prioritize: they are inflexible, growing out of monocultural form in a passive audience manner; and internal migrants to Tijuana though residing in the city. On the other hand, the young *Tijuanenses* view themselves as open to change, with a conscious construction of identity that is culturally pragmatic so as to improve, in a very general frame, the quality of life in the border.

The semiotic figure below presents a narrative summary of the opposition axes:

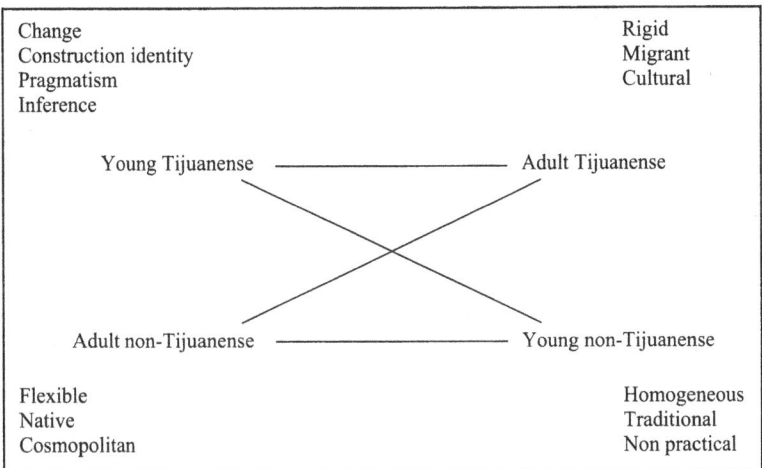

YOUNG VIEWER VERSUS NONVIEWER

Young viewers associated themselves with fun, something they have learned to code from television. Viewing youth assume a state of euphoric, playful, and entertaining connection with the television actors. This subject position implicitly assumes that young nonviewers are at odds with fun, identity construction, and comprehension inherent in U.S. programs. They are attributed phrases such as "Oh, I do not see it because I don't understand." Explicitly young viewers assume that not to know the English language precludes the entertainment, education, and understanding factors of television viewing, a noneuphoric connection within my semiotic model. This disjuncture takes the form articulated by the following question: "How is something that you don't understand going to entertain you?" As such it appears that the knowledge, the language, and the understanding of U.S. culture by TV audiences are juxtaposed to knowledge and competence of the nonviewers of U.S. television.

This process suggests that the audience enacts implicit rules or procedures that grant certain segments of the audience more competent than others and renders them subject of the fun intentional effect of the narrative route of the U.S. version of entertainment. First, the youth audience defined the need to learn from U.S. television. This rule makes it possible to detect frequent television viewing and the type of interaction of the youth audiences achieves through playful repetition. Second, youth speak of competence. In spite of frequent TV viewing, the greater achievement, over and above fun, is the learning and understanding of U.S. television narratives. U.S. television, through of multiple genres, has few "standard" codes that allow for understanding beyond mere translation.

U.S. VERSUS MEXICAN TELEVISION

Youth conceive the television audience of both countries as opposite as far as programs and technology. They link U.S. television to more variety (than the Mexican) and better reception of the signal (which in turn means better transmission technology). In this sense, when speaking of the inferior traits of Mexican television, youth implicitly code it as noneuphoric speech, which is boringness according to my model. Youth establish the notion of greater variety by means of certain values that they consider necessary for television. On the other hand, the lack of variety ascribed to Mexican television is noted by only three genres: soap operas, news, and sports (especially soccer). U.S. television is categorically juxtaposed against Mexican television. Diagramming this articulation yields the following set of oppositions:

```
Better signal               Bad reception/signal

U.S. TV      ----------------    Mexican TV

Greater Variety             Lack of variety
```

This results in a positive perception of U.S. television based on perceived better access to its diverse channels, which in turn suggests more options than Mexican television. Youth interpret program selection as a complex television agenda structured by means of genres or styles. U.S. option is juxtaposed against Mexican lack.

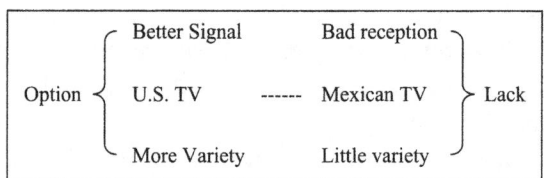

U.S. VERSUS MEXICAN TELEVISION HUMOR

Humor is important, linked to a major axis of opposition and reason that articulates the reasons to watch U.S. television. Whereas U.S. television humor represents fun and entertainment for young *Tijuanenses*, Mexican television represents the simple and ordinary—that is, the culture of central Mexico. This construct works to develop difference between the border/transnational, modern, fun youth, and the traditional/backward, internal/country bound, no fun, older Mexican nationals. Components like *double entendre* (the singular meaning of sexually implicit jokes) are perceived as the backbone of Mexican television, a form of simplistic humor. From the point of view of the entertainment, youth express a preference for U.S. and against Mexican television. Nonetheless, Mexican television humor does not apply to real situations, since in the daily world confrontations are observed that contradict the Mexican television cosmo-vision. On the other hand, youth interpret U.S. television humor as a form that laughs at itself, with no need of explanations.

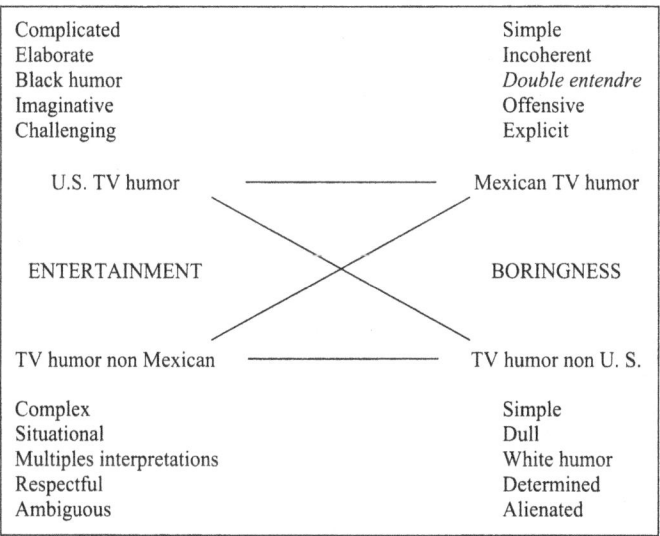

U.S. VERSUS MEXICAN TELEVISION NEWS FORMAT

The fifth opposition relates to television genres, in particular the information formats. This is the last opposition between U.S. and Mexican programs and articulates interpretation of news content. Isolating this confrontation produced a relevant manner of understanding two different approaches to the coverage of national and regional realities.

Youth indicate in their group discourse that U.S. television conforms a desirable object of information related to collective memory, or at least thus it seems to establish the continuity of violent news in the television. Whereas Mexican news "has accustomed us to the forgetfulness." These added elements aim at a sense of the social conscience that has a collective memory. This suggests that they see in

U.S. news a continuity in themes and stories that contextualizes them. Whereas in Mexican news they see episodic accounts of robberies and others without contextualization or link to previous robberies or such issues and themes. This form attributed to Mexican adds depression and forgetfulness to endemic violence, although not explicitly formulated but inferred when noting the exaggeration of "news like these," robberies, shots, and assaults. In such sense, the deep logic of the discursive expression of youth rests on the accumulated collective memory by the U.S. (and border) audience. However, this social memory is activated by means of the recognition of one of the most powerful dimensions of the news: the spectacular dramatization of information—what is also called sensationalization.

It is possible to add that youth discourse, in depth, constitutes the objection to the projected national reality value from Mexican news, that they attribute its informative subjects and qualities. There is a taste for U.S. news because they include different cultural elements, whereas Mexican news is depressing because they only broadcast robberies, assaults, and murders. This opposition in the perception of the group, evoking a television reality that transmits daily insecurity and violence in Mexico, while in the United States, the news of assassinated and assault is scandalous and therefore not routine. This also implies a total credibility on U.S. television, since "many seem to think that if is heard in English it is true."

CONCLUSION

It is of particular relevance that youth perceive a disjuncture within television of the border. The entertainment axis articulates and fractures elements of humoristic gratification: U.S. and Mexican. This disjunctive implies a *double competence* operating at the border, which serves as a basis for appraisal of two national television systems. This double television cultural competence implies, at the end of the day, to "grow up watching in English" also means to grow up watching in Spanish. Youth have to be bilingual to express preference and desire for one system over the other.

Young viewers confirm the legitimacy of U.S. television because, for them, it allows greater playfulness, education, strategic, and pragmatic uses than Mexican television. This implies that to acquire transnational cosmopolitan visions [i.e., to be a subject in the contemporary neoliberal global regime] one needs cultural competence in the negotiation and "balance" of meaning. These reconciled consequences are the affirmation of the border location that tends to differentiate the practices of television audiences. It is evident that U.S. television legitimacy is relevant in the border because it emerges from providing justifications of comparisons, not always discontinuous (the discontinuity is against determinism), mainly between those defined as "properly Mexican" and "American." This partly explains the type of formulations made by the *Tijuanenses* is always from a position of "*Mexicanidad*" (Mexican way of seeing things) or, rather "*Tijuanidad.*" Yet as this research suggests, *Tijuanidad* is itself a transnational position, rooted in Mexico/Tijuana but certainly incorporating a familiarity with U.S. television and at the very least a psychic mobility in terms of the physical and symbolic border (González, 2007a).

In this game of intense oppositions, the disjuncture articulates a tension that youth audiences experience at the border. Where and how to derive meaning from television messages in a place where it is necessary to survive under the logic of several nations? One answer, partial and still incipient, formulated by Renato Ortiz (1998) insists to think of the planetary audience: "all of them" as not interested in the programs "worldwide" but as they circulate in a "youth stratum that transcends national borders. Its importance resides in the fact that they generate a space of legitimacy of an international popular culture" (p. 96). This category of "space of legitimacy of an international popular culture" proposes to articulate a new understanding of social phenomena, although very open and incomplete (this resonates with the concept of superculture suggested by James Lull [1995]), it has great potential as it indicates my attempt to revitalize the area of youth popular culture by infusing it with the study of youth border culture much like the work of Bejarano (2005) and Mayer (2003).

As with other forms of mass media, U.S. television's bid to worldwide reach is buttressed not only by the sheer amount of content it produces and distributes but also by the pervasiveness of its formats and genres. This case study suggests that we can identify some clear implications that these processes have had on Mexican youth as far as their expectations about technology, commercial models, and genres, especially in the border region. This in turn influences their identity in relation to the United States, the world, and, most alarmingly, in rejection of their own adult Mexican people. This type of finding deserves further study, as it suggests not just the cosmopolitan effects so touted by globalization supporters, but also an internal rejection that threatens to undermine national unity and efforts to consolidate some sort of Mexican togetherness or belonging. But perhaps, if we take a cynical approach, this is precisely the desired effect of contemporary globalization—to alienate youth from its own adults and toward a commercial and transnational popular culture. In this process, border youth would seem to be a litmus test for future and more pervasive effects of neoliberal globalization, especially as applied to mass media in general and television in particular.

U.S. television is an industry that dynamically seeks economic prominence in a transnational environment (through publicity, marketing research, sports, music, among other components). NAFTA has not increased the production of Mexican programming to be exported to the United States and Canada, but rather has opened the border to more U.S. circulation—a circulation that was extensive to begin with. To forget this historically specific effect of multilateral agreements is to underestimate the complexity of the expansive commercial nature of transnational capital in general and U.S. television in particular. But its expansion is also cultural. Television is a forum and device of dreams that almost nobody evades—certainly not heavy television viewers as many media studies authors have noted and certainly not the middle-class border Mexican youth on whose shoulders much of future Mexican policies will be enacted.

NOTES

1. Language does not in principle, by itself, represent a barrier that detracts from the attractiveness of television programming. For example, Telemundo and Univisión, both US companies, use Spanish yet mix values, beliefs, patterns, and conduct that seek to interpellate both U.S. Latina/os and Latin Americans, including Mexicans.
2. Tijanuenses is a term that refers to those living in or from Tijuana.
3. In the Greimasean model, the diagonal arrows represent relations of contradiction, while the vertical arrows represent relations of implication.

REFERENCES

Alegría, T. (1992). *Desarrollo urbano en la frontera México-Estados Unidos*. México: Conaculta.

Bejarano, C. L. (2005). *Que Onda? Urban youth culture and border identity*. Arizona: University of Arizona Press, 2005

Bustamante, J. (1989). Frontera México-Estados Unidos; reflexiones para un marco teórico. *Frontera Norte, 1*(1).

Crovi, D. (1995). Entretener y vender, ¿fatal destino de la television mexicana? En *Anuario de Investigación de la Comunicación CONEICC II*. Guadalajara: Consejo Nacional para la Enseñanza y la Investigación de las Ciencias de la Comunicación (CONEICC).

García Canclini, N. (1990). *Culturas híbridas*. México: Grijalbo.

Giddens, A. (1986). *The constitution of society*. Berkeley: University of California Press

Giddens, A. (1991). *The consequences of modernity*. Stanford, CA: Stanford University Press

González, D. (2006). Televisión y frontera: el espacio audiovisual en Tijuana. En Manuel Ortiz (Coor.), *Los medios de comunicación en Baja California* (pp. 143–156). México: Universidad Autónoma de Baja California/Porrúa.

González, D. (2007a). Aquí, allá y en todas partes: las audiencias juveniles en la frontera norte. En Guillermo Orozco (Coor.), *Un mundo de visiones. Interacciones de las audiencias en múltiples escenarios mediáticos y virtuales* (pp. 117–131). México, DF: Instituto Latinoamericano de Comunicación y Educación (ILCE).

González, D. (2007b). *El sueño americano en México. Televisión y audiencias juveniles en Tijuana*. Mexicali, Baja California: Universidad Autónoma de Baja California.

Ibarra, A. (1998). La agenda televisiva infantil en Guadalajara. *Comunicación y sociedad*, 32. Guadalajara: Universidad de Guadalajara

Jensen, K. B. (1987). Qualitative audience research: Toward an integrative approach to reception. *Critical Studies in Mass Communication*, 4(1), 21–36.

Juárez, R. E. (1992). *Las chapuzas del lector. Análisis semiótico de la recepción.* Guadalajara: ITESO.

Lozano, J. C. (1995/1996). Oferta y recepción de television extranjera en México. *Comunicación y Sociedad* (pp. 25–26). Guadalajara: Universidad de Guadalajara.

Lozano, J. C. (2000). Oferta y consumo de contenidos televisivos transnacionales en México. En *Estudios sobre las culturas contemporáneas*, Época II, 6(12). Colima: Universidad de Colima.

Lull, J. (1995). *Media, communication, culture. A global approach.* New York: Columbia University Press.

Mayer, V. (2003). *Producing dreams, consuming youth: Mexican Americans and mass media.* New Jersey: Rutgers University Press

McAnany, E. & K. Wilkinson. (Eds.). (1997). *Mass media and free trade: NAFTA and the cultural industries.* Austin: University of Texas Press.

Ortiz, R. (1998). *Otro territorio.* Bogotá: Convenio Andrés Bello.

Reguillo, R. (1995). En la calle otra vez. Las Bandas: identidad urbana y usos de la comunicación. Guadalajara: ITESO.

Sánchez, E. (1995). La agenda televisiva en Guadalajara. In D. Crovi (Coord.), *Desarrollo de las industrias audiovisuales en México y Canadá.* México: UNAM.

Sánchez, E. (1996). El nuevo carácter de la dependencia: Globalización y el espacio audiovisual. En Guillermo Orozco (Comp.), *Miradas latinoamericanas a la Televisión.* PROIICOM, 2. México, DF: Universidad Iberoamericana.

Straubhaar, J. (1991). Beyond media imperialism: Asymmetrical interdependence and cultural proximity. *Critical Studies in Mass Communication*, 8, 39–59.

Valenzuela, J. M. (1993). Ámbitos de interacción y consumo cultural en los jóvenes. García Canclini (Coord.), *El consumo cultural en México.* México: Conaculta.

Wilkinson, K. (1995). *Where culture, language and communication converge: The Latin American cultural-linguistic television market.* Unpublished doctoral dissertation. University of Texas at Austin.

APPENDIX OF TABLES

Table 1. Television channels seen in Tijuana by open-air signal

Channel	Companies	Hours of transmission	Type of programming	Nationality
Channel 3	IPN Channel 11	24	National (certain places)	Mexican
Channel 6	Fox	24	National/Regional/Local	United States
Channel 8	CBS	24	National/Regional/Local	United States
Channel 10	ABC	24	National/Regional/Local	United States
Channel 12	Televisa (Local)	24	National/Regional/Local	Mexican
Channel 15	PBS	24	National/Regional/Local	United States
Channel 21	TV Aztec 7	24	National	Mexican
Channel 27	TV Aztec 13	24	National/Regional/Local	Mexican
Channel 33	Telemundo	24	National/Regional/Local	United States
Channel 36	Univision	24	National/Regional/Local	United States
Channel 39	NBC	24	National/Regional/Local	United States
Channel 45	Independent/Galavision	24	National/Regional/Local	Mexican
Channel 51	Independent- UPN	24	National/Regional/Local	United States
Channel 57	Televisa XEW	24	National	Mexican
Channel 69	Warner Brothers	24	National/Regional/Local	United States

Table 2. Profile of the three mains types of weekly programming from 6:00 a.m. to 12:00 a.m. (Pacific time) of channels seen in Tijuana or San Diego by over-the-air signal

Channel	Total: Hours by week	First rank Genre	First rank Hours	First rank %	Second rank Genre	Second rank Hours	Second rank %	Third rank Genre	Third rank Hours	Third rank %
3 Channel 11	126'	Reportage/documental	44'	34.9	Children	22'30"	17.8	Movies	18'30"	14.6
6 FOX	126'	Sitcoms	46'	36.5	Sensational	24'	19.0	News	17'30"	13.8
8 CBS	126'	News	34'30"	27.3	Soap opera	17'30"	13.8	Varieties	14'30"	11.5
10 ABC	126'	News	27'30"	21.8	Sensational	17'	13.4	Sports	13'30"	10.7
12 Televisa	126'	Soap opera	25'	19.8	Varieties	21'30"	17.0	Movies	20'	15.8
15 KPBS	126'	Reportage/documental	49'	38.8	Children	39'	30.9	Educative	21'	16.6
21 Tv Azteca	126'	Movies	55'	43.6	Paid program	38'	30.1	Sensational/sitcoms	7'30"	5.9
27 Tv Azteca	126'	Varieties	34'	26.9	Soap opera	22'30"	17.8	Sensational	21'	16.6
33 Telemundo	126'	Sensational	46'30"	36.9	Soap opera	25'	19.8	News	20'	15.8
36 Univision	126'	Soap opera	38'	30.1	Varieties	27'	21.4	Sensational	26'	20.6
39 NBC	126'	News	31'	24.6	Varieties	22'30"	17.8	Soap opera	15'	11.9
45 Galavision	119'30"	Movies	30'	25.1	Series with plot	21'	17.5	News/Sensational	20'	16.7
51 KUSY	126'	News	37'30"	29.7	Sensational	29'30"	23.4	Varieties	22'	17.4
57 Televisa	126'	Varieties	35'30"	28.1	Soap opera	30'	23.8	News	22'30"	17.8
69 WB	126'	Sitcoms	35'30"	28.1	Sensational	30'	23.8	Children	20'	15.8

Table 3. Global percentages by television genre on the US-Mexico border

Rank	Televise genre	Global percentage	Percentage in English Language	Percentage in Spanish language	Contribution of Univision and Telemundo*
1	News/informative	14.80%	59.00%	41.00%	11.50%
2	Sensational/Reality shows	13.90%	47.00%	53.00%	27.60%
3	Varieties	11.20%	39.00%	61.00%	15.80%
4	Soap operas	10.00%	25.30%	74.70%	33.50%
5	Movies	9.60%	17.00%	83.00%	9.90%
6	Sitcoms	7.10%	86.00%	14.00%	0.00%
7	Reports/documentaries	6.90%	54.00%	46.00%	1.10%
8	Cartoons	6.50%	61.00%	39.00%	6.00%
9	Sports	5.50%	47.00%	53.00%	6.70%
10	Dramatic series	5.00%	56.00%	44.00%	8.00%
11	Paid program	4.50%	30.00%	70.00%	1.70%
12	Contests	2.10%	67.00%	33.00%	12.50%
13	Educational	1.30%	87.00%	13.00%	0.00%
14	Debates or analysis	1.00%	0.00%	100%	0.00%
15	Mexican comic program	0.60%	0.00%	100%	50.00%

* The percentage in this column corresponds to its total of the percentage in Spanish.

CHAPTER ELEVEN

Survival Aesthetics: U.S. Latinas AND THE Negotiation OF Popular Media

MARÍA ELENA CEPEDA

To paraphrase an often-cited text by Susie Orbach (1990), hair, skin, makeup, and clothing—much like fat—are feminist issues. That said, in the wake of the so-called Latin(o) music "boom" of the late-1990s, a new, far more visible prototype of the global Latina popular music star has emerged, as exemplified in the careers of Shakira, Thalía, Christina Aguilera, Paulina Rubio, Jennifer Lopez, and Olga Tañón, among others. Reincarnated as blonder, thinner, and (in some cases) bilingual versions of their former selves, these women have been (re)inserted into the global market as heavily cross-marketed, more "polished" (i.e., Anglo consumer friendly) products of the Miami-based Latin(o) music industry. Whereas the academic research to date has primarily focused on Latina/o "crossover" in linguistic and/or racial terms,[1] this project centers on the highly gendered, classed, and racialized aesthetics that inform the marketing of Latina popular music stars, and the contradictory ways in which mainstream feminist beauty politics shape U.S. Latina college students' interpretations of the visual media narratives constructed around these women.[2] Of further interest are these young women's attitudes toward fandom itself, which exhibit a simultaneous rejection and adoption of traditional portrayals of fandom as "a chronic attempt to compensate for a perceived lack of personal autonomy, absence of community, incomplete identity, lack of power and lack of recognition" (Jenson, 1992, p. 17). The tensions generated by the internalization of long-standing negative attitudes toward fandom, in combination with the young women's acute awareness of their own marginalized subjectivities, clearly manifested themselves during the focus groups I conducted.

Yarbro-Bejarano (cited in Luibhéid, 2002) notes that social relations foment the construction not just of Latina attitudes about their own bodies, but the very bodies themselves. Therefore, if English acts as the global lingua franca, do blond hair, blue eyes, light skin, slim thighs, and a flat stomach serve as its aesthetic counterpart? Employing Latina-centered reception scholarship as a point of departure, we must also ask ourselves: How do young Latina fans consume and interpret the visual texts put forth by the global music industry and popular media? Who are the Latina "tastemakers," and how do the "politics of cultural exclusion" inform young Latinas' understanding of Latina popular music stars? (Storey, 2003, pp. 43–45). And perhaps most importantly, as Figueroa (2003) queries in her analysis of normative constructions of Latina beauty in recent films and media, "if [Latina] bodies are for sale and consumption, how can they be claimed for ownership?" (p. 271).

As Valdivia (2000) observes in her critique of existing models of female spectatorship, few reception studies of women of color exist, particularly with respect to U.S. Latina audiences. As such, this project revolves around a series of focus group discussions with Latina students at the University of Minnesota in Minneapolis-St. Paul, Minnesota, and Mount Holyoke College, a small, private women's college in rural South Hadley, Massachusetts. As I foreground these two regions in which the Latina/o population is rapidly increasing, yet often overlooked, my goal is to engage in Latina-centered reception scholarship, or research whose parameters are dictated primarily by informants. As opposed to researchers such as Báez (2007) and Casillas & Cepeda (2002), this approach thereby constitutes a "move away from an implicit paternalism in which the intellectual knows best and may speak on behalf of the audience which she does not have to consult" (Hermes, 2002, p. 387). As García (2004) notes in her discussion of Latina feminist thought and practice in contemporary university classrooms, the practice of building upon what Cherríe Moraga and the late Gloria Anzaldúa (1981) aptly term "theor[ies] of the flesh" (p. 23)—that is, theories rooted in the physical realities of women of color—appears to play a central, if at times unacknowledged, role in the epistemological practices of many young Latinas. It is at this juncture that we might begin to think about the relationship between these "theories of the flesh" and the "survival aesthetics" that emerge from the tensions between sanctioned modes of mainstream U.S. feminist thought regarding the personal aesthetics and the everyday material and symbolic practices of many young Latinas.

As defined here, the concept of survival aesthetics refers to an alternative form of gendered, classed, and racialized behavior grounded in young women's (specifically, young Latinas') acute awareness of the socially charged, potentially risky relationship between "modes of displaying the body and social response" (Lewis, 1990b, p. 94). Previously, Chicana feminist theorists such as Fregoso (1999) have delineated the ways in which marginalized figures such as the World War II–era *pachuca* and the latter day homegirl have skillfully employed the politics of personal aesthetics and space as a means of oppositional practice. Building on Fregoso's conceptualization of the political potential underlying individual or communal aesthetics, in addition to a recognition of the economic opportunities (and obstacles) that personal style may present for young women of color, the analysis of survival aesthetics offered here draws on the "anthropological conceptualization of culture as the lifeways of people that are the consequence of the conditions to which they must adjust" (Bettie, 2003, p. 119). Much like Latina/o linguistic practices, survival aesthetics represent an alternative, if not adversarial, ethos "constituted by everyday aesthetic practices ... that in the current historical juncture do not amount to subalternity, but rather to a way of prying open the larger culture, by making physical, institutional, and metaphorical borders indeterminate, precisely what we have seen the dominant culture fears" (Flores & Yúdice, 1997, p. 189). In this chapter, I posit that Latina personal aesthetics (as represented in the mainstream U.S. media and as part of lived, bodily experience) pose a unique challenge to prevailing "feminist antibeauty ideologies," through which mainstream feminist leaders possessing greater educational and institutional privileges have imposed homogeneous definitions of what "true" feminists must wear (or not) in order to achieve "liberation" (Scott, 2005, p. 2). I also argue that despite the often contradictory nature of their responses to popular media imagery of Latinas, the young women I encountered more often than not recognized the oppositional potential of these depictions.

As Scott (2005) notes in her counterhistory of the contentious relationship between feminism and fashion, white/heterosexual/upper-class feminist ideals have traditionally supported the interpretation of fashion and personal aesthetics as a means of female oppression promoted by males, often linking the politics of personal appearance to (hetero)sexual provocation.[3] Such a perspective, which fails to take into account differences of race, ethnicity, class, national origins, and sexual orientation, promotes a decontextualized, dehistoricized interpretation of the myriad ways in which images, sexuality, consumption, self-representation, and ultimately power function within distinct U.S. cultural milieus. Moreover, as the most widely circulated scholarly and anecdotal means of reading the Latina body and Latina personal aesthetics, this mode of feminist thought provides only a partial lens through which to understand what we wear, why we wear it, and how to interpret Latina aesthetics within both the local, global, and/or transnational contexts. For as Frith (1996) reminds us, "[t]he experience of identity describes both a social process, a form of interaction, and *an aesthetic process*" (p. 110; emphasis mine).

Two recent studies inspired this project: the first, Lowe's 2003 scholarship on Nashville, Tennessee "tweens," focuses on the ways in which adolescent girls negotiate the contradictions underlying media depictions of pop star Britney Spears. During her focus group conversations with adolescents, Lowe is struck by the anger her respondents express regarding the "no-win" virgin/whore dichotomy (or *marianismo*) endemic to readings of Spears' public persona. Significantly, Lowe (2003) describes this as their "feminist consciousness colliding with a postfeminist culture" (p. 125). The second study, conducted by Rojas (2004), centers on issues of *Latinidad* and gender among U.S. Latinas and Latin American women in Austin, Texas. Interestingly, Rojas' interpretation of her informants' reactions lies squarely in between a purely populist perspective of cultural consumption (typically known as "active audience" theory), and an interpretation of informants' reactions that elides audience agency (see Báez, this volume; Casillas & Cepeda, 2002; Grossberg, 1992; Rivero, 2003; Valdivia, 2000). As Rojas (2004) notes, while we must recognize that U.S. Latinas are indeed conceded media space, we must ask ourselves "What *type* of space is that and *how is it perceived* by the Latino community?" (p. 147; emphasis mine) As Rojas' work illustrates, a reception-based focus on the Latina community might well offer the opportunity to embark on the type of multidirectional theoretical project outlined by Aparicio and Chávez-Silverman (1997), while simultaneously signifying a move away from the Anglocentric comparative focus that often pervades U.S. Latino Studies.

COMMUNITY AND METHODOLOGICAL CONSIDERATIONS

Though historically of mostly Mexican origin, the Minnesota Latina/o community is rapidly growing more diverse, as noted in the increased presence of new Puerto Rican, Colombian, Cuban, and Ecuadorian family businesses, among others. The well-established Mexican population has multiplied four times since 1980 to number more than 95,000 in the 2000 census, enough to merit a visit to Minneapolis-St. Paul by Mexican president Vicente Fox in June of 2004 and the opening of a Mexican consulate in 2005. However, this figure does not include an estimated 60,000 undocumented individuals (Nelson, 2004). Within the Twin Cities, St. Paul's historic West Side and various Minneapolis neighborhoods have been home to a vibrant *mexicano* community since early in the twentieth century (Valdés, 2000), though in recent years the Latina/o and Chicana/o population of St. Paul's East Side and Minneapolis' South Side (specifically, the Lake Street corridor) have experienced marked growth, due not only to an increase in Latin American immigrants but also to those moving north from states such as Texas, California, and Illinois (Nelson, 2004). Despite this increased Latina/o presence, the University of Minnesota-Twin Cities, the flagship campus of the 60,000 student-plus, 5-campus University of Minnesota system serves a relatively small Chicana/o and Latina/o population (*University of Minnesota, Twin Cities,* 2003). According to the university's fall 2002 "Undergraduate Enrollment Profile" on Chicana/o and Latina/o students, out of the 11.5 percent student of color (primarily Asian) population on the Twin Cities campus, only 1.5 percent self-identify as Chicana/o or Latina/o; 52 percent of the Latina/o or Chicana/o students are women ("Office for Multicultural and Academic Affairs," 2003).

In contrast, South Hadley, Massachusetts, home to Mount Holyoke College, is located in the largely rural Pioneer Valley. With approximately 17,000 residents, South Hadley forms part of the Springfield, Massachusetts metropolitan region. According to the 2000 census, South Hadley residents overwhelmingly characterize themselves as White (94 percent); however, the nearby cities of Holyoke and Springfield are both home to significant Puerto Rican and Dominican communities. Mount Holyoke, a private college founded in 1837, is the United States' oldest continuing institution of higher learning for women, and consistently ranks among the nation's top liberal arts colleges. As of 2006, the college served 2,125 undergraduate students, and one of every three students was an international student, a domestic student of color and/or multiracial. Of these students, 108 self-identified as Latina, or slightly more than 1 percent of the Mount Holyoke's student population (*epodunk*, 2006; "Facts about Mount Holyoke College," 2006).

Despite the methodological limitations of the privilege implied not only by access to higher education, but to the internet as well, I elected to conduct my first focus group on the UM campus in the fall of 2004. The following factors, among others, led to my selection of the University's Twin Cities and Mt. Holyoke campuses: my newcomer status in the Twin Cities (and later on, in Western Massachusetts), the impossibility of working with students at my home institution, the existence of a long-standing (since 1972) Chicano Studies program at the University of Minnesota-Twin Cities (Valdés, 2000), and the relative ease of making academic contacts with fellow Ethnic Studies colleagues and students at a neighboring institution. My approach to the construction of both focus groups was rather straightforward: after having identified several courses and/or extra-curricular student organizations that were likely to attract Latina undergraduates, I contacted individuals and organizations potentially interested in participating in the project via e-mail. The resulting focus groups then met on campus one evening each, for approximately one and a half hours total. The meetings began with a brief introduction and a request to audiotape the group's conversation; participants were then asked to provide basic demographic information about themselves and their families, which provided them with the opportunity to self-identify (albeit in nondirect fashion) in terms of race/ethnicity, class, and national origins. Next, the women viewed a variety of photographic images of Latina celebrities, and were asked to complete individual short-answer and "free-writing" exercises in which they recorded their immediate responses to these images as well as more direct questions regarding the photos' Latina subjects. Finally, during approximately the final half-hour of the focus group, the students engaged in an open-ended discussion session about the images and their own opinions about U.S. Latina media representation.

The unique composition of these groups became clear with a cursory glance at Lowe's (2003) study and its complete absence of any Latina, non–middle class perspectives. Indeed, Lowe's study contained only one African-American participant. However, I level this critique keeping in mind the privilege associated with access to U.S. higher education, and mindful of the fact that there were no Afro-Latina participants in either of my focus groups—a reality that likely underscores the lesser amount of racial discrimination faced by non–Afro-Latinas relative to their darker-skinned sisters. As Segwick notes, "the person who is disabled through one set of oppressions may *by the same positioning* be enabled through others" (cited in Bury, 2005, p. 13; emphasis in original).

One critical reason to conduct this type of research, as Hall observes, is that "*experience* directs us to ask certain questions of particular theory which the theory alone does not lead us to ask" (cited in Chabrám, 1990, p. 242; emphasis in original). Such an approach necessitates the oftentimes frustrating process of working from an outline, painstakingly constructing open-ended questions, and dealing with the obvious logistical difficulties and pitfalls of conducting focus groups comprised of living, breathing, rather unpredictable human beings (who, despite my doctoral degree and years in "the field," don't always agree with me.)[4] Moreover, I found it essential, though at times difficult, to contextualize English and Spanish-language media within the appropriate cultural, economic, and political spheres, as well as to question the frequent portrayal of ethnic media as bastions of diversity (Beltrán, 2002; Johnson, 2003; Johnson, Prabu, & Huey-Ohlsson, 2003). Perhaps most challenging was the process of negotiating the divide between "neutral" focus group facilitator and my desire to switch to "fellow fan mode" (Gallager, 2003, p. 24). The potential dilemmas (or advantages, for that matter) posed by my own role as a "halfie" observer/participant/critic/fan demanded that I "travel uneasily between speaking 'for' and speaking 'from,'" thereby destabilizing the standard distinction between self and other so integral to the traditional anthropological exercise (Abu-Lughod, 1991, p. 143; Zavella, 1996).[5] However, as Hills rightfully suggests in his analysis of the "fan-scholar," any belief in the inherently rational academic, or in the inherently "self-absent" fan, is sorely misplaced (2002).[6] All of these factors, and in particular the distinctive, if uneven, power differentials regulating the relationship between fan and fan-scholar, led me at times to question if a truly nonlinear approach to audience studies were even possible.[7]

Although my subject role as a non-Chicana/*mexicana* undoubtedly influenced the dynamics of the University of Minnesota focus group, which was entirely Chicana/*mexicana*, my position as a Latina of Caribbean descent proved to be a factor in the Mount Holyoke group as well, for while that population proved far more heterogeneous (most likely the product of targeted secondary school recruitment efforts and East Coast demographics), Caribbean-origin Latinas students still predominated. However, the veracity of any sort of instantaneous "panfemale solidarity" generated by the focus group exercise was perhaps most severely tested by my status as a middle-class, Latina/o Studies professor, which served as constant reminder of the power differentials between participants and facilitator, and to a lesser extent, among the participants themselves (Cahill, 2004; Cahill & "Fed Up Honeys," 2004; Dávila, 2001; Gallager, 2003; Haymes , 2004; Hermes, 2003; Parameswaran, 2003; Zavella, 1996, p. 140). In this regard, Bettie (2003) reminds us that the importance of engaging in a "radical" reflective ethnography, or that which foregrounds the academic's privilege as moderator, author, and editor, cannot be overestimated.

UNFASHIONABLE FASHION

As McRobbie (2002) and Puwar (2002) contend, fashion culture and aesthetics remain understudied arenas given the fact that prevailing notions of the political don't often encompass agents of production and consumption (both coded as stereotypically feminine activities), thereby precluding the possibility of engaging in oppositional practice within feminine "consumption work." Such perspectives also disregard the ways in which the market itself acts as a means of "female symbolic expression," or the genuine possibility of employing personal aesthetics as "material stepping stones of escape" (Lewis, 1990a, pp. 99, 101; Bettie, 2003, p. 43). The feminine/*feminized* nature of the fashion industry inevitably comes into play here, in addition to the ever-shifting location of Latinas/os within the U.S. racial hierarchy, as reflected in contemporary entertainment industry dynamics (Beltrán, 2002; Molina Guzmán & Valdivia, 2004). The young Latinas in the focus groups, however, appeared sensitive to the issues of agency (or lack thereof) that formed the subtext of our conversations. Marta, a student at the University of Minnesota, offered a firm opinion to this effect, as she observed that Jennifer Lopez "seems really manipulated by her company ... I don't really see a flavor; I don't really see her spirit come through," ironically echoing the popular use of the term "flavor"/ "*sabor*" as an adjectively applied indiscriminately to all objects and individuals "Latina/o." Later on in the session she reiterated this stance, albeit in modified form: "It's hard because it's a very complex thing, because you can't take agency away from them, because, they [the performers]—they do have choices." Indeed, more nuanced opinions regarding the agency of the Latinas discussed appeared in both focus groups, as the Mount Holyoke students acknowledged that while the Latina performers discussed were being "used" (by the media/entertainment industries), the very same performers were also engaged in "using" (the media/entertainment industries).

Current research suggests that for many Latina university students, adopting a feminist stance implies a concomitant abandonment of their cultural and ethnic/racial identities as Latinas (García, 2004). This pattern, which I myself have observed in anecdotal fashion among both undergraduate and graduate-level Latina students, underscores a key tension that emerged in the first focus group conducted; though the words "feminism" or "feminist" never crossed these young women's lips, they nonetheless felt free to openly criticize the Latina performers in the images (pronouncing them "objectified, fetishized," "trivial," and "trashy," among other comments). These young women were clearly well instructed in the usage of terms typically associated with feminist readings of popular media representations, and therein lay one of the supposed contradictions of the focus groups' reactions.

As exemplified by the focus group conversations, the discursive inconsistencies embodied in the rejection of the "feminist" label by Latina "third wavers"[8] may well extend beyond general cultural and ethnic/racial identity politics to a more specific rejection of the "lingering second wave politics of appearance" (Scott, 2005, p. 8). This abandonment of feminist nomenclature on the part of young women of color is even more striking, given the fact that for most current female college students, issues related to body image have dominated the mainstream feminist platform throughout their lifetimes. In this regard, Munford (2004) suggests that widely employed terms such as "girl power" may be interpreted in a variety of ways: on one hand, they may be read as depoliticized rhetoric; on the other, they may be seen to function as a "code" indicative of a postfeminist mindset. Notably, the rhetoric of girl power can be interpreted as a means of claiming a space both *within* and *against* feminism. As Munford (2004) points out, "third wave" feminists are often accused of privileging style over substance, and the individual over the collective. Again, this perspective ultimately runs counter to mainstream feminism's claims of inclusion, as it implies that personal style and aesthetics are somehow anathema to feminist identity.

FANDOM AND VISUAL NARRATIVES OF TRANSFORMATION

The difference between *looking* as opposed to *being looked at* (Stacey, 1994) references a host of power differentials, among them hierarchies of gender, class, race, and sexual orientation. As Luibhéid (2002, pp. 83, xxii) notes in her critique of gender, sexuality and U.S. border control policy, "the visual or that which gets seen, is driven by and redeploys particular cultural knowledges and blindnesses." She explains that the notion that bodies of color "look" a certain way was initially constructed by scientific racism, and then widely disseminated into the U.S. popular consciousness. Indeed, as recent Latina/o Studies media scholarship demonstrates (Johnson, 2003; Johnson et al., 2003; Martínez, 2004; Rojas, 2004), the disproportionate representation of white Latinos in Spanish language and Latino media is rooted in the centrality of whiteness as an unmarked racial identity, or the societal belief in whiteness as a (seemingly) invisible constant (Lipsitz, 1998). More succinctly stated, when we study brownness or blackness, we are also studying whiteness (Parameswaran, 2003). In this context, the "white gaze" functions as a strategy of containment, and as in the Latin(o) popular music industry the power to (de)construct "other" ethnicities remains in White hands (Beltrán, 2002; Cepeda, 2003). From this (de)constructive privilege emerges the type of media visual narrative protagonized in the images displayed to focus group members.[9]

This dialectic also plays itself out in the tension that emerges between women of color hailed as "beautiful" and reigning white beauty standards, or the "differ[ing] versions of femininity … integrally linked to and inseparable from … class and racial/ethnic performances" (Beltrán, 2002; Bettie, 2003, p. 5). A most vivid example of this dynamic is the latest trend in plastic surgery, or what have become known as "Latin" or "Brazilian" butt lifts designed to enhance one's posterior, at roughly $20,000 per operation (Singer, 2006). The comparatively less wealthy or *bisturí* (scalpel)-phobic in search of a J.-Lo.-like rear simply need seek out the costly new blue jeans designed to lift and separate through the use of complex seam work and strategic padding. Conversely, we may also witness the phenomenon that one of Rojas' (2004) respondents dubs "el trauma latino" [the Latina/o trauma], or the perpetual inferiority complex rooted in many Latinas' desire for blondness/whiteness (p. 143). In this regard, while they expressed an awareness of the socioeconomic and racial privileges associated with blonde hair and its attainment/maintenance, University of Minnesota focus group participants did not offer a monolithic reading of the newly blonde locks of Latina icons like Shakira: as one student stated, Shakira simply bleached her hair in order to "mock Britney Spears," thereby ascribing a more oppositional stance to the singer's personal aesthetics.

Given the visual's ability to communicate beyond language or community-specific cultural signifiers, visual images of Latinas/os in the media "teach" both Latinos and non-Latinos more about what it means to be a U.S. Latina/o. In this way, media "body language" performs a vital function in the creation and circulation of prevailing notions of pan-Latinidad and Latina femininity (Johnson, 2003). As the photo of the young fan of Colombian singer-songwriter Shakira demonstrates, a fan's personal aesthetics can provide the opportunity to "respond" to a given star, and to thereby participate in a "visual conversation" of sorts (Lewis, 1990a, p. 97) (see Figure 1).

Among the Mount Holyoke College students, however, the politics of fandom were not always understood in such empowering terms. One student, immediately after providing the group with an impressively long list of the Jennifer Lopez films that she had viewed, proceeded to criticize Lopez' talents, prompting the following exchange:

María Elena: So you're criticizing her [Lopez] but it sounds like ...

Norma: (interrupting) No, no, no ...

ME: ... you've seen a lot of her movies.

N (in a defeated, almost confessional tone): I, I have. I really have. I mean, I watch a lot.

ME: Are you, do you consider yourself a fan of hers?

N (insistent): I'm not a fan.

Figure 1. Linda, born in Cali, Colombia, and raised in Miami, waits in line for an autograph from Shakira at an event celebrating the release of Shakira's first English-language album. Her naturally dark hair is dyed blonde, much like that of her idol. Photograph by M. E. Cepeda.

In spite of their contradictory nature, Norma's comments here do not illustrate an isolated incident, as focus group participants tended to assume an "us" versus "them" mindset toward fandom in general. While these attitudes hinted at the largely unacknowledged dividing lines of status and class that form the basis of social distinction between cultured aficionado (us) and mere fan (them), they also reflected the inherently contradictory nature of the fan experience (Hills, 2002). Indeed, for Norma, as for many other focus group members, fandom was clearly associated with the brand of excessive indulgence verging on the pathological that prevailed in earlier scholarly writings on the subject. I remark on these dynamics not to berate these young women, but rather to highlight their (un)conscious awareness of the unspoken behavioral norms that pervade mainstream higher education. As high-achieving young women of color who have learned to "play by the rules" successfully enough to gain entrance into one of the nation's most elite colleges, they are well aware that "[t]hose who exhibit [a] charged and passionate response are believed to be out of control; those who exhibit [a] subdued and unimpassioned reaction are deemed to be superior types" (Jenson, 1992, p. 24). Given that passivity, excessiveness, and an overly excitable nature are all traits that are widely coded as female and/or "Latina/o," it is no wonder that many of the Latina students resisted labeling themselves (or each other) as fans.

At times, focus group participants also drew on their insightful observations of Spanish-language media in their commentary on the Latina stars under discussion. For example, many in the group remarked on their enjoyment of Jennifer Lopez' recent romantic comedy *Maid in Manhattan* (2002). In turn, Norma correctly located one of the sources of the movie's familiarity to Latina/o audiences, noting, "It's a *novela* [Spanish-language soap opera]. She's a *maid*." Her brief commentary not only succinctly identified the key convention uniting Lopez' English-language romantic comedy with its Spanish-language counterpart, but also offered a terse criticism of both genres' limited portrayals of the working-class, women of color, and women in general.

CONSUMPTION OF/AND "LA OTRA"

As Molina Guzmán and Valdivia (2004) argue, Latina iconicity may be read as evidence of Latinas' popular culture presence and "postcolonial exigency" rooted in the fluid nature of Latina racial, ethnic, and cultural subjectivities. However, this iconic status may also prove a mixed blessing (in the sense that as access to these images increases, so does the possibility of their homogenization), as Latina icons are "caught in the dialectic between agency and the objectification of identity that operates within many mediated products" (pp. 205–206, 214, 219). As previously stated, many of the Mount Holyoke focus groups members in particular declined to categorize themselves as fans of the Latina celebrities under discussion, and few if any of claimed to own an entire CD by any of the artists. Nevertheless, technological advances, the widespread use of cross-marketing techniques, and the increasingly porous boundaries between the advertising and entertainment spheres in general have removed some of the choice out of contemporary consumption habits (see Cashmore, 2006). Thus, for "fans" and "nonfans" alike, Latina celebrities *are* products under constant consumption, for besides their most easily recognizable commercial ventures (music and film), they are also associated with global brands such as Pepsi-Cola, Nokia, Verizon, Calvin Klein, Versace, Louis Vuitton, Sketchers, Revlon, L'Oreal, and M. A. C. cosmetics, as well as personal perfume, lingerie, clothing, and jewelry lines, among other items. As the myriad celebrity/brand associations here attest, one of the principal connections between star and fan is via commodity consumption (of images as well as products). In this scenario, feminine identity is under constant negotiation in a culture that casts women as both the subjects and the objects of popular commodity exchange (Stacey, 1994).

Echoing García Canclini's (1995) critique of market expansion and hegemonic legitimization wrapped in the guise of "prolonging shared traditions" and "societal renewal" (p. 107), Puwar (2002) traces multiculturalism's (and multicultural capital's) position at the heart of globalized economic markets. Rooted in the consumption of the so-called third world, the ahistorical frameworks that govern much popular media ultimately feed dominant consumers' attraction to the more "digestible" elements of Latin(o) América (pp. 64, 66). Within this dynamic, new trends are necessarily generated by *la Otra* (the Other Woman) and production of difference acts as cornerstone of the fashion industry. In this sense, the consumption of difference permits the dominant classes the opportunity "to recode and neutralize long-standing tropes while simultaneously intensifying them" (Root, cited in Puwar, 2002, p. 71), engaging in an aesthetic tropicalization of sorts (see Aparicio & Chávez-Silverman, 1997). A potential result of this dynamic is the "representational tension" that emerges from the interstices between hybrid Latina bodies and their symbolic resistance and commodification, or what we might otherwise classify as a simultaneous movement toward celebration and objectification (Beltrán, 2002; Molina Guzmán & Valdivia, 2004). In this regard, the young women interviewed appeared well aware of the racial tensions faced by Latina celebrities, and even more strongly attuned to the symbolic and concrete impacts of such conflicts in their own lives. As Mount Holyoke student Cate remarked, "Latinas … we're used to bridge the gap" [between black and white]. Indeed, many focus group participants viewed the United States' rigid black/white racial paradigm as a source of "impossibility"; and noted that as a result of this binary categorization, Afro-Latinas in particular are the subject of negligible media representation, and white Latinas, despite their disproportionate media presence, are cast as a contradiction in terms.

The popular notion of woman as "sign" and the related theorization of the woman of color's racialized body as a "boundary" or marker of difference renders the clothing, hair, and makeup present in media representations of Latinas some of the most readily identifiable markers of their "difference." According to Beltrán (2002), "media representations of the Latina body thus form a symbolic battleground upon which the ambivalent place of Latinos and Latinas in this society is acted out" (p. 82). This ambivalence surfaces even in the problematic ways in which Latina identity is assigned (and claimed) within the mainstream *and* ethnic media, as focus group participant Inés bitterly remarked. (I noted with interest that no one spoke of singer Christina Aguilera specifically in terms of her Latina identity, perhaps a reflection of what many Latinas/os perceive as her opportunistic, unilateral adoption of a "Latina" identity in recent years (see Cepeda, 2001). Furthermore, the Latina body itself—by some mainstream standards an abject body—introduces an element of vulnerability such as that identified by Rojas' informants, who readily recognized the pitfalls inherent in claiming a Latina identity for oneself, given the pervasive commodification of the Latina body within U.S. society (2004). Thus emerges the "assimilative pressure" on Latina stars to embrace "unmarked" styles or to engage in "nonethnic" forms of dress (Puwar, 2002, p. 77). These everyday practices could well be interpreted as a form of (un)conscious Latina "survival aesthetics," such as those seen in the photographic narratives displayed to participants.

AMBIVALENCE AND BEYOND

Latinas' challenge to prevailing racial paradigms shapes our perceptions of visual/media culture, and the ways in which variables such as race/ethnicity, gender, sexual orientation, class and religion are visually coded in mainstream media and society (Valdivia, 2004). But what about the possibility, as suggested by University of Minnesota focus group participants, of signs existing in a "free-floating" fashion? And how might Latinas consumers interact with star culture on their terms? (Puwar, 2002). As such, the often-theorized relationship of seduction and power, in which "no single practice or manner always suggests either power or oppression" (Scott, 2005, p. 12), was a persistent source of interpretive tension within both groups. As University of Minnesota focus group participant Alicia observed, "if you want to be successful and you're Latina, like there's always that stigma of, you know, sexuality and seduction." The Mount Holyoke students responded to what they described as the "very sexual" choreography of performers such as Shakira in much the same way, consistently treating it as cause for alarm. Although comments like these offer a realistic portrayal of current mainstream media practices and their objectification of the Latina body, they also fail to recognize the oppositional potential underlying the "weapons of the weak" (see Hartman, 1999).

Perhaps the most striking aspect of Lowe's (2003) work on "tweens" and their readings of Britney Spears was that despite the girls' vociferous objections to much of Spears' public persona (including her appearance), they were clearly capable of separating their disapproval from their enjoyment of Spears' texts, as evidenced by their familiarity with the minutia of Spear's life and music. Unlike Lowe's respondents, however (which were all, with one exception, white and middle-class), the young women of color in the Mount Holyoke and University of Minnesota focus groups I conducted are more often confronted with mainstream fashion's potential to entice emotions "beyond ambivalence-rage" (Puwar, 2002, p. 64). In my dialogues with these students, at times I noted an oppositional response that moved toward the consumption of "images and texts outside the [tropicalized] matrix," yet didn't ignore the "symbolic and physical violence of the stereotype" (p. 64). During a discussion of Jennifer Lopez' shifting romantic partners and the impacts that they have had on her public persona, Mount Holyoke students Norma and Inés provided the group with a brief, yet telling, description of the various public "roles" that Lopez has played, ranging from simply "Latina" to "ghetto girl from the block" to "dancer body" to "sophisticated" to "the housewife." Each of these periods were defined primarily by noticeable alternations in Lopez' hair color and style, clothing, and body shape. These categorizations might speak to widely internalized notions of race, gender, class, and beauty standards, in that each of Lopez "characters" mentioned were defined in conjunction with her romantic partner at the time, and his racial and class origins (i.e., Lopez was a "ghetto girl" when dating an African-American, "sophisticated" when with a white partner, and a "housewife" when married to a Puerto Rican man). However, the problematic nature of these depictions was further complicated by the fact that the focus groups participants then described Lopez' shifting public persona as the combined result of professional demands and personal conflicts. In other words, they recognized that the changes in hairstyle, clothing, and body shape were a reflection of the particular brand of survival aesthetics practiced by arguably the most visible Latina performer in the world today. This example highlights the focus group participants' struggles to negotiate what many interpreted as problematic (hegemonic) images of Latina celebrities with their oppositional potential. Furthermore, as Paz-Frydman (2006) notes, "underlying most criticism is a sense of pride and identification with these artists, an identification which occurs not based on the physical but on the emotional appeal of Latinidad and 'the common struggle,' regardless of whether this common experience is actually imagined or not" (p. 15).

Clearly, the most recent Latin(o) music boom has emerged as a key site for the display of Latina bodies, just as the selective deployment of the term "crossover" has historically indexed the racial, ethnic, and cultural fault lines that are simultaneously represented and perpetuated within U.S. popular media. As Poran's (2002) psychological research on cultural standards and perceptions of beauty among college-age women proposes, Latinas in particular appear to possess a complex attitude toward dominant imagery, accompanied by an acute understanding of U.S. consumer culture, much like the elements of "ambivalence and distinction" noted by Rojas (2004). This is not to suggest, however, that fans constitute an entirely unproblematic resource regarding their own media consumption, or that employing the "right" method(s) will yield transparent results (Bird, 2003, p. 9; Hills, 2002). Nor can we assume that the semiotic, enunciative, and textual products of fandom are inherently oppositional, as the oppositional nature of fan readings are determined by factors external to the fan/fan text relationship itself (Sandvoss, 2005).

The young Latina students I encountered were highly sensitized to alternative conceptualizations of Latina beauty, quotidian aesthetics, and their subordinate location in relation to dominant U.S. cultural mores. I found this to be the general case in both focus groups, despite the considerable class, geographic, cultural, and institutional differences between the two sites. However, the need for more broad-based reception studies focusing on Latina/o fans persists, given that "a map that colours in only small sections of the territory may be accurate as far as these sections is concerned, yet of lesser value in navigating through the territory at large" (Sandvoss, 2005, p. 6). In an age when we appear to have exhausted the "Civil Rights politics of visibility" (Fregoso, 2004), moreover, it is essential that Media Studies, Ethnic Studies, Cultural Studies, and feminist scholars as well strive to locate popular aesthetic practices within their historical, social, and cultural contexts, or else run the risk of reinscribing the very of gatekeeping measures that U.S. feminisms are theoretically and practically intended to challenge.

ACKNOWLEDGMENT

Muchísimas gracias a las mujeres de la Universidad de Minnesota, Twin Cities and Mount Holyoke College for your generosity, intelligence, and sense of community. Many thanks to Scott Morgensen and the members of Macalester College's

2003–2004 faculty seminar on Race, Sexuality, and the Transnational for their helpful insights regarding an earlier version of this research. Special thanks are also due to Jillian Báez, Dolores Inés Casillas, Caitlin Cahill, Cate Costa, Inés Leal, Rachel Martínez, Louis Mendoza, Rogelio Miñana, Silvia Paz-Frydman, Marylyn Scott, Lise-Anne Strohschank, and Angharad Valdivia for their kindness and invaluable assistance at various stages of this project.

NOTES

1. A notable exception is Beltrán's (2002) insightful article on Latina media "crossovers," which asks, "Does crossover necessarily involve containment? Must it ultimately be hegemonic?" (p. 73). For a related topic, see Cepeda (2001).
2. Despite the predominance of Chicana/mexicana students in the University of Minnesota focus group conducted for this study, I have elected to use the terms "Latina/U.S. Latina" here, as they provide the greatest degree of linguistic and cultural inclusivity for the project at hand. In addition, all participants' names have been changed when requested.
3. Consult Scott (2005) for a more complete historical account of mainstream U.S. feminism's relationship to fashion and grooming, from the "first wave" to the present. In this regard, Scott's adept counterreading of U.S. feminist history and media prove very convincing; however, her general failure to contextualize the aesthetic experiences of U.S. women of color in a more informed fashion runs the risk of eliding difference, much in the same way for which she critiques feminist elites.
4. Here I refer to an expanded notion of "field" and "fieldwork," such as that proposed in Chapter 1 of Bird (2003).
5. According to Abu-Lughod (1991), "halfies" are those "individuals whose national or cultural identity is mixed by virtue of migration, overseas education, or parentage" (p. 137).
6. A foundational discussion of the complex dynamic underwriting the fan/scholar relationship and its impact on academic research can be found in Jenkins (1992).
7. For examples of recent groundbreaking, Latina/o Studies reception research models, see Aparicio (1998, Chaps. 11–12) as well as Dávila (2001, Chap. 6). Further discussion of specifically nonlinear reception scholarship can be found in Casillas and Cepeda (2002), and Báez (2007).
8. As Gillis (2004) notes, the labels "postfeminism" and "third wave" are employed virtually interchangeably. Moreover, she observes that the competitive, "wave-based" model upon which contemporary feminist theory is based allows little room to construct a collective, "wave-based" experience among feminists.
9. Focus group participants were shown a variety of photographic images of Latina celebrities (almost exclusively popular music stars), ranging from advertisements to magazine covers to more "candid" personal photos. However, I was most interested in participants' reactions to a three specific photo collages focusing on Shakira, Jennifer Lopez, and Christina Aguilera (these are referred to in the preceding subheading as "visual narratives of transformation"). Each of these recently published collages consisted of a chronological series of several images focusing on the physical changes that the female celebrities had undergone in recent years. Without exception, each of the Latina stars had dyed their hair lighter and lost weight as part of what were described as "improvements" in the commentary accompanying the collages.

REFERENCES

Abu-Lughod, L. (1991). Writing against culture. In R. Fox (Ed.), *Recapturing anthropology* (pp. 137–162). Santa Fe, NM: School of American Research Press.

Aparicio, F. R. & S. Chávez-Silverman. (1997). Introduction. In F. R. Aparicio & S. Chávez-Silverman (Eds.), *Tropicalizations: Transcultural representations of Latinidad* (pp. 1–18). Hanover, NH: Dartmouth/University Press of New England.

Báez, J. M. (2007). Mexican (American) Women Talk Back: Audience Responses to Latinidad in U.S. Advertising. In A. N. Valdivia (Ed.), *Latina/o Communication Studies Today*. New York: Peter Lang.

Beltrán, M. C. (2002). The Hollywood Latina body as site of social struggle: Media constructions of stardom and Jennifer's Lopez's "cross-over" butt. *Quarterly Review of Film and Video 19*, 71–86.

Bettie, J. (2003). *Women without class: Girls, race, and identity*. Berkeley, CA: University of California Press.

Bird, S. E. (2003). *The audience in everyday life: Living in a media world*. New York: Routledge.

Bury, R. (2005). *Cyberspaces of their own: Females fandoms online*. New York: Peter Lang.

Cahill, C. (2004). Defying gravity?: Raising consciousness through collective research. *Children's Geographies, 2*(2), 273–286.

Cahill, C. & "Fed Up Honeys." (2004). Speaking back: Voices of young urban women of color using participatory action research to challenge and complicate representations of young women. In A. Harris (Ed.), *All about the girl: Culture, power and identity* (pp. 231–242). New York & London: Routledge.

Cashmore, E. (2006). *Celebrity/culture*. New York & London: Routledge.

Casillas, D. I. & M. E. Cepeda. (2002). *How Tejas arrived at La Isla: Jennifer López, Selena, and the construction of a Latina iconography*. Paper presented at the Puerto Rican Studies Association, Chicago, IL.

Cepeda, M. E. (2001). "Columbus effects": The politics of crossover and chronology within the Latin(o) music "boom." *Discourse, 23*(1), 242–267.

Cepeda, M. E. (2003). Shakira as the idealized, transnational citizen: A case study of Colombianidad in transition. *Latino Studies, 1*, 211–232.

Chabrám, A. (1990). Chicana/o studies as oppositional ethnography. *Cultural Studies, 4*(3), 228–247.

Dávila, A. (2001). *Latinos, Inc.: The marketing and making of a people*. Berkeley: University of California Press.

Figueroa, M. P. (2003). Resisting "beauty" and *Real women have curves*. In A. Gaspar de Alba (Ed.), *Velvet barrios: Popular culture and Chicana/o sexualities* (pp. 265–282). New York: Palgrave Macmillan.

Flores, J. & G. Yúdice. (1997). Living borders/*Buscando América*: Languages of Latino self-formation. In A. Darder, R. D. Torres, & H. Gutierrez (Eds.), *Latinos and education: A critical reader* (pp. 174–200). New York & London: Routledge.

Fregoso, R. L. (1999). Re-imagining Chicana identities in the urban sphere, *Cool Chuca* style. In C. Kaplan, N. Alarcón, & M. Moallem (Eds.), *Between woman and nation: Nationalisms, transnational feminisms, and the state* (pp. 72–91). Durham: Duke University Press.

Fregoso, R. L. (2004). *Money talks: The politics of U.S. Spanish language and bilingual media*. Comments presented at the American Studies Association, Atlanta, GA.

Frith, S. (1996). Music and identity. In S. Hall & P. Du Gay (Eds.), *Questions of cultural identity* (pp. 108–127). London: Sage.

García, E. (2004). *Are Latinas feminists? A critical look at Latina feminist thought and practice.* Paper presented at Latin American Studies Association, Las Vegas, NV.

García Canclini, N. (1995). *Hybrid cultures: Strategies for entering and leaving modernity.* C. L. Chiappari & S. L. López (Trans.). Minneapolis: University of Minneapolis Press.

Gillis, S. (2004). *New and improved! The branding of (third wave) feminism.* Paper presented at the American Studies Association, Atlanta, GA.

Grossberg, L. (1992). Is there a fan in the house?: The affective sensibility of fandom. In L. A. Lewis (Ed.), *The adoring audience: Fan culture and popular media* (pp. 50–65). London & New York: Routledge.

Hartman, S. (1999). Seduction and the uses of power. In C. Kaplan, N. Alarcón, & M. Moallem (Eds.), *Between woman and nation: Nationalisms, transnational feminisms, and the state* (pp. 111–141). Durham: Duke University Press.

Haymes, M. (2004). Hearing girls' silences: Thoughts on the politics and practices of a feminist method of group discussion. *Gender, Place, and Culture, 11*(1), 105–119.

Hermes, J. (2003). Practicing embodiment: Reality, respect, and issues of gender in media reception. In A. N. Valdivia (Ed.), *A companion to media studies* (pp. 382–398). Malden, MA: Blackwell.

Hills, M. (2002). *Fan cultures.* London & New York: Routledge.

Jenkins, H. (1992). *Textual poachers: Television fans & participatory culture.* New York: Routledge.

Jenson, J. (1992). Fandom as pathology: The consequences of characterization. In L. A. Lewis (Ed.), *The adoring audience: Fan culture and popular media* (pp. 9–29). London & New York: Routledge.

Johnson, M. A. (2003). Constructing a new model of ethnic media. In A. N. Valdivia (Ed.), *A companion to media studies* (pp. 272–292). Malden, MA: Blackwell.

Johnson, M. A., D. Prabu, & D. Huey-Ohlsson. (2003). Beauty in brown: Skin color in Latina magazines. In D. I. Rios & A. N. Mohamed (Eds.), *Brown and black communication: Latino and African American conflict in mass media* (pp. 159–173). Westport, CT: Praeger, 2003.

Lewis, L. A. (1990a). Consumer girl culture: How music video appeals to girls. In M. E. Brown (Ed.), *Television and women's culture: The politics of the popular* (pp. 89–101). London: Sage.

Lewis, L. A. (1990b). *Gender politics and MTV: Voicing the difference.* Philadelphia: Temple University Press.

Lipsitz, G. (1998). *The possessive investment in whiteness: How white people benefit from identity politics.* Philadelphia: Temple University Press.

Lowe, M. (2003). Colliding feminisms: Britney Spears, "tweens," and the politics of reception. *Popular Music and Society, 26*(2), 123–140.

Luibhéid, E. (2002). *Entry denied: Controlling sexuality at the border.* Minneapolis: University of Minnesota Press.

Martínez, K. (2004). *Latina* magazine and the invocation of a panethnic familia: Latino identity as it is informed by celebrities and *Papis Chulos. The Communication Review, 7:2,* 155–174.

McRobbie, A. (2002). Fashion culture: Creative work, female individualization. *Feminist Review, 71,* 52–62.

Molina Guzmán, I. & A. N. Valdivia. (2004). Brain, brow, and booty: Latina iconicity in U.S. popular culture. *The Communication Review, 7:2,* 205–221.

Moraga, C. & G. Anzaldúa. (Eds.). 1981. *This bridge called my back: Writings by radical women of color.* Brooklyn: Kitchen Table Press.

Mount Holyoke College. *Facts about Mount Holyoke College.* Retrieved June 6, 2006, from http://www.mtholyoke.edu/cic/about/facts.shtml

Munford, R. (2004). *(En)gendering "girl" identities: Third wave feminism and popular culture*. Paper presented at the American Studies Association, Atlanta, GA.
Nelson, T. (2004, June 13). President's visit highlights Minnesota's growing Latino population. *Saint Paul Pioneer Press*, p. A1.
Orbach, S. (1990). *Fat is a feminist issue: A self-help guide for compulsive eaters*. Berkeley: Berkeley Publishing Group.
Parameswaran, R. E. (2003). Resuscitating feminist audience studies: Revisiting the politics of representation and resistance. In A. N. Valdivia (Ed.), *A companion to media studies* (pp. 311–336). Malden, MA: Blackwell.
Paz-Frydman, S. (2006). *The Latina body and the entertainment industry: The practices of resistance, hegemony, and identity construction*. Unpublished manuscript, Williams College.
Poran, M. A. (2002). Denying diversity: Perceptions of beauty and social comparison processes among Latina, black, and white women. *Sex Roles, 47*(1/2), 65–81.
Puwar, N. (2002). Multicultural fashion … stirrings of another sense of aesthetics and memory. *Feminist Review, 71*, 63–87.
Rivero, Y. M. (2003). The performance and reception of televisual "ugliness" in Yo soy Betty la fea. *Feminist Media Studies, 3*(1), 65–82.
Rojas, V. (2004). The gender of Latinidad: Latinas speak about Hispanic television. *The Communication Review, 7*, 25–153.
Sandvoss, C. (2005). *Fans: The mirror of consumption*. Cambridge: Polity Press.
Scott, L. M. (2005). *Fresh lipstick: Redressing fashion and feminism*. New York: Palgrave Macmillan.
Singer, N. (2006, March 2). How to stuff a wild bikini bottom. *The New York Times*, p. 3.
South Hadley, MA. Retrieved June 7, 2006, from http://www.epodunk.com/cgi-bin/popInfo.php?IocIndex=3136.
Stacey, J. (1994). *Star gazing: Hollywood cinema and female spectatorship*. London & New York: Routledge.
Storey, J. (2003). *Inventing popular culture*. Malden, MA: Blackwell.
University of Minnesota, Twin Cities. (2004). *University of Minnesota, twin cities*. Retrieved October 19, 2004, from http://www.umn.edu
University of Minnesota, Twin Cities: Office for Multicultural and Academic Affairs. (2003 May). *Undergraduate enrollment profile, Chicano/Latino students*. Retrieved October 19, 2004, from http://www.oma.umn.edu/committees.html
Valdés, D. N. (2000). *Barrios Norteños: St. Paul and Midwestern Mexican communities in the twentieth century*. Austin: University of Texas Press.
Valdivia, A. N. (2000). Women of color in the audience: Reception analysis meets frustration theory. In *A Latina in the land of Hollywood and other essays in media culture* (pp. 149–170). Tucson: University of Arizona Press.
Valdivia, A. N. (Ed.). (2003). *A companion to media studies*. Malden, MA: Blackwell.
Valdivia, A. N. (2004). Latina/o communication and media studies today: An introduction. *The Communication Review, 7*: 2, 107–112.
Zavella, P. (1996). Feminist insider dilemmas: Constructing ethnic identity with Chicana informants. In D. L. Wolf (Ed.), *Feminist dilemmas in fieldwork* (pp. 138–159). Boulder, CO: Westview Press.

CHAPTER TWELVE

Mexican (American) Women Talk Back: Audience Responses TO Latinidad IN U.S. Advertising

JILLIAN M. BÁEZ

> Yvette: I think gender inequality has been going on forever and I think it's so.
> Isabel: It's so right.
> Monica: And advertising—
> Isabel: That's not going to help them [Latinas].
> [They all talk over one another].
>
> —Focus Group (February 2005)

As Latinas are increasingly desired as a niche market by transnational media industries, Latina audiences are ever aware of how their subjectivities are mediated. Since the 1980s, the "Hispanic" advertising industry[1] continues to capitalize on the "buying power" of Latina/os in the United States through constructing a largely homogenous Latinidad.[2] Much media and industry attention is placed on the "buying power" of Latina/os as more and more products and services are being created for and/or targeted to this population. For example, according a University of Georgia study, the 38 million Latina/os in the United States hold 8 percent of U.S. purchasing power—a number that has increased almost 30 percent in the past three years (Humphreys, 2006). As such, "Hispanic" advertising has grown substantially with an increase in the amount of agencies and advertisements targeted to Latina/os. With this increase in Latina/o representation within advertising—one of the most visible forms of representation in mass media—the

Latina body functions as a hypervisible commodity. Thus, Latinidad becomes gendered as feminine within an already homogenized identity constructed by niche-marketing specialists. This chapter asks how Latina audiences, specifically Mexican (American)[3] women, respond and/or "talk back" to these contemporary representations of commodified Latina femininity and sexuality.

By combining feminist media studies and transnational feminist theory, this chapter examines the relationship between Latinidad, consumer culture, and the female body. Extending the work of Arlene Dávila (2001, 2002), this chapter interrogates how Latinidad is constructed by the U.S. "Hispanic" advertising industry and how women of Mexican origin make meaning of these media texts. In other words, I am interested in how Latinidad is constructed both from within and outside–that is, by both Latina/os and by the government, media and other social institutions. As such, this study primarily pursues the following question: Given the increased visibility of Latina/os in U.S. advertising and other popular culture, especially the female body, how do women of Mexican origin make meaning of these representations? More specifically, how is Latinidad (as a panethnic construction of identity) deployed both from within and outside, that is, by both Latina/os and the advertising industry? Finally, how does the Latina body figure into this process? To begin answering these questions, this study employs focus groups with young women of Mexican origin in order to make meaning of representations of Latinidad, especially within the context of the increased visibility of the Latina body in contemporary popular culture.

While much contemporary research focuses on the construction of Latinidad in popular communications (see Aparicio & Chávez-Silverman, 1997; Dávila, 2002; Flores, 2000; Levine, 2001; Valdivia, 2000, 2003a, 2003b), there is little scholarship that examines specific nationalities' (e.g., Mexican, Cuban, Colombian, etc.) responses to Latinidad as it is constructed in the media. Further, there is little audience research on Latinas, and women of color in general (Bobo, 1995; Valdivia, 2000). This chapter builds on and extends burgeoning Latina audience scholarship that foregrounds the intersectionality of race, ethnicity, class, and gender (Aparicio, 1998; Báez, 2007; Cepeda, this volume; Mayer, 2003; Rivero, 2003; Rojas, 2004; Vargas, 2005, 2006, this volume). It specifically seeks to intervene in this literature on Latina audiences by investigating the ways in which popular culture can mediate relations among Latina subgroups.

A THEORETICAL FRAMEWORK FOR STUDYING LATINA AUDIENCES

This chapter largely draws from feminist media and cultural studies and transnational feminist theory. Feminist media and cultural studies offer a framework for understanding the intersection between gender, representation, and audience uses and interpretations. Germinal work on female audiences such as the work of Ien Ang (1985), Jacqueline Bobo (1995), Andrea Press (1991), and Janice Radway (1984) among others, provide ways in which to think about audiences as active and interpretive. This scholarship argues that meanings are not just located within texts, but are produced through audiences' interactions with those texts. As such, audiences may use and interpret media differently than the producer's intent. However, this does not suggest that audiences are always resistant; in fact, they may have readings that are consistent with the producer or a negotiation of it.[4] Instead, the usefulness of this framework lies in its understanding that audiences are producers of meaning (Hall, 1980; Valdivia, 2003a) and that they may interpret texts in unexpected ways.

Transnational feminism assumes that intersectionality—or how axes of difference such as race, nation, gender, class, and sexuality all overlap to form our identities and the oppressions we face in our everyday lives—is central to understanding our social position in the world. Transnational feminism, especially as it is articulated in the work of Chandra Talpade Mohanty (2003), Ella Shohat (1998), and Angharad Valdivia (2004), provides an appropriate framework for studying Latinas as female, transnational subjects who experience often painful, uneasy hybridity in their everyday lives (Valdivia, 2004). In particular, it provides a template for studying how transnational flows intersect with everyday life in an increasingly more globalized world. This approach examines issues of power and agency across difference, understanding that identities are not monolithic, and sometimes can be contradictory and competing. Transnational feminism highlights the fluidity, mobility, and also immobility of people and cultural products. This perspective attempts to understand how commodified culture may traverse borders, while the people who produce these products continue to be unwelcome (Fusco, 1995; Lugo, forthcoming). Transnational feminism also leaves room for women's agency and resistance within dominant global structures. Ultimately, transnational feminism is extremely useful for a project such as this one that examines the overlaps, convergences, and divergences between representation and the lived experience of Latinas.

THE POLITICAL ECONOMY OF THE LATINA BODY IN "HISPANIC" ADVERTISING INDUSTRY

In order to situate the women's responses to representations of gendered Latinidad in advertising, it is imperative to understand the industry in which these texts are produced. Though "Hispanic" advertising, or that which is targeted to Latina/o consumers, has existed in the United States since at least the mid-1960s, it was not until the mid-1980s, called "Decade of the Hispanic," that this niche-marketing industry becomes full-fledged (Dávila, 2001; Peñaloza, 1997; Turow, 1997). Pioneer "Hispanic" advertising agencies were initiated by Cuban immigrants in New York City focusing on Caribbean Latina/o consumers in the Northeast. The agencies later grew to include other markets such as South Florida, California, and Texas with a growing emphasis on marketing to Mexican Americans. With this expansion of the Latina/o market, ownership also opened up in terms of ethnicity, with other Latina/o groups and Anglos controlling the industry. Within the past decade both news media and advertising trade publications have placed much attention on the growing Latina/o population in the United States, their status as the largest minority, and ultimately how this translates into their potential buying power. As such, Latina/os are now coveted as one of the most profitable consumer blocks (Castañeda Paredes, 2003; Dávila, 2001; Rodriguez, 1999).

Since its inception, "Hispanic" advertising has employed the trope of "tropicalization" (see Aparicio & Chavez-Silverman, 1997), a trope in which differences within Latinidad are flattened to tropical settings, Caribbean music, bright colors, male Latin lovers, and Latina spitfires. Overall, Latina/os are exoticized under the trope of tropicalization as the perpetual foreign Other. Part of this trope of tropicalization has focused on gendered representations, particularly the use of Latinas' bodies to sell products and services. Traditionally, "Hispanic" advertising represented Latinas as the asexual, self-sacrificing mother confined to the kitchen or laundry room (e.g., Goya commercials) (Dávila, 2001). More recently, advertising recalls the archetype of the Latina spitfire dominant in other U.S. popular culture, namely Hollywood film (ibid.). The Latina spitfire is hypersexual, loud, aggressive, and usually young. She is present in many contemporary advertising campaigns for large corporations such Coca-Cola, Pepsi, and Tecate. In this way, Latinas' bodies have come to stand in for Latinidad in advertising falling within a women-as-nation trope (Shohat & Stam, 1995; van Zoonen, 1994), or in this case, woman-as-panethnicity trope. Aside from reproducing the virgin/whore dichotomy, these two representations (the mother and the spitfire) in advertising reify the dominant tropes of feminine Latinidad within mainstream media, that is, the binary of the submissive, (in)visible, and often undocumented, Mexican female immigrant (Ruiz, 2002) and the tropicalized hypervisible, oversexed Latina (Aparicio & Chavez-Silverman, 1997). More so, this shift from asexual to hypersexual representations of Latinas underscores the erasure of *mexicanidad* and foregrounding of tropicalized bodies and commodities in contemporary mainstream popular culture.

Not only are Latina bodies commodified within the representational realm in order to sell specific products and services to Latina/o and non-Latina/o global audiences, but transnational media corporations also consider Latina audiences a commodity. Just as Latina/o and female consumers are vied for as niche markets, advertisers and other media professionals are increasingly considering Latinas to be a potentially lucrative consumer block. This is evident in the increased visibility of Latina celebrities and media products targeted specifically to Latina audiences that range from films to books to magazines to shoes. As such, not only are Latinas' bodies commodified by the advertising industry in order to represent and sell Latinidad to Latina/o consumers, but transnational media corporations also construct Latina audiences as commodities in order to appeal to advertisers.

EMPLOYING ETHNOGRAPHIC FOCUS GROUPS:
A BRIEFING ON METHODOLOGY

As with other women of color, Latinas are an understudied group within audience studies (Bobo, 1995; Valdivia, 2000, 2004) despite their status as the second largest population of women in the United States (U.S. Census, 2003). Burgeoning Latina audience studies (see Aparicio, 1998; Cepeda, this volume; Mayer, 2003; Rivero, 2003; Rojas, 2004; Vargas, 2005, 2006, this volume) point to the significance of studying Latinas as a gendered and racialized group. These scholars argue that Latinas are a heterogeneous, hybrid group that often times have different experiences from that of other women, especially Anglo women. These experiences also range depending on geography, class, race, nation, sexuality, and religion among other axes of difference. These authors also point to how audience studies, like other qualitative research, allows for Latinas to speak back, against, and to mainstream institutions such as media and provide a space in which scholars can consider the delicate balance between the structural forces of media industries and the agency that Latinas potential can exert. These types of studies also allow for women to express frustration, not just pleasure (Valdivia, 2000), with media representations and re-write pleasure from seemingly oppressive depictions (Aparicio, 1998). Finally, these studies discuss how Latina audiences negotiate representations in complicated, uneven ways that are in accordance with their transnational, hybrid subjectivities. This study draws upon and extends this burgeoning body of work by focusing how Latina audiences' intersectionality shapes how they interact and interpret media texts. I especially consider how a particular ethnic group,[5] in this case Mexican (American) women, understands and relates to Latinidad as it is represented in advertising and practiced in everyday life. Studying Mexican (American) women in particular provides an important case study given that Mexican Americans are often erased and excluded in mainstream popular culture in favor of a tropical discourse (Valdivia, 2003a). In this way, this study contributes to this body of literature by considering intra-ethnic relations among Latinas and is ethnic-specific as opposed to studying Latinas within a broader panethnic context.

Similar to the methods used by Meenakshi Gigi Durham (2004) and Andrea Press and Elizabeth Cole (1998), I employed focus groups to understand how women of Mexican origin produce meanings about representations of Latinas in advertising. Focus groups were selected as a method for the following reasons: (1) they allow the researcher to gather a great amount of qualitative data within a relatively short amount of time (Morgan, 1997); (2) one can observe social interaction in discussing the given topic (ibid.); and (3) as some feminist research has argued, it allows for a more balanced power relation between the researcher and the informants (in comparison to individual interviews) given that there are more group members than the researcher (Madriz, 2000). Furthermore, Ester Madriz identifies focus groups as an especially useful method for studying women of color as historically these women have resisted oppression through talking to one another. In this way, focus groups potentially provide a liberatory space for the informants to engage with one another and perhaps make it easier for these women to feel comfortable speaking to a researcher.

In particular, I drew upon Press and Cole's (1999) methodology of "ethnographic focus groups." Unlike traditional focus group methodologies that draw from market research that seeks to obtain generalizable information from a large and/or diverse sample pool, Press and Cole argue that ethnographic focus groups seek to gain an *in-depth* understanding of the social interaction between participants and their meaning making practices among a small sample that already has formed relationships with each other (e.g., as friends, family members, or co-workers). In this way, ethnographic focus groups challenge traditional methodologies by studying participants who already know one another as opposed to randomly selected participants who have never met before the session. Also, researchers using this methodology try to have participants host the focus group sessions in an effort to shift from traditional method of conducting them in a sanitized, institutional, impersonal environment such as the university. In addition, rather than studying several groups of people in different sessions, I chose to conduct two focus group sessions with the same women to build upon the rapport we had established and to follow-up on topics and ideas we had discussed in the previous session. In this sense, this can be considered a study of "longitudinal groups" (Morgan, 1997, p. 69), or an in-depth exploration of one group's perspectives over the course of more than one session in contrast to researching several groups' that meet only once.

Before recruiting focus group participants, I collected 25 print advertisements from February 2003 to February 2005 depicting Latinas from *Latina* magazine, a women's magazine that targets 18–45-year-old, middle-class, professional Latinas.[6] Advertisements were selected on the basis that they visually depict bodies marked as Latina at least from the neck up. From this sample, I randomly selected seven advertisements to be presented to the participants during the focus group sessions. Five of the advertisements are full body poses (showing the model from at least the waist up) and two are close-up, headshots. The texts were selected from *Latina* given its wide distribution across the U.S. and bilingual content. *Latina* also serves as an appropriate source from which to draw texts for this study given its construction and celebration of Latinidad as a panethnicity (Martinez, 2004). In particular, advertisements have been increasingly central to *Latina* over the span of the magazine's life (Garcia, 2005). Today, advertisements often comprise over half the pages of the publication.[7]

After selecting the advertisements, I organized a focus group with five Mexican (American) women recruited using snowball sampling with the input of a key informant that I met previously through activities held at a university cultural center. The women already knew one another well as they are all members of the same Latina sorority. I held the first focus group session in May 2004 in a room in a university cultural center. Although I had wanted to meet in a noninstitutional environment, given that I did not know the women well, they felt that it was a safe and convenient place we could meet as a group. Nonetheless, it provided the women a somewhat comfortable space since it was a student environment and they held previous sorority meetings and functions there. I organized another focus group session in February 2005 to follow-up with the women and focus more on their conceptualizations of how Latinidad and media intersect in their everyday lives. At this point, one of the women offered her apartment for the focus group to meet, which provided a more intimate and comfortable environment for the group. During this second session, one of the original women could not make it and another sorority sister participated in her place.

All of the participants are women of Mexican origin who also identify as Latina and/or Hispanic from the Pilsen/Little Village area, also known as "the heart" of the Mexican American community in Chicago. During the time of the last focus group, the women were all 4-year college students ranging in rank and ages 18–24. All the women are second generation (their parents emigrated from Mexico) and two of the women have dual Mexican and U.S. citizenship. Although all the women identified as working-class, they are still a segment of *Latina*'s target group of mainly college-educated, middle-class Latinas ranging from ages 18–45 (Martinez, 2004) given their socioeconomic mobility as college students.

Each session lasted about two and a half to three hours and consisted of open-ended questions to allow me to conduct a nonlinear approach, or one in which the research was dictated by the informants, not the researcher. At the first session, I showed the women three of the selected advertisements to provoke discussions on representations of Latinas and their bodies in advertising.[8] The focus group was structured so that first the participants could informally engage with the advertisements and then were asked specific questions about their interpretations of the texts. For the second session, I brought the other four selected advertisements and followed the same procedure, except that I allotted for more time at the end for the women to engage with the role of Latinidad in their everyday lives in general, not just as represented in media texts. At each session all participants were provided with a description of the study and signed an informed consent form. The participants selected their own pseudonyms that are used in this chapter to protect their confidentiality. All the women were compensated for their time by receiving $20 each in cash.

What follows is a thematic analysis of recurring topics and patterns in the focus group data that I collected with this particular group of women of Mexican origin. Though there were many themes, particularly centered around femininity, upward-class mobility, family, and sexuality, I chose to focus on three interrelated and overlapping themes that came up several times throughout the course of the two focus group sessions: (1) their frustrations with representations of Latinas' sexuality in advertising and other mass media; (2) their reading of the advertisements as a lens through which to understand their desire for upward-class mobility; and (3) their disavowals of an "authentic" Latina body and simultaneous identification and tension with non-Mexican Latinas. These themes are inextricably intertwined with the women's hybrid and transnational subjectivities in an increasingly globalized world in which the movement of people, products, and ideas flows unevenly and under the constraint of a largely capitalist political economic system. In a world in which the Latina body is commodified and circulated both physically and symbolically by transnational corporations (Molina Guzmán & Valdivia, 2004), these bodies function simultaneously as objects of desire and repulsion (Durham & Báez, 2007). As such, it was unsurprising that most of their responses were complicated and sometimes contradictory and competing.

VOICING FRUSTRATION: TALKING BACK TO COMMODIFICATION OF THE BODY

Similar to Viviana Rojas' (2004) findings, the most recurring theme that occurred during the course of the focus groups was frustration with the way that Latina femininity and sexuality are constructed in the advertisements and media in general. Though the women appreciated that there are more representations of Latinas in mainstream U.S. media today than in the past, they took issue with the prevalent unidimensional images of Latinas as hypersexual—sexually proficient, insatiable, and available (Valdivia, 2000)—that reify a colonial legacy of the commodification of racialized sexuality (Barrera, 2002; Durham & Báez, 2007; Hobson, 2005; Molina Guzmán, 2001). In particular, the women pointed to the prevalence of scantily clad and provocatively dressed (usually wearing the color red and *tacones*[9]) models and actresses in advertising, television, and film. For example, upon viewing a print advertisement for Coca-Cola (see Figure 1) featuring the backside of model walking in an ambiguous street wearing a red dress and tacones, Isabel (age 20, junior) complained that it revealed "too much skin." Anjelica (age 19, sophomore), later added, "How could a girl be dressed like that to walk down the street?" Isabel responded in the same fashion to Jennifer Lopez's *Glow* ad (see Figure 2) rhetorically asking "why is she naked?" and "why can't she have clothes on?" Similarly, in reference to another ad for JC Penney (see Figure 3) featuring a model wearing a camisole-like top and short skirt with tacones, Yvette (age 21, senior), joked that the model "needs to stop shopping in the kid's section." Through these types of the comments the women contested hegemonic depictions of Latinas' as mere racialized sex objects.

Furthermore, they argued that these types of representations are not isolated in media texts and are present in discourses of their employers, professors,

Figure 1: Source: Latina, October 2003

Figure 2: Source: Latina, February 2003

classmates, and friends. In particular, Yvette recounted a story of how one of the university's famous basketball players, a black young man, would try to pick up Latinas at a local bar by telling them "how much he loved Latinas and them talking to him in Spanish." Some of the other women then chimed in that they have had similar experiences, particularly with black men, of being desired for appearing "exotic." These types of discourses of desire for the Other hark back to dominant representations of the tropicalized, hypersexual Latina. As such, the fetishization of the Latina body is ubiquitous and intersects in both popular culture texts and everyday life practices across the ethnic spectrum.

While the women's act of "talking back" to depictions of Latinas in media and other discourses can be interpreted as transgressive given that they are countering exoticized and fetishized representations of their bodies, they can also serve to police Latina bodies by desiring for models/actress' to dress less provocatively. One of the participants, Monica (age 24, senior) expressed this contradiction toward the end of the second focus group session when the following conversation ensued:

> Monica: Hold on, hold on. You have a lot of people in the group saying, oh, well you know, my parents, they, they're, you know, very traditional you know. And they didn't

Figure 3: Source: Latina, February 2003

let me do this and that. But then when you get back to these advertisements everybody complains about the girl who is half-way naked. And, oh, she should be covered up and blah, blah, blah.

Isabel: But then you dress like that? (laughing and pointing to Figure 2).

Monica: So then, yet, you're complaining about the parents saying that they're too traditional, but you yourself, you're saying it's ok to be traditional in the—any advertisement. I find that—to me that's such a contradiction …

Alejandra: I just wish there was more of a balance within the magazines …

Yvette: Cause, I don't think that, you know how you [Monica] were saying, like traditional—it's weird to see how we're breaking out of this conservative—and how Latinas are becoming more sex—sexualized. You think that before they were portrayed as traditional and now they're being portrayed as—

Monica: Nah, I mean, I'm just saying, looking at these advertisements as Latinas—Latinas were never even portrayed period. But I'm saying society itself thought of Latinas as you should be this traditional—because some people when you think of Latinas they've romanticized it. You know, oh, sexy—

Isabel: Right.

Monica: ... But when you really think of what a Latina should be like, you think a Latina should be conservative—

Yvette: Within the eyes of Latinas? Or Latinos? Or within the eyes of American society?

Monica: No, no, no. I don't know because, see, American society kind of looks at Latinos overall, not just Latinas, like Latino culture as *crazy*, you know, like sexualized.

Here the women begin to flesh out the virgin/whore binary inherent in their own discourses of the Latina body. Monica points out how these intersect with other discourses present in their everyday lives such as advertising, their own patriarchal families, and U.S. society at large. Though the virgin/whore binary is present in representations of women of all ethnicities, for these women it is particularly salient for Latinas because it signifies a racialized and transnational discourse of both media representations and their families. In their readings of the ads, the women were also complicit in the reproduction of the virgin/whore binary through their discourses of *la mujer de la calle* (embodied in the Coca-Cola ad) and *la mujer de la casa*. While *la mujer de la calle* is epitomized in these ads and other popular culture as a sign of desire for *la mulata* (see Aparicio, 1998), *la mujer de la casa* is idealized by their families because she is relegated to and sheltered within the domestic sphere. As such, the women felt tension between their families' expectations of chaste femininity and heterosexual male and non-Latina/o's "intercultural desire" (ibid.) of hypersexualized Latina bodies. The participants simultaneously policed Latina bodies, yet struggled to define Latina femininity and sexuality beyond the confines of the virgin/whore binary.

Overall, "talking back" is a competing and contradictory enterprise that is at once transgressive as it is hegemonic. The women critiqued hypersexual images of Latinas at the expense of policing other Latinas' sexuality and femininity. The women's investment in the desire for a particular image of Latinas, while rejecting hegemonic hypersexualized representations, is nonetheless imbued with specific notions of decency and desire for upward mobility. In the next section, I explore how the women's current class positions and desires to become "professionals" shaped their readings of the advertisements.

DREAMS OF UPWARD MOBILITY:
CLASS AND THE POLICING OF SEXUALITY

While the women critiqued most of the advertisements for reproducing representations of Latinas as hypersexual, these readings also were embedded in raced and classed notions of what are appropriate displays of sexuality. In particular, most of the participants preferred "decent," conservatively dressed, and professional representations of Latina femininity. The ideal of the conservative Latina recalls colonial discourses in Latin America that hold aristocratic and bourgeois white women as superior to poor mulata, indigenous, and black women (see ibid.). While aristocratic and bourgeois women were deemed as "pure" *mujeres de la casa*, poor women of color were associated with the erotic and dangerous due to their construction as *mujeres de la calle* (ibid.). In this way middle-class and upper-class white women are placed in opposition to poor women of color. In some ways, the women's readings of the texts draw upon and reproduce these colonial discourses of race, class, sex, and gender.

The desire to view more conservative and professional depictions of Latinas was voiced by most of the women. For example, Anjelica argued that these representations were crucial, especially for children because "there are no professional Latina women, conservative women" in popular culture. For her, hypersexual images such as those in some of the selected ads are "the wrong role models." Instead, Anjelica and most of the other women preferred Salma Hayek's more conservative and upper-class representation in Figure 4. This was the advertisement that the women identified with the most because she was perceived as classy, sophisticated, and "wearing clothes." This perhaps can be attributed to their class background— working-class, first-generation college students aspiring to be professionals. The women also claimed that they "liked" the advertisement because it is different from most of the other roles that Hayek has been relegated to play, namely the spitfire. Alejandra (age 19, sophomore) pointed out that even the three cars, "cada a tu estilo" (each to your style), was a metaphor for the multiplicities inherent in Hayek's hybridity, including that she was more than just a sexual being. The following conversation is revealing about their reading of this ad:

Isabel: She's covered up.

Alejandra: They're not showing her body at all.

Frances: And her beauty is there.

Alejandra: And she could be more revealing ... It's more of a subtle advertisement. It's not too out there.

Jillian: So, you were saying that we don't normally see Salma like this—

Alejandra: Like she's not just one way ... she can be different ways ...

Isabel: She's very conservative, like a Latina. Like here [pointing to Figure 2] JLo got nothing. And that matters. I like the way she's covered up. She's [pointing to Figure 2] not ... That [Figure 3], on the other hand, I would not want my daughter to see that and say oh, Mommy, you know, I want to grow up to be like her. More like this [pointing to Figure 3]. I like this. This is respectful.

As Isabel alludes to, the concept of "respect" is also central to their ideas of appropriate Latina femininity. For example, Alejandra commented that advertising

> ... would be more respectful towards women if they would show them more covered or doing activities. Like regular just posing ... If it was only in an office setting or somewhere like, I don't know, where they have status and where they're recognized or something that they're doing that's not according to the physical aspect or anything like that. If they would just put them in an office setting wearing glasses and advertising for nail polish while writing.

These desires for more "respectful" ads depicting conservative, professional women seem to speak to the women's desire for upward socioeconomic mobility; a mobility they felt is constrained by hypersexual discourses of the Latina body in popular culture and other discourses. This desire is complicated by colonialist discourses of gender, race, class, and sexuality. Some of the participants idealize the

Figure 4: Source: Latina, August 2003

disembodied woman who is prized for her mind, not body—recalling the construction of the white, aristocratic/bourgeois *mujer de la casa*. This reminiscence of the *mujer de la casa* is renegotiated through the calling for more representations of Latinas in the office. The office can be read as a negotiation of the binaries of public/private space that the *mujer de la casa/calle* inhabit respectively. Instead, the office signifies an in-between space in which *la mujer* can be outside the domestic sphere, but not totally unprotected in the public sphere of the street. This notion of the office as negotiated space also intersects with some of their suggestions for a more "balanced" representation that would depict Latinas as sexual subjects, physically attractive, yet also intelligent and competent in education and work. While these women still desired some use of the body in representations of middle-class and upper-class women, others completely rejected the commodification of Latina bodies as a method for class advancement and disavowed any use of the body. In this way, they divorced the mind from the body simultaneously reinscribing and countering the Western mind/body binary. For example, consider the following debate:

> Monica: I mean, it's good to see Latinas out there you know. That they're actually going somewhere getting ahead …
>
> Anjelica: Yeah, but the only way they're doing it here is through their body … They're not business women.
>
> Monica: Well, we don't know who they are.
>
> Several women: They're models. Yeah.
>
> Alejandra: How do you know?
>
> Isabel: Because I know them [smirking].
>
> Alejandra: They could be a lawyer. She [Figure 3] could be a pageant model.
>
> Anjelica: But they're not using that. Who cares if she's that. It's just the body type.
>
> Alejandra: It's not just the body.
>
> Isabel: No, they don't. But they're not there with their briefcase.

This excerpt reveals how the women are negotiating the binary of mind/body through debating whether it is more empowering to emphasize the body (hence sexuality) or the mind (signified by the briefcase).

However, the women also critique hypersexual representations that commodify Latina bodies because some view them as a violation against Latina/o cultural norms. Alejandra argued that the scantily clad woman is not appropriate within Latina/o cultures "… because traditionally in the Latina/Latino culture that wouldn't be acceptable exposing your body … that's seen as a very negative thing." While this statement can be read as essentializing Latina/o cultures and could be applicable to females from other ethnic groups, what is significant here is

Alejandra's perception of this policing of women's dress as specific to Latinas. In other words, Alejandra and the other participants perceived that they experienced more policing of their bodies than non-Latinas within their own Latina/o communities, particularly within their transnational Mexican (American) families.

Part of this desire for more representations of professionals is also because so little of these exist in contemporary popular culture. Isabel argued that

> Women are generalized still right here [her hand at stomach length] and men up here [her hand above her head]. Whereas, you know, women, you know, they're getting their shit together. They're getting degrees, working in offices, you know, and so forth. But, it's like, why can't we see that already?

Thus, their notions of gender liberation both within and outside the advertising texts intersect with their desires for upward socioeconomic mobility. The women perceived that less hypersexual representations of Latinas would allow for more advancement in higher education and the professional workplace since it is a sexuality that is marked as deviant because it is marked as working-class and as nonwhite. As will be discussed in the next section, their notions of class mobility, gender, and sexuality were also complicated by norms of Latina femininity imposed both within and outside Latina communities and intra-ethnic tensions among different Latina subgroups.

BOTTLE-SHAPED FIGURES, CURVES, AND BOOTIES: THE "AUTHENTIC" LATINA BODY

Accompanying the women's frustrations of hypersexualized representations of the Latina body and their call for more professional depictions of Latinas in popular culture, there was a discussion of how an "authentic" Latina body is constructed both within and outside the advertising texts. This "authentic" body is constructed and celebrated in popular and everyday discourses as a voluptuous hour-glass figure that includes wide hips and a generous derriere. However, participants were clear that though this "authentic" body is "curvy," it is still a thin body—larger bodies are still constructed as unattractive and encouraged to be disciplined through diet, exercise, and plastic surgery. The participants expressed concern with this homogenous depiction of Latina bodies prevalent in the selected advertisements. In reference to the Coca-Cola ad Alejandra said, "I find it ironic that Coca-Cola says 'de verdad,' but then it's not true because every Latina is not like that. And not only Latinas have that body. There are also other races are also very bottle-like … have bottle-like figures." This discourse of Latinas having "bottle-like figures" harks back to the legend in Latin

America that the Coca-Cola bottle was made in the likeness of Latina/Latina American women.

These discourses of an "authentic" Latina body also speak to the larger homogenization of Latinidad in mainstream popular culture. Yvette mused that

> I think it [the "authentic" Latina body] goes into the whole thing where a lot of people think that Latinos are just a category. A lot of people don't know there's necessarily Puerto Ricans or Cubans. They assume, oh, everyone's Mexican or everyone's Latino ... Maybe the people in their advertising department are—they're advertising these general Latinas because they many not know, obviously, ethnicities and cultures within Latinos or Latinas.

Similar to Yvette's idea of the strategy of advertising "general Latinas," Monica expressed frustration that there is only "one Latin look" in popular culture—referring to olive-skinned, dark-haired, and voluptuous Latinas. This idea of widespread use the "Latin look" in advertising has also been discussed by Arlene Dávila (2001) in her ethnographic research with "Hispanic" advertising professionals. Ultimately, these representations of the "authentic" Latina body in the advertisements suggest a homogeneous Latinidad embodied in the models' bodies that do not allow for differences in race, class, femininity, and ethnicity.

The women also disrupted these notions of an inherent, natural, "authentic" Latina body when they speculated that most of the images were digitalized, or "messed with" as Monica put it. In particular, they suspected that the ads cut down the waists to make the models' hips and buttocks appear larger. While Yvette argued that there are indeed some women who have this body type, most of the women were convinced that it was rare. Some of the women expressed "pressure" to conform to these beauty standards, though most of the women felt that these were impossible bodies to achieve, even if one were to discipline the body with diet, exercise, and/or plastic surgery. Furthermore, they argued that the commodities being promoted in the ads would not help them obtain those bodies, despite the ad implicitly making this connection. For example, Isabel ended the first focus group saying, "You're not gonna drink Coke and look like that, that's all I'm saying." As such, though the women may feel anxiety over fitting into this ideal body type, they also were cognizant that these products would not assist them in obtaining it. In fact, the women lamented that it may be impossible to attain this body shape and in some ways it was pointless to try.

At the same time, some participants saw a transgressive aspect to the increasing visibility of the curvy Latina body in popular culture. Yvette pointed out the following:

> There's actresses that are coming out now that don't care if they have a big butt or like JLo, you know, for example. She does exercise a lot of whatever, but literally like

how it used to be in Hollywood—it used to this real skinny, no, you couldn't have a butt. You couldn't have—your breasts had to be a certain size and you had to be so skinny to the point where it was just—it was just really skinny. And now people are like, you know like—see, there's little changes. I mean, I think, a little bit, you know. There is at least a little bit of change where women feel that it's ok ... So that's like a great improvement. I mean, it's not a big change because you still see women that are the stereotypical skinny, white female, but at the same time, there's just a little bit of change where you do see some women have some type of curves—some type of body weight other than the typical looking.

In addition, most of the women also had their own notions of Latina authenticity, often invoking similar stable, fixed notions of Latina femininity. For example, the women associated the Lincoln Mercury ad with Salma Hayek with being more authentic than the model in the Coca-Cola and Lopez's in her *Glow* ad. This discourse of authenticity can be framed around other media discourses, including conflicts between Hayek and Lopez themselves. In particular, these discourses suggest that Hayek is more authentic than U.S. born Lopez, because of her original Mexican citizenship (only recently has she received U.S. citizenship) and her accent. Valdivia and Molina Guzmán (2004) argue that these debates over authenticity are directly related to how Lopez and Hayek differ in how their sexuality has been racialized. They contend that "unlike Lopez whose sexualized image primarily foregrounds her racialized booty, sexualized representations of Hayek center on her body as the stereotyped performance of Latina femininity" (p. 212). The reading of Hayek as more "authentic" is further reinforced by the background in the ad that resembles a "hacienda" in either Latin America or the U.S. southwest. The "hacienda" background invokes the "Spanish fantasy heritage" (see Habell-Pallán, 2005; Garcia, 2001) that traps Mexican (Americans) in the past in an idyllic, pastoral setting of Mexico or missionary California and does not locate them in the present. In this way, these women simultaneously rejected notions of Latina authenticity in popular culture, yet at the same time were invested in their own definitions of Latina femininity embodied in Hayek and located in a nostalgic, colonial past.

The participants' investment in Hayek as an icon of Latina authenticity may also be due to an ethnic identification with this Mexican actress. Given that *mexicanidad* is often marginalized in mainstream popular culture representations of Latinidad, Hayek's presence may have filled this void for the participants. Though they explicitly expressed a class identification with Hayek because she embodies their desires for upward mobility, it can be speculated that the women also identified with Hayek because of her representation of Mexican femininity. This is evident when considering their distancing and critiques of another Latina icon, Jennifer Lopez who is of Puerto Rican descent. Perhaps because there are so few Mexican (American) women's bodies are celebrated in mainstream popular culture the women identified with Hayek the most in order to not be erased from the (trans)national imaginary.

Discussions of the ads also provoked discussions about differences in racialized beauty standards and practices within Latina subgroups. For example, Alejandra thought that Colombian and other South American women "tend to take care of themselves more" than other Latinas. She pointed to South American women's visibility in international pageants and argued that they were more likely to be invested in changing their appearance to fit hegemonic beauty standards. She added, "They [South American women] place so much important on it [beauty] that if there's something wrong I know that they'll have surgery. They'll change their hair, body structure, face and so forth." Monica also pointed out that these South American beauty queens tend to be "light-skinned" or "tanned," thus erasing the indigenous and African presence in Latin American countries. These comments demonstrate the women's perceptions of themselves in relation to other Latinas and their imaginations of the Other.

The participants' reflections on other Latinas went beyond beauty practices and the ads also elicited discussions of differences in how sexuality is viewed and displayed among different Latina nationalities. In particular, some of the women perceived Puerto Ricans to be more "sexually liberated" and less machista than Mexicans. For example, the following discussion arose when discussing Latina authenticity:

> Monica: A Latina is looked at like you should be like this [by the Latina/o community]. Like you should fit the traditional archetype …
>
> Yvette: I think it depends on ethnicity because I know a lot of—I'm not being stereotypical or nothing like that. I think it depends on ethnicity because I think a lot of, I think Mexicans are more, I think within a lot of Latinos are more machismo, but we hear more about Mexican machismo than any other ethnicity. And I know that for—not to be stereotypical or nothing—but Puerto Ricans. They're not, like I don't hear machismo as much as I do with Mexicans. And I've noticed and I've met—because when I went to Washington and I was a sophomore in high school and four girls that were Puerto Rican went, they were my roommates. They were Puerto Rican and they were dressed with short shorts. I mean, tight. You know what I mean? I just think it depends on the ethnicity.

While Yvette was trying to destabilize a homogeneous rendering of Latinidad, at the same time, she inscribed Mexican culture as more patriarchal while reproducing Puerto Rican culture as more accepting of overt displays of sexuality. When I probed Yvette further about how she interpreted these Puerto Rican women in Washington she said,

They traveled to Washington from Puerto Rico, from their high school, and they were very liberal. And I even asked them, guys, do your parents?—because I was shocked. Because I do understand that with Latinos there is machismo within any ethnicity in Latinos alone, but I was shocked, you know—

These perceptions of Puerto Ricans women as less oppressed by patriarchy (read: machismo) and sexually liberated and Mexican women as more submissive and traditional are especially salient within discourses among Latina/os in Chicago, particularly between Mexicans and Puerto Ricans (see De Genova & Ramos-Zayas, 2003; Pérez, 2003). They disrupt hegemonic discourses of Latinidad as an undifferentiated group and highlight tensions that exist among Latina subgroups. Though the women identify as Latina and can relate to other Latinas' experiences of oppression, they also differentiate themselves from non-Mexican women. In particular, the women mapped specific beauty practices onto the bodies of women from specific nationalities (e.g., makeup and plastic surgery for South Americans and provocative dress for Puerto Ricans). In this way, the women were able to distinguish themselves from other Latinas, albeit in a still problematic and monolithic manner in which other Latina groups are essentialized.

CONCLUSION

Valdivia (2000) argues that women of color audiences do not always experience the pleasure that psychoanalytic and early audience studies scholars suggested in the 1980s and 1990s. Instead, most often women of color audiences have conflicted experiences with media texts that amount into frustration. The women in this study expressed this frustration by talking back to the simple and limiting representations of Latina femininity and sexuality so rampant in mainstream and Latina/o media. In this way, the women's engagement with the ads functions as awareness of and resistance to a colonial legacy of the commodification of racialized sexuality and contemporary expectations of sexualized performances. This production of meaning is significant given that Latinas historically have had limited access to media representation in both the United States and Latin America and safe spaces to express these frustrations within the public sphere.

While there is a wealth of research on gender and advertising, such as the work of Susan Bordo (1993), Jean Kilbourne (1999), and Vicki Routledge Shields (2002), among others, little focuses on nonwhite women. Furthermore, there continues to be a dearth of research on Latina audiences' relationships to media and popular culture, particularly advertising. In this chapter, I have explored the experiences of women of Mexican origin and their interpretations of advertisements that commodify the

Latina body. In particular, their transnational and hybrid subjectivities significantly informed their complicated, and at time contradictory, responses to print advertisements. Overall, they struggled with negotiating Western gendered binaries such as virgin/whore and mind/body along with both reproducing and rupturing notions of hegemonic Latina femininity and sexuality.

In their struggle for more hybrid representations of Latinas, the women expressed frustration with the prevalence of hypersexualized images of Latinas in advertising and other popular culture and insisted on the creation of more representations of Latina professionals. While there are far too few representations of professional Latinas in mainstream media, the women's desire for seeing "la profesional" privileges middle- and upper-class women over working-class women. Similarly, the women critiqued static notions of the "authentic" Latina body as curvy with wide hips and large buttocks, yet at the same time were invested in a rigid sense of Latina authenticity. In other words, they contested or "talked back" to hegemonic representations of the Latina body, but found it difficult to imagine an unproblematic image of Latina identity. In these ways, the women struggled with redefining Latina femininity and sexuality as hybrid and transnational, yet also found themselves constrained by using hegemonic discourses, notions of authenticity, and their shifting class identities. This speaks to the difficulty we all face in using language, which is largely structured within binaries, to express our hybrid subjectivities.

This chapter also demonstrated some of the ways intra-ethnic conflict occurs. In this case, these Mexican (American) women identified as Latina while speaking of the Other, or other Latina women. This is especially salient when considering that Mexican (American) women are a marginalized audience despite Mexicans being the largest Latina/o group in the United States because mainstream popular culture continues to exclude representations of *mexicanidad* in favor of a tropicalized Latinidad. While dominant representations of Latinidad may be homogenous, they are uneven. Some ethnic groups are deemed to be more commodifiable than others. There was also heterogeneity and dissidence in their readings of the ads. As such, there is also conflict within this relatively homogenous group of working-class, young Mexican (American) female college students. Ultimately, these women's discourses point to the difficulty of ensconcing a flexible identity within a global and local situation that impedes flexibility, especially for racialized women who already experience what Valdivia (2003a) calls a "radical hybridity."

ACKNOWLEDGMENT

I thank Angharad Valdivia, Maria Elena Cepeda, Coco Fusco, and Isabel Molina Guzmán for their invaluable feedback and the women who participated in this study for sharing their perspectives and experiences with me.

NOTES

1. Here I use the term "Hispanic" in quotes because this is how the niche advertising industry that targets Latina/o consumers refers to this population. However, I prefer to use "Latina/o" over "Hispanic" to refer to people of Latin American and Spanish Caribbean descent living in the United States given that the latter term was self-imposed by the U.S. government and privileges ties to Spain over indigenous and African strains within Latina/o culture.
2. By Latinidad I am referring to the cultural practices of being and identifying as Latina/o.
3. I use Mexican (American) in this chapter instead of Mexican, Mexican American or Chicana to refer to women of Mexican origin because the participants varied in how they identified themselves in terms of ethnicity. The women identified as either Mexican or Mexican American, and not Chicana (which they understood as a "Southwest thing"; a phenomenon that is prevalent among the Mexican [American] community in the Midwest).
4. Stuart Hall's (1980) encoding/decoding model suggests there are three ways to decode or read texts. First, the dominant or preferred reading refers to an interpretation that is consistent with the intended message of the producer of the message. The second potential reading is an alternative or oppositional interpretation of the text that rejects the producer's intended message. Finally, a negotiated interpretation is an amalgam of the first two and acknowledges both the intended message of the producer as well as the personal experience of the reader.
5. However, in doing so, I do not attempt to essentialize the female Mexican (American)/Chicana experience. I recognize that even with the Mexican origin population there exists a multiplicity of perspectives based on social location (e.g., gender, color, class, sexuality, age, religion, etc.) and individual experience. The point is to consider issues of Latinidad within the context of one particular ethnic group as opposed to a panethnic study.
6. See Calafell (2001), Garcia (2005), and Martinez (2004) on the emergence of Latina magazine, its role in fostering Latinidad, constructing Latina femininity, and its function in simultaneously providing hegemonic, alternative and hybrid subjectivities for its readers.
7. I discovered this when my class "Latina/o Media in the U.S." performed a content analysis of 6 Latina issues ranging from 2003 to 2006 during an in-class content analysis exercise.
8. Although I do not perform textual analysis of the selected advertisements in this chapter due to space limitations, it is equally necessary to do so in order to understand the larger discursive formation on the Latina body. I analyze them elsewhere in my forthcoming dissertation.
9. "Tacones" means "high heels" in many Latin American countries. See Hedrick (2001) for a more detailed discussion of how tacones signify "authentic" Latina femininity and sexuality in popular culture discourses.

REFERENCES

Ang, I. (1985). *Watching Dallas: Soap opera and the melodramatic imagination*. New York: Methuen.
Aparicio, F. (1998). *Listening to salsa: Gender, Latin popular music, and Puerto Rican cultures*. Hanover, NH: University Press of New England.
Aparicio, F. & S. Chávez-Silverman. (Eds.). (1997). *Tropicalizations: Transcultural representations of Latinidad*. Hanover: University Press of New England.
Báez, J. M. (2007). Speaking of Jennifer Lopez: Discourses of iconicity and identity formation among Latina audiences. *Media Report to Women, 35*(1), 5–13.

Barrera, M. (2002). Hottentot 2000: Jennifer Lopez and her butt. In K. M. Phillips & B. Reay (Eds.), *Sexualities in history: A Reader* (pp. 407–417). New York: Routledge.

Bobo, J. (1995). *Black women as cultural readers.* New York: Columbia University Press.

Bordo, S. (1993). *Unbearable weight: Feminism, Western culture, and the body.* Berkeley: University of California Press.

Calafell, B. M. (2001). In our own image?!: A rhetorical criticism of *Latina* magazine. *Voces: A Journal of Chicana and Latina Studies, 3*(1/2), 12–46.

Castañeda Paredes, M. (2003). The transformation of Spanish-language radio in the United States. *Journal of Radio Studies, 10*(1), 5–16.

Dávila, A. (2001). *Latinos, Inc.: The marketing and making of a people.* Berkeley and Los Angeles: University of California Press.

Davila, A. (2002). Talking back: Spanish media and U.S. Latinidad. In M. Habell-Pallán & M. Romero (Eds.), *Latino/a popular culture* (pp. 25–37). New York & London: New York University Press.

De Genova, N. & A. Y. Ramos-Zayas. (2003). *Latino crossings: Mexicans, Puerto Ricans, and the politics of race and citizenship.* New York & London: Routledge.

Durham, A. & J. M. Báez. (2007). A tail of two women: Exploring the contours of difference in popular culture. In S. Springgay & D. Freedman (Eds.), *Curriculum and the cultural body* (pp. 131–145). New York: Peter Lang.

Flores, J. (2000). The Latino imaginary: Meanings of community and identity. In *From bomba to hip hop: Puerto Rican culture and Latino identity* (pp. 191–203). New York: Columbia University Press.

Garcia, M. (2001). *A world of its own: Race, labor and citrus in the making of Greater Los Angeles, 1900–1970.* Chapel Hill: University of North Carolina Press.

Garcia, E. (2005). *Reading Latinas: A cultural analysis of beauty, gender and empowering models for and by Latinas.* Unpublished Dissertation, University of Michigan, Ann Arbor, MI.

Habell-Pallán, M. (2005). *Loca motion: The travels of Chicana and Latina popular culture.* New York & London: New York University Press.

Hall, S. (1980). Encoding/decoding. In S. Hall, D. Hobson, A. Lowe & P. Willis (Eds.), *Culture, media, language: Working papers in cultural studies, 1972–79* (pp. 128–138). London: Hutchinson.

Hedrick, T. (2001). Are you a pura Latina? or, menudo every day: Tacones and symbolic ethnicity. In S. Benstock & S. Ferris (Eds.), *Footnotes: On shoes* (pp. 135–155). New Brunswick, NJ: Rutgers University Press.

Hobson, J. (2005). *Venus in the dark: Blackness and beauty in popular culture.* New York: Routledge.

Humphreys, J. M. (2006). The multicultural economy 2006. *Georgia Business and Economic Conditions, 66*(3), 1–15.

Kilbourne, J. (1999). *Can't buy my love: How advertising changes the way we think and feel.* New York: Simon & Schuster.

Levine, E. (2001). Constructing a market, constructing an ethnicity: U.S. Spanish language media and the formation of a Latina/o identity. *Studies in Latin American Popular Culture, 20,* 33–50.

Lugo, A. (forthcoming). Inspecting border crossings: The case of the Ciudad Juárez-El Paso region. In M. Garcia, A. N. Valdivia, & M. Leger (Eds.), *Geographies of Latinidad.* Durham: Duke University Press.

Madriz, E. (2000). Focus groups in feminist research. In N. Denzin & Y. Lincoln (Eds.), *Handbook of qualitative inquiry.* Thousand Oaks, CA: Sage Publications.

Martinez, K. Z. (2004). *Latina* magazine and the invocation of a panethnic family: Latino identity as it is informed by celebrities and *papis chulos*. *The Communication Review, 7,* 155–174.

Mayer, V. (2003). Living telenovelas/telenovelizing life: Mexican American girls' identities and transnational novelas. *Journal of Communication* (September), 479–495.

Mohanty, C. T. (2003). *Feminism without borders: Decolonizing theory, practicing solidarity.* Durham, NC: Duke University Press.

Molina Guzmán, I. (2001, April 9–14). *Commodifying Latinidad: A case study of Hollywood films featuring Jennifer Lopez and Salma Hayek from 1995 to 1999.* Paper presented at the National Conference of the American Studies Association/Popular Culture Association Annual, Philadelphia, PA.

Molina Guzmán, I. & A. N. Valdivia. (2004). Brain, brow or bootie: Iconic Latinas in contemporary popular culture. *The Communication Review,* 7(2), 205–221.

Morgan, D. (1997). *Focus groups as qualitative research.* Thousand Oaks, CA: Sage Publications.

Peñaloza, L. (1997). ¡Ya viene Atzlan! Latinos in U.S. advertising. In D. Everette & E. Pease (Eds.), *The media in black and white* (pp. 113–120). New Brunswick, NJ: Transaction Publishers.

Pérez, G. (2003). "Puertorriquenas rencorosas y mejicanas sufridas": Gendered ethnic identity formation in Chicago's Latino communities. *Journal of Latin American Anthropology,* 8(2), 96–125.

Press, A. L. (1991). *Women watching television: Gender, class, and generation in the American television experience.* Philadelphia: University of Pennsylvania Press.

Press, A. L. & E. R Cole. (1999). *Speaking of abortion: Television and authority in the lives of women.* Chicago: University of Chicago Press.

Radway, J. (1984). *Reading the romance: Women, patriarchy, and popular literature.* Chapel Hill: University of North Carolina Press.

Rivero, Y. M. (2003). The performance and reception of televisual "ugliness" in Yo soy Betty la fea. *Feminist Media Studies,* 3(1), 65–81.

Rodriguez, A. (1999). *Making Latino news: Race, language, class.* Thousand Oaks, CA: Sage Publications.

Rojas, V. (2004). The gender of Latinidad: Latinas speak about Hispanic television. *The Communication Review,* 7(2), 125–153.

Ruiz, M. V. (2002). Border narratives, HIV/AIDS, and Latina/o health in the United States: A cultural analysis. *Feminist Media Studies,* 2(1), 37–62.

Shields, V. R. (2002). *Measuring up: How advertising affects self-image.* Philadelphia: University of Pennsylvania Press.

Shohat, E. (Ed.). (1998). *Talking visions: Multicultural feminism in a transnational age.* Cambridge: MIT Press.

Shohat, E. & R. Stam. (1995). *Unthinking Eurocentrism: Multiculturalism and the media.* London & New York: Routledge.

Turow, J. (1997). *Breaking up America: Advertisers and the new media world.* Chicago: University of Chicago Press.

Valdivia, A. N. (2000). *A Latina in the land of Hollywood and other essays on media culture.* Tucson: University of Arizona Press.

Valdivia, A. N. (2003a). Radical hybridity: Latina/s as the paradigmatic transnational post-subculture. In D. Muggleton & R. Weinzierl (Eds.), *The Post-subcultures reader* (pp. 151–165). New York: Berg.

Valdivia, A. N. (2003b). Salsa as popular culture: Ethnic audiences constructing an identity. In A. N. Valdivia (Ed.), *Media studies companion* (pp. 399–418). Oxford: Blackwell.

Valdivia, A. N. (2004). Latinas as radical hybrid: Transnationally gendered traces in mainstream media. *Global Media Journal,* 4(7). Retrieved September 12, 2006, from http://lass.calumet.purdue.edu/cca/gmj/refereed.htm.

van Zoonen, L. (1994). *Feminist media studies.* London, Thousand Oaks & New Delhi: Sage Publications.

Vargas, L. (2005). Media and racialization among working-class Latina immigrant young women. In H. W. J. Peacock & C. A. Matthews (Eds.), *The American South in a global world* (pp. 39–58). Chapel Hill: University of North Carolina Press.

Vargas, L. (2006). Transnational media literacy: Analytic reflections on a program with Latina teens. *Hispanic Journal of Behavior Sciences, 28*(2), 267–285.

About the Authors

Jillian M. Báez is a doctoral candidate at the Institute of Communications Research at the University of Illinois at Urbana-Champaign. Her research interests lie in media ethnography, feminist theory, and Latina/o Studies. She is currently working on her dissertation that explores representations of the Latina body in advertising and Latina audiences' interpretations of these texts. Ms. Báez is currently a Ford Foundation Predoctoral Fellow and has published in *Centro: Journal of the Center for Puerto Rican Studies* and the *Journal of Popular Communication*. She has a B.A. in Media Studies and Puerto Rican/Latino Studies from Hunter College-City University of New York.

Mary Beltrán is Assistant Professor of Communication Arts and Chicana/o & Latino/a Studies at the University of Wisconsin-Madison. Her research is focused on Latino/a, mixed-race, and other nonwhite representation, participation, and celebrity in U.S. film, television, and popular culture. Books include *Hollywood Latinidad: Latina/o Stars, Shifting Borders*, University of Illinois Press (2009), and *Mixed-Race Hollywood: Multiraciality in Film and Media Culture*, an anthology coedited with Camilla Fojas, New York University Press (2008).

Dr. Bernadette Marie Calafell is Assistant Professor of Human Communication at the University of Denver. She received her Ph.D. in Communication Studies with a focus on queer Latina/o performance at the University of North Carolina at Chapel Hill. Her research focuses on Latina/o and Chicana/o representation, performance, and identity. She is particularly interested in finding ways to bridge differences across Latina/o groups through explorations of affective coalitions and performances that occur on the level of the everyday and in popular culture. Her research work has been published in *Latino Studies, Critical Studies in Media Communication, Text and Performance Quarterly,* and *The Communication Review*. Her forthcoming book is titled *Latina/o Communication Studies: Theorizing Performance* (Peter Lang, 2008).

Dolores Inés Casillas was a University of California President's Postdoctoral Fellow in the department of Latin American and Latino Studies at the University of California, Santa Cruz, and is now Assistant Professor of Chicana and Chicano Studies at the University of California, Santa Barbara. She is completing a book that chronicles the cultural history of U.S. Spanish-language radio. In 2006, she received her Ph.D. in American Culture from the University of Michigan, Ann Arbor. Currently, she researches and teaches in the areas of Latina/o media, immigration policy, language politics, and popular culture.

Mari Castañeda (Ph.D. 2000, University of California, San Diego) is an Associate Professor in the department of Communication, the Center for Latin American, Caribbean, and Latino Studies, and the Center for Public Policy and Administration at the University of Massachusetts Amherst. Her fields of study include Spanish-language and Latina/o media, media and cultural policy, and digital media and the political economy of communication. She is currently working on a project that examines the cultural politics and property creation of Latina/o media in the United States

María Elena Cepeda is Assistant Professor of Latina/o Studies at Williams College, where she specializes in Latina/o popular culture, media, language politics, "New" Latina/o communities, and community-based pedagogical approaches. She has published in the journals *Popular Music and Society, Latino Studies,* and *Discourse*, among others, and served as editorial assistant for *Musical Migrations: Transnationalism and Cultural Hybridity in Latin(o) America* (Ed., Cándida F. Jáquez and Frances R. Aparicio (Palgrave, 2003). Cepeda is currently completing *Musical Imagi/Nations: The U.S. Colombian Diaspora and the Latin(o) Music "Boom"* (NYU Press, 2008).

David González Hernández is the coordinator of the Communications program in the School of Humanities at the Universidad Autónoma of Baja California, Tijuana. He is also a member of the Asociación Mexicana de Investigadores de la Comunicación where he has been coordinating the reception studies group with Dr. Guillermo Orozco since 2005. In 2004, he won the Consejo Nacional de la Enseñanza y la Investigación en Ciencias de la Comunicación award for best M.A. thesis, in Communication from the Insituto de Estudios Superiores de Occidente (ITESO, Mexico). His research focuses on viewers' reception of television and history of the media in the U.S.- Mexico border.

Katynka Z. Martínez is an Assistant Professor in the department of Raza Studies at San Francisco State University. Her research on *Latina* magazine and the Latin Grammys has been published in the journals

The Communication Review and *Latino Studies*. Her work on HBO Latino can be found in the edited anthology *Cable Visions: Television Beyond Broadcasting* (New York University Press). Prior to joining the SFSU Raza Studies department, Martínez served as a postdoctoral researcher associated with the MacArthur funded study "Kids' Informal Learning with Digital Media: An Ethnographic Investigation of Innovative Knowledge Cultures." Publications based on her research with Los Angeles Latino youth are forthcoming.

Isabel Molina Guzmán (Ph.D., University of Pennsylvania, 2000) is a Research Associate Professor of Communications at the Institute of Communications Research and Latina/o Studies Program, and a faculty affiliate of the Gender and Women's Studies Program at the University of Illinois Champaign-Urbana. Her research examining media discourses of Latinidad and its intersectionality with gender, sexuality, race, and ethnicity has appeared in journals such as *Critical Studies in Media Communication, Latino Studies, Communication Research, Critical Inquiry, Journalism: Theory, Practice, Criticism*, and many edited anthologies. Her book tentatively entitled *Consuming Latina Bodies: Global Media Representations of Latinidad* is forthcoming from NYU Press.

Shane Moreman is a Communication faculty member at California State University, Fresno—the department's first and currently only Latina/o professor. His research focused on the communicative and performative aspects of cultural identity expression, with particular emphasis on the changing discourse around Latina/o populations. He is currently coediting a special issue on Latina/o performativities for *Text and Performance Quarterly* with Bernadette Calafell. Forthcoming publications include works on memoirs, qualitative interviewing, and a performance ethnography of *Women in Black*. Being at a teaching university, much of his time is wonderfully spent in the classroom. In collaboration with *Universidad Xochicalco*, he recently took a group of students to Baja California to study how Mexican-U.S. border discourses of tourism shape the tourist experience.

Angharad N. Valdivia is a Research Professor at the Institute of Communications Research with appointments in Media Studies, Gender and Women Studies, and Latina/o Studies. Her research, teaching, and publications focus on the intersection of Media Studies with international and transnational issues, especially in the area of popular culture, foregrounding issues of gender and ethnicity. Her books include *Feminism, Multiculturalism and the Media* (Sage, 1995), *A Latina in the Land of Hollywood* (Arizona, 2000), *A Companion to Media Studies* (Blackwell, 2003, 2006, 2008 in Chinese), *Latinas in Popular Culture: Uses and Abuses of Hybridity* (Blackwell, forthcoming), and Geographies of Latinidad (Duke, forthcoming).

Lucila Vargas is an Associate Professor in the School of Journalism and Mass Communication at the University of North Carolina, Chapel Hill. Her teaching and research interests are international communication, Latino media studies, and communication for social change. She wrote *Social Uses and Radio Practices. The Use of Radio by Ethnic Minorities in Mexico* (Westview, 1995), edited the anthology *Women Faculty of Color in the White Classroom* (Peter Lang, 2002), and has published in numerous academic journals. She holds a *licenciatura* degree from the Universidad Autónoma de Chihuahua, and an M.A. and Ph.D. from the University of Texas, Austin.

Index

advertisement[s]
155, 200, 252, 257, 262-64, 267-8, 272-3, 276-78
African American[s]
10, 17, 46, 55, 79, 82, 94, 98, 119, 242, 250
agency
44, 76-77, 87, 106, 127, 129, 156, 168-9, 173, 193, 240, 240, 244, 247, 259, 261
agency and structure
7, 18, 110, 138
Anzaldúa, Gloria
14, 86, 93, 95, 97, 101, 107, 178, 196, 208, 238
Aparicio, Frances
9, 13, 86, 137-9, 143, 153, 177, 258, 261, 168
Aparicio, Frances and Susanna Chavez-Silverman
12, 127, 240, 248, 258, 260
Asian American[s]
10, 184, 190, 207
authenticity
20, 103, 106-7, 137, 274-7
authority
117, 126-7, 129, 164-5, 172, 192, 214

autonomy
237
beauty
17, 33-36, 40, 42, 45, 104, 106, 137, 139, 151, 153-4, 168, 170, 188, 196, 201-2, 204, 210, 237-8, 224, 250-1, 269, 273, 275-76
Beltran, Mary
9, 11-13, 16, 137, 139, 242-3, 245, 248-9
blackness
8-9, 46, 106, 246
body
17-8, 36, 71, 74, 79, 81-5, 92-103, 131, 139, 141, 149-56, 193, 201, 210, 239, 244-5, 249-50, 258, 261, 269, 271, 274-5
body, Latina
12, 18, 137-8, 156, 238, 249, 258, 259-277
bootie
272
buttocks
210, 273, 277
butt
20

bracera
190, 201, 213-4
Chicana/o
17, 69-73, 75, 80, 84-86, 141, 145, 150, 196, 240-1, 243
Chicana/Mexicana
243
commodification
20, 97, 103, 104, 154, 248, 249, 264-5, 271, 276
consumption
55, 154, 221, 238-40, 243, 247-48, 250-1
Cuba
12, 64, 1115-136 (Chapter 6), 146, 152
Cubans
115-8, 149-50, 240, 248, 260, 273
Cuban-US or Cuban American
18, 1116-8, 145
Cuban-US [relations]
12, 116

Dávila, Arlene
17, 56, 60, 147, 187, 243, 258, 260, 273
discrimination
46, 58, 119, 242
Dominican Republic
152
Dominican[s]
118, 143, 145, 150, 235

fashion
29, 34-5, 104, 138, 150-1, 154, 172, 188, 196, 201-210, 239, 241, 243-50, 265
femininity
20, 29, 46, 106, 117, 124, 128-9, 138, 152, 154, 157, 187-8, 196-7, 199-214, 245, 248, 264, 268-77
Fregoso, Rosa Linda
12-3, 177, 187, 238, 251

gay
91, 97-108
gay, Latina/o
17, 92, 103

Gutiérrez, Félix
12, 17, 21, 163
heterosexuality
71, 210
hybridity
9, 11, 17, 20, 24-5, 86, 92-3, 95, 97-8, 99, 102, 105-6, 108, 110, 152, 187-8, 193, 196, 213, 217, 259, 269, 277, 280, 284-5
hypersexuality
118

immigration
8, 17, 29, 31, 51-2, 61-4, 69-90 (Chapter 4), 115, 119-20, 124, 128, 131, 163, 166-7, 175-6, 189

Jennifer Lopez
8, 13, 27, 137-9, 153-6, 237, 242, 246-7, 250, 265, 274

Lupe Vélez
28, 31-2, 35, 37
M
Marisleysis Gonzalez
125, 127-9
masculinity
18, 29, 117, 161-186 (Chapter 8), 188, 196-7, 210
masculinity, Latino
18-9, 27
Mexican
28, 31, 33,-4, 37, 41-2, 51-2, 55-6, 70-2, 75, 81, 83-5, 91-3, 95-7, 100-3, 106-9 118-9, 138, 145, 163, 166-7, 172, 177, 257-82 (Chapter 12)
Mexicanidad
8
Mexicanness
41, 103
Mexican American
19-20, 28, 30-1, 33, 37-8, 46, 55, 71, 85, 139, 148, 194, 257-281 (Chapter 12)
Mexico
8-9, 16-7, 19, 28, 30-45, 55-6, 58, 63, 75, 96-7, 132, 152, 168, 176-7, 190, 209, 219-236 (Chapter 10), 263, 274

Mexico/San Diego/US Border
19, 55, 93, 100, 195
Mexico City
85, 91-2, 96-8
miscegenation
38, 139, 172
Molina Guzmán, Isabel
5, 8-13, 18, 53, 65, 116, 124, 139, 148, 243, 247-8, 264-5, 274

national imaginary
8, 18, 64, 77, 79, 275
nationalist
9, 72, 172, 174, 219, 220
Native American[s]
10, 138

Paulina Rubio
17, 91-113 (Chapter 5), 243
Puerto Rican[s]
61, 69, 118, 139, 140-1, 148, 155, 240-1, 251, 273-6
Puerto Rico
107, 149, 152, 190, 276

race
33, 92-5, 101-3, 117, 203, 252, 271
race, mixed
9, 11
race and class
36, 167-8, 193, 204, 244, 250, 259, 261, 260-70, 273
race and ethnicity
4-5, 7-8, 14, 30, 38, 86, 92, 94, 96, 108-9, 117-9, 241, 249, 258

raced
71, 116, 268
racialization
28, 32, 37, 129, 190
racism
15, 58, 69, 71-2, 221, 245

Salma Hayek
12, 20, 129, 269, 272, 275
sexuality
7, 14, 20, 78, 94, 98, 106, 109, 141, 169, 193, 195, 213, 239, 245, 249, 252, 258-9, 261, 264-72, 274-5
Shohat, Ella
12, 259-60
Subervi-Vélez, Federico
11-2, 115, 117, 194

transnational, transnationality, transnationalism
5- 6, 8, 10-1, 14, 16-7, 52-64, 104-107, 154, 162-168, 176-7, 187-218 (Chapter 9), 229-32, 239, 256-60, 264, 268, 272, 277

Valdivia, Angharad N.
8-12, 20, 32, 86, 139, 177, 196, 214, 252, 258

whiteness
9-10, 14, 17-8, 29, 31-2, 36, 46, 80-1, 91, 94, 102, 110, 116-20, 130-2, 139, 245

youth
11, 19, 24-5, 55, 95-6, 122, 188, 190, 196, 199, 202, 219-236 (Chapter 10)